THE HISTORY OF THE "PROLETARIAT":
The Emergence of Marxism in the
Kingdom of Poland, 1870–1887

───────

NORMAN M. NAIMARK

EAST EUROPEAN QUARTERLY, BOULDER
DISTRIBUTED BY COLUMBIA UNIVERSITY PRESS
NEW YORK

1979

EAST EUROPEAN MONOGRAPHS, NO. LIV

Norman M. Naimark is Assistant Professor of History at
Boston University

Printed in the United States of America

EAST EUROPEAN MONOGRAPHS

The *East European Monographs* comprise scholarly books on the history and civilization of Eastern Europe. They are published by the *East European Quarterly* in the belief that these studies contribute substantially to the knowledge of the area and serve to stimulate scholarship and research.

21. *The Crises of France's East-Central European Diplomacy, 1933–1938.* By Anthony J. Komjathy. 1976.
22. *Polish Politics and National Reform, 1775–1788.* By Daniel Stone. 1976.
23. *The Habsburg Empire in World War I.* Robert A. Kann, Bela K. Kiraly, and Paula S. Fichtner, eds. 1977.
24. *The Slovenes and Yugoslavism, 1890–1914.* By Carole Rogel. 1977.
25. *German-Hungarian Relations and the Swabian Problem.* By Thomas Spira. 1977.
26. *The Metamorphosis of a Social Class in Hungary During the Reign of Young Franz Joseph.* By Peter I. Hidas. 1977.
27. *Tax Reform in Eighteenth Century Lombardy.* By Daniel M. Klang. 1977.
28. *Tradition versus Revolution: Russia and the Balkans in 1917.* By Robert H. Johnston. 1977.
29. *Winter into Spring: The Czechoslovak Press and the Reform Movement 1963–1968.* By Frank L. Kaplan. 1977.
30. *The Catholic Church and the Soviet Government, 1939–1949.* By Dennis J. Dunn. 1977.
31. *The Hungarian Labor Service System, 1939–1945.* By Randolph L. Braham. 1977.
32. *Consciousness and History: Nationalist Critics of Greek Society 1897–1914.* By Gerasimos Augustinos. 1977.
33. *Emigration in Polish Social and Political Thought, 1870–1914.* By Benjamin P. Murdzek. 1977.
34. *Serbian Poetry and Milutin Bojic.* By Mihailo Dordevic. 1977.
35. *The Baranya Dispute: Diplomacy in the Vortex of Ideologies, 1918–1921.* By Leslie C. Tihany. 1978.
36. *The United States in Prague, 1945–1948.* By Walter Ullmann. 1978.
37. *Rush to the Alps: The Evolution of Vacationing in Switzerland.* By Paul P. Bernard. 1978.
38. *Transportation in Eastern Europe: Empirical Findings.* By Bogdan Mieczkowski. 1978.
39. *The Polish Underground State: A Guide to the Underground, 1939–1945.* By Stefan Korbonski. 1978.
40. *The Hungarian Revolution of 1956 in Retrospect.* Edited by Bela K. Kiraly and Paul Jonas. 1978.
41. *Boleslaw Limanowski (1835–1935): A Study in Socialism and Nationalism.* By Kazimiera Janina Cottam. 1978.
42. *The Lingering Shadow of Nazism: The Austrian Independent Party Movement Since 1945.* By Max E. Riedlsperger. 1978.
43. *The Catholic Church, Dissent and Nationality in Soviet Lithuania.* By V. Stanley Vardys. 1978.
44. *The Development of Parliamentary Government in Serbia.* By Alex N. Dragnich. 1978.

45. *Divide and Conquer: German Efforts to Conclude a Separate Peace, 1914–1918*. By L. L. Farrar, Jr. 1978.
46. *The Prague Slav Congress of 1848*. By Lawrence D. Orton. 1978.
47. *The Nobility and the Making of the Hussite Revolution*. By John M. Klassen. 1978.
48. *The Cultural Limits of Revolutionary Politics: Change and Continuity in Socialist Czechoslovakia*. By David W. Paul. 1979.
49. *On the Border of War and Peace: Polish Intelligence and Diplomacy in 1937–1939 and the Origins of the Ultra Secret*. By Richard A. Woytak. 1979.
50. *Bear and Foxes: The International Relations of the East European States 1965–1969*. By Ronald Haly Linden. 1979.
51. *Czechoslovakia: The Heritage of Ages Past*. Edited by Hans Brisch and Ivan Volgyes. 1979.
52. *Prime Minister Gyula Andrássy's Influence on Habsburg Foreign Policy*. By János Decsy. 1979.
53. *Citizens for the Fatherland: Education, Educators, and Pedagogical Ideals in Eighteenth Century Russia*. By J. L. Black. 1979.
54. *The History of the "Proletariat": The Emergence of Marxism in the Kingdom of Poland, 1870–1887*. By Norman M. Naimark. 1979.

To my parents

Contents

Tables

Preface

The following study focuses on a number of themes at once. First and most directly, it reconstructs the history of the "Proletariat" (1882–1886), an underground party of Polish intelligentsia and workers known as the "Wielki" or "Great Proletariat" to distinguish it from later, less significant groups of the same name. The Proletariat established the theoretical foundations of Polish Marxism and communism while participating in the revolutionary movement in the Russian Empire. Second, the volume explores the national history of Poles in the Kingdom of Poland (commonly called the Congress Kingdom), in European Russia, and in the borderlands of the Ukraine, Belorussia, and Lithuania during the period between the aftershocks of the 1863–64 rebellion and the development of modern Polish political movements in the early 1890s. In this relatively short span of time, the Polish industrial revolution — the third area of my concern — recast the social and economic life of the Congress Kingdom to the point where the working class would stand at the center of any subsequent internal solutions to the "Polish question." In addition, the period witnessed important shifts in the course of Polish political thinking, which too are of major interest in this volume. It is only in the context of the activities of the Proletariat, Russian occupation, rapid industrialization, and new forces in Polish intellectual life, that the emergence of Polish Marxism can be illuminated, the fifth and final task of this book.

It is appropriate at the outset to discuss several conceptual problems that influence the organization and argument presented in the following pages. Generally, this study can be included within the framework of Russian and Polish history. In a strict sense, however, the subject matter is distinct from both fields. Developments in Austrian Galicia and in the Prussian Grand Duchy of Poznań are touched on only insofar as they influence the history of the Congress Kingdom. By the time of the emergence of the Proletariat in 1882, the Congress Kingdom can be considered an integral part of the Russian Empire, administered and organized according to the same principles as any other area of the empire. Yet social and intellectual integration was not completed. Considerations of internal Russian history in the post-emancipation period often do not influence Congress Kingdom developments, and in these cases are omitted from this study. One of the premises herein is that the Congress Kingdom in the last half of the nineteenth century was a distinct historical entity with its own culture, its own national economy, its own forums for public expression, and as unlike its brother partitions in its internal life as it was dissimilar to Russian territorial units.

A further series of problems come to the fore as a result of these observations. In the nineteenth century, Polish socialism was a complex of socialisms of Poles in Galicia, Poznania, Silesia, the Congress Kingdom, European Russia, Paris, London, Switzerland, and the New World. Similarly, Poles in dispersed population centers were self-proclaimed followers of Marx. The Proletariat is distinguished from these Marxists and from the earlier history of Polish socialism as a whole owing to its character as a broadly-based and indigenous movement among the Polish population in the Polish lands — the first such socialist movement in the history of Poland. Other prior or contemporaneous socialist groups and other Marxists are unquestionably significant in the history of Polish Marxism and communism, and as far as they affect the Proletariat will be discussed. But my interest here is in the internal sources of Polish Marxism, and for those, one must concentrate on the Proletariat and its history in the Congress Kingdom.

The subject matter of the Proletariat must also be distinguished from the history of the Russian revolutionary movement. To be sure, geographical proximity and the same autocratic opponent facilitated the undertaking of common actions. Cultural affinity and a common educational establishment encouraged an extensive cross-fertilization of ideas and the actual exchange of revolutionary personnel. Polish *narodniki* ("populists") and *narodovol'tsy* (members of the terrorist party Narodnaia Volia — "People's Will") were instrumental in the foundations of the Proletariat just as the Polish Marxists played a crucial role in the development of Russian social democracy. The Proletariat can even be considered the first *Russian* Marxist party because it operated almost exclusively within the borders of the Russian Empire. Nevertheless, this study approaches the Proletariat as a *Polish* party of the Congress Kingdom, with its roots sunk deep into the soil of the history of that geographically and politically well-defined region.

The sources for this reconstruction of the history of the Proletariat are primarily archival. The concern of the Russian police and judicial authorities about the growth and influence of the underground party is amply reflected in the detailed papers of the Warsaw Prosecutor (AGAD, PWIS), the Warsaw Gendarme Administration (AGAD, WGZŻ), the Department of Police (TsGAOR, f. 102–DP), and the Ministry of Justice (TsGIA, SSSR, f. 1405). A judicious reading of the reports, letters, confessions, indictments, and other materials contained in these collections can produce, in and of itself, an accurate picture of revolutionary activities during this period. In addition, from these archival sources, it was possible to compile a statistical collective biography of the arrested socialists between 1878 and 1886. This material (presented in written and table form in the book's appendix) is sometimes cited in the text to evaluate various historiographical generalizations concerning the social, educational, religious, or occupational determinants of the revolutionary movement in these years.

This study has also benefited from the rich tradition of Polish socialist historiography of the Proletariat. Since the 1890s, Polish socialists have shared a common devotion to elevating the Proletariat from persistent obscurity to its proper place in Polish history and in the history of European socialism as a whole. The plethora of Proletariat memoir literature and the existence of lengthy factual accounts of the party's history can be attributed to the efforts of these historians. However, the intense topicality of the Proletariat left its historiography shot through with politically motivated interpretations and omissions. The most provocative work in this tradition — Rosa Luxemburg's 1903 "In Memorium to the 'Proletariat'" — used the party to assail her terrorist and nationalist opponents. Leon Baumgarten, in the most reliable and extensive treatment of the party, *The History of the Great Proletariat* (1966), examined the Proletariat on behalf of the Polish United Workers Party (PZPR) in search of concrete antecedents and historical legitimization. In the case of Luxemburg and her contemporaries, the "mistakes" of their political opponents became the "mistakes" of the Proletariat. Baumgarten and his contemporaries in the People's Republic of Poland identified the "mistakes" of the party not in terms of political opponents, but as elements of Proletariat theory or practice that contradicted the shifting tenets of party rule in post-1945 Poland.

Western scholarship, it should be noted, has played a lamentably insignificant role in the historiography of the Proletariat. Similarly, nineteenth-century Polish social and economic history has suffered from a lack of interest in the West for problems not strictly associated with the independence movement. My intention in writing this book, then, is to provide the reader with the first chapter of the history of Polish Marxism as free as possible from interpretations of post-1945 developments in Poland and to engage the closely related problems of social and economic development in the Congress Kingdom with the hope of stimulating further research in these crucial fields.

I have used the standard American system of transliteration for the Russian, except for generally accepted English spellings of common Russian names, places, and terms. Also, in the names of provinces and provincial capitals, the soft sign has been eliminated. Names of Russian revolutionaries and imperial officials of non-Russian descent are rendered in Russian unless their affiliations are primarily with a non-Russian organization. On the sensitive question of the spelling of place names in the Polish territories and in the borderlands, I have chosen what I consider to be a consistent, though not necessarily ethnically accurate, system that reflects the political divisions of late nineteenth-century Poland. All place names in Galicia, the Grand Duchy of Poznań, and the Congress Kingdom are given in Polish. (Only Warsaw has been Anglicized.) All other place names follow the official Austrian, Prussian, or Russian spelling. For the sake of consistency, I have modernized both the Russian and the Polish spelling. Dating follows the modern calendar unless otherwise noted.

Parts of two articles appear in revised form in this book: "Warsaw Positivism and the Origins of Polish Marxism," *Canadian-American Slavic Studies* (Fall, 1976); "Problems in the Historiography of the 'Proletariat'," *East European Quarterly* (Summer, 1978).

The greatest portion of the research for this book was carried out under the auspices of the Stanford University–Warsaw University Exchange Program. I owe a great debt to the staffs of the archives and libraries of Warsaw, particularly Archiwum Główne Akt Dawnych. In addition, thanks are due the archivists of the Tsentral'nyi gosudarst-vennyi istoricheskii arkhiv SSSR, the Hoover Institution, and the International Institute of Social History. At various stages of the research for this project, I have been fortunate to have received financial support from Stanford University, the International Research and Exchanges Board (IREX), and the Fulbright-Hays Program. The Russian Research Center of Harvard University provided a quiet office and conducive atmosphere to work on the manuscript. Generous grants from the Alexander von Humboldt Foundation, which supported a year at the Osteuropa Institute of the Free University of Berlin, and from Boston University's Graduate School and Office of the Provost made possible the book's completion.

To Wayne Vucinich and Terence Emmons of Stanford University, to Dietrich Orlow, Nancy Roelker, Arnold Offner, and John Gagliardo of Boston University, and to Gregory Freeze and David Powell of the Russian Research Center of Harvard University, I owe the inestimable debt of encouragement, care, and example. I am also beholden to those colleagues and friends who read parts or all of the manuscript and provided sound criticisms and helpful comments: John Ackerman, Stanislaw Blejwas, Jeffrey Brooks, Terence Emmons, David Powell, Thomas Simons, Frank Sysyn, and Tadeusz Szafar. I would especially like to thank William Freeman; as friend, colleague, and editor, he was a true partner in this endeavor. Naturally, I am alone responsible for the book's shortcomings.

I

The Background

In the mid-1870s, the Congress Kingdom was a politically incon-sequential Russian dependency. Even by the standards of the Russian Empire, its intellectual life was stagnant and its economy under-developed. The defeat of the 1863–64 rebellion had shattered the political vibrancy of radical Poland, and the Russian administrative repression that followed denuded the Congress Kingdom of the few remnants of autonomous self-government.

Still, the Russian partition represented the direct historical and spiritual descendant of the great Polish-Lithuanian Commonwealth, which had been devoured by its powerful neighbors at the end of the eighteenth century. Warsaw, the seat of the Russian administration in Poland, remained as it had been since the end of the seventeenth century, the heart of Polish civilization and the focus of Poland's ambiguous historical mission. Since the disastrous Kościuszko up-rising in 1794 and the final partition in 1795, the fate of Warsaw and that of the Polish nation rested precariously in the hands of con-querors and congresses, its own enfeebled noble class, and émigré diplomats. With Warsaw at the forefront, Poland rose in two great revolutions, 1830–31 and 1863–64, and attempted to regain its great-ness, only to be crushed and left once again to the mercy of its own immense social chaos and the machinations of European great power diplomacy. The Polish *szlachta* (gentry), the conscious bearers of Polish nationhood, the once great flower of the European nobility, steadily declined as a force able to protect the rights of class or state-hood. After the 1863–64 uprising and the tsarist reforms in the Con-gress Kingdom, the *szlachta* remitted the unquestioned respect and faith of the Polish people as well as that of a segment of European public opinion. The Russians repressed the national aspirations of the Polish nobility and confiscated much of their land. Demoralized, exhausted, and landless, the *szlachta* lost the vigor to resurrect a Polish state or lead the Polish nation. The appearance of democratic, socialist, and other antinobility political theories in 1830–31 and

1863–64 portended a new content as well as a new standard-bearer of Polish nationhood in the half-century following 1863. In fact, the 1860s in the Congress Kingdom witnessed the culmination of the gradual transferral of the social locus of Polish national aspirations from the *szlachta* and its magnate leadership to the new urban intelligentsia and middle class, the theorists of modern socialism and nationalism.

Polish Utopian Socialism

Polish socialists of the first half of the nineteenth century left to their heirs a romantic and idealistic legacy shaped both by the influence of Western utopian socialists (especially Saint-Simon, Buonarotti, and Owen) and by the extraordinary strength of the international forces that gravitated against Polish nationhood. After the defeat of the 1830–31 rebellion, the Polish student was a dreamer, wrote a rather unsympathetic English observer: "Dissatisfied with what was, [he] solaced himself with chimerical visions of a future which will never be. Crude and impracticable theories of socialist scribblers, wild notions of ultra-theoretical liberalism, dreams of impossible changes, . . . filled his mind and animated his exertions."[1]

From this generation of Polish student youth came the great representatives of Polish utopian socialism — Joachim Lelewel, Stanisław Worcell, Adam Mickiewicz, Edward Dembowski, and Jarosław Dąbrowski.[2] They and their followers shared no common vision of the future Poland, nor did they agree on the best means to realize their goals. They did, however, consistently reemphasize a set of political axioms shared as well by Western European socialists.[3] First of all, they insisted that the partitioning powers must be resisted, thrown out of Poland, and that an independent Polish state be reestablished. Secondly, at the core of this new state, as its fundamental social, political, and economic unit, would stand the Polish peasant commune — the *gmina*. Finally, the Polish socialists demonstrated an all-encompassing passion for democracy and republicanism, which united them in their efforts to abolish the *pańszczyzna* (corvée), the financial and juridical basis of Polish serfdom.

What distinguished Polish utopian socialism from the general European pattern was its admixture of intense religio-mystical messianism. As the "Christ of Nations," Poland suffered to save mankind and would be resurrected to be its redemption. This is the familiar theme of the works of the Polish utopians, among them the poet Adam Mickiewicz and the writer Zenon Świętosławski.[4] Piotr Ściegienny, a Catholic priest, and Edward Dembowski, the leader of the bloody Galician peasant revolution of 1846, preached a different form of utopian messianism in the Polish countryside, one that synthesized primitive communal Christianity and revolutionary socialism.[5] Robed in priestly white and carrying a cross, Dembowski was killed leading a group of unarmed Galician poor into battle against Austrian troops in 1846.

The most important organizations representing Polish utopian socialism — the "Towarzystwo Demokratyczne Polskie" (Polish Democratic Association) (1830–31), the "Gromada Rewolucyjna Ludu Polskiego" (Revolutionary Commune of the Polish People) (1835), and their offshoots inside Poland — crumbled even before the defeat of 1863–64.[6] It would be inaccurate to assert, as some Polish historians do, that Polish utopian socialism ceased to exercise any influence on the political development of the Congress Kingdom.[7] Certainly, the rallying cry of Polish utopian socialists and democrats alike — the abolition of the *pańszczyzna* — evaporated with the promulgation of the 1864 Polish emancipation and the establishment of a form of peasant self-government in the countryside. Rather than disappear, Polish utopian socialism underwent a profound transformation. Its concern for social issues diminished, its distinct socialist identity of the pre-1863 period faded, and it gradually merged with the independence movement as a whole. In the post-emancipation period, note the historians Lidia and Adam Ciołkosz, "Polish socialists . . . considered that it was the national obligation of a Pole to be a revolutionary and even a socialist."[8] This new identification of socialism and patriotism forged in the ranks of Polish utopian socialism became one of the most significant political ideologies in modern Polish history, advocated by Piłsudski the revolutionary and Piłsudski the dictator, as well as by ideologues in contemporary Poland.[9]

Although socialist organizations disappeared in the Congress Kingdom prior to the uprising of 1863–64, émigré socialism (now most accurately described as socialist-patriotism) continued to flourish. In fact, the identification of socialism and patriotism in emigration served to strengthen the numbers of socialists abroad. The "Zjednoczenie Emigracji Polskiej" (Union of Polish Emigrants) (1866), renamed in 1868 the "Zjednoczenie Demokracji Polskiej" (Union of Polish Democrats) had 1,500 members and became the major center of activity for émigré radical Poles. Among its members were the leading Polish participants in the Paris Commune — the generals Jarosław Dąbrowski and Walery Wróblewski — as well as the famous publicist

Zygmunt Miłkowski (T. T. Jeż). This group fostered the idea, already articulated by the Polish utopians of the earlier generation, that all European revolutionary struggles, national and social, were inextricably bound to the Polish liberation movement. In the case of the Polish Communards, then, the struggles of the French proletariat served the cause of Polish independence and therefore of Polish socialism.

Marx and Engels, like the Polish socialists themselves, ignored the contradictions inherent in this ideological package. During the 1840s, Joachim Lelewel maintained contacts with them; during the 1870s, Wróblewski, as the secretary of the Polish section of the first International, was an intimate confederate of the pair.[10] Both Marx and Engels shared the Poles' inclination to view the liberation movement as a socialist phenomenon. Engels wrote to Wróblewski in 1875, "je verrai toujours dans la délivrance du prolétariat europeen et sur tout de la délivrance des autres nationalites slaves."[11] Marx himself consistently and unequivocally supported the Polish liberation movement and welcomed its members into the European socialist community. In his view, the reestablishment of an independent Poland would constitute a severe if not fatal blow to the European status quo by freeing the Western proletariat of its most bitter enemy, the reactionary Russian autocracy.[12]

With Poland at the crux of Marx and Engels's strategy for European revolution, Western socialists lent their full support to Polish émigré socialist-patriots throughout the decades of the 1870s and 1880s. The irony of this situation became apparent in the early 1880s when an indigenous Polish Marxist movement appeared whose identity rested partially in a strident disaffiliation with its émigré utopian socialist predecessor. Much to the surprise and chagrin of the Congress Kingdom Marxists, Marx and Engels, as well as the Western socialist community, continued to lionize the émigré utopian circles and support the cause of the Polish independence movement.

Still, Polish Marxists of the 1880s owed a large debt to their utopian forebears. There can be little question that the literary works of Krasiński, Mickiewicz, and Słowacki, all of whom shared the dreams of utopian socialism, kept alive the spirit of democracy and independence even in the most hopeless periods of Polish history. These poets of Polish freedom, read clandestinely in the Congress Kingdom and discussed in hushed whispers, brought countless members of the Polish literate classes into the socialist struggle.[13] Even more significant to the future of Marxism in Poland was the absolute integration of utopian socialism into the patriotic movement. The attempt of Polish socialists of the 1870s and 1880s to unravel the national and social struggles and to deal with each of these struggles separately (much like Rosa Luxemburg's attempts of the following decades) constantly confronted the omnipresent socialist patriotic ideology of Polish pre-Marxist socialism. The strength of this ideology forced nineteenth-century Polish Marxism into the corner of extreme internationalism and led to its ultimate failure to erase socialist-patriotism from the history of Polish socialism.

Russianization

The extremism of both the messianic expectations of Polish utopian socialism in the post-1830 generation and the identification of the social and national struggles among the post-1863 emigration can be traced in part to the hard political facts of Russianization in the Congress Kingdom. It would be misleading, however, to view Russianization as a historically consistent attempt by the "Muscovites" to eliminate the Polish nation.[14] Russianization was neither simply an administrative tool by which the autocracy hoped to integrate its Polish population, as A. L. Pogodin wrote, nor was it an attempt to make Poles into Russians.[15] Lacking an official definition and depending rather on a spectrum of definitions which originated in various centers of political power in the empire, Russianization can be generally described as a series of related, but qualitatively varied, attempts to make loyal subjects of the Russian Empire out of a resentful Polish population. Especially in the borderlands, Russianization reached the proportions of forced assimilation.

Between the defeat of the 1830–31 insurrection and 1863, Russianization in the Congress Kingdom consisted exclusively of administrative measures meant to abrogate the rights of autonomy granted by the 1815 constitution. After the 1863–64 rebellion, however, Russian liberal opinion turned violently against the Poles, and the autocracy, now virtually unopposed, implemented a virulent anti-Polish policy, which brought to an end all vestiges of Polish autonomous civil life in the Congress Kingdom. The first step was the Polish peasant reform of 1864, which cut the umbilical cord tying Russian rule in the Congress Kingdom to the Polish gentry. In 1866, the Russians eliminated the Administrative Council, the Council of State, the independent budget administration, and combined the functions of these bodies into the existing ministries in St. Petersburg. After the death of Viceroy Berg in 1874, the autocracy created a completely new Russian administrative apparatus for the Congress Kingdom. A Russian governor-general who supervised an all-Russian administrative staff now ruled the *"Privislanskii Krai"* ("Vistulaland"), which consisted of ten *gubernii,* organized like the other *gubernii* of the empire. The final steps in the administrative integration of the Congress Kingdom came between 1876 and 1886, when the extra-ministerial organizations for Polish affairs — the Chancellorate, the State-Secretariat of the Kingdom of Poland, and the Committee for the Affairs of the Kingdom of Poland — were abolished. By the mid-1880s, as Pogodin wrote, "the 'Privislanskii Krai' was simply turned into one of the Russian governor-generalships."[16] Ludicrous administrative orders were enforced forbidding any official or public use of words or expressions that would indicate that Poles were foreigners to the empire or that a Poland in any way existed in the present or in the past.[17]

Polish fears that behind this extensive reorganization of administration and nomenclature loomed a serious attack on the Polish nation were justified by the Russian administration of Polish affairs in the borderlands of the empire. "The Poles should be ejected at any price from Russia's western provinces," exhorted the Slavophile Mikhail Pogodin in 1867; "they should be smoked out, expelled, deported with all their money and Russian bonds, with their priests, with all their belongings and grief, with their movable properties. That soil is ours, it is native Russian soil — not an inch of it should belong to Poland."[18] The governor-general of Lithuania, Mikhail Muraviev (called by Kucharzewski the "Vilna demon of revenge with the bulldog face") followed Pogodin's advice and, with brutal systematic reprisals against the Polish gentry in Lithuania, earned his historical appellation, the "Hangman."[19]

Russian terrorization of Poles in the borderlands corresponded in part to the pressure exerted on Poles in the Congress Kingdom to discontinue the use of the Polish language. According to the *ukazes* of 1868 and 1869, all administrative institutions were to use the Russian language. From 1867 Russian was to be the only language of instruction (and conversation) in the middle schools. From 1871 all entrance examinations into the gymnasia were to be given in Russian only. The Warsaw Szkoła Główna (Main School), which had been the primary center of Polish learning and culture since its foundation in 1862, was reintegrated into the Russian university system as Warsaw University in 1869. These measures and others intended to curtail Polish national

feeling proved fruitless. To be sure, the autocracy had totally transformed the civil life of the Congress Kingdom in the years 1864 to 1880.
But as Governor-General Albedynskii reported to the tsar in 1880,
these measures did not touch the Polish nationality itself. Both
"materially and morally," wrote Albedynskii, national feelings appear
"even stronger than before."[20]

Albedynskii was the last governor-general in Warsaw who pleaded
the case for Polish cultural autonomy under Russian rule. The decade
of the 1880s in the Congress Kingdom was characterized instead by a
new and more brutal era of Russianization, which the Soviet historian
P. A. Zaionchkovskii justifiably terms "zoological nationalism."[21]
These new policies of national repression emanated primarily from the
chambers of K. P. Pobedonostsev, the ober-prokurator of the Holy
Synod and chief advisor to Alexander III in the first half of the 1880s.
They were carried out in the Congress Kingdom by the new Governor-
General I. V. Gurko and by the Curator of Schools A. L. Apukhtin.[22]
As military governor of the St. Petersburg region, General Gurko had
earned a reputation in the Russian administration for his military
prowess and his tough-minded, though uninspired, administrative
abilities. "To be sure," noted Pobedonostsev, "he is no genius."[23] A. A.
Polovtsev recorded in his diaries the increasing displeasure with which
the liberal camp of the Russian administration viewed Gurko's policies: "With such foolish lawlessness is Poland administered under the
influence of Gurko."[24] The laws introduced in the 1860s and 1870s to
induce Polish integration into the empire were used by Gurko to
Russianize the Polish population, especially Polish youth. In the
school system, wrote Gurko, the Polish student should be vilified. He
should be "reproached for his Polish origins, insulted in his national
feelings," and his religion should be treated as "contemptible." His
mother tongue should be relegated to the place of a foreign language,
and at that, after French and German. "From the Polish child . . . is
demanded a better knowledge of the Russian language and of its gram-
matical rules than from Russians themselves."[25]

The Curator of Schools Apukhtin also began his career in the military and, like Gurko, could count on strong support from conservative
court circles.[26] Before coming to Warsaw, Apukhtin had already
proved his mettle as a thorough conservative in school affairs. If anything, Apukhtin's Great Russian chauvinism and Polonophobia went
further than Gurko's, and he quickly earned his reputation among
Polish youth as the "beast."[27] In fact, Apukhtin can be considered the
first of a lamentable series of foreign racist politicians who attempted

to deprive the Poles not only of their statehood, but of their nationality. In the schools he unleashed a reign of terror that encouraged an atmosphere of hate. Polish school children were beaten if caught speaking Polish; at Warsaw University and in the other schools of higher education, Polish professors were relieved of their duties as were Polonophile Russian professors. All courses, even those on Polish law, literature, and history, were now to be taught in Russian, by Russians, from a Russian point of view.[28]

Roman Dmowski, the leader of Polish National Democracy and a brilliant observer of late nineteenth-century Polish affairs in the Congress Kingdom, carefully distinguished the form of Russianization carried out by Apukhtin from that of his predecessor of the 1870s, S. S. Witte. Witte, wrote Dmowski, instituted a period of "formal Russianization," in which the schools "were transformed into Russian schools, everything which was Polish being expurgated from them." When Witte died in 1879, Dmowski continued, the schools were totally Russianized, and almost half of the teachers in the schools were Russians. In Apukhtin, Witte's successor, the "brutal force" was found to translate formal policy into actual attempts at denationalization. For the schools, Dmowski concluded, "a new period was introduced, a period of unbelievable suppression." No new reforms were introduced. Still this period "weighed more heavily on the fate of our younger generation" than did the previous one.[29]

Following Dmowski's analysis, the post-1863 history of Russian rule in the Congress Kingdom can be divided into three fairly distinct periods. Between 1863 and 1866, the Russian authorities fought, then crushed the Polish revolt and instituted legalistic reforms to curtail any further outbreaks of Polish national feeling. The second period, roughly 1867 to 1879, corresponded to the reform period as a whole and saw the gradual formal Russianization (as well as rationalization) of government institutions and public forums in the Congress Kingdom. The final period, 1879–1886, the period of most direct concern to this study, was the high point of Russianization. In this period, the autocracy, determined to subjugate the Polish to the Russian nationality and to make loyal imperial citizens out of recalcitrant Poles, resorted to methods of denationalization and re-education. The school system of the Congress Kingdom became the focal point of the attack. Using repeated and excessive beatings, expulsion, and vilification as their means, Apukhtin, Gurko, and the tsarist administration succeeded only in creating an entire generation of violently anti-Russian Polish educated youth.

The struggle between tsarist administrative demands and nationalist policies, on the one hand, and Polish cultural resilience and socialist patriotic traditions, on the other, permeated the history of the Congress Kingdom in the last half of the nineteenth century. No political ideology or social movement could ignore the basic political problem of Pole versus Russian and still be effective. In the immediate post-1863 generation, however, the consensus among educated Poles that the autocracy must be violently resisted fell apart. A whole new series of problems emerged as a result of rapid Polish industrialization after 1863, not the least among them the burgeoning political importance of the Polish labor force. A new mood swept the Polish educated classes as well, one that demanded reconciliation, peace, and economic progress. The glories of the Polish past immortalized in the works of Mickiewicz or Kraszewski faded in comparison to the awesome power of modern factories and commercial banking establishments. That the mood of peaceful progress did not last and that the benefits of modernization did not quell but rather fed the sources of national discontent can in part be attributed to the autocracy's anti-Polish policies of the 1880s and the viciousness with which Gurko and Apukhtin carried them out.

II

The Industrialization of the Congress Kingdom and the Formation of the Polish Working Class, 1864–1885

Although Russianization was a politically motivated and politically implemented process, it nevertheless exerted a profound influence on the economic history of the Congress Kingdom. Both Russia and the Congress Kingdom, as underdeveloped areas ruled by a common economic as well as political system, experienced rapid industrialization as a result of similar variants from, or in Alexander Gershenkron's model "substitutions" for, major building blocks of the industrial revolution in more advanced countries. However, the nature of the "substitutions" that occurred in Polish industrialization were determined by the lack of an independent political administration as well as by its degree of backwardness.[1] The Russian factory expert I. I. Ianzhul and after him Rosa Luxemburg argued that without its integral ties to Russia, the Congress Kingdom would have been severely handicapped in its industrialization drive.[2] Most modern Polish economic historians argue, on the other hand, that the benefits of Russian markets and economic policies were outweighed by the absence of a forceful and centralized Polish political administration, one that would have encouraged even more rapid and certainly more diversified economic development.[3]

Whether or not the tsarist political administration of the Congress Kingdom eventually hindered or encouraged Polish economic development, it is clear that the history of industrialization in the Congress Kingdom can be examined only within the broader context of industrialization in the empire itself. The benefits and encumbrances of tsarist financial and industrial planning (or lack of planning) influenced the pace and the extent of industrialization in the ten *gubernii* of the Congress Kingdom as they did that of Russia as a whole. The Congress Kingdom, then, was simply another industrial area of the Russian Empire, or, as Engels wrote in 1892, "the great industrial region of the Russian Empire."[4] Its most important industrial *guber-nii*, Warsaw and Piotrków, corresponded in some measure to the St. Petersburg and Moscow industrial regions.[5] In each case the former region concentrated primarily on metal manufacturing and the latter on textile production. From this point of view, the individuality of these regions was determined by their particular geographical, demographic, resource, and transportation configurations.[6]

At the same time, there exists a separate history of the "national economy" of the Congress Kingdom distinct from the economic history of the empire. This is in part because the same Russian administrative measures elicited different economic responses in the various industrial regions of the empire. Moreover, because of political considerations, tsarist economic policies toward the Congress Kingdom often differed radically from those designed for the rest of the empire. Also, although the rapid industrialization of the Congress Kingdom took place independently of economic developments in Austrian Galicia and Prussian Poland, interpartition economics cannot be ignored. The development of the industrial sector in each partition was affected by the labor, products, buyers, and capital that found their ways across partition borders. Even more important to the economic development of the three partitions were the entrepreneurial and political ideas that spilled over borders more easily than either labor or capital.

With these reservations to approaching the economic history of the Congress Kingdom in an all-Russian context in mind, this chapter focuses on those aspects of the history of Polish industrialization in the post-1863 period that directly and indirectly influenced the formation of the Proletariat. Polish Marxism, like its European counterparts, was both an affirmation of and protest against the new industrial age; its specific characteristics can be examined only against the background of tsarist economic policies, the growth of Polish factories and towns, and the development of the Polish working class itself.

The Industrial Revolution in the Congress Kingdom

The most important factor prompting rapid industrialization in the Polish partition was the Polish peasant emancipation (*uwłaszczenie*) of 1864, in which the Russian authorities attacked the economic predominance of the Polish *szlachta*. In the final section of this chapter on the formation of the Polish working class, the *uwłaszczenie* will be considered in greater detail. For now, it is enough to note that *uwłaszczenie,* unlike its 1861 Russian counterpart, provided the legal and financial framework for the destruction of gentry farming, the consolidation of peasant landholding, and the formation of an urban work force.

Also crucial for the development of Polish industry were imperial railway building programs. The strategic location of the Polish partition and the political decision to tie the Congress Kingdom by rail to European Russia encouraged investment in the Polish railway system. In 1865 and 1866 the "Łódź-Factory" station was completed, linking Łódź to the Warsaw-Vienna line and facilitating the transportation of goods between the Łódź region and Warsaw. In 1866, the most important section was finished — from Warsaw to the eastern border of the Congress Kingdom at Terespol. The direct ties between Warsaw and Moscow through Brest (Brześć) were completed in 1872. Warsaw was also linked to Kiev in 1873 with the completion of a line between Kiev and Brest. By 1877 an east-west Congress Kingdom line connected the Russian border at Terespol-Brest with the Prussian border in the west, and from there on to Poznań. Between 1870 and 1880, a second track was built on the Warsaw-Vienna line, and between 1883 and 1886 on the Warsaw-Terespol line. The "Vistula Line" was completed in 1877, facilitating the transportation of goods and labor within Warsaw *guberniia* itself.[7] Along with improvements in the Warsaw-Vienna and Warsaw-Poznań lines, these imperial railway projects not only tied all the major and even secondary economic centers of the Congress Kingdom to one another by the late 1870s, but also tied them to markets in Prussia and Austria and, more significantly, to markets in central Russia.[8]

The effect of the new and improved railway links on the industrial boom in the Congress Kingdom between 1864 and 1878 is difficult to gauge exactly. Still, the role of the railways in the boom is apparent from the rapidly rising figures of product transport on these lines. The tonnage of goods transported on the Warsaw-Vienna line increased six times from 1864 to 1884, on the Warsaw-Terespol line five times from 1867 to 1884, and on the Warsaw-Łódź line ten times from 1867 to 1884.[9] In the short span of five years, 1866 to 1871, the income from the Łódź-Factory line quadrupled from 28 to 115 thousand rubles.[10] Consumption of iron ore and coal produced in the Dąbrowa Basin was concurrently stimulated by the railway building. On the Warsaw-Vienna line, which served the Dąbrowa mines, the amount of coal transported increased between 1860 and 1870 from 3.5 million puds to 17.6 million. (1 pud = 16.38 kg.) By 1877, the amount of coal transported reached 35 million puds and by 1880, 77.7 million puds.[11] In its predominantly political decision to integrate the various areas of the empire by rail, the tsarist administration inadvertently placed in the hands of Polish industry the powerful stimulant of an efficient and modern transportation system. Even more significantly, tsarist tariff policies, which were intended to integrate the Congress Kingdom economically into the empire, also unwittingly stimulated the overall industrial growth of the Congress Kingdom. Perhaps more than any other single factor, imperial tariff policy brought to a close a four-century-long Polish tradition of grain export and inaugurated an era in the late 1860s where, in Stefan Kieniewicz's formulation, instead of exporting grain to the West the country now supplied Russia with textile goods.[12]

Before the Crimean War, the Kankrin policy of high protective tariffs erected an insurmountable obstacle to the rapid development of trade between Russia and the West and between the Congress Kingdom and the West. Kankrin also preserved the tariff barriers between Russia and the Congress Kingdom. Although Russian industry made some gains under this system in the beginning of the 1850s, Polish industry continued to depend on specialized artisan production, sometimes illegally exported by Jewish tradesmen.[13] In the 1850s and 1860s, Congress Kingdom sugar appeared on the St. Petersburg market, but this export was curtailed by rapid strides in the Polish-owned Ukrainian sugar industry.[14] In 1857 and then again in 1868, prohibitive empire import tariffs were reduced, which provided a needed shot in the arm for both Russian and Polish industry by reducing the costs of imported machinery.

The most significant imperial tariff act in the history of Congress Kingdom industrialization was promulgated in 1877.[15] This act, by reintroducing high import tariffs on all finished products, effectively eliminated the competition of nonempire producers. At the same time, it knocked down the tariff wall between European Russia and the Congress Kingdom. The ability of Polish manufacturers to compete on equal footing with their Russian counterparts for markets in the empire vastly increased and proved to be both a short-run and long-run gain for industry in the Congress Kingdom. German investment now began to pour into Congress Kingdom industry. Some German industrialists quite simply moved their factories to the Congress Kingdom, imported raw materials at low duty rates, and manufactured the finished products, which could then enter the internal Russian market tariff-free.[16] Sosnowiec, on the German border, became an industrial center overnight. Between 1877 and the late 1880s twenty-three new German-financed and German-managed factories were built in the Congress Kingdom.[17] In only the two years following the tariff act, 1877–1879, the value of production of the Polish textile industry more than doubled, from twenty-six to fifty-eight million rubles.[18]

The investment of foreign capital in the Congress Kingdom in the 1870s and 1880s was facilitated and sometimes even initiated by the rapid expansion of Warsaw private banks and investment companies.[19] The Bank Handlowy (Trade Bank) and the Bank Dyskontowy (Discount Bank), chartered in 1871 and 1872 respectively, erected the machinery to finance the industrial boom of the next three decades and played a crucial role in attracting foreign investment. According to W. Kula, foreign-owned factories accounted for 25 percent of the total number of Congress Kingdom enterprises, employed 54 percent of the total number of workers, and manufactured 60 percent of the total worth of production.[20] The Russian factory expert I. I. Ianzhul, to whom the historian owes many of the first statistics on Congress Kingdom industry, expressed his alarm at this mushrooming growth of foreign-owned factories in the Congress Kingdom. In no way, Ianzhul warned, could the state consider this growth beneficial.[21]

The combination of the tariff act, the accelerated pace of investment in Congress Kingdom industry, and the empire-wide railway building spurt of the 1870s led to a marked increase of the role of Congress Kingdom export to Russia, especially to central Russia, and through central Russia to the Far East.[22] By the 1870s, one-quarter of all Congress Kingdom cotton goods production was exported to Russia.[23] By the mid-1880s, approximately one-half of all Congress Kingdom industrial production, and by the end of the 1880s three-quarters of all cotton-mill production, was likewise exported to Russia.[24] Ianzhul despaired, as did the textile manufacturers of the Moscow region, that the entire Russian textile market would soon be completely dominated by the cotton mills of Łódź, Zgierz, and Tomaszów and the linen factories of Żyrardów.[25] The Asian market had already fallen to the Poles, claimed Ianzhul; Kharkov and Kiev had quickly succumbed to Polish industrial goods; and even in Moscow itself, Polish textiles were successfully competing with Muscovite textiles.[26]

Quantitative Aspects of Polish Industrialization

Between 1864 and 1880, the Congress Kingdom evolved from a traditional economic unit whose national income derived almost exclusively from grain export to a semi-industrial unit whose 1878 industrial and mining income of 150 million rubles accounted for 23 percent of its total income.[27] In the years 1860 to 1879, the number of textile factories in the Congress Kingdom increased by 4,000, the number of textile workers by 10,000, and the value of textile production quadrupled from 14 to 58 million rubles.[28] Notable progress was registered as well in the metal industries of the Congress Kingdom.[29] In 1870 the Polish metallurgy industry produced a value of 2.8 million rubles and consisted of 97 factories employing 3,000 workers. By 1880 the number of factories doubled to 181, the number of workers increased 2½ times to 7,500, and the value of production quadrupled to 9.3 million rubles.[30] In the highly specialized machine-building industry, which does not normally lend itself to extremely rapid expansion, remarkable strides were made between 1870 and 1880. The number of factories increased from 46 to 72, and the number of workers increased from 2,100 to 4,400. The value of production more than tripled from 1,765,000 rubles to 5,492,000 rubles.[31]

With available statistical information, it is impossible to calculate accurately for this period the rate of industrial growth in the Congress Kingdom or for that matter in the Russian Empire as a whole.[32] If we take, however, Ianzhul's statistics on the value of industrial output, which are generally corroborated by those few studies of Polish economic growth in the immediate post-emancipation decades, and compare them to estimates of European Russian growth during the same period, the relative magnitude of Congress Kingdom industrial expansion becomes clear. Between 1863 and 1879 Russian industrial output rose from a value of 247,614,000 rubles to 541,602,000 rubles, a sixteen-year increase of 119 percent. Congress Kingdom industry in the sixteen-year period 1864–1880 produced a value of 50,034,000 rubles in 1864 and 171,414,000 in 1880, an increase of 242 percent.[33] Therefore, while the value of Russian industrial production in these years was growing at a very high rate of 7.5 percent per year (without adjusting for currency variations), the value of Polish industrial output was growing at twice that rate, a phenomenal 15.1 percent per year.

The marked superiority in the growth of the *value* of Polish industrial production cannot be attributed to such factors as growth of factory population, urbanization, factory size, or factory concentration — Russian growth in almost every case matched or outstripped that of the Congress Kingdom.[34] Neither can one attribute this superiority to machine-intense industry. In the cotton manufacturing sector, where the Poles made the most notable strides, the number of spinning machines per factory and per shop remained, in both Russia and the Congress Kingdom, at a steady fifty machines per institution (1877–1886).[35] What did affect the higher value increases in the Polish economy versus the Russian was the historical pace of industrialization in both areas.

If we turn to the crucial textile industry, for example, we see that in 1815 there were virtually no cotton goods produced in the Russian partition of Poland. Finished textiles of all kinds were imported from Germany and Russia and paid for by Polish grain export.[36] At the same time Russia possessed a small but significant cotton industry of 198 factories.[37] In the 1820s and 1830s, with the encouragement of Polish Minister of Finance Lubecki, thousands of craftsmen, Germans and Poles, poured into the Congress Kingdom from the Prussian partition and initiated a handicraft-based cotton industry in the Łódź region.[38] By the mid-1850s, however, because of an overall expansion of Russian industry stimulated by the needs of the Crimean War, the Russian textile industry remained clearly superior to the Polish. From about 1858 to the mid-1860s, the empire as a whole experienced a serious economic crisis; factories closed, the work force was drastically reduced, and production plummeted.

The economic recovery that European Russia experienced beginning about 1867 was rather more a beginning for Congress Kingdom industry, and the advantages of Polish backwardness became readily apparent. Ianzhul later observed:

> Judging from such rapid development of industry, one could come to the conclusion that in the Congress Kingdom, as a place of much more favored industrial development than the empire, this industry should be older, and its development should have taken a more natural and correct road. . . . We would not be making the least error if on the other hand we maintain that in general the industry of Poland is younger than the Russian.[39]

Ianzhul's observations are supported by available statistics on the ruble output per worker in the Congress Kingdom and European Russia between 1860 and 1890.[40] In the immediate post-emancipation period the individual Russian worker produced about 50 rubles more than his Polish counterpart, but by 1880 the individual Polish worker produced over 300 rubles more than the Russian. The crucial change came in 1869–70, when Polish industrialization quite literally "took off."

Although the Russians renovated old machines and continued to encourage the purchase of machinery manufactured in sometimes second-rate St. Petersburg factories, German and Polish factory owners preferred to import modern and more efficient German machinery. In the short span of seven years, at the outset of modern Polish industrialization, 1868–1875, the value of machinery imported into the Congress Kingdom increased over nine times from 520,000 rubles to 4,620,000 rubles.[41] These Congress Kingdom entrepreneurs not only imported new machines but also hired Western managers and foremen who were better acquainted than their Russian counterparts with modern industrial techniques.

In addition, Polish factories were newer and had better facilities than the Russian establishments. If one compares statistics for the pace of new factory building for Moscow and St. Petersburg *gubernii* with the figures for Warsaw and Piotrków *gubernii* during the same period, the relative newness of Congress Kingdom industry becomes apparent. In St. Petersburg and Moscow *gubernii,* about 30 percent of the factories were built before 1870. In Warsaw *guberniia* fewer than 25 percent and in Piotrków *guberniia* 12 percent of the factories were built before 1870. In the years 1876 to 1886, eighteen new German-owned and German-financed factories were built in Łódź alone.[42]

The results of the Congress Kingdom's relative newness to industrial production show up not in comparative figures of rising urban and working-class population or of increased industrial concentration in larger factories in fewer industrial centers, but in the increased worth of the final product. In fact, as Olga Crisp suggests, there may be a reverse relationship between the size of the Russian factory and its modernity.[43] Taking the official statistics for the empire's machine-building industry, one sees that although the Russian factories were much larger than the Polish — 143 workers per factory to 70 per factory in the Congress Kingdom — the individual Polish worker in these factories produced a value of 1,313 rubles per year to his Russian counterpart's 923 rubles per year. Russian factories were twice as big, and still the Poles produced over 25 percent more than the Russians.[44]

Other factors of Congress Kingdom superiority — easier access to better raw materials, greater efficiency and care of the individual worker, and better marketing procedures — are difficult to gauge, but undoubtedly played a role in the more valuable Polish product. In any case, in less than twenty years, 1867–1885, the Congress Kingdom achieved a remarkable feat of economic advancement, jumping from industrial obscurity into a highly mechanized industrial economy dominated by textiles and metals. It advanced from a moderate consumer of Russian industrial production to a superior competitor in many industrial sectors and, in textiles, to a major threat to the Moscow industrial region's textile markets.

Towns and Factories

The demographic structure and quality of life in the Congress Kingdom were altered drastically as a result of this rapid economic expansion. Between 1876 and 1886 the Congress Kingdom participated in the spiraling population growth of the Russian Empire as a whole. Although between 1840 and 1863, the population of the Congress Kingdom grew from 4.5 to 5 million — a twenty-three year increase of 11 percent — in the next twenty-three year period, from 1863 to 1886, it rose from 5 to 7.9 million, an increase of 58 percent.[45] Most of this growth was concentrated in Congress Kingdom cities and towns, which expanded from 1,354,000 in 1866 to 2,125,000 in 1886.[46] The population of Warsaw almost doubled between 1863 and 1886, from 212,000 to 407,000, and the population of Łódź tripled, from 33,000 in 1866 to 117,000 in 1886.[47] Some towns, such as Sosnowiec on the German border and Żyrardów outside of Warsaw, were essentially created by the industrial boom. In 1866 Żyrardów was a sleepy artisan town of several hundred. By 1886, Żyrardów's population had reached 10,000, 90 percent of whom were linen workers and their families.[48]

The industrial work force grew at an even more rapid pace than the urban population as a whole. Between 1863 and 1883 the number of industrial workers increased at the highest estimate from 50 to 150 thousand, or by three times, and at the lowest estimate, by 2½ times.[49] By the late 1880s industrial workers and their families accounted for 8 percent of the total population of the Congress Kingdom.[50] The growth in the number of industrial workers was accompanied by a slight increase in the number of factories and works and therefore by an overall increase of the size of individual factories. In 1870 Congress Kingdom industry employed 67,595 workers in 9,433 factories and workshops; in 1880, it employed 118,831 in 9,606 factories and workshops, a rise of from 7.2 workers per institution to 12.4 workers per institution. In the highly concentrated Warsaw metal industry during the same period, the number of workers per factory and workshop rose from 28 to 63. In 1870, the three largest cotton mills in the textile city of Łódź employed an average of 150 workers. A decade later, the five largest Łódź cotton mills employed an average of 560 workers.[51]

Both Łódź and Warsaw experienced a rapid development of the use of modern factory machinery. Capital investment poured most heavily into these booming industrial centers. By the end of the 1870s, Łódź textiles accounted for 60 percent of the total Congress Kingdom industrial product (in contrast to 32 percent in 1870).[52] This new Manchester of the Russian Empire aroused both fear and awe among visiting Russian officials. The factory inspector V. V. Sviatlovskii wrote of Łódź: "Without a doubt, neither in Moscow nor in St. Petersburg is there such a concentration of purely factory workers. In this sense, Łódź is totally unique within the boundaries of our country, to be likened only to several factory centers in Western Europe."[53] The monuments to the new era of capitalism in Łódź were the factories Scheibler and Poznański. Almost 60 percent of the total number of Congress Kingdom spindles were at work at Scheibler. Between 1870 and 1875 alone, the worth of the machinery here quadrupled, the number of workers grew from 333 to 1,175, and the worth of production increased from 600,000 rubles to 1.8 million rubles. Poznański's factory, built in 1873, quadrupled its number of mechanical looms between 1874 and 1879; at the same time, its work force increased from 294 to 700 and its worth of production from 412,000 to more than 1.5 million rubles.[54]

Warsaw's metal industry similarly benefited from the new concentration of capital and workers. Though containing only one-quarter of the Congress Kingdom's machine-building factories, Warsaw nevertheless employed three-quarters of that industry's workers and produced four-fifths of its income.[55] In 1876 the Warsaw and Łódź industrial regions accounted for 60 percent of the total worth of Congress Kingdom industrial production — 28 million rubles in the former, 22 million in the latter. After the tariff acts of 1877, however, the increasing importance of the textile industry pushed Łódź further ahead of Warsaw. By 1885 Łódź industry employed 23,000 workers who produced a value of 40 million rubles.[56]

The Formation of the Polish Working Class

Where did the Polish working force come from? Which factors in its formation influenced its participation (or lack of participation) in the social and political movements of the late 1870s and 1880s? In order to answer these questions and others involving the first generation of Polish industrial workers, we need to turn back to the emancipation statutes of 1864, the *uwłaszczenie*.[56a] In contrast to the short-term effects of the 1861 Russian emancipation, *uwłaszczenie* rapidly altered the structure of landownership in the Polish partition. Smallholding peasants sold their meager possessions and along with the landless peasantry migrated, often permanently, to the cities. Middle and lower-level *szlachta* also lost or sold their estates and looked to the cities for work. This movement of the Polish nobility to the cities not only swelled the urban professional classes but also forced poorer members of the *szlachta* into the working class.[57] The primary beneficiaries of the *uwłaszczenie* were the middle-level peasants who bought out their smallholding compatriots. Altogether, the Polish countryside witnessed a marked improvement in the living standard of peasant landholders.

Through *uwłaszczenie,* the autocracy provided the groundwork for the development of an urban working class. With the proverbial stroke of a pen, Congress Kingdom industry was provided with cheap and available labor (from the peasantry) and potential skilled labor (from the *szlachta*). Tsarist fears of an urban proletariat, so pervasive in the formulation of the Russian emancipation, were disregarded in the Polish case owing to the first priority of eliminating the political power of the *szlachta* in favor of a loyalist grouping of small and middle-level farmers on the one hand and urban entrepreneurs on the other.

In European Russia, as is well known, the rapidly expanding industrial proletariat remained half-peasant. Bound to the land by communal obligations and cultural patterns, Russian peasants were not forced into a new social grouping by the combination of emancipation and industrialization as were their Polish counterparts. Neither did the Russian nobility rapidly lose their economic and social status as did the Polish *szlachta.* (Russian nobles also made up a much smaller percentage of the population than did the oversized Polish nobility.) Careers in the expanding tsarist bureaucracy (now difficult if not impossible for Poles to pursue), government loans and mortgages, and a favorable land settlement prevented the Russian nobility from being forced into the industrial proletariat. In this sense, then, the Russian emancipation held back social change — the Polish emancipation prompted it.

Another aspect of social change in the Congress Kingdom stimulated by rapid industrialization was the transformation of Polish artisans into factory workers.[58] This transformation was shared to some extent by the Russian artisans employed in the *kustar'* or home industry sector.[59] That is, many of the craftsmen who had formerly worked in *kustar*s sought employment in factories. However, the Polish and Russian artisans who entered their respective industrial work forces brought with them different sets of historical experiences. Most important for the development of the Polish working class was the fact that the Polish artisans were overwhelmingly urban and had been involved in the Polish urban insurrectionary tradition.[60] The Russian artisans, on the other hand, were predominantly peasants. The transition from peasant-artisan to peasant-worker in Russia paralleled the transition from urban artisan to urban worker in the Congress Kingdom. Both transitions involved the alienating and degrading process of workers confronting machines, crowded and unhealthy work conditions, and the strictures of impersonal wage earning. Yet the Russian artisan-worker often returned to his peasant home at least part of the year and maintained his ties with the communal village.

Because urban artisans and even noble-born workers were available to fill the expanding factories, Polish peasants had a much more difficult time than the Russian *muzhik* finding work in large, mechanized factories. Instead, the Polish peasant was employed primarily in the most primitive industries on a day-labor basis or in the unskilled building-trades industry. After achieving some minor skills, the peasant could then go on to earn his living in the new factories. Still, these peasants, unlike the Russian peasant-workers, generally severed their ties to the land and became permanent city dwellers.[61] The economic significance of the transformation of Polish peasants and artisans into permanent urban workers in the post-emancipation period is partly reflected by the above-cited individual production advantage of the Polish over the Russian worker. Certainly, one of the most important factors in this advantage was the fact that the Polish peasant-worker had learned the skills of an urban factory worker, participated in urban culture, and severed his economic, if not psychological, ties with the village. The Russian peasant-worker, on the other hand, rarely assimilated into urban life, thus impeding the development of a skilled and industrially advanced labor force in European Russia.

Living and Working Conditions of Polish Labor

The average gross wages of the Polish worker were subject to wide variations, depending upon the geographical area and the type of enterprise. On the whole, Warsaw metalworkers were the best paid not only in the Congress Kingdom but also in the Russian Empire as a whole. Between 1877 and 1882, the average Warsaw worker's wages steadily rose from 226 rubles a year to 286 rubles a year, about 50 rubles a year higher than his St. Petersburg counterpart.[62] In the textile region of Piotrków *guberniia,* the average wage came to 188 rubles a year, about 20 rubles less than the Moscow average. Throughout the Congress Kingdom in 1880, the average male earned 204 rubles a year, the average female slightly more than half of that sum.[64]

It is of course extremely difficult to translate these gross wages into a reasonable portrait of the Polish worker's daily existence. Expenses for housing, for instance, varied widely throughout the Congress Kingdom. Though less often than his Russian counterpart, Polish workers sometimes lived in factory barracks, costing between six and thirty-six rubles a year.[65] In Warsaw, where few such barracks existed, a worker had to pay five to six rubles a month or around sixty to seventy rubles a year for a rented room located about an hour walk outside the city.[66] The socialist newspaper *Równość* concluded from these high rental payments that a Warsaw worker "was not in a position to keep his family from hunger." On the other hand, in Żyrardów, where many of the 5,000 workers lived in barracks, the average wage was half that of a Warsaw worker.[67]

Another variable that complicates the problem of wages in the Congress Kingdom was the extent to which the worker was tied to the land. Factory Inspector Mikhailovskii, for instance, calculated that the Russian worker was actually better paid than the Polish worker because of his high nonfactory income.[68] The phenomena of the peasant-worker and nomad-worker common to Russia were sometimes present as well in the Congress Kingdom. Thousands of Warsaw workers from the surrounding counties rose as early as two in the morning to make the six o'clock factory whistle. To be sure, those Polish workers who lived on the land not only paid less rent but also were able to save on food and clothing costs. Polish workers in the mines and ironworks were paid a bonus for their horses.[69] However, it is unlikely that, as Mikhailovskii suggests, these peasant-workers were financially better off than their urban counterparts. They were paid much less, and a good portion of that income went to maintaining their plots of land.

Another aspect of assessing the real wages of the Polish worker is the fact that the actual pay received ranged from between one-third and one-half of his gross wage. Subtracted was not only his debt to the factory store, where he bought (on credit and most often at higher prices) his groceries and clothes, but also penalties for allegedly poor work.[70] Even according to Mikhailovskii, an apologist for the tsarist factory system, one-third of the workers' wages in the 1880s were attached because of penalties.[71] Among unskilled ironworkers of the Congress Kingdom, 78 rubles out of their wages of 112 rubles a year went for clothes, food, lighting, rent, and taxes, just for a man and wife. Out of the remaining 34 rubles expenses for children had to be paid, which often exceeded this sum.[72] If one then takes into account the penalties, it becomes clear that debt to the company store was the rule rather than the exception.

Still, the Polish worker was considered "privileged" among workers in the empire because of his shorter average working day — according to Ianzhul ten to twelve hours a day versus twelve to fourteen in European Russia. Rosa Luxemburg quoted a factory commission report that came to the same conclusion:

> Although in Moscow factories a 13 to 14 hour workday is very widespread, this is the case only in nine factories in Poland, and in three cases only in single sections of these factories. Generally in 75 percent of the [C.K.] factories, work is carried on 10–12 hours, and one can consider 11 hours as the average workday for Poland. In Moscow the average workday is more than 12 hours. In Poland night work appears to be a rare exception, in Moscow it is very widespread.[74]

Factory Inspector Sviatlovskii also noted this disparity. "Six in the morning to six in the evening seems to be the general rule for the Polish worker," he wrote, and in contrast to Russia, "we did not once see in the *Privislanskii Krai* a sixteen hour day or higher."[75] At the same time, it was not uncommon that the factory manager demanded overtime as well as lunchwork from his employees. Neither the six-day week nor even religious holidays were consistently honored.

Indeed, before the Factory Laws of 1888, wrote Mikhailovskii, the factory owners "had the right to use the labor of workers of both sexes and various ages on all days of the year [and at any hour of the day] not excluding Sunday and other holidays."[76] Youngsters beginning at age six and seven and female labor were employed throughout the Polish partition and were the most severely affected by the lack of factory legislation.[77] Their pay, as we have seen, was one-third to one-half that of the men, and sometimes for the same work. In times of economic difficulties, they were the first to be laid off. Their jobs were sometimes less skilled and more taxing than those of the men. Women in the

Żyrardów factory, for instance, were ill twice as often as the men.[78]

Perhaps more telling in the outlook of Polish workers toward revolutionary propaganda and life itself than the extraordinarily long working day and low real wages were the conditions in the factories themselves. Here, Factory Inspector Mikhailovskii's reports of well-lighted, well-ventilated factory barracks, where workers made use of libraries, baths, medical clinics, and schools, were clearly fictional, poorly disguising the appalling conditions of labor in the Russian Empire.[79] The Polish workers lived under only slightly less poor circumstances than did the Russians. Factory Inspector Ianzhul recalled that "although in all of Russia, as well as the Congress Kingdom, in the eighties of the last century, one very rarely saw charitable institutions, but nevertheless, more often in Polish than in Moscow factories."[80] Factory Inspector Sviatlovskii was especially disturbed by the unfortunate state of health standards in the Congress Kingdom factories, which, he added, were nevertheless better than those of Russian factories. He attempted to investigate the number of illnesses caused by factory conditions, but without success "because there did not exist a person who was responsible for such a matter, that is, there were no factory doctors." The newly built factories, Sviatlovskii complained, "far from always pay attention to the needs of proper hygiene," and "in old factories and especially in small enterprises, these needs are *always* and blithesomely ignored, and they never have accommodations for ventilation or for the removal of dust." Lighting, continued Sviatlovskii, was terrible. Sanitation facilities were inadequate. Protection against industrial accidents was nonexistent. "Similar discomforting conditions can be seen in our factory institutions at every step."[81]

In smaller individual workshops, conditions were even more difficult. Competition from factory products induced the small shop managers to force their workers to labor longer hours at lower wages. Machinery, lighting, sanitation, and ventilation in Warsaw's thousands of basement workshops were primitive. Often, because of low wages, young boys served as the backbone of a shop of five to fifteen workers. One master and a few journeymen would supervise the strenuous work of a contingent of badly fed and overworked youngsters.[82]

One of the few notable exceptions of government indifference to the plight of factory workers was an 1883 directive from the Department of Trade and Manufacture asking for information on the number of industrial accidents in factories and workshops for the stated purpose of developing "measures for the safeguarding of workers and their families in case of injury or death of workers at the time of carrying out work at factories, works and in other industrial institutions."[83] The responses to the department's questionnaire varied, but the theme of local Congress Kingdom official reports was generally the same — industrial accidents had reached dangerous proportions. Even though most accidents — in the view of these officials — were the workers' own fault, caused, that is, by their "carelessness," still too many families of injured workers were left destitute. One Łowicz *uezd* official (Warsaw *gub.*) suggested that because of the already "extreme destitution of the poor class of the population" it would be a "humanitarian act" of the government to establish compensation regulations for maimed workers. These industrial accidents angered and frustrated the workers, added the official, and it would be in the government's political interest to institute factory regulations. Strict enforcement "would inevitably decrease the number of dissatisfied, and socialist propaganda, which would have a great foundation, would lose any meaning and cause."[84]

Even the most modern metalworking factories had staggering numbers of industrial accidents. A Praga official wrote to the Warsaw governor that "in the years 1879–1883 in only two metal factories in the Praga region, employing 1,508 workers, 2,240 accidents were reported, four of them fatal."[85] Another report of the Warsaw *guberniia* commission concluded that during the five years, 1878–1883, in eighty-one factories in which 25,157 workers were employed, there was "one accident for every nine workers." 2,634 workers were injured, 66 or 2.5 percent of them fatally. The report concluded by stating that 99 percent of these accidents were the result of carelessness of workers, 0.3 percent the fault of the owner, 0.19 percent the fault of foremen, and 0.23 percent the fault of malfunctioning machinery.[86]

Periods of unemployment were especially tragic for workers in the factories of the Congress Kingdom. Even the governor of Warsaw was shocked by the misery of the city's workers at the onset of 1882 (at the same time as the formation of the Proletariat).

> As a result of the present unemployment . . . , the extreme poverty-stricken situation of the majority of families of laborers, factory workers and masters in the city of Warsaw is especially noticeable in the suburbs of the city: New Praga, Wola, and others. Here, congested in stinking housing the refuse of the Warsaw working class, its very lowest part, become embittered and are near despair . . . children roam

out from their slums by foot at night naked for lack of clothes; families who have for several days gone without food.[87]

Those workers who had jobs during periods of unemployment were badly underpaid. In an anonymous letter to the director of the Żyrardów factory Ogden, one worker wrote: "We strongly implore you, Sir, to grant the favor of providing us with better pay, for among us is quite simply poverty, destitution . . . know that it is many who with wives and with children have nothing to eat."[88]

Besides sheer hunger and even starvation, the lack of decent housing was perhaps the most difficult problem for the Polish workers. The rapid growth of city populations, doubling in Warsaw and tripling in Łódź from 1863–1886, crowded industrial workers' quarters and swelled the number of families living in a single dwelling.[89] In factory barracks workers were crowded into small rooms on bunk beds with little other than sleeping space; workers who lived in their own rooms were only slightly better off than those in barracks. These rooms, wrote the Warsaw health expert Jan Heurich, were "too cramped," very small, with low ceilings and usually a single small window. "In a word, there was neither fresh air nor light, nor healthy water, the most important conditions of health and life did not exist in these uncivilized workers' quarters."[90] The health of the inhabitants of these workers' dwellings was abysmal, continued Heurich. In Warsaw 45 out of every 1,000 in the population died every year because of improper sanitation; in London only 13 out of 1,000 die of such causes. These conditions, he added, are the fundamental cause of the "lamentable moral decadence" that pervaded the life of the Polish working class.[91] "Family existence is being torn at the core and perishing," Factory Inspector Sviatlovskii wrote. "The workers return to their hovels with loathing and at the first possibility run to the pubs!" Among the women and children, Sviatlovskii added, there is no such thing as a "home life."[92]

The picture of the home life of Congress Kingdom labor as it emerges from the reports of the tsarist factory inspectors is one of relative misery, relative poor health, relative crowded and unsanitary housing, of hunger and even of starvation. The metalworkers of Warsaw were somewhat better off than the linen workers of Żyrardów, and the latter were somewhat better off than the Łódź textile workers. Further down on this scale of the factory inspectors came the ironworkers of the Dąbrowa region and the textile workers of European Russia. At the "model factory" of Helle and Dietrich in Żyrardów, wrote Sviatlovskii: "The people were pale, thin, their muscles limp; on the whole [they were] undernourished; healthy types were the exception; the children gave an especially clear impression of anemia."[93] Still, Sviatlovskii noted, the condition of the Żyrardów workers was much better than that of Łódź textile workers, and they in turn were "unquestionably better off" than the workers in Russia. At least in Łódź, there were blankets and beds, rarely seen in Russia, and the Łódź workers were better dressed and less often reduced to vagabondage.[94] Factory Inspector Bezobrazov also came to the conclusion that the destitute Łódź workers were nevertheless doing better than Russian workers. They stand "incomparably higher" than their Russian counterparts in their "intellectual development," in their "accomplishments," and in their "better conditions of existence." They are "more ambitious" and "they are not content with low earnings." "Still," adds Bezobrazov, "their work is found to be less expensive than that of the Russians."[95]

Bezobrazov's observations are supported by those of Ianzhul. The most telling difference between the Polish and Russian worker, he wrote, is that the Polish worker is "more intelligent and educated." In the Moscow industrial region, he estimated, literacy among the working class ranged from 22 percent to 36 percent, and in the Congress Kingdom it ranged from 45 percent to 65 percent.[96] To be sure, within the Congress Kingdom, literacy among workers varied from region to region. In the southwestern ironworks, especially among older workers, noted one contemporary, "almost without exception, [the workers were] illiterate." Warsaw workers, noted the same author, "stand on a higher cultural rung."[97] According to the 1881 Warsaw census, very little variation in literacy existed between different sections of the city (all about 50 percent literate), indicating that Polish urban workers, unlike their Russian counterparts, were generally as literate as the rest of the urban population.[98] The pattern of literacy in the Congress Kingdom followed that of the Russian Empire as a whole. Polish metalworkers were more literate than textile workers, male workers more literate than female workers, and workers in cities more literate than those in the provinces.[99]

Industrialization and the Development of Polish Marxism

As has been shown above, the industrial revolution in the Congress Kingdom depended to a large extent on tsarist administrative measures with broad-ranging economic consequences — namely, on the uwłaszczenie, the railway concessions, and tariff policies. By the end of

the 1880s this combination of factors had brought the Congress Kingdom to the classic first stage of the industrial revolution, the creation of
a substantial textile industry. Various statistical measures show the
progress of industrialization in this period; suffice it to reiterate here
that thanks to the rapid pace of industrialization, the Congress Kingdom became a major exporter in several industrial sectors and thus a
competitor to Russian industry. As industrialization proceeded apace,
so did the inevitable concomitants. Many Congress Kingdom cities,
especially Warsaw and Łódź, grew rapidly. New factories, especially in
cotton textiles and metallurgy, sprang up. And a new factory working
class, drawn primarily from peasants and artisans, appeared on the
scene. As in many countries undergoing industrialization, the Polish
worker found the conditions of his life and work unacceptable.

What conclusions can be drawn from the path that industrialization
took in the Congress Kingdom? To what extent does it explain the
emergence and early development of Polish Marxism? Historically,
there have been many answers to these questions. Rosa Luxemburg
gathered some of the above data on the better conditions of the Polish
worker and the superior growth of Congress Kingdom industry, compared these data to data on the Russian situation, and set up an economically deterministic argument that theoretically explained the
emergence of the Marxist-oriented party, the Proletariat.

> Social conditions in the Congress Kingdom in the eighties provided a
> completely appropriate foundation for a workers' movement in the
> European sense of the word. The blossoming of industry after the
> defeat of the last uprising and the peasant reform achieved the final
> triumph of capitalism in the cities as well as, in part, in the country-
> side. . . . Modern class contradictions, economic distinctions, and the
> social significance of the industrial proletariat visibly came to the fore.

The "objective conditions" for a Marxist party were fulfilled, and the
"natural path" of the Proletariat was a Marxist path.[100] "When we
retrace the history of the Proletariat," Luxemburg asserted, "it represents a fully logical development. Social relations in Poland, produced
by already well-developed capitalism, as well as the influence of
Western Europe, brought Polish socialism to the position of social
democracy already in 1881."[101]

Rosa Luxemburg was neither the first nor the last to tie the sophistication of Polish socialism to the development of industrialization and
the working class. J. Uziembło ("Amerykanin"), a veteran of the
Polish movement, also linked the "advanced" revolutionary ideology

of the Polish Left to the relatively mature state of the Polish proletariat:

> I became quickly convinced of the extent to which the Warsaw worker was more developed than the Russian. Whereas in Russia those workers were exceptions who, invited to circle meetings, ventured to speak — here [in the C.K.] most spoke. There it was more often limited to asking questions. Here the worker in his speech often straightened out the error in the speech of the intelligentsia.[102]

The Soviet historian A. El'nitskii agrees with both Uziembło and Luxemburg. Already by the end of the 1870s, writes El'nitskii, many Polish workers were conscious socialists: "The Polish worker in this regard very favorably distinguished himself from his Russian and Jewish comrades. He was significantly more cultured than the worker of native Russia, lived under better circumstances, and worked in better conditions."[103]

Even government officials took note of the special dangers that socialism posed for the Polish partition. As early as 1873, the Third Section warned Congress Kingdom officials to take extraordinary precautions against the influence of the Paris Commune and the First International: "Of all the areas of the empire, the Congress Kingdom, more than others, constitutes a receptive ground for the actions of the International. The reason for this is both its geographical position as well as the aggregation of a significant number of workers in few industrial and mining centers."[104] The government *Chronicle* also warned that the Polish workers were "easily inflamed" by these "new theories" because of their concentration in few centers. Therefore, concludes the *Chronicle,* "these new ideas are directed in a straight line to the Polish center, to the lower ranks of the Warsaw . . . masters and workers."[105]

The primary weakness of all these arguments, Luxemburg's included, is that they take no account of the wide regional variations within Russia and the Congress Kingdom. If one accepts the proposition that the Congress Kingdom indeed was ahead of Russia and behind Western Europe in the rush toward modernity and that Polish industrial output was in general increasing more rapidly than that of European Russia, one cannot forget that St. Petersburg industry was actually the most powerful in the empire and that in terms of numerical and sometimes percentage increases, Russia was moving toward modern industry more quickly than the Congress Kingdom. Even if one accepts Luxemburg's argument that the Congress Kingdom underwent the industrial revolution during the late 1870s and 1880s and Russia not until the mid-1890s, one need not accept her conclusion that workers' consciousness was greater in the Congress Kingdom than in Russia.[106] In fact, St. Petersburg workers more often than not were better paid, lived under better conditions, and worked in more modern industrial surroundings than either their Warsaw or Łódź counterparts, though clearly, the Congress Kingdom worker was generally better off in these areas than his average all-Russian counterpart. Indeed, some role in the greater involvement of Polish workers in the labor movement[107] and the revolutionary movement[108] as well as the greater success of Marxism in the Congress Kingdom versus Russia can be attributed to a measured industrial superiority and an equally measured superiority in "conscious" workers. More important to the relatively greater success of a workers' socialist and revolutionary movement in the Congress Kingdom, however, were the social and intellectual changes associated with Polish modernization — derived as much from autocratic political decisions as from the process of industrialization and the numerical growth of the proletariat.

III

Warsaw Positivism and the Origins of Polish Marxism

The history of Polish political thought in the last third of the nineteenth century is closely tied to the spectacular successes of Polish industrialization as well as to the crushing defeat of the 1863–64 insurrection. The locus of political prestige and intellectual vibrancy shifted from the Polish *szlachta* and its magnate leadership to the new Polish urban alliance of bankers and merchants on the one hand and liberal professionals, many of *szlachta* origin, on the other. This alliance, which both promoted and reflected the values of industrial capitalism, revived the political slogan of Organic Work and espoused the antirevolutionary philosophy of Warsaw Positivism. With its stress on social harmony, national reconciliation, and economic progress, Warsaw Positivism overcame the lingering influence of Polish utopian socialism and by the mid-1870s, dominated the political consciousness of educated Poles.

The historiography of both Warsaw Positivism and of the Proletariat has treated the liberalism of the former and the Marxism of the latter as completely separate and antagonistic intellectual movements.[1] Yet much like the general pattern of nineteenth-century European intellectual history, Polish Marxism developed on the fringes of entrenched liberalism. The purpose of this chapter, then, is to examine the influence of Warsaw Positivism on the development of Polish Marxism. The often maligned political program of the positivists is examined in the first section by tracing its intellectual origins and discussing its maturation in the positivist press. As the second section of the chapter attempts to demonstrate, it was especially the positivist press that cleared an intellectual path through Polish political thought for the emergence of Marxism. Just as the defeats of Russian liberalism in the post-emancipation period retarded the development of Russian Marxism, the strength of Warsaw Positivism in the same years abetted the early successes and vitality of Polish Marxism.

Warsaw Positivism and Organic Work

Organic Work was a concept of social action that can be dated to the immediate postpartition period, when a small, educated minority of Poles began to think of the future of Poland not in terms of revolt and the insurrection of an independent Poland, but rather in terms of the building of the cultural and material wealth of the Polish people.[2] As the slogan for a broad antiinsurrectionary political program, Organic Work first appeared in the Grand Duchy of Poznań in the 1840s. In Poznań, a number of Polish landowners and professionals took advantage of the advances of German liberalism and instituted programs of social and cultural betterment for the Polish population. Karol Marcinkowski, a distinguished Poznań physician, and Andrzej Zamoyski, a Congress Kingdom magnate, also encouraged the foundation of fundamentally liberal and noninsurrectionary associations, brotherhoods, and publications for the improvement of national life in partitioned Poland.[3] The feeble alliance between the liberal magnates and the incipient urban bourgeoisie that promoted the programs of Organic Work crumbled with the advent of the revolutionary situation before 1863. Nevertheless these activists firmly implanted Organic Work in Polish political thinking as a future alternative to the recurrence of insurrectionary optimism.[4]

Although most historians of Polish political thought trace the intellectual roots of Warsaw Positivism to the early nineteenth-century advocates of Organic Work, others concentrate on the influence of Galician stańczycy, especially the editors of *Przegląd Polski* (Polish Review): Józef Szujski, Stanisław Tarnowski, Stanisław Koźmian, and Ludwik Wódzicki.[5] Together with historians at the universities of Kraków and Lwów, the stańczycy founded the conservative school of Polish political thought and historiography, which glorified monarchism, rejected the Polish conspiratorial and insurrectionary past, and lauded triloyalism — the political idea that each Polish patriot owed obedience to his respective imperial government.[6] The stańczycy represented primarily the interests of the Polish Galician nobility, whose social conservatism and readiness to cooperate with the Austrian authorities brought them considerable political power. But although the Warsaw Positivists shared the stańczyk antipathy for insurrectionary activities, they were neither conservative nor, as members of a growing urban bourgeoisie, interested in preserving the predominance of the nobility in Polish political life. As the noted historian of Polish politics Wilhelm Feldman rightly observed, the stańczycy and the Warsaw Positivists shared few common social or ideological characteristics and can be historically linked only by their program of "changing the national psychological type" by "imbuing it with realism."[7]

The primary intellectual sources of Warsaw Positivism are to be found not in stańczyk literature but in the positivism of Comte and Littre, the "evolutionism" of Darwin, Mill, and Spencer, and the scientific materialism of Ludwig Büchner.[8] The diverse theories of these and other representatives of Western European positivism flowed together in the Congress Kingdom into one intellectual stream out of which the Poles formulated a number of simplified axioms.

Those Polish intellectuals who wrote positivist theory were not philosophers, but sociologists, economists, and most often simply journalists, dedicated to formulating a new concept of Polish political and social action rather than to developing any kind of comprehensive philosophical school. Their understanding of the subtleties of Western positivist theory was quite limited. "Society" was their central concept, and "society" found its definition and its mission in scattered products of Western European positivism that found their way into the Congress Kingdom.

If there was one overriding philosophical principle of the Warsaw Positivists, it was the strict, unimpeachable materialism of Büchner, which "rejected every kind of supranaturalism and idealism in the explanation of natural events."[9] Büchner also satisfied the Poles' inclination to attach a moral imperative to materialism. It is a "gratuitous assertion," wrote Büchner, "to pretend that the materialism of science changes all grand and noble ideas into vain dreams, that materialism has no future and no morality."[10] For Büchner, morality existed only with the recognition of the hegemony of "material" in all phenomenological explanations.

The Polish positivists were also enamored of Comte, particularly of his attacks on all forms of revolutionary political and philosophical thinking. Because Comte included radical and revolutionary theorists in what he called the "metaphysical school" of social science, his works reaffirmed the positivists' immediate goals of discrediting Polish insurrectionary political thought.[11] Ultimately, however, the Poles were more interested in philosophical affirmation of nonrevolutionary social action than in social criticism, and it was here that Comte proved most helpful. Although Comte ostensibly established irreversible and objective laws of social statics and dynamics, he, like Büchner, affirmed the ethical superiority of materialism. According to Comte, the moral lives of individuals were fulfilled by their active participation in science and progress. To a certain extent, as many scholars of positivism have noted, Comte was as much a reformer as he was a "scientist," and the philosophy of Warsaw Positivism, like that of Comte, though supposedly rejecting all idealist and grandiose philosophies of history, in fact established a new ideal — that of "Progress."[12]

The ideology of "Progress," combined with the theories of Darwin and Spencer, which confirmed for the Poles the organic development and unity of society, developed into a powerful philosophic justification for the indigenous Polish tradition of Organic Work and a soothing remedy for the traumatic consequences of the unsuccessful 1863–64 Polish insurrection. Warsaw Positivism and Organic Work acquired further impetus from the moderate successes of the anti-insurrectionary Galician stańczycy,[13] the apparent liberalism of Tsar Alexander II, and the increasing vitality of Polish industrialization.

The crushing defeat of the 1863–64 uprising engendered a collective psychological depression among the population of the Congress Kingdom. The cumulative effects of such defeats since that of Kościuszko weighed especially heavily on the public consciousness of educated Poles. For those members of the upper classes who experienced the bitter struggles of the insurrection yet managed to retain their privileged economic position in the Congress Kingdom, social conservatism and political triloyalism appeared the only answers to the problem of political action.[14] For the new post-1863 urban middle class, that generation of Poles who did not personally participate in the uprising, the literature of romantic nationalism and the grandiose schemes of the radical democratic and utopian socialist émigré organizations were shelved in favor of materialism and progress. These Poles also rejected the conservative ideas of Polish nationhood proposed by the stańczycy and by the Russian-Polish triloyalist periodical *Kraj* in favor of Warsaw Positivism. In 1866, Adam Wiślicki established the positivists' first public forum — *Przegląd Tygodniowy* (Weekly Review) — and it was soon joined by other positivist-oriented periodicals — *Atheneum, Nowiny* (News), and *Prawda* (Truth).

Aleksander Świętochowski, the "Zarathustra of his times" and an alumnus of the Szkoła Główna, directed the struggle of the positivists to capture the allegiance of educated Poles.[15] Feldman called Świętochowski a "magnificent dialectician" and "cool rationalist."[16] The Third Section noted that Świętochowski was known in liberal circles "as a learned and gifted man."[17] Beginning his career with Wiślicki and *Przegląd Tygodniowy*, Świętochowski then edited with his own publication, *Prawda*. In the introductory article to the first number of *Prawda* in 1881, Świętochowski wrote:

At the beginning of this newly formed locus of Polish thought, we welcome our dear readers who gather about us in the name of Truth, in the name of independent knowledge, freedom of belief, enlightenment, the well-being of the entire people and national rights, in the name of our own and of world civilization. Today we can be summoned by nothing else but by the sincere desire to serve sensibly and honestly the general public.[18]

Świętochowski and his colleagues, though not always in full agreement on the methods of achieving these general goals, shared an ebullient faith in progress and enlightenment.

The Positivist Critique

Erazm Piltz, the editor of the triloyalist *Kraj* (Homeland), criticized Świętochowski and the Warsaw Positivists for their negativism: "Their positivism was not positive work, but only theory, criticism, opposition, negation. They were capable of demolishing, but they lacked the strength to build political knowledge, enlightenment."[19] In one sense, Piltz was correct; the positivists did launch brutal attacks on clericalism, conservatism, conspiracy, anti-Semitism, obscurantism, and socialism. At the same time, they defended the salutary merits of criticism from a philosophical position that accorded criticism a crucial role in the advancement of culture and civilization, much in the manner of Comte and the Russian Lavrov. In an article on Herbert Spencer in *Atheneum,* Władysław Kozłowski wrote that if one were to attempt to classify contemporary society, the "most corresponding [name] would be 'realistic,' for today's trends are based mainly on the fact that thought and feeling, which were up to this time not always in accordance with reality, are now approaching it."[20] Using typically positivist nomenclature, Kozłowski concluded that Poles were approaching the "natural" end of the "metaphysical and romantic direction" of their civilization and that the new age of realism would be ushered in by "rejecting all established ideas and conceptions, all forms of *a priori* reasoning."[21]

The Catholic church was one of the positivists' primary targets of critical abuse. In an article "Who Is to Blame?" Wiślicki vehemently castigated clericalism for perverting Christ's words and sacrificing the good of Poland. The real Christians, he maintained, were to be found in the "progressive alliance of the liberal camp."[22] In conjunction with their attacks on obscurantism, the positivists consistently criticized manifestations of anti-Semitism. In an effort to combat the popular demonology of Polish Jewry, the positivists provided sympathetic histories of the Eastern European Jewry. In other more polemical articles, the positivists lashed out at socialism for creating the bases for anti-Semitism in the Congress Kingdom.[23]

The positivists directed the bulk of their criticism, however, against the Polish aristocracy and the *intelligencja wiejska* ("rural intelligentsia"). Three extensive articles in *Przegląd Tygodniowy* — "Without Leaders," "What Do We Need?", and "The Task of Our Intelligentsia" — attacked the inertness of members of the Polish upper class and proposed that they accept new roles as educators, progressives, and social activists.[24] "With sadness and with shame we must recognize that from any point of view . . . the landed intelligentsia does not stand in a high position — and therewith abdicates the immensely important position that it should properly occupy because of its greater maturity."[25] The level of public consciousness, *Przegląd Tygodniowy* complained, is "so little developed here, that one might boldly say that it doesn't exist at all."[26] The task, concluded "What Do We Need?" is "to look into ourselves and attempt to create in us civic virtues which we now still lack."[27] Wiślicki also wanted to create good citizens, but he was less hopeful about the aristocracy. "In a word, our goal is . . . the transformation of the entire populace of our country into citizens of sensitive heart and head." "Our aristocrats," he added, "do not help us at all, for they have empty heads, empty hearts, and even empty pocketbooks."[28]

In "The Tasks of Our Intelligentsia," Wiślicki derided the intelligentsia "caste" of *szlachta* Poland, which had remained neutral between noble and peasant during the Polish peasant emancipation. "And today," he noted, "things are not much different."[29] Because the role of the intelligentsia is so "decisive for the fate of the people . . . it must have self-knowledge."[30] In Wiślicki's view, the intelligentsia could achieve this self-knowledge, throw off its caste heritage, and serve as the consciousness of the Polish nation by merging with and leading the people.

> Therefore, first of all, the intelligentsia must stand totally together with the villagers, must, one might say, grow into them, to a certain extent derive strength from them so as to be able to affect their lives, and most of all to represent their world not with words but with deeds.

Until this is accomplished, the intelligentsia cannot fulfill its most important, most essential destiny.[31]

For the positivists, the task of the intelligentsia was both to "go to the people," the slogan of the Russian intelligentsia, and to "study the people." Educated Poles must learn to speak the language of the people, gather their songs and jokes, decipher their needs and wants. The intelligentsia, Wiślicki wrote, "must learn to speak to the people [*lud*] in a language they can understand, even better, in the language of their interests and their aspirations."[32]

Wiślicki nevertheless made it quite clear in this same article that he was not advocating socialism. "Naturally, this matter has nothing to do with the abrogation of differences in the social structure deriving from a difference in abilities, or differences in the economic conditions of existence, for these not only are not harmful, but stand as fundamentals of social harmony."[33] Elsewhere, Wiślicki also categorically rejected socialism and stated that "our society either will be liberal, or it will not be at all."[34] The positivists' stubborn devotion to liberalism is also omnipresent in Świętochowski's *Prawda*. The article "The Way Out," which discussed questions of Warsaw local self-government, effectively eliminated workers, peasants, and, in part, the Jews, from the democratic process by advocating that the rights of voting should be held "only by those independent and long-term residents of the city who are capable of reading and writing in the country's language and who finished general elementary school."[35]

Influenced by Western materialism, the rapid growth of industry in the Congress Kingdom, and their own perceptions of the wisdom of political liberalism and realism, the positivists focused their attention on the benefits of economic activism. Władysław Wściekły wrote in *Prawda* that equality was neither immediately attainable nor necessarily desirable. "Our only task is a sure thing, and that is that economic progress must always and constantly be a precursor of political progress."[36] Karol Dunin added: "Of all the aspects of the life of society, the economic aspect undeniably possesses the greatest vitality and strength. . . . Economic advancement clears the way for any other [advancement]."[37] Bolesław Prus wrote that "every time and every country has its own slogan or idea which the majority would happily see realized . . . , ours is 'Acquire Credit.'" It is no joke, stated Prus in the same column, that "we would be ready to give up half our land . . . if we could get notes with low interest."[38]

As a part of their ultimate devotion to the benefits of industrialization and liberalism, the positivists publicized the plight of Polish workers and lobbied for the improvement of their circumstances. "With noble humanitarian ideas, believing in the equal right of all people to happiness," Wściekły wrote, "we cannot look quietly at those glaring discrepancies of position that in our view divide the masses of working people from the happy chosen of fate. . . . Our goal . . . is to correct the relationship among the people as a whole. . . . In this will be the basis for the 'kwestia społeczna' [social question]."[39]

Prus, in his column "Monthly Chronicle" as well as in his novels and stories, drew special attention to the destitution of the factory workers and artisans of Warsaw. He was particularly disconcerted by their ignorance. The worker, Prus wrote, is "frightfully impoverished intellectually." Not only does the worker not understand basic concepts and slightly complex language, Prus complained, but he "isn't able to listen and desires only to entertain himself."[40] Still, in article after article, Prus reported the modest gains of factory legislation, always confident that the reprehensible conditions of the working class were steadily improving.[41]

Prus's immediate concern, as well as that of the majority of positivist critics of the deprivations suffered by Polish labor, was to establish better factory health care and some form of industrial accident insurance: "The worker needs assistance in the case of illness, a special bonus in case of sickness or death . . . this need should be fulfilled with the help of a forward-looking institution of the type of the proposed society for mutual help."[42] The first such institutions in the Congress Kingdom were established in the sugar industry in 1878. Nowiny expressed the hope that "shortly, other sugar factories, as all the large factories in the country, will also speedily imitate them [the mutual help societies]."[43] In addition, the positivists repeatedly voiced their concern about health standards in factory districts and towns. In an article "From Żyrardów," Nowiny deplored the miserable sanitation in the textile mills and workers' quarters in this factory center outside Warsaw.[44] At the same time, the positivists rejected regulations on industry such as a minimum wage law or price controls. Their method of improving the condition of the working class consisted of providing health and accident insurance while allowing the capitalist system time to alleviate other inequities through the "improvement of management" and the "perfection of production methods."[45]

According to the positivists, the eventual solution to the problems of the Polish working-class population was to be found in European-style factory legislation. "Progress" had brought to Western Europe a maximum twelve-hour working day, child-labor laws, and health and insurance programs; "Progress" in the Congress Kingdom would bring the same results. In Western Europe, *Prawda* noted, "the promulgation of factory legislation became the *inevitable means* of protecting the working classes."[46] The positivists also produced several empirical studies that ostensibly demonstrated that the lot of the Western European proletariat was rapidly improving. Wściekły concluded from data on the age structure of Western countries that with the development of European civilization and the growth of large industry, "the condition of the working classes constantly improved."[47] For the positivists, factory legislation was the final step that would insure the improvement of the workers' conditions, but one that could only accompany the eventual hegemony of "Progress" in the Congress Kingdom. By adopting this passive, long-range stance toward the pressing issues of Polish labor, the positivists renounced any possible political role they might have played in the development of the Polish workers' movement.

The Positivists and the National Question

Although the problems of greatest concern to the positivists were those of economic progress, enlightenment, and the amelioration of the most obvious deficiencies of modern industry, the question that dominates the historiography of Warsaw Positivism is its stand vis-à-vis the national question, the *"kwestia narodowa."* The debate over whether the positivists were patriotic derives primarily from modern historians' understandable though often myopic fascination with Polish patriotism. In fact, in response to patriotic critics of their own period, the positivists clearly, if somewhat contritely, explained that they considered the economic and cultural advancement of the Polish people the highest form of patriotism in an era of impossibly difficult political circumstances. "We understand," wrote the positivists, "that an epoch of patience does not illuminate the history of the people as does an epoch of good fortune. In it there is less to publicize . . . but still, both the people and the social classes . . . , though without a crown of laurels, are capable of making advances in their spiritual life."[48] To the positivists, patriotism could be silent as well as vocal, patient as well as agitated, and, most importantly, politically passive as well as insurrectionary. Bolesław Prus wrote, "everything has its time . . . and we therefore do not make a call to action as is usually done in similar situations and always to no end."[49] In an article entitled, "Is Positivism an Anti-National Movement?" W. Kozłowski similarly emphasized the advisability of dispassionate analysis in Polish political thinking. We are interested only in science and methods of science, he wrote, and "scientific discussions are by nature clearly abstract." "Perhaps with time it will occur that what we take as the truth is false."[50] "Tradition," Kozłowski stated, "is not something permanent and unalterable. It, too, goes through phases of growth and setbacks — and in every historical period it takes the form the demands of the times and the influence of civilization gives it." Correctly summarizing the positivists' view of patriotism, Kozłowski continued: "The position of our people is different today from what it was several decades ago; therefore, its needs are also different. Idealism is of no use to us today. Moreover, a sad realization convinces us that its slogan — measure strength according to goals, not goals according to strength — is basically false."[51]

The Warsaw Positivists' stand on the national question was shaped by their thorough disaffection with the patriotism of the Polish *szlachta* as well as by their devotion to rationality and scientific reasoning. According to the positivists, the national tradition had always been the exclusive property of the Polish gentry, and though this tradition in itself should be preserved and cultivated, gentry predominance had to be terminated in order to keep Poland from going down "a false and mistaken road." The "aristocratic tradition" will be replaced, they claimed, by "that great mass of people who most persistently maintain their national character."[52] The positivists' goal should be to "make possible their [the masses] education, not to develop in them the national feeling they already have, but [to develop] their national self-consciousness." "This goal and this task is to enlighten broader circles of the people, to educate, and to recognize every educated person's right to a voice and influence on the matters of the whole without considering whether he belongs to the gentry, worker or peasant estate."[53] The positivists' answer to the national question was therefore a form of Organic Work in the national sphere — an attempt to make the Polish masses, the *lud*, aware of their own national traditions.

The opponents of positivism and its national policy have directed their harshest criticism at Aleksander Świętochowski and his article "Political Advice" in the 1882 *Ognisko* (Hearth) collection dedicated to T. T. Jeż (Z. Miłkowski). After belittling the "loud and empty

patriotism" of the past, Świętochowski announced in this controversial article the coming of a new generation that would ignore
"messianic prophecies" and "oracles of providential purpose." No
longer would Poles be shackled to idealistic visions of salvation; no
longer would they cling to the symbols of the "chosen people of God"
escaping the "Pharaoh's troops" as a result of impossible miracles.[54]
Świętochowski, like his fellow positivists, described the critical importance of realistic internal work and the necessity to involve all the
people in the life of the nation:

> We expect nothing from political revolution, wars, pacts, the granting
> of favors from foreigners, but we believe only in our vitality. . . . Today
> we must attempt to replace dreams of regaining outward independ-
> ence with efforts of internal self-dependence. This self-dependence
> can only be possible as a result of the strengthening of intellectual and
> material forces, the synchronized, multifaceted growth of the people
> with general progress, as well as with the democratization of society.[55]

Polish historiography's primary criticism of the national program of
Świętochowski and the positivists centers on their cooperation with or
at least toleration of tsarism.[56] "He [Świętochowski] fought for every
possible freedom," wrote Feliks Perl, "except for one — political." The
positivists, continued Perl, struggled "with God, with tradition, with
romanticism, with the gentry, just not with tsarism."[57] For Ludwik
Kulczycki, the main weakness of positivism was that it chastised "conspiracy and the illegal work that are natural in an absolutist structure."[58]

Świętochowski denied in his memoirs that he was antipatriotic and
called the attention of his critics both to the limitations imposed by
Russian censorship and to those articles in his periodical supporting
South Slav nationalism, which he claimed indirectly encouraged
Polish nationalism.[59] The hindsight of Świętochowski aside, there was
little question in the minds of the positivists that the forms of Polish
national feeling that had dominated political thinking throughout the
previous century were, in the post-1863 period, outdated, irrelevant,
and even insidious. National consciousness, if it indeed were to be truly
national, had to come from the education of the common folk and the
democratization of society — processes that required peace, unity, and
economic progress.

To be sure, Warsaw Positivism was an eclectic and sometimes self-
contradictory jumble of progressive and liberal philosophic declara-
tions. Yet it served as a convenient and highly successful framework

for social action in a beaten, disheartened, and self-deprecating nation. "Despite everything," Kulczycki recalled, "Polish life strongly pulsated, the national culture and intellectual currents deepened. It is therefore no wonder that at the time we were not pessimists."[60] The positivist press glorified and expounded the intellectual watchwords of the day: science, progress, capital, and the people. In the context of the national question, the positivists were far less concerned with denying the attributes of Polish nationhood than with vilifying all forms of Polish idealism and ushering in an age of national realism. In addition to their emphasis on industrialization, public spirit, and social welfare, they also indirectly lobbied for the democratization of Polish society— a process that did not include any tampering, legally or underground, with the locus of political power, the Russian imperial government. Rather, democratization meant sharing the material and cultural benefits of national life with the masses of Polish peasants and workers as well as terminating *szlachta* domination of Polish society.

Positivism and Socialism in the Congress Kingdom

Warsaw Positivism pervaded the consciousness of the urban intelligentsia in the Congress Kingdom until the late 1870s. Especially in Warsaw itself, Polish intellectual life revolved around the positivist press. Because other public forums resided securely in the hands of the Russian authorities, clubs, salons, and university circles, as well as the censored Polish press, became centers for the formation of Polish public opinion. These small and mostly legal circles were devoted to "self-education" and to the discussion of articles in the positivist *Przegląd Tygodniowy, Prawda,* and *Atheneum.* Roman Dmowski, the future leader of the Polish nationalist movement, noted that the positivist discussion circles clearly dominated Warsaw's intellectual life. Especially at the university, he wrote, "a fashion was established among the youth, the so-called programs of self-education."[61] In these circles, Dmowski continued, the "cult of reason" reigned supreme, the successful outgrowth of Warsaw Positivism.[62] Other commentators also attest to the remarkable strength of positivism among educated Polish youth of the 1870s. The intellectual fashions of those times, wrote Jan Offenburg, were dictated by "the fanatics of materialism." "With its important victories in the scientific field, materialism was dominant — this impressed the youth to such a great extent that a cult of reason and of science became their religion."[63]

No single historical factor explains the transfer of the intellectual allegiance of part of the Polish urban intelligentsia from positivism to Marxism at the turn of the 1880s. Dmowski now complained not about the "cult of reason" as he had of the 1870s, but about the "cult of politics" and the "tremendous spread of socialism among our university youth."[64] Although Dmowski, like the noted memoirists of the period, Stefan Koszutski and Stanisław Czekanowski, attributed the rapid spread of Polish socialism to the indirect example and direct influence of Russian socialism, he nevertheless also recognized the important impetus that Warsaw Positivism provided to the development of Polish socialism.[65] In Dmowski's view, it was the positivists' determinedly critical posture vis-à-vis the Poland of the past and their decisively progressive and liberal notions of Poland's future that facilitated the rapid spread of socialism. "The positivists' movement," Dmowski wrote, "unusually strong in its time, provided such a powerful reforming impulse to the young generation, that its activities . . . maintained among youth the persistent need to defy the whole society."[66]

By the beginning of the 1880s, socialism had attracted adherents within the working class as well as among the young intelligentsia. Throughout the period 1876–1881, economic conditions in the Congress Kingdom steadily deteriorated, unemployment rose, and a depression, corresponding to that of the empire as a whole, heightened industrial tensions. In general, the Congress Kingdom experienced, as did European Russia, the development of a "revolutionary situation." Intensified national and social tensions characterized the decade of the 1880s in the Congress Kingdom — a condition that the positivists had attempted to avoid and that subsequently led to their demise as the predominant political force in Poland.

The increase of intelligentsia and working-class socialism at the end of the 1870s and the activities of the underground Marxist Proletariat in the years 1882–1886 did not go unnoticed by the positivist press. In *Przegląd Tygodniowy, Prawda, Atheneum,* and *Nowiny,* the positivists took up the challenge of socialism and sowed, in an almost classical Marxist sense, the seeds of their own destruction. The positivists themselves helped to popularize Marxism in their press by repeated references to Marxist theory and to the activities of Western Marxist parties. The measured respect they accorded to Marx himself was reflected in his obituary printed in *Prawda,* 24 March 1883: "The socialist messiah is dead. A man died, who like Samson, shook the economic pillars of the civilized world, who although not responsible for the individual outrages of his followers — placed and entrenched continuously exploding dynamite under Europe."[67] Numerous articles in the positivist press, though critical of various aspects of Marxist theory, generally concluded that Marx had indeed made numerous "enduring contributions to political economy."[68]

The positivist press also contributed to the popularization of socialism in the Congress Kingdom by consistently overemphasizing the role of Western European socialism in European politics. A. J. Cohn, an unrelenting positivist critic of socialism, wrote a brief history of Western socialism that began: "Today, everyone is talking about socialism and socialists."[69] Another *Prawda* article, which described Western European child-labor laws, stated: "Today, Europe can be viewed as a split picture: on the one hand the mass uprisings of socialism, and, on the other, the introduction of changes conceived by it."[70]

Certainly, the emergence of a socialist movement in Poland stimulated the positivists' manifold interest in the history and politics of Western European socialism. In fact, positivist commentators suggested that the economic issues raised by socialism were justified even while they implied that in order to prevent the spread of the socialist malaise in the Congress Kingdom, it was imperative to take these issues away from the Polish socialists. In an article about socialism in England for instance, the positivists clearly advocated economic reform in the Congress Kingdom and, in effect, warned the Russian administration of the dangers of Polish socialism.

> If Europe is affected in the near future with some revolution, it will surely be neither a broad political nor religious revolution, but an economic one. . . . Therefore all signs that augur that storm, all manifestations of great social convulsions, are subjects of special attention for the public and for journalism. . . .
>
> We will consistently reiterate economic questions — to solve them is possible only by economic means: with the help of legislative changes, reforms, or, where the conflict is too stubborn — by revolution. The genuine aspiration of governments should be that these questions not be settled in a bloody court.[71]

In a similar vein, Bolesław Prus implicitly warned the authorities that although conditions were rapidly improving among Warsaw workers, time was short; Polish labor was distressingly susceptible to those "false theories, which are spreading among the working classes in the West and are coming closer and closer to our country."[72]

In addition to reporting most major occurrences in the West European socialist movement,[73] the positivist press periodically alluded to socialist activity in the Congress Kingdom itself. Generally, however, very little material on Polish socialism filtered through the censor's office onto the pages of the Warsaw press. Świętochowski in his column "Liberum Veto" vaguely referred to socialist agitation in Warsaw.[74] Similarly, *Prawda* circumspectly reported the events of the Warsaw-Vienna railway workers' disturbances in the spring of 1882. The article, "Sad Page," was able only to quote a letter of explanation from the management of the railway workshop and to mention that "public opinion of our city was very disturbed to hear of the violent actions of the workers . . . against the head mechanics."[75] The socialists' involvement in the fighting and the strike was omitted. A positivist "Report on the Conference of the International at Chur," a crucial milestone in the history of Polish socialism, made no reference to Congress Kingdom socialism or to its leaders — Waryński, Dłuski, et al. — and only perfunctorily noted the presence of Polish socialists in Poznań and Galicia.[76]

The positivists repeatedly disavowed any concern that their own position might be undermined by the spread of socialism in the Congress Kingdom. Yet their press, especially during the formative period of the Proletariat, 1881–1883, was obsessed with socialism. Certainly the socialists were acutely aware of the campaign carried out against them. In an article written for the sixth and unpublished number of *Proletariat,* the author complained, "We cannot escape from the attention of the quasi-liberal organs." Especially, "the progressive *Prawda* . . . carries on a crusade against us."[77] Although in the 1870s the positivists concentrated their critical articles on the aristocracy and patriotism, by the 1880s the socialists and socialism were of paramount concern. In these later articles, the positivists attempted to separate socialism as a "catechism of agitation" from socialism as "the scientific theory";[78] they anathemized the former and tolerantly criticized the latter.

Świętochowski, in an article aptly entitled "Sharks," explained that Poles completely rejected socialist internationalism. "Despite every trick," Świętochowski wrote, "the socialist wolf" will not find his way into Poland.[79] In another article on Bismarck and the German socialists, Świętochowski somewhat less polemically assessed the dangers of Polish socialism.

We believe therefore that it [socialism] is a theory immensely susceptible to accommodating itself to the service of a dictator for the infliction of shackles on the free development of work and civilization. We are not blind to the insufficiencies and faults of private owner- ship . . . [yet] no one to this time has been able to eliminate the question of whether extreme socialism will crush humanity with far greater oppression. This is a genuine Pandora's box.[80]

In general, the positivist press indicted revolutionary socialists as mis- guided murderers, liars, or knaves. In an article about a Viennese socialist terrorist, N. Stillmacher, *Prawda* concluded: "It seems that he is a cruel, brutal, possessed though chaste fanatic who was obsessed by the thought of improving the fate of workers and who demanded justice for them."[81] The positivists labeled the Russian socialists "apostles of barbaric evangelical nihilism."[82] Socialism was often similarly impugned for its disregard of the human personality. "Socialism," wrote one author, "does not know psychology and does not want to know it."[83] "A social democratic state, the state of the future," wrote W. Wściekły in "Apostasy in the Church," "is an absurdity, an impossibility."[84] Other articles also attacked socialism for demonstrating the same totalitarian characteristics as ultra- montanism and for encouraging European anti-Semitism.[85]

Świętochowski's first major article on the socialist question, "So- cialism and Its Mistakes," is a paradigm of the service the positivist press provided the socialist cause. Ostensibly examining German social democracy, Świętochowski introduced to the Warsaw public the tenets of Polish socialism that had been articulated in the underground "Brussels Program" of the 1877-1878 Warsaw socialist movement: "Socialism proposes a social structure in which private capital would become public capital, that is, in which all means of production would belong to every individual. . . . The main premise upon which socialism bases its theoretical scaffolding is the idea of the elemental equality of people." Świętochowski described a socialist system of production consisting of collective workshops and commonly owned factories. He straightforwardly presented the socialist program, but he also bitterly derided socialism as a "fantastic dream" and an "impossible fairy tale." If successful, Świętochowski claimed, socialism would bring into the life of the people, "no other institutions but factories, no other people but workers." "We [the positivists] care about the equalization of the segments of society, we try to enrich the poor, enlighten the ignorant, bring up the lowly; socialism in contrast tries to pauperize the rich, blend the enlightened, and flatten the high."[86] From this article and others in the positivist press, the Polish intelligentsia could extrapolate the major tenets of the socialist program: social equality, common ownership of the means of production, and cooperative workshops. If they were disposed to the positivist position, they could, like Świętochowski, discard socialism as an unlikely dream or as an undesirable solution to contemporary problems. If, however, the readers of the positivist press were disillusioned with their liberal political program, they were able to turn to the hitherto unknown or unexplained solution of socialism.

The positivist press also demythologized socialism by lifting it out of the fearsome primordial underworld of the Russian terrorists and by intellectually binding socialism and liberalism to a common materialistic and humanistic tradition. Several articles in the positivist press even suggested to the Polish intelligentsia that the Western schools of positivism "aspired to the same ends as socialism, only by different roads."[87] The Polish intelligentsia of the 1880s was in search of a new road to political action, and, in part, the positivist press provided the signposts.

The Polish Legal Marxists and the Positivists

The most significant contributions of the positivist press to the socialist cause came not from its own editors and staff writers, but from a group of Polish Marxist intellectuals led by a Warsaw University political philosopher, Stanisław Krusiński.[88] Other noted members of the "Krusiński circle" ("Krusińszczycy") included the sociologist Ludwik Krzywicki and the literary critic Bronisław Białobłocki.[89] Krusiński and his collaborators, though closely allied with the Proletariat, rejected the underground party's devotion to the political struggle against tsarism. They concluded that the tsarist administrative machinery and the backward conditions of the Polish working class precluded the possibility of a genuine socialist movement.[90] Socialist intellectuals should therefore concentrate their efforts on both propagandizing the essentials of Marxism among the intelligentsia and perfecting a rigorously Marxist approach to Polish conditions.[91]

Although Krusiński severed formal ties with the Proletariat in 1883 as a direct result of a confrontation with Waryński over the question of cooperation with the Russian movement, his group nevertheless served an important function as the Legal Marxist wing of the underground Proletariat.[92] Initially, the Krusiński circle intended to publish its own Marxist journal. But the difficulties of such a venture soon prompted Krusiński, Krzywicki, and Białobłocki to turn their attention to challenging the intellectual hegemony of Warsaw Positivism in the legal press and in legal discussion circles.

Ludwik Krzywicki initiated the Legal Marxist assault on the positivist program in a series of articles in *Prawda* entitled "Behind the Scenes." In these articles, Krzywicki subtly but convincingly juxtaposed the positivists' assertion that the Congress Kingdom was experiencing gradual economic improvement with a description of the desperate plight of Polish industrial workers and artisans. He chose as his subjects the sugar industry, touted by the positivists as the most progressive of Congress Kingdom enterprises, and the flower sellers, the most visible small tradesmen on the streets of Warsaw. Despite innovations in health care and workers accident compensation in the sugar industry, Krzywicki found that the workers suffered from extreme poverty and from arbitrary treatment by factory foremen and managers. "Therefore," he concluded, "the question of the improvement of the conditions of workers in the sugar enterprise is tied together with the question of the liberation of the entire working class."[93] After exposing the deprivation of sugar workers in this supposedly progressive sector of the economy, Krzywicki turned to an analysis of the complicated business hierarchy of the flower-selling industry, from the half-dozen profit takers to the hundreds of beggared girls who peddled flowers on the street corners of Warsaw. He concluded his analysis of the flower-selling operation, much as he had that of the sugar enterprise, with a surprisingly explicit statement on the necessity of an economic revolution: "In our opinion, to eliminate the poverty of the flower-selling girl workers, as in general the entire working people, . . . it is necessary to completely change the basic contemporary system of production."[94]

Krzywicki concentrated his efforts on disproving the positivists' economic arguments; Bronisław Białobłocki attacked their liberal notions of the role of the intelligentsia in Polish society. The old idealistic intelligentsia, Białobłocki claimed, had been replaced by another equally useless group, the "bourgeois" positivist intelligentsia. The "young generation" was dissatisfied with both idealistic and bourgeois formulations of the role of the educated youth in Polish society and was embarking on a new era of Polish social thought. Socialism, Białobłocki implied, was the inspiration for and the ethos of this, "the new intelligentsia."[95]

The journalistic confrontation between positivism and Marxism culminated in a series of harsh polemics carried on the pages of *Przegląd Tygodniowy*. The Krusińszczycy, represented by Krzywicki, and the positivists, represented primarily by A. Głowacki (B. Prus), were joined in these polemics by Adam Zakrzewski, the leader of a small legal populist group.[96] Adam Wiślicki, the editor of *Przegląd,* summarized the two primary issues debated by all three groups: (1) whether society was an organism, as Spencer had concluded, or whether it was the sum total of disparate and conflicting elements, and (2) whether individual societies, in accordance with the tenets of Marxism, must pass through a capitalist phase, or whether certain aspects of particular societies could cause a deviation from this "natural" path.[97] The first question found the Krusińszczycy and Zakrzewski in opposition to the positivists. The second question allied the positivists and the Krusińszczycy against Zakrzewski.

The Marxists' assertion that Polish society, like all others, was divided into competing and irreconcilable class formations was particularly threatening to the positivists' position that peaceful economic and cultural improvement served the interests of all Poles. In the positivists' view, the society of the Congress Kingdom was not a product of class conflict, but a unified nation with the common goal of advancement for all members of that nation. This organic unity of the nation was not founded on racial, religious, or ethnic unity, but on a peculiarly positivist "social" unity. "To be a Pole," the positivists asserted, "is not identical with being a member of the *szlachta;* Poles are even non-Catholic and nonnoblemen."[98] Bolesław Prus was the most articulate advocate of this organic world view in his columns in *Atheneum* and *Przegląd Tygodniowy.* A member of society, he wrote, could no more separate himself from the "organic being" of that society "than man can separate himself from the planet on which he lives."[99] In turn, Krzywicki responded to Prus's theories of societal unity by taunting the talented Polish writer with the question of whether "the struggle that is now taking place between the bourgeoisie and the proletariat of Western countries . . . is a proof of unity, which is supposed to exist between individuals for the development of the social organism."[100]

Krzywicki's repeated invocations of Marx and Marxism in his attacks on Prus in the positivist press elicited the response of Adam Zakrzewski, a Polish populist. Zakrzewski was particularly disturbed by Krzywicki's implication that the social clashes occurring in Western Europe would soon, of necessity, engulf the Congress Kingdom. He criticized Krzywicki and the other "democrats of the future" (the Krusińszczycy) for following the teachings of Marx too literally. At the same time, he noted that the positivists like the socialists were advocates of Marx and "fight with those same weapons." Citing Marx's "Letter to a Friend in the East," Zakrzewski claimed that even the "father of scientific socialism" realized that his theories "did not have universal validity." In the case of the Congress Kingdom, Marxist theory was not applicable because Poland's agricultural structure was based on small holdings. Like the Russian populists, Zakrzewski claimed that this unique agricultural situation, combined with the paucity of Polish industry, made it possible to avoid capitalism in the Congress Kingdom. At present, Zakrzewski added, "we lack the broad foreign markets for home products which, as is known, is the first and natural condition for the development of capitalism."[101]

The civilized debates between the positivists and Marxists over the social consequences of industrialization were jolted by the insertion of Zakrzewski's populist heresy, which questioned the materialistic foundations of both arguments. This time, the leader of the Polish Legal Marxists, Stanisław Krusiński, assumed the responsibility for discrediting Zakrzewski's "antimodern" challenge. Quite simply, Krusiński wrote, his populist opponent had "misread *Das Kapital*" and misunderstood Marx. "In fact," Krusiński added, "it is not worth discussing at great length the inevitability of the capitalist phase." Although Polish capitalism was still admittedly behind that of Western Europe, "one would have to look through rose-colored glasses or be blind" not to note the "rapid, multifaceted development of capitalism in the Congress Kingdom."[102] Krusiński concurred with Zakrzewski's statement that Marx had exempted Russia from his general European developmental scheme, but he added that "the latest results of research on the great Russian *obshchina*" demonstrate that even "the *obshchina* was strongly shaken by the unheard-of rapid capitalistic growth in Russia. After several years . . . the *obshchina* will be a fact of history."[103] Despite Krusiński's admonitions, Zakrzewski steadfastly reiterated his populist view that capitalism was an evil that could and should be avoided in Poland. "Our society," he insisted, "does not have to go through the same economic development that Western Europe experienced."[104]

No conclusions were reached in the polemical exchanges among the positivists, the Marxists, and the populist Zakrzewski. In various forms, populism remained a steady, though tertiary political force in the Congress Kingdom and in modern Poland. Both the positivists and Marxists were confident that they could vanquish their opponents by intellectual argument and thereby eliminate them from Polish political thought. Neither camp was decisively victorious, but the elevated tone of the battle itself brought legitimacy and respectability to the previously profaned or ignored advocates of Marxism.

Convinced of the impossibility of significant political change in the Russian Empire, of the demonstrated counterproductivity of revolutionary activity, and of the enormous advantages of materialism, Polish positivists attacked the romantic, messianic, patriotic, and insurrectionary heritage of the Polish past. In successfully combating, though not ultimately conquering, these deep-rooted traditions in the Congress Kingdom, the positivists provided a valuable set of social, economic, and even political principles upon which the socialists could build. While stressing the progressive political and even ethical merits of investment capital, efficient factory management, and the development of trade, the positivists concomitantly directed the attention of Polish educated society to the plight of the urban working class. In fact, it was Warsaw Positivism that initially identified not only the characteristics of the Polish working class but also its existence as a unified and coherent social formation. Factory legislation, social welfare, and workers' education were issues first identified by the positivist press and positivist-dominated university and intelligentsia circles.

The positivists contributed to the rapid spread of socialism in the Congress Kingdom in other, more immediate fashions. Their press directly summarized and quoted Marx's ideas either in sympathetic articles by their positivist contributors or in articles by the Krusińszczycy. Even in their sometimes specious attacks on socialism, the positivist periodicals popularized the very ideas they attempted to denigrate. It was also positivism that first applied Marx and the vocabulary of Marxism to the dynamics of industrialization in Poland, and the Krusińszczycy contributors to the positivist press were the first to translate Marx into Polish. Finally, the positivist press helped to accelerate the spread of socialism by overstating the revolutionary potentialities of Western European socialist movements. Clearly, the positivists hoped to avoid industrial strife and socialist gains by counterposing the exaggerated dangers of revolutionary socialism to the benefits of progressive labor legislation. Instead, they inadvertently supported the Proletariat's recruitment of intelligentsia members by confirming the party's utopian pronouncements of imminent, Europeanwide socialist revolution.

Under conditions of heightened national and social tensions that characterized the period 1878–1883, passive sympathizers and sometimes active participants were won from the positivist to the socialist program. The positivists had maintained that the rejection of the national struggle coupled with cautious reform and diligent economic and social work were required to resolve the dilemmas of Polish nationhood and the debilitating byproducts of industrialization. From this program, the young Polish intelligentsia of the 1880s took the single step, in part prepared by the positivists themselves, to the Marxist position that liberal policies could not allay the increasingly obvious social and national antagonisms and that the only solution resided in an international socialist revolution.

IV

Polish Socialism in Russian Schools and in the Congress Kingdom, 1876–1881

Until the mid-1870s, Warsaw Positivism and its liberal political ethos held exclusive dominion over the intellectual life of the Congress Kingdom. Before 1875, wrote the distinguished Polish sociologist, Ludwik Krzywicki, "there was no talk of socialism in Warsaw."[1] No single factor explains why the spell of positivism waned. Certainly, the immediate cause was the influx into the Congress Kingdom of radicalized Polish students from Russian schools, beginning in 1876 and reaching its apogee in 1879–1880.[2] These students found a willing audience among sections of the disgruntled Warsaw working class. Positivism remained almost exclusively an intelligentsia and middle-class phenomenon; Warsaw workers, on the other hand, maintained a vague "insurrectionary" mentality. It is to these initial contacts between radicalized youth from Russia and Warsaw workers' circles that the origins of the Polish socialist movement can be traced.

The socialist ideology propagated in the first workers' circles was based on the experience of Polish youth in the *kresy*, the borderlands of European Russia, and especially in the southwestern Ukrainian *gubernii* of Podolia, Volhynia, and Kiev. In these areas, industrialization was too limited and concepts of organic development too irrelevant for positivism to maintain any more than a scattered and uninfluential following. Instead, Polish youth lived under conditions more attuned to the experiences of their Russian school comrades. At the same time, the *kresy*, as a border region, was the scene of an almost incredible conjuncture of social and national interests. The peasant population was overwhelmingly Orthodox and Uniate (even though formally abolished in 1839), Lithuanian, Belorussian, and Ukrainian; the towns were heavily Jewish; and the nobility, both rich and poor, were primarily Polish or Polonized and Catholic. In Podolia and Kiev *gubernii*, the Polish *szlachta* lived under far better conditions than the *szlachta* of Lithuania or the Congress Kingdom. The magnates of the south, unlike those of Lithuania, did not unilaterally support the 1863 uprising and therefore were not subject to the same terrifying measures of Russianization experienced by the Lithuanian *szlachta* under Muraviev. Many of the old Polish "tężyzny" (the "tough ones") continued to assert economic and social leadership in the Ukraine. Some memoirists attributed the energetic involvement of the youth of Podolia and Kiev *gubernii* in cultural and political activities to their traditional hardheaded independence as well as to the new economic prosperity of the *szlachta*-dominated sugar industry.[3] In any case, the Polish youth of this area, more enculturated into Russian life than their Lithuanian or Congress Kingdom comrades, better off economically, and better educated, immersed themselves into the Russian student movement of the 1870s and received their initial revolutionary training from Russian *narodniki.*

Poles in the Russian Schools

Some members of the 1870s generation of Polish *szlachta*-radicals came into contact with underground social patriotic or positivist circles at the local gymnasium, but most at this age were, like Ludwik Waryński, the future leader of the Proletariat, a *"panicz* [young master] in every sense of the word."[4] It was only with their arrival at Russian university centers that the majority of radical Poles acquired their first taste of and for revolutionary thinking. Waryński, like many of his *kresy* counterparts of modest means, chose a technical university as an educational ladder to a successful professional career.[5] Other, usually wealthier, young noblemen chose the medical and law faculties of Russian universities.[6] Strikingly, the youth of the *kresy* avoided Warsaw University; it was considered to be both an instrument of Russianization as well as of a lower intellectual caliber. Not without an element of social snobbery, *kresy* Poles looked toward St. Petersburg as an ideal place for schooling. The later socialist notable, Edmund Płoski, wrote in his memoirs:

> Russian students were accepted into Warsaw University — from the so-called religious seminaries ... or from the sixth and seventh class of the gymnasium . . . even without their *matury* ["gymnasium diplomas"]. . . . At the same time, at St. Petersburg University, the question to which nationality students belonged did not exist at all. Relations with the university authorities, with professors, and above all else, with the Russian youth . . . were in this matter absolutely correct.[7]

By the mid-1880s, Poles accounted for nearly 10 percent of the student body of St. Petersburg University and 20 percent of the capital's technical and medical schools.[8] The Poles who left their *kresy* estates for St. Petersburg as well as other university centers were immediately drawn into the cauldron of science and politics that dominated Russian student life in the 1870s. "Even the most apolitical students," wrote N. A. Borodin, "were unable to remain outside of politics."[9] Płoski recalled that "already in the first year" at the university, he formed a circle with other leftist Poles.[10] Edward Piekarski wrote that upon entering Kharkov Veterinary Institute (another center for radical Poles), he "at once" became involved in revolutionary activities.[11] "In the matter of a few months" after entering the university in Odessa, wrote Kazimierz Długski, "we formed a Polish circle."[12]

In contrast to the scattered gymnasia secret circles, which tended to dismiss socialism, at the university the Poles began to study this new ideology so widespread among their Russian colleagues. "Here for the first time," wrote Płoski, "I became interested in this movement. For it was clear that the so-called nihilists had goals and fundamentals for which they risked their lives."[13] Soon, the writings of Pisarev, Chernyshevskii, and Dobroliubov were better known to the Polish students than were the positivist writers in Warsaw. Neither were the *kresy* Poles immune to the attractions of Russian populism. Especially the writings of Lavrov in *Vperëd*, remembered Długski, influenced his circle's work.[14] Ludwik Waryński's biographer noted that it was a difficult struggle before Waryński "was freed from the influence of this ideology [populism]."[15] The *kresy* Poles were also introduced to Marx, Lassalle, and the literature of Western socialism by Russian *narodniki*. The Russian translation of the first volume of *Das Kapital*, Długski wrote, "passed from hand to hand."[16] N. I. Ziber's (1844–1888) popularizations of Marxist economic thought were read and discussed by Polish and Russian students alike.[17]

The intellectual searchings and social psychology of the Polish students in the schools of the empire never crystallized into a comprehensive socialist ideology. They retained definite ties to Polish culture while they emulated popular Russian heroes. Their socialism was a great deal more libertarian than scientific. Most significantly, they experienced no profound call to political action. Their confused progressivism and essential eclecticism is apparent in the diaries and papers of Włodzimierz Butkiewicz, a Polish leftist student at Moscow University. In his album, Butkiewicz asked his friends Obuchowski, Ptak, and Zagórski to record their preferences in ten categories of questions. Stanisław Ptak's preference of government reflects a typical Polish leftist dilemma of the 1870s, a devotion to the homeland combined with a strong *narodnik* bias: "There doesn't exist one that I like, that is, composed of independent communes. If I should have to choose among those in existence, I would choose my own fatherland which is everything dear to me." Interesting, too, is the almost positivist tenor of Ptak's values — "industry," "work in the name of Progress," and "society before the individual" — and his favorite poet is Nekrasov and his hero, Vera Zasulich. Obuchowski, an admirer of Admiral Nelson (!), chooses Switzerland as his preferred country "because there the proletariat suffers less than in other nations," and Zagórski finds the United States the most attractive because of its "equality and independence." In the arts, all three are devoted to realism as well as to the national culture (in the painting of Matejko). Two list Karl Marx and Chernyshevskii among their favorite authors and Nekrasov among their favorite poets; Dobroliubov, Pisarev, and Thomas Buckle are also mentioned.[18]

Polish youth were caught up in the activism of Russian students as well as in the influence of populist literature. A friend of Ptak's wrote to him of masses of students demonstrating in Moscow, St. Petersburg, and Odessa in 1878, "all of this is a wonderful sign of the times. You know Russia [*Rus*] reminds me at this moment of Rome in the time of its fall."[19] The frenzied activity and liberating chaos that Ptak's friend described also swept through Polish student groups. The authorities questioned Płoski about the reason he attended an illegal student gathering in 1879. He answered, "because of curiosity and a feeling of colleagual solidarity."[20] A friend persuaded Zygmunt Heryng to attend the Kazan Cathedral demonstration. "From that time," wrote Heryng, "I felt as if I were a participating socialist activist, and others also began to see me as one."[21] The direct terrorist struggle of the Russians against tsarism likewise aroused the Polish studentry. In this struggle, recalled Płoski, "the entire sympathy of our youth, regardless of their political views and affiliations, was on the side of the revolutionaries." For Płoski, it was the attempt of Soloviev on the life of the tsar that was crucial for his involvement.[22] For Stanisław Stempowski, Maria Bohuszewiczówna, and many others, it was the 1881 assassination of Alexander II that touched off their involvement in socialist activities.[23]

The Russian movement unquestionably influenced Polish youth in the universities; this does not mean, as Kucharzewski asserted, that the Poles were "hypnotized by the growth of the Russian revolutionary movement during the reign of Alexander II."[24] Kon noted in his memoirs that the Poles carried their own heavy psychological burdens as Poles and democrats in a Rusian and autocratic state: "This contradiction between cult and actuality, between word and deed must have been flung before the eyes of the younger generation, must have been placed there by discussions unknown to the earlier generation."[25] Both the example of the Russians and the "burdens" of their own position encouraged the formation of secret Polish circles in St. Petersburg in early 1874, and soon thereafter in Kiev, Odessa, and Moscow. It would be an exaggeration to call all of these circles "socialist" as do the historians Emil Haecker and Stanisław Walczak.[26] Polish students (including Waryński, E. Kobylański, and B. Wysłouch) did organize one socialist circle at the St. Petersburg Institute of Technology in 1874, but most were circles of self-education (samokształcenie) and mutual help.[27] These latter groups served more as social institutions for Poles and had almost nothing in common with political action.

The Gminas

Under the influence of the prestigious Institute of Technology socialists, Polish semilegal, self-help groups evolved by the end of the 1870s into larger circles with varying degrees of socialist involvement. Among Polish students during this period, wrote Heryng, the "spiritual atmosphere" changed radically. Very few Poles were interested simply in "making a career."[28] Instead, they organized themselves by school and then again by geographical area (Kiev, the Congress Kingdom, Belorussia, Lithuania, and Podolia), studied populist literature, and engaged in ideological discussion. Loris-Melikov's ascension to power in 1880 and several liberalizing measures undertaken by Minister of Education Saburov provided the opportunity for these circles to become legalized under the rubric of the zemliachestva — large, regionally oriented student organizations concerned with mutual help. Polish students avoided the Russian zemliachestva and instead formed Gminas ("communes") in all large Polish educational centers of the empire: St. Petersburg, Moscow, Vilna, Kiev, and Warsaw. Although they existed barely a year, the Gminas were a significant watershed in the history of Polish socialism. In them, Polish students combined the organizational security of the zemliachestva, their increasing sympathy for socialism, and their still strong desire to remain separate from Russian organizations.

Heryng interpreted this desire on the part of the Poles to remain separate as a tactical manoeuvre reminiscent of Von Moltke's *zertrennt marschieren, zusammen schlagen* ["march separately, attack together"].[29] Aleksander Rodziewicz, in his confession to the police, stated that the Gminas had nothing in common with the Russian social revolutionary party and simply served the needs of Polish students.[30] The desire to remain separate from the Russians was so strong, recalled Aleksander Dębski, that Polish activists even attempted to draw other Poles away from the Russian socialist organizations. "We went into this work," wrote Dębski, "with the idea that we should help the Russians as an organization, as a collective body, and not as individuals."[31] This desire for separation was tempered, however, both by the overwhelming sympathy the Poles felt for the Russian movement and by the well-established personal ties between members of the Gminas, especially the St. Petersburg Gmina, and the Russian populist comrades.[32] The official government *Chronicle* of the revolutionary movement asserted that the Polish Gminists Józef Hłasko and Marian Wilczyński, the former a member of Narodnaia Volia ("People's Will") and the latter a member of Chernyi Peredel ("Black Partition"), maintained contacts between the Gminas and these two Russian populist organizations.[33] The Soviet historian S. S. Volk claims that by the winter of 1880, the St. Petersburg Gmina was an intimate ally of Narodnaia Volia and that several of the Poles carried on negotiations with A. P. Mikhailov, A. I. Barannikov, and N. N. Kolodkevich, leaders of the Executive Committee.[34] But arrests halted these negotiations, and by the spring of 1881, the Gmina ceased to exist.

The Gminas were in fact wary of ties with Narodnaia Volia for just such a reason. Their activities were based not so much on conspiratorial actions with the Russians as on the spread of a mixed-bag ideology of socialism and Polish democracy among their Polish comrades and friends.[35] Social conservatism had not totally disappeared from Polish student circles; the primary enemy of the Gminists was not the Russian autocracy but the antisocialist Polish student group — the "Ujeżdżalna" ("riding school").[36] Therefore, according to the St. Petersburg prosecutor, the Gmina was primarily a propagandistic organization, and its leaders, Edmund Płoski and Stanisław Kunicki, spent their major efforts trying to organize self-help circles among nonaligned Polish students in St. Petersburg educational institutions.[37] The Gminas also attempted to extend contacts and form alliances with Polish groups in and outside the empire.[38] The gendarmerie in Warsaw were especially concerned with these efforts, which had already begun in 1878 by the Gminist Ludwik Straszewicz, who "while attending St. Petersburg Technological Institute, belonged to the social revolutionary party, whose goal was the undermining of the present social and economic structure of the Kingdom of Poland, and, on behalf of his cohorts, traveled in December 1878 from Petersburg to the cities of Warsaw, Kraków, and Lwów in order to recruit local student youth into revolutionary activity."[39] The network of Polish student groups that Straszewicz established spread even further during the Gmina period owing primarily to the efforts of Zygmunt Balicki and Kazimierz Sosnowski.[40]

Despite these widespread contacts in the Polish as well as Russian revolutionary world, the Gminas were able neither to draft a unified ideological program nor to publish a common platform of principles. An all-Gmina meeting was planned for June 1880 in Warsaw, at which the editors of the émigré publication *Równość* were to be challenged on their socialist program. But no representatives arrived from Geneva, and a programmatic settlement was therefore put off until July 1881. But the July meeting was never held. It, like the spring 1881 programmatic discussions planned in Vilna, fell victim to the mass arrests beginning in February and March 1881.[41]

In his report on Gmina activities, the prosecutor of the St. Petersburg district Muraviev did refer to a draft "Gmina program." As its first plan of action, Muraviev wrote, the program advocated:

> peaceful propaganda of socialist principles and work on the development of the scientific theory of socialism. And, at the same time, taking into consideration the conditions of the population, it recognized as one of the tasks of the organization active agitation among the working class of the countryside and cities, as well as the preparation of an organization followed by a political and economic revolution.[42]

This programmatic document was never approved by the Gmina structure as a whole, and no copies of it have so far been located. The only extant political document of the Gminas is a Russian translation of a proclamation in an 1880 issue of *Narodnaia volia* entitled, "From the 'Gminas' of Polish Socialists on the Occasion of the 50th Anniversary of the Uprising of the Polish People." This proclamation, composed by the Warsaw and St. Petersburg Gminas, mixed socialist ideals with aspirations for Polish nationhood:

> We love our fatherland no less than those fighters of 1830, but we understand this love differently: to us is dear not the fate of the privi-

leged, dear to us is the fate of the Polish people.... Therefore, we want national independence, equality of members of the communes; put before all else; [however,] as the precondition for all this, [we desire] economic equality, which in turn may occur only when the means of production and the land come into collective ownership of the people and not of separate individuals.[43]

The new Poland would therefore be built on communal foundations. It would somehow be brought about without the "useless struggle" — class warfare — with which the revolution "is connected in Western Europe."[44]

The most difficult historiographical problem in an examination of the Gminas is the placement of these groups within the history of Polish socialism. The two most accomplished modern historians of the period 1878–1886, the Soviet T. G. Snytko and the Pole Leon Baumgarten, disagree precisely on this question. Baumgarten tends to view the Gminas as regressive organizations, less socialist and more patriotic than the circles formed in Warsaw in 1878, and he assigns them a separate period in the early history of Polish socialism as an anachronistic outburst of "social patriotic" ideology. The Gminas' concern for national independence is due, in Baumgarten's view, to the influence of Narodnaia Volia's national program, which, unlike that of Zemlia i Volia, recognized the legitimacy of national entities.[45] Snytko, on the other hand, insists that one can neither establish a separate period for the Gminas nor convincingly demonstrate that they were any more patriotic than the Warsaw groups of 1878–79. The Gminas, in Snytko's view, were "social revolutionary" rather than "social patriotic."[46]

Both historians' arguments have some validity, but they fail to capture the essence of the Gminas' role in this period. First of all, one must delineate between the Gminas in Russia and the Warsaw Gmina. In Warsaw, as we shall see, the Gmina was influenced by a different set of conditions than were the Gminas of other Russian university centers; namely, workers' circles, Polish strikes, and a short history of working-class socialism played a significant part in the organization and ideology of the Warsaw Gminists.[47] Warsaw socialists had formulated a firm platform — the "Brussels Program" — with which the Warsaw Gmina was forced to come to terms. The other Gminas — Vilna, Kiev, Moscow, and St. Petersburg — represented rather the culmination of a decade-long process of involvement of *kresy* youth, primarily from the *szlachta*, in socialist circles. These young radicals did not solve the problem of political action until returning to the fatherland and the "people" to whom they pledged their fates. More and more deeply, recalled Dłuski, "the notion spread that the ideas of socialism should be propagated by Poles not in Russia, but in their own country . . . in its capital — in Warsaw."[48] The Gminas were neither strictly social revolutionary nor social patriotic; they were, quite simply, loose confederations of Polish radicals who shared a vague dream of a communal Poland, a dream that did not seem realizable until returning to Warsaw.[49]

Poles and Russians

The influence exerted by the Russian revolutionary movement on Polish studentry in the 1870s was instrumental in the emergence of a full-scale Polish movement in the 1880s. The literature of the Russian movement, the example of its deeds, and the contacts it established among Polish youth, combined with the particular background of the *kresy* youth, helped inaugurate the Gmina movement. This movement itself culminated in the mass infiltration of *kresy*-born radicals into the Congress Kingdom. But another dimension of Russian influence on the development of Polish socialism (as well as Poles on Russian socialism) was the direct participation of Poles in the Russian revolutionary movement of the 1870s.[50] In emigration, Kacper Turski was a crucial contributor to *Nabat* (Tocsin) and an important influence on the Russian Jacobin, Petr Tkachev. A Polish circle led by Leon Dmochowski was involved in the "going to the people" movement of 1873–74.[51] Aleksander Więckowski was an editor of *Nachalo* (Beginning) and a leader of Zemlia i Volia.[52] The brothers Izbicki, Ludwik Kobylański, and Walerian Osiński similarly played important roles in the Russian terrorist movement.[53] Poles in Odessa participated in the Southern Workers' Union and attempted to form a section of the International on the prompting of the Polish Communards.[54]

Far more interesting and of far greater consequence for the history of Polish socialism was the new national type of revolutionary Pole emerging from the circumstances of the *kresy*. The generation of *kresy* youth who grew up in the postinsurrectionary era under the influence of Russian socialism in the universities began, in some senses, to lose their national identity as Poles. "Even in the Gmina," wrote Płoski, "there were numerous persons who were Russified to such an extent that they were not fluent in Polish, and only in Warsaw learned to talk and write in Polish."[55] In his analysis of the intelligentsia of the *kresy*, Z. Łukawski writes that these Poles worked and lived so closely with the other ethnic groups that a national transition often occurred. "Poles became Ukrainians, Lithuanians, Russians, and also White Russians."[56] Many Polish socialists who were born in the *kresy* and were educated in Russian universities — among them, Ludwik Janowicz, Tymoteusz Abramowicz, the Daniłłowicz brothers, Cezaryna Wojnarowska, and even Ludwik Waryński — were remembered for their bad Polish, full of "Russianisms."[57] Russianization extended even to matters of dress and style. Zygmunt Balicki, the later ideologue of National Democracy, pranced about St. Petersburg in his Russian "red" outfit — a worker's shirt and pantslegs tucked into his boots.[58] It was easy to tell a "Russian" Polish student on the Warsaw streets by the radical styles. Long hair for the young men, short hair for the girls, and red shirts set off those whose Russian university training indicated a fashionable radical sophistication.[59]

An awareness of the gradual denationalization of some *kresy* Poles in matters of thought, language, and dress can be profitably applied to the problem of estimating the numbers of Poles involved in the Russian movement. T. G. Snytko, for instance, describes these Russianized Poles as unquestionably Polish and therefore counts over a thousand "Polish" *narodniki*.[60] Ludwik Bazylow, on the other hand, sees them as denationalized citizens of the Russian Empire, more Russian than Polish. Populism was a peculiarly Russian phenomenon, claims Bazylow, and experienced very little Polish support. Using Bazylow's criteria (Catholic religion, Polish name, Polish language), probably no more than fifty Poles were involved.[61] In addition, there was an insolvable ethnic problem for the Polish *narodniki* in Russia; the *kresy* had very few Polish peasants or workers. If the Poles went "to the people" at all in this region, it was to Belorussians or Ukrainians.

The background of one *kresy* Pole, Ignacy Hryniewiecki, the assassin of Alexander II, illustrates the central problem of the Polish nationality argument. Snytko, in fact, attacks Bazylow for hedging on the *polskość* ("Polishness") of Hryniewiecki and instead describes the young *narodovolets* as a "Polish patriot."[62] Born in Minsk, the son of a landless nobleman, Hryniewiecki attended secondary school in Białystok and then entered the Institute of Technology in St. Petersburg. At the institute, he led a small circle of Narodnaia Volia sympathizers and was noted for his propagandistic abilities. Soon he became deeply involved with the terrorist Executive Committee, which led him to his role in the March 1 assassination plot.[63]

Hryniewiecki spoke Russian a great deal better than Polish and called himself a Lithuanian, though he may well have been of Belorussian ancestry. Dłuski recalled that Hryniewiecki had almost no contact with the Polish colony in St. Petersburg. "Neither I nor, as far as I know, any of my close friends ever met him, even at the school[the heavily Polish Institute of Technology], which we both attended."[64] Hryniewiecki himself has been quoted as stating that despotism must first be destroyed in order to build "a free and socialist Russia and Poland."[65] In response to the question of a fellow Pole, asking why he did not fight for Poland, Hryniewiecki reportedly answered, "When you go to the woods [take up arms], I will come to you. Now I'll fight here, for here our blows are more effective."[66] The position of the Russianized Pole, like that of Hryniewiecki, approached but did not equal the denationalized position of many Jewish revolutionaries of the 1870s and early 1880s. In part, this can be attributed to the vigor of the Polish national myth. Only a very small minority rejected that myth, and those who did often returned to it in times of national resurgence.

The denationalized minority of *kresy* Poles, as Ludwik Krzywicki noted, often took a deprecating view of their own national past and maintained that Polish society was "incapable of aspirations of a democratic nature."[67] Snytko adds that even the Russians were disturbed by this overly cosmopolitan, antipatriotic attitude of the Poles. "The *narodniki* tried to show the Polish socialists their errors in the national question, of their underrating the national liberation movement."[68] In the 1870s, Snytko's somewhat too paternalistically Soviet assessment aside, the Poles, even the most Russianized, had no more clear idea of how to handle the national question than did the Russians. As Boris Itenburg quite correctly writes, the revolutionary populist movement lived under the stars "of ideological searching and differences, sharp contradistinctions, heavy quarrels, expressing the persistent hope of its participants to find the correct path of revolutionary action."[69]

The programs of Zemlia i Volia were at best ambiguous toward the Polish question. The first program (1876–1877) did not mention Poland specifically but called for the "dividing up of the Russian Empire in sections according to local wishes."[70] On the supracommunal level, one can assume, the empire would remain intact, albeit with a new social, economic, and administrative structure. The two drafts of the second program (1878) affirmed the need to recognize the unique interests of the nationalities. Poland was viewed by these drafts as "ready at the first chance to separate" from the empire. In the first draft, the *zemliavol'tsy* wrote, "we should not hinder the partition of the contemporary Russian Empire," and in the final draft they added, "therefore our duty is to promote the partition."[71] Lev Tikhomirov later bitterly complained about Russian populism's willingness to chop up the empire: "Our cosmopolitan in reality was not even a cosmopolitan, for in his heart, not all nations were equal, but all were palatable except for his own."[72] Ludwik Waryński, Kazimierz Dłuski, Maria Jankowska, and other Polish *kresy* youth brought this cosmopolitanism (in part derived from their own denationalization) to the Congress Kingdom and, with it, the foundations of Polish internationalism.

Russian revolutionaries affirmed the *kresy* youth's distaste for the autocracy, encouraged their aspirations for autonomy, welcomed them into their movement, provided them with a solution to social problems, and shared with them the vast indigenous and translated literature of science and socialism. Polish radical youth responded in various ways, but all respected the Russian movement, were knowledgeable in its literature, receptive to its social solutions, and convinced of its future. A few Poles completely submerged into Russian culture and into the Russian movement. The majority remained tied — some more, some less — to their Polish national consciousness. Several participated in both cultures and served both movements. Few who entered political activity through *narodnik* gates left social action in one final form or another.

The Socialist and Patriotic Movements in Warsaw, 1876-77

Most historians and memoirists, as well as the Russian police, date the beginnings of the socialist movement in Warsaw to 1876.[73] This 1876 movement, the Warsaw prosecutor later wrote, was the product of "local elements . . . tied directly to the party of the Russian revolutionary movement . . . [who] aimed to spread as widely as possible social revolutionary views." The prosecutor added that these Polish socialists were mostly propagandized by the Russian movement and were youth "from the southwest and northwest lands [the *kresy*] . . . graduates of Petersburg and Moscow scientific schools."[74]

When they arrived in Warsaw, the Polish radical youth embarked on a variant of the "going to the people" movement. Ludwik Waryński arrived in Warsaw in November 1876 and immediately went to work in the city's largest metal factory — Lilpop, Rau, and Lowenstein.[75] Ludwik Krzywicki learned cabinetmaking and latheturning.[76] Kazimierz Dłuski became a metalworker, and even Stanisław Mendelson, the son of a wealthy Warsaw banker, worked as a tailor.[77] Kazimierz Hildt, while still attending school, spent all his free time laboring in a carriage factory and learning the habits of the Warsaw working class.[78] These and other efforts by the Polish revolutionary intelligentsia, in contrast to those of their Russian brethren of 1873–74, met with relative success among a labor force partially conscious of politics and of social questions due to the recent history of an urban rebellion in 1863–64.

The small discussion groups initiated by these propagandists would have been much less successful without those well-born artisans and workers who entered the ranks of the proletariat through the unpleasant path of economic necessity.[79] Henryk Dulęba and Wacław Sieroszewski, both unable to continue in the gymnasium, were forced into industrial professions. Dulęba became a soapmaker and later worked in a railway workshop; Sieroszewski became a metalworker. Both maintained contact with their intelligentsia friends, yet both were integrally tied to the working class.[80] Dulęba especially, partly because of his personal persuasiveness but also because of his position as a worker and intelligentsia member, was able to establish important ties between working-class and intelligentsia socialist circles.

In addition to these first propaganda efforts among the Warsaw working class, other Polish socialists, especially those from Kiev, entered into Warsaw University student political circles, devoted at this point to positivist and patriotic squabbles. Władysław Izbicki from the Kiev Medical School, Aleksander Rodziewicz also from Kiev, and Kazimierz Dłuski from Odessa prodded Warsaw University students with the new and soon fashionable ideas of socialism.[81] At one meeting, recalled Dłuski, he talked about the principles of revolutionary socialism and "of the inevitability of organizing socialist circles among the studentry of Warsaw." All of this was taken in by the students "with a certain curiosity" but also "with general indifference to our endeavors." Then a young medical student jumped to the center of the hall and shouted, "Every socialist Pole is a traitor!"[82] The student was Józef Pławiński, who a year later was one of the most active socialist agitators among Warsaw educated youth.[83]

Pławiński's conversion represents an early example of the conversion of an entire generation. After his apathetic reception in Warsaw in 1876, Dłuski left the Congress Kingdom; on his return in the fall of 1877, he found "a completely different mood among the progressive group of students."[84] Prosecutor Pleve and the Russian police also noted a rapid increase in student socialist agitation at the end of 1877.[85] By this point, the rudimentary beginnings of a socialist organization had been formed with about thirty students from various faculties of the university.[86] No formal organization was set up in 1876–77 either among the university students or among the workers, and no ties were established between their circles. The socialism that was propagated was a mixture of Russian populism, Polish utopian socialism, and the Western socialism of Lassalle and Marx.[87] On the other hand, the fact that within a year socialism could spread with such rapidity greatly encouraged the dreams and determination of its advocates, as well as prompted the anxiety of the Russian authorities.

The acceleration of socialist activities among Poles in 1876–77 was accompanied by the reemergence of the patriotic movement. In the Congress Kingdom, states an Okhrana history of Polish nationalism, "all was quiet and orderly" until 1876. In that year, continues the author, "circles were formed among the students of Warsaw University for the purpose of raising patriotic feeling . . . which led to propagandistic and illegally based agitational actions."[88] Despite the social and theoretical strength of antiinsurrectionary Warsaw Positivism, Polish dreams of an independent nation revived with the advent of the Russo-Turkish War of 1877–88, as they had during numerous earlier breaks in the European order. As Ludwik Kulczycki recalled, "The Eastern War aroused a strong echo throughout Poland. . . . A significant part of Polish society awaited its outcome in the hope that it might lead to a shift in the international order. The optimists expected that Russia would lose the war, and then the existing governmental system would have to be changed."[89] Once again, in a well-rehearsed pattern, an adversary Western power — this time, England — turned to the exile Poles, to Z. Miłkowski (T. T. Jeż) and probably also to General Wróblewski, for the organization of military action in the Congress Kingdom. Miłkowski correctly assessed the widespread antiinsurrectionary sentiments among the Polish population and turned down the English offers.[90]

As a result of the outbreak of the war and the reemergence of patriotic hopes, a new "national government" was hastily put together in Lwów under the leadership of Prince Adam Sapieha.[91] The law student Adam Szymański was named by the so-called "government" to serve its interests in the Congress Kingdom.[92] Szymański and his main co-workers — Jan Popławski in Warsaw and Adam Miński in Lublin — set out to organize a complex system of local, regional, and national groups that would prepare the national uprising.[93] In fact, the

"Szymański conspiracy" lasted five months and could recruit only about thirty members (mostly friends and relatives of Szymański) to the cause of national rebellion.[94] A grandiose plan with less than meager results, the "Szymański conspiracy" nevertheless provides interesting insights into the political tenor of the Congress Kingdom in the last half of the 1870s. It would be misleading to interpret the conspiracy as an "activization of the national liberation movement" in the Congress Kingdom, as does Snytko, or as proof that there was "no interruption of the political traditions after the January [1863] uprising," as does Kulczycki.[95] Szymański was the last and the most impotent of Polish intelligentsia revolutionaries to depend exclusively on international involvements and the idea that the Poles were at any moment ready to leap to the barricades. "One cannot improvise an uprising" — this, wrote Wilhelm Feldman, was the lesson of Szymański.[96] Warsaw Positivism and tsarist repression had done their work well; the Polish people would not suffer another uprising during this period. Even Adam Miński, Szymański's close confederate, complained about the "total apathy" of the populace and of the conspirators themselves.[97]

Although exemplifying the lack of interest displayed in the Congress Kingdom for national insurrection, the "Szymański conspiracy" also demonstrated that socialism had made considerable inroads into Polish political life by 1878. Szymański himself was in and out of contact with Warsaw University socialist circles in 1877. His papers and those of his cohort Miński display an acute and defensive awareness of the attraction of socialism and the social question to Poles during this period. Eventually, Miński wrote, the social order must be altered. But to us, he added, "the social question is in second place, the first place belongs to the concern to save our national political existence."[98] In his confessions to the police, Szymański attempted to use the fear of socialism in his favor, suggesting that his group meant only to salvage the morale of the Polish nation "and paralyze the social movement."[99] The abysmal failure of his group discredited once again the insurrectionary mentality. At the same time, it brought new recruits into the socialist movement from small radical circles indirectly tied to the patriotic quest.[100]

The Dawn of a New Age, 1878-79

At the outset of 1878, with patriotic insurrection discredited and positivism losing its hold on Polish youth, socialism came to the Congress Kingdom with enormous force and captured the attention of a substantial segment of Polish studentry, intellectuals, and working-class intelligentsia.[101] Their socialism was, however, far from mature and sophisticated. Adam Próchnik accurately portrayed the young propagandists as "missionaries" who viewed the coming of socialism in terms of "one gigantic act, one powerful and all-encompassing revolution."[102] Not only did these 1878 socialists believe in an explosive social situation, they also believed in its absolute immediacy. "Who of us at the time," Dłuski wrote, "doubted that in three or at most four years a fierce social revolution would break out."[103] "We then believed," he noted elsewhere, "totally sincerely and also naively, that in a few years there would occur a social revolution in all civilized nations."[104] In a letter to A. Grużewska, A. A. Drobyszewski wrote, in a typically allegoric style, "Here all is quiet, but a perceptive person can easily see the clouds on the horizon; a storm will break out, but let it do so, for it will have good results, the air will be cleaned and freshened."[105] These views of the proximity of the revolution, though indeed naive, were founded in part on the growth of a "revolutionary situation" the empire experienced in 1878. Especially the lost war evoked revolutionary dreams. "The war is finished. Russia is defeated," wrote A. Wiśniewski in his diary. "The war made possible the rapid growth of revolutionary forces. . . . With this war, Russia brought ever closer the death of autocracy."[106]

Conscious only of the dawn of the new world, the 1878 socialists immersed themselves in propaganda "taking into account neither their enemies nor their own strength and means."[107] Impromptu meetings were held all over Warsaw — by factory gates, in taverns, at the university, and in the workers' quarters themselves.[108] At larger gatherings, Dłuski and Waryński broadly outlined to the workers the economics of factory labor and the involvement of the autocracy in capitalist exploitation. They glowingly described strikes and workers' organizations in Western Europe, encouraging their listeners to join the *kasy oporu* ("defense treasuries") which were to be the grass-roots organizations of the Polish workers' movement. The inspiration for the *kasy* came from the West and from the International which advocated their formation as crucial links in the struggle of the working class against capital (*caisses de résistance* or *Widerstandskassen*).

The larger meetings were supplemented by meetings among the workers themselves led by Feliks Tomaszewski, Kazimierz Kobylański, Karol Redlich, Kazimierz Dąbrowski, Wacław Sieroszewski, and other members of the working-class intelligentsia.[109] Waryński and Filipina Płaskowicka propagandized as well among women workers, but as Tomaszewski admitted, "this was simply unsuccessful."[110] (Płaskowicka, a devotee of Lavrov, had already in 1876–77 served as the only major socialist to take propaganda to the Polish countryside, where she achieved considerable success among the peasants as a schoolteacher.)[111] Among previously existing patriotic circles, especially among the politically conscious railway workers, Henryk Dulęba led the propaganda efforts.[112] Still, it was Waryński who was at the heart of the 1878 movement. Variously referred to in police reports as the "tall blond," "Jan Buch," the "smooth-talker," or simply as "Ludwik," Waryński's attractive character and dedication clearly served as an inspiration for the entire movement. His gymnasium friend Edmund Brzeziński wrote:

> Physically, he was the typical *kresowiec* — a tall blond, strongly built, very nearsighted, always wore glasses. He was very handsome and from the first sight captivated people. He was extraordinarily courageous, firm in decisions, and loyal in friendships. He was well-read and adjusted quickly, articulate and ably discussed, punctuating his arguments with expressive gesticulations. He had tremendous influence on those around him.[113]

Waryński's method of propaganda, soon followed by his comrades, was (wrote Sieroszewski), "No political innuendoes! . . . Talk only of economic matters of exploitation and oppression of the workers, of capital, of the fact that work is the only basis of wealth and gives worth to products, of 'surplus value,' etc."[114] This propaganda of what certainly can be called vulgar Marxism remained almost strictly oral until May 1878, when Waryński organized the smuggling of newly translated socialist literature into the Congress Kingdom from Poznań.[115] It was at this point as well that an indigenous Polish socialist literature began to take shape in the books and pamphlets of Szymon Dikształjn and Bolesław Limanowski.

The response of the Warsaw working-class population to propaganda efforts of the first six months of 1878 was encouraging to Waryński and his cohorts. By May the *kasy* had 150 enrolled members, by June 300.[116] Even during the summer of 1878, when the authorities arrested the most visible intelligentsia socialists and others (including Waryński) were forced into exile, the workers' *kasy* remained strong and intact.

Despite the arrests, the intelligentsia leadership quickly replenished its ranks. By the fall of 1878, Ludwik Dziankowski, Samuel Rogalski, Zygmunt Heryng, and Józef Uziembło took over the responsibilities of

intelligentsia propaganda.[117] The old *zemliavolets* Aleksander Więckowski returned to Warsaw as did the brothers Piechowski.[118] A
revolutionary center was formed at the home of the socialist Albin
Kowalski, and with the help of his children's tutor, Dionesy Certowicz,
continuity in the socialist movement was maintained.[119] Socialist
circles continued to gather strength until the spring of 1879, when the
Russian police launched a second series of arrests. By July and August
1879, with the final group of arrests, the initial Polish socialist movement ceased to exist.[120]

The Warsaw prosecutor Trakhimovskii classified this 1878–79
group of socialists as a "social revolutionary association" (*soobsh-
chestvo*) and claimed that "all persons deriving from the intelligentsia
and implicated in the investigation of radicals are tied closely to one
another, and do not act as individuals but in complete agreement with
one another."[121] If the organizational efforts of these socialists were
well coordinated, their ideological views ranged the entire gamut of
European and Russian socialist thought. There were anarchists, wrote
Dębski, and there were Lassalleans.[122] There were those who, like
Waryński, advocated agitation and others, like Uziembło, who fought
for pure propaganda. Jan Paszke admitted to the police that he stood
"on the same principles as the German party"; Dziankowski looked to
the Russian movement for inspiration.[123] One socialist document of
this period, "Dear Comrade," spelled out what the author considered
to be the three dominant characteristics of Polish socialism: "We
unconditionally recognize the common character of property, which is
the social force par excellence. . . . Second, our foundation is cooperation. . . . Next comes anarchy, which we understand in the broadest
terms as the decentralization of power and full self-determination."[124]

The composite ideological nature of Warsaw socialism in these years
is also reflected by its program, entitled "The Principles of the Social
Revolutionary Union of Poles."[125] Here the authors combine the
populist sense of social revolution, present as well in "Dear Comrade,"
with a Marxist analysis of the evils of contemporary capitalism. The
problem of agitation versus propaganda is solved by advocating both.
All possible methods for gaining influence among the people were to
be employed — "uprisings, that is, protests, demonstrations, and
active fights in the spirit of our principles."[126] On the national question, the program advocates the same kind of organization of ethnic
communes for the Lithuanians, Belorussians, and Ukrainians as for
the Poles and Russians.

Unlike the programs of either Zemlia i Volia or Narodnaia Volia, the "Principles" contain an unambiguous indictment of the failings of the capitalist mode of production and a call for the workers to overthrow it. At the same time, the program makes no mention of the necessity for tight conspiracy nor does it contain an apology for terrorism. Organizational problems are, in fact, totally ignored. Still, the "Principles," much like the program of Narodnaia Volia, call the Polish people to a political struggle against "the evil government, which unites unheard-of national oppression with economic exploitation" and concludes that "a bloody social revolution is unavoidable."[127]

In their everyday attitudes as well as in their program, the 1878–79 Polish socialists demonstrate an affinity more for the later terrorist Narodnaia Volia than for Zemlia i Volia. Waryński, the "brilliant organizer" and "smooth-talking" agitator, also "ran about all of Warsaw with a revolver in his pocket and a dagger in his belt."[128] At an 1878 meeting, Dłuski is reported to have put his revolver on the table and stated, "in the case of arrest, shoot."[129] When a worker is harassed by the police, exhorted Waryński, "then all should join in! Don't be afraid of them! . . . Let them be afraid of us!"[130] At Jan Paszke's home, as well as in many other secret party centers around Warsaw, the police turned up revolvers, knives, and chemical preparations for explosives.[131]

The Russians and the Congress Kingdom Movement, 1878–79

Prosecutor Trakhimovskii assumed from the style, the program, and the social origins of the leading 1878–79 socialists that "the forces that lead the [local] elements into the movement are external to Polish society and that these contemporary socialist circles grew up under the influence of the Russian revolutionary party." We are not worried, concluded Trakhimovskii, for "the *gubernii* of the Congress Kingdom . . . do not provide the proper basis for the development of social revolutionary propaganda."[132] To be sure, although the socialists managed to formulate a draft program, their movement in 1878–79 remained scattered, diverse, and in a political sense, inconsequential. The persistent call in the personal papers of the revolutionaries for the formation of a great workers' party "which already had been completed in other countries" reflected the need for and lack of just such a party in the Congress Kingdom.[133] Many politically conscious workers were still tied to socialist patriotic circles;[134] intelligentsia socialists continued to be torn both on the question of patriotism and on the role of propaganda and agitation.

Yet Trakhimovskii's assessment of the exclusivity of Russian influence (not to mention his Pollyannalike vision of the total absence of indigenous roots of socialism) needs to be revised. That the vast majority of intelligentsia leaders of the party had contact with, if not directly participated in, the Russian movement is unquestionable.[135] That Russian revolutionary literature provided the dominant intellectual stimulus for Polish radicalism is also beyond doubt.[136] Nevertheless, the Russian revolutionary ideology, confused enough in its own country, became even more confusing in conditions alien to its origins, and the Poles turned to the West for ideological solutions. Zygmunt Heryng translated Liebknecht; Wojnarowski studied and translated Lassalle; and Dziankowski translated Draper, Spencer, and Renan.[137] More important than both Russian and Western literature in translation were the new efforts at providing an indigenous Polish socialist literature, which answered questions directly relevant to Polish reality. "What is socialism?" asks one of these pamphlets aimed at the Polish working class, and "Does socialism contradict our patriotic feelings?"[138]

The common enemy of Russian and Polish revolutionaries, the autocracy, provided a common cause; but dissimilar environments necessitated separate solutions. The first Polish attempt to integrate student groups in the Congress Kingdom into the Russian movement occurred in 1875. "This proposition was not accepted," wrote Kazimierz Hildt, "because it was opposed by the influence of those students [Szymański was one] who upheld the national liberation direction."[139] Even though *kresy* Poles maintained active contacts with the Russian movement, there were notably few further attempts to unite the two movements.[140] Viktor Obnorskii of the "Northern Workers' Union" traveled to Warsaw and Kraków in 1878 in an attempt to establish ties with Polish workers' circles, and A. Drobysz-Drobyszewski, a veteran of Obnorskii's group, spread the Union's literature among Warsaw circles in 1878-79. Numerous Polish translations of the "Program of the Northern Russian Workers' Union" circulated among Polish worker circles.[141] Still, no concrete measures resulted from these efforts. In fact, the only result of Russo-Polish contact was an exchange of salutory letters in 1879, which was, in Leon Wasilewski's words, the "first public manifestation of mutual sympathy between socialists of the two peoples."[142]

The most talked about attempt to unite Polish and Russian revolutionary circles in this period occurred in 1878 with the visit of S. Stepniak-Kravchinskii to Warsaw.[143] Although he came to Warsaw for the purpose of escaping to the West, at the same time he proposed the unification of Polish circles into the Russian organization.[144] (The Poles were to have one delegate on the Russian Executive Committee.) "The Poles, however, decided to remain in their own organization and limit themselves to the friendly exchange of mutual help with the Russians."[145] One of the results of Kravchinskii's visit and his meetings with several circles, recalled J. Uziembło, was that some Poles advocated a greater use of terrorism, but this was rejected by the majority.[145] The reports of visits by Obnorskii and Kravchinskii to Warsaw as well as the documented ties of Petr Lavrov and Vera Zasulich to the Poles lead one to the conclusion that though many links existed between the two movements, the Polish circles of 1878–79 can be by no means considered (in the prosecutor's words) "one of the offshoots of Russian socialism."[146]

The Russian administration in the Congress Kingdom added yet another dimension to the history of Polish socialism in 1878–79 by imprisoning the first generation of Polish socialists in the Tenth Pavilion of the Warsaw Citadel. Although in shambles owing to three sets of arrests (which resulted in the "Trial of the 137"), the movement persisted in the prison cells. When the prison authorities mistakenly thought the young socialist Józef Beuth intended to escape, they shot and killed him, precipitating a prison riot and creating the movement's first martyr.[147] Inside the Citadel, under the leadership of Filipina Płaskowicka and Józef Pławiński, the socialists issued three numbers of a handwritten newspaper entitled *Głos Więźnia* (Prisoners' Voice). Filled mostly with poetry, short news articles, and satirical cartoons, *Głos Więźnia* called on socialists in and out of prison to continue the movement despite widespread arrests. Our movement is like early Christianity, we are like the apostles, the paper wrote, no matter how we are persecuted, "our message of good" will win out.[148]

Although a few socialists left political activity upon imprisonment, most became even more determined as did Płaskowicka that "the struggle is not yet over ... we are also at war."[149] The police intercepted coded letters to and from jail that expressed the heightened political consciousness of the internees. These letters also reflected the close familial aspect of the movement.[150] Sisters, brothers, husbands, wives, and even parents were entrusted with carrying out the activities of their imprisoned relatives.[151]

It would be impossible to estimate the propagandistic effect of the imprisonment and martyrdom of the 1878–79 socialists. For the first time since the 1860s, Russians arrested Poles en masse for political reasons, and these socialists could now be pushed forward as the new Polish national heroes. A handwritten piece found on the worker Leon Bielecki in July 1879 reflects the propagandistic potential of the mass imprisonment. "The people who think of us [the workers] and want to help us, who want to sacrifice their lives for our future are the Socialists. These people . . . are painted in black colors by a government which only beats them over the head."[152]

The Poznański Circle

Arrests of the 1878-79 socialists and the resulting "Trial of the 137" forced a hiatus in the continuity of the movement. However, the first Polish socialists had provided a firm foundation for later social revolutionary activities. Propaganda in workers' circles continued unabated; Warsaw University was still agog with the literature of socialism; and contacts with the Russian movement persisted. A new set of Polish student radicals, also educated in Russian schools, now, once again, began the arduous task of organizing and coordinating the activities of scattered socialist groups. Zygmunt Poznański, Feliks Ostaszewski, and Bolesław Wysłouch, all of whom had been in St. Petersburg, and Zofia and Roman Piechowski from Kiev, assumed the new leadership of the Congress Kingdom socialist movement.[153]

Poznański ("Professor" to the workers), advocated the spread of propaganda as the only means to bring about the final and "inevitable goal — the change of the economic structure of society." In addition, he proposed a form of maximum and minimum program and even suggested that it might not be necessary for the revolutionaries to use force.[154] Poznański's gifts did not reside in revolutionary theorizing, which he left mostly to Wysłouch, but in the active propagandizing of workers. "Almost every Sunday [he] gave talks or held discussions in workers' circles and, with his fervor and omnipresence, drew entire groups of converts into circle life."[155] The gendarmerie wrote of one such meeting: "Poznański collected in his room his workers and in the guise of a lecture introduced into their midst social revolutionary ideas; after the lecture he gave the workers books and brochures of social revolutionary content."[156]

Poznański's confession to the police reveals no specific theoretical sources for his socialism. (Usually, the propagandists were delighted to talk about theory rather than practice.) Yet his constant emphasis on economic issues, the importance of propaganda, and in general, his evolutionary approach to the problem of accomplishing socialist goals bespeak a considerable debt to Lassalle. His closest confederate, Roman Piechowski, wrote: "It seems to me that no laws could be established that would be more just than those written by the workers themselves. . . . These laws would not be thought up, but taken from real life."[157] Poznański, too, was frenetically involved in the everyday concerns of the industrial work force. To know their grievances, he felt, was to build the socialist movement. The goal of his work was a massive study of Warsaw factory workers.

Poznański's devotion to the working people is also evident in his contempt for what he called the "slumbering lethargy" of the Warsaw intelligentsia. These "spiritless masses" of "our educated society" need to be shaken by any means, by propaganda or by agitation. "In their time," wrote Poznański, "Pisarev, Chernyshevskii, and many others did the same."[158] Most important, however, was the work among factory labor. In March 1879, in a letter to his friend L. Straszewicz concerning the planned publication of a new journal, Poznański wrote: "As much as I can gather from what you write, . . . it will be a periodical for the intelligentsia . . . would it not be of more worth to found a paper for the people, wouldn't that be better . . . we must place the people [*lud*] and its interests always and consistently on the first order of business, as the only goal of our activities."[159]

Under Poznański's leadership, workers' circles, once confined to metal and railway workers, now spread throughout Praga and even as far as Żyrardów, the linen center outside of Warsaw.[160] Emil Gostkiewicz, Michał Żynda, Sikorski, and Jaworowski, as workers themselves and as associates of Poznański, were crucial figures in spreading propaganda among noninitiated workers. The socialists, under Poznański's direction, aimed this propaganda at the most fundamental worker grievances. As one worker testified to the police: "He [Gostyński] asked me in what condition I now found myself, to which I answered that my matters were going very badly, that I had no job at this time, and that until I found some kind of work I would remain basically without any means to live. Then Gostyński told me of some rich Russian people who would give me enough to supply me daily sustenance." At this point, Gostyński gave him printed literature from these people who called themselves "socialists" and departed.[161]

Together with its Lassallean form of working-class socialism, the Poznański group also incorporated an element of socialist patriotic thought, expressed primarily in intelligentsia circles and in the writings of Bolesław Wysłouch.[162] Wysłouch was not alone in his desire to combine the tenets of socialism with traditional Polish patriotism; in 1880 the police repeatedly found examples of Polish national liberation literature in the homes and on the persons of socialists.[163] Krzywicki suggests that Poznański was in fact the only internationalist among the leadership of his group and that he alone provided the link between internationalists of the 1878–79 groups and those of the Proletariat.[164] One might add that Wysłouch himself was a crucial transition figure in that he helped tie the socialist-patriotism of the 1860s to that of the 1890s.

With Poznański at work among Warsaw laborers, Wysłouch led the internecine attack on the "Program of Polish Socialists," known as the "Brussels Program," for its antipatriotism.[165] In his private papers he completely dismissed the program as useless and unscientific.[166] In a handwritten paper passed among socialist leaders entitled "Notes on the 'Program of Polish Socialists,'" Wysłouch criticized the authors of the program for their "insufficient love of the nation." The spirit of their program, he insisted, was "not the people but capital." Wysłouch added that patriotism in the hands of the Polish working folk could only be a progressive force and that the "cosmopolitanism" of the "Brussels Program" ignores "an entire category of suffering and national interests." "Cooperation," he wrote, "depends on the intensity of culture," common landholdings, on some kind of borders. Though a strong proponent of Polish independence, Wysłouch, like his self-proclaimed forefather, the radical democrat Piotr Ściegienny, favored the formation of Lithuanian and Belorussian national units.[167] All of these units, the Poles included, would be organized on a confusing concept of industrial cooperatives. These cooperatives would have a socialist base, would be democratically governed, and would include not just workers but also intelligentsia, bourgeoisie, and nobility.[168] Wysłouch's suspension of the class struggle and insertion of patriotism into the ideology of infant Polish socialism never gained wide support outside of the Poznański group and its successor, the Warsaw Gmina. Still, his brand of socialist-patriotism appeared sporadically throughout the 1880s; by the 1890s, linked to the rise of modern Polish nationalism, it blossomed into a full-scale movement.

The Warsaw Gmina

After the arrests of Poznański and most of his confederates, the social revolutionary circles in Warsaw joined with circles throughout the empire and, under the leadership of St. Petersburg University graduates Zygmunt Balicki and Kazimierz Sosnowski, took the name of the Warsaw Gmina. The split personality of the Poznański-Wysłouch group reappeared in several ways in the Balicki and Sosnowski-dominated Gmina. Balicki was a devoted national revolutionary, as shown by his later adherence to National Democracy. Sosnowski, on the other hand, was an ideologue and propagandist of workers' socialism, not unlike his forerunner Poznański.

The dual character of the Warsaw Gmina and its unique position among the empire's Gminas as a whole are evident in its messages to the 1880 "Conference of the Fiftieth Anniversary of the 1830 Revolution" in Geneva. The section of the Warsaw Gmina headed by Balicki conformed to the inclination of the Gminas in Russia to reject class warfare and seek a society of "mutual help as well as justice and equality." The struggle for freedom and independence was to be based "on all-Polish cooperation." Our goal, stated the Balicki-inspired proclamation, "is economic, social, and political emancipation."[169] The two proclamations from the Sosnowski-led sections of the Warsaw Gmina, including most of the workers' groups attached to it, stressed the importance of the class struggle within Poland as well as the need for Polish independence. "We therefore firmly believe that only a basic change from the contemporary socioeconomic organization (actually, disorganization) to a socialist structure will bring about the complete emancipation of our people."[170] The "Polish Workers under the Rule of the Tsar" (attached to the Gmina) wrote that although the slogan should be "equality and independence," "we are not concerned whether or not we extricate ourselves from the rule of foreign governments, because, in general, we, the oppressed and working men, don't want anyone to rule over us."[171]

Even though the leadership of Warsaw socialism had changed, there was little indication of a break in continuity between the Poznański and Warsaw Gmina socialists. To the dismay of the authorities, the workers' circles continued to spread and function. Oral propaganda and the infiltration of socialist literature at all levels of society persisted. By 1880 socialism had become the common property of the entire Polish intelligentsia, to be attacked or accepted, but in few cases to be ignored. The Warsaw Positivists, the conservatives, the tsarist authorities, and even the Polish national-insurrectionists in one way or another were forced to take a stand on the spread of socialism. A purely patriotic organization, the "Polish Club of the Sons of the Fatherland," reflected the respect the socialist cause had garnered among Poles since 1876 when it wrote to Narodnaia Volia: "Our brothers, the socialists of Poland, told us . . . that you, brother Russians from the revolutionary party, would like to establish relations with us." The letter continued by suggesting that the Russians publicly recognize the right of Polish national existence and, in exchange, the "Sons" would happily join in a political alliance.[172]

Polish socialism had perceptibly gained support since its meager beginnings in 1876–77. The optimism of its initial proponents — Waryński, Dłuski, Uziembło, and others — was in part justified. The Congress Kingdom indeed provided fruitful soil for the growth of socialism. As its adherents increased and its influence spread to diverse segments of society, the need for a strong ideological basis became more profound. In the years 1876–81, radical democracy, *narodnik* socialism, Lassallean workers' socialism, and a form of vulgar Marxism mixed in a rainbow of socialisms composed of variegated, generalized, and sometimes contradictory elements. By 1880 it was not even clear whether social antagonisms, the national struggle, or various combinations of both provided the impetus for socialist action.

The original intention of the founders of the Polish socialist movement was to spread the gospel to the working classes that injustice — national, economic, and social — could be attributed to the capitalist mode of production and the autocracy that supported it. They assumed that the mere realization of these facts by the workers would spark an immediate social revolution, which would bring with it communal ownership and social justice. The word was spread. But the revolution was stillborn. It was now up to the founders, as a result of repeated arrests and the diminishing returns of propaganda, to channel the movement into an organization and to formulate for that organization a unified and comprehensive ideology.

V

The Development of the Ideology of Polish Socialism in Galicia and Switzerland, 1878–1881

The first wave of arrests of Polish socialists in 1878 spurred an exodus of revolutionary leaders from the Congress Kingdom to the relatively safe Galician towns of Lwów and Kraków and then finally to the peaceful haven of Switzerland. For the leaders of Polish socialism, exile in the Austrian partition fostered an unwelcomed but valuable ideological gestation period in which they could absorb their practical experiences in the Congress Kingdom and could argue the issues of socialism with members of the infant Galician socialist movement. Of even greater significance for Polish socialism was its debut on the stage of international socialism in Switzerland. Open contacts with the Russians proved especially stimulating and consequential. Free from the specter of police surveillance and arrest, and free from conspiratorial and propagandistic obligations, Polish socialists had the opportunity to study West European socialism and reflect on its implications for their own struggle in the Congress Kingdom. The removal of external constraints also brought to the surface inchoate ideological contradictions. Those who were forced to band together in order to perform the everyday tasks of propaganda among the working class now quarreled over minor issues, split into camps, and competed in the international arena for the leadership of Polish socialism.

The "Brussels Program"

The first socialist leaders to emigrate to Switzerland from the Congress Kingdom were Szymon Diksztajn, Stanisław Mendelson, Kazimierz Długi, and Kazimierz Hildt. Along with Maria Jankowska, already in Switzerland, these members of the Polish intelligentsia formed the editorial board of the first Polish socialist newspaper, *Równość* ("Equality"). Soon thereafter, in October 1878, Ludwik

Waryński also fled imminent arrest and made his way to Lwów. On leaving the Congress Kingdom, Waryński wrote Prosecutor Pleve a sarcastic and threatening note, promising his return.

> You can persecute us, Sir, as you wish, you are paid for that, but I warn you that if that persecution loses its weak yet still human quality . . . that will call forth measures from our side that will not be very comfortable for the paid executive organs. Somehow, however, we must defend ourselves. We cannot give you more money, for we don't have it for you. We therefore have to arouse fear in you. You very much value your life, for its convenience you don't hesitate to step over dead bodies, and you are incapable of sacrificing that life for anything.[1]

Both Waryński and the first *Równość* editorial board upheld the principles of the "Program of Polish Socialists," the so-called "Brussels Program." The authors of the program intended to deceive the police by stating that it was first printed in Brussels in 1878. In fact, the "Brussels Program" was drafted in Warsaw perhaps as early as September 1878 and appeared in the first number of *Równość* in October 1879.[2] The preparation of the "Brussels Program" initiated an ideological dispute among Congress Kingdom socialists, prompting the two minority documents discussed in Chapter 4, the "Principles" of Więckowski and Uziembło and the "Notes" of Wysłouch.[3] Although these latter programmatic statements provide interesting insights into the variegated intellectual components of Polish socialism in 1878–79, it was the "Brussels Program" that most precisely expressed the ideology of those who fled the Congress Kingdom during this period.

Like the "Principles" and the "Notes," the "Brussels Program" affirmed an unequivocal commitment to socialism: "The triumph of the principles of socialism is the natural condition for the prosperous future of the Polish people; the active participation in the struggle against the established social order is the duty of every Pole who places the fate of millions of Polish people [*lud*] over the interests of the gentry-capitalist portion of our nation." Although the program addressed itself to Poles and spoke of a Polish nation, it advocated the "complete social equality of citizens without regard to sex, race, and nationality" and, in contrast to the "Principles," rejected the advisability of a national struggle or a political revolution. In even sharper contradistinction to the "Principles," the "Brussels Program" discarded an evolutionary or legal path to socialism: "The above program, in view of the impossibility of a legal road, can be accomplished only by means of a social revolution." The "Brussels Program" and the

"Principles" did agree on the necessity of organization, propaganda, and agitation as the proper means to accomplish a social revolution. They also agreed "that the emancipation of the workers should be the act of only the workers themselves" and "that the struggle for their [the workers'] emancipation should not aspire to the formation of a new ruling class, but to the institutionalization of equal rights and equal obligations for all."[4]

In a series of articles in the 1879 and 1880 numbers of *Równość* entitled "Our Program," the Polish socialists explained each aspect of their platform and jousted with their critics. "Our Program" expressed a clearly antiauthoritarian and, its authors' protests to the contrary, utopian and anarchist vision of the future.[5] It described a society that would have "glorious buildings, centers for science and recreation, museums, literature, and art for the use of all." Contemporary art and learning, which existed only at the sufferance of the rich and powerful, would be replaced by popular culture.[6] Political oppression would be eliminated by a "free and equal union of working people." "All authority imposed from above, all paternal direction" would be crushed in face of the principles of free choice, solidarity, and the working people's "active participation in public life."[7]

Równość also made it clear that the "Brussels Program" did not exclude the possibility of a resurrected Poland, as so many of its critics have asserted. The fundamental social unit indeed would be the *gmina,* a "productive cooperative," but "naturally the *gminas* would enter into federative ties among themselves." These federations of *gminas* would be called "lands," and "a union of lands could become the foundations of a 'country.'" Even further, these countries were free to vary the closeness of their international ties.[8] Besides "economic, geographical, as well as other conditions of public life" that could serve to bind one *gmina* to another, there "exist also moral, ethical, national, ethnographic reasons" for the reconstitution of a country. There is no way to ascertain, concluded the authors, "how far these federative organizations will go" — it all "depends on economic, geographic, or national conditions."[9]

The economic credo of the "Brussels Program" — that "the means and instruments of work" should be transferred from the hands of individuals to the common ownership of workers — was explained by "Our Program" in patently Marxist terms. The history of economic relationships, wrote *Równość,* demonstrated that the violent struggle for ownership of the means of production dominated the transition from the ancient communal to the capitalist world. Similarly, the capitalist system could be overthrown only by "a radical restructuring of the entire previous system of production."[10] Not unlike the movement from which it derived, the "Brussels Program" can be described as Marxist in its historical analysis, Lassallean in its working-class socialism, Lavrist in its view of making a revolution, and anarchist in its vision of the future. The roots of this eclectic working-class anarchism can be traced primarily to the Russian tutors of the *kresy* intelligentsia. At the same time, the "Brussels Program" exhibited a number of characteristics specifically derived from its authors' experiences in the Congress Kingdom. The strength of the liberal, gradualist forces of Warsaw Positivism accounts, at least in part, for the "Brussels Program's" omission of any minimum program. In order to distinguish themselves from the positivist liberals, for instance, the socialists could not adopt constitutionalism as a practical demand. Similarly, their lack of open concern for the national struggle must be seen in the context of their need to remain separate from the deeply rooted traditions of democratic and patriotic insurrectionist movements.[11]

Waryński in Lwów

Just as the "Brussels Program" grew out of the concrete experiences of Polish socialists in Russian schools and among Congress Kingdom workers, the program's future depended on the widening perspectives of its proponents. Ludwik Waryński, the leading figure of Polish socialism in these years, fled Warsaw for Lwów in the fall 1878. There his encounter with Galician socialism was an important stage in his further development as a socialist theorist. Conditions in Lwów and Galicia differed markedly from those in Warsaw and the Congress Kingdom; a working class, per se, was almost nonexistent, and the vast majority of Polish peasantry lived in squalid and ruinous conditions. The two major urban centers of Galicia — Kraków and Lwów — contained no large factories and no distinguishable urban proletariat. Kraków was ruled by Polish clerical and conservative elements to whom the Austrians had granted a modicum of political autonomy in 1867. The capital city of Lwów, on the other hand, supported a substantial democratic intelligentsia and an urban artisan class. It was from these latter groups that Galician socialism recruited its membership.

In the 1860s Galician democrats and artisans, most noticeably the typesetters of Lwów, organized a protosocialist group, "Gwiazda" (Star), which published the newspaper *Rękodzielnik* (Craftsman). However, Galician socialism "really first began with the arrival of Bolesław Limanowski in Lwów in 1870."[12] Limanowski, a veteran of the 1863 uprising, spent the years 1865–66 in Siberian exile reading Comte and Lassalle. An advocate of positivist and Lassallean self-help institutions for workers and a defender of the inseparability of the national and socialist struggle, Limanowski influenced and shaped an entire generation of Lwów socialists through his immense intellectual gifts and constant publicist activities.[13] The Lwów typesetters, under the leadership of Antoni Mańkowski, Józef Daniluk, and August Skerl, joined their own artisan socialism with that of Limanowski and published a new socialist newspaper, *Czcionka* (Type). Limanowski and the typesetters turned Lwów into a major center (along with Leipzig) for the printing and distribution of Polish socialist literature.[14]

Upon his arrival in Lwów, under the pseudonym of "Antoni Lipski," Waryński and his friend Maria Jankowska found their way to Limanowski's apartment.[15] The meeting, reported Limanowski, was friendly and congenial: "Waryński and Jankowska, arriving in Lwów, came to acquaint themselves with us and remained for the evening for tea. Waryński was a rather good-sized, articulate, handsome young man. Jankowska was young, pretty, elegant, and well-mannered. Both left a very pleasant impression."[16] Several sources indicate, however, that Waryński's short stay in Lwów was due to his ideological differences with Limanowski and the Lwów socialists as well as to his inability to operate in a semilegal framework.[17] Bolesław Jędrzejowski wrote that Waryński was so accustomed to underground work that he felt uncomfortable in Galician conditions.[18] Emil Haecker also noted that "Waryński did not like the nature of the work of the Lwów socialists . . . , where at that time not one socialist brochure had been confiscated, where it was possible to organize an open workers union and under a constitution carry on broad socialist propaganda."[19] Uziembło stated simply that Waryński did not want to submit to the authority of the Lwów socialists and therefore "left for Kraków where, with his characteristic energy and carelessness, [he] organized broad secret circles."[20]

Still, Waryński's exposure to legal socialist activity altered his views of socialism as a whole. Until his Lwów experience, Waryński, like most *kresy* socialists, had been under the immediate tutelage of Russian populism. In Lwów, Waryński came into direct contact with a form of Western trade-union socialism, which accounts in part for the gradual change from his "Brussels Program" apoliticism and anarchistic socialism to a more Western socialist orientation.

The Kraków Trial

In Kraków, Waryński lived with Hieronim Truszkowski and worked under the name of Ludwik Trzciński. In a letter to his sister, Waryński described his Kraków activities: "For three months I have lived in Kraków, and for this entire time I have been involved with agitation, with propaganda, in a word, with every kind of work which comes under the rubric of revolutionary activity.... Unremitting surveillance forces me to change names constantly."[21] Although the university remained firmly in the hands of the conservative stańczycy, as did Kraków's primary intellectual organs, socialism had gained considerable support among both gymnasium students and the city's skilled artisan groups.[22] Kraków socialists, like those in Lwów, formulated a program on the basis of trade unionism and Limanowski's socialist-patriotism. One Kraków socialist, S. Mikołajski, wrote, "I am convinced that socialism would not have found seed in Kraków if Limanowski's theory of the close ties between the struggles for national independence and for the economic emancipation of working people had not cleared the way."[23] A letter from an ex-positivist Kraków Pole also emphasized Limanowski's great influence in Galicia: "Positivism, which led me to a certain theoretical stage of socialism, in the hands of the clever, talented doctor of philosophy Bolesław Limanowski, was a thunderbolt — very successfully destroying old objectives."[24] The legal work of Limanowski and the underground efforts of Waryński in Kraków led to the formation of a small but significant circle of socialist sympathizers, among whom, wrote the same commentator, "one can notice a greater desire to end the old type of conflict between the Russian Ivan and the Polish Jan."[25]

However, Waryński's activities in Kraków lasted only a few months; on the night of 9 February 1879, he and his most important co-workers — H. Truszkowski, W. Piekarski, Stanisław Mendelson, and J. Uziembło — were arrested. At their trial, which lasted from 16 February to 16 April 1880, (the "Trial of Ludwik Waryński and his 34 confederates"), the Kraków prosecutor accused Waryński not of socialism — that in itself was not illegal under Austria law — but of the crime of "disturbing the public peace."[26] The prosecution's strategy was to demonstrate that Waryński and his colleagues made up a branch of the Russian social revolutionary party determined to turn all

Slavic peoples in Austria-Hungary, especially in Galicia, against the monarchy. There is little doubt that in the indictment, and perhaps even in the course of the trial itself, the Russian authorities in the Congress Kingdom played a cooperative if not an initiatory role. Throughout the Kraków proceedings, Russian police from Warsaw examined evidence and searched letters for information that might help them in prosecutions in the Congress Kingdom.[27]

Because Waryński accepted the responsibility to speak for most of his codefendants and because his career was the most crucial for the future of Polish socialism, his trial defense is an important document on the state of Polish socialism in early 1879. To counter the prosecution's allegations that the socialists worked to overthrow the government, Waryński brilliantly and, to be sure, also somewhat disingenuously, used the apoliticism of the *Równość* program, maintaining that the Dual Monarchy was irrelevant to his propagandistic aims. "Socialism," he affirmed, "is a purely scientific pursuit, and is based only on science." The kind of socialism that is practiced depends "on the structure of the country under which it finds itself." In general, he explained, "the program of Polish socialists published in Brussels is my profession of belief," and this program "does not advocate revolution, but foresees it." The immediate struggle is for a form of parliamentarianism — "This is the struggle Lassalle began."[28]

In answering the prosecutor's inquiry about the difference between the "Brussels Program" and the "Principles" (referred to at the Kraków proceedings as the "Lwów Program"), Waryński once again emphasized that the "Brussels Program" was accepted

> mainly because socialists do not play around with politics. Our goal is an economic revolution; we recognize that after the introduction of reform in the economy . . . the political structure must also change, but this should occur without any force, simply in the historical course of events. . . . Naturally in a country where all personal freedom is unknown, we must take into account political conditions, but that is only a change in the methods of action, and not a change of principles.[29]

Waryński cleverly disclaimed all ideological ties to the Russian revolutionaries, repeatedly stated his affinity with Lassalle, and, in regard to the socialist vision of the future, indicated that the *gmina* organization would succeed the economic revolution.

The prosecution tried to portray Waryński as a crazed and pernicious nihilist, single-mindedly intent on overthrowing the political system of the Dual Monarchy. In support of his case, the prosecutor read to the court and jury a communique from the Russian authorities, which stated that Waryński "belongs to the most extreme anarchist party and is a person very dangerous to all governments and nations."[30] Waryński successfully countered this exaggerated characterization of himself by appearing calm, collected, and neat and by carefully articulating his answers to the prosecutor in a scientific context. The obvious discrepancies between the wild-eyed revolutionary Waryński of the prosecutor's indictment and the equally exaggerated professorial pose that Waryński convincingly assumed in the courtroom resulted in the verdict of "not guilty" to the most serious count of political subversion. The Kraków authorities expelled the Russian citizens from Galicia, Waryński included, and sentenced the others to short jail terms. The verdict stood as a tremendous victory for the socialists.

The Kraków trial was a victory not so much in the sense of the socialists' struggle against the governments of Austria-Hungary and Imperial Russia, but in terms of their attempts to gain sympathy, adherence, and recognition from Polish society. Even the conservative Polish Kraków newspaper *Czas* (Time), in an editorial of 17 April 1880, wrote that this "overly long trial was a social, political, and national defeat. The most barbaric theory of revolution was not condemned, and, in the persons of its advocates, was today declared not guilty." Our national life, the editorial concluded, is in serious danger.[31] Indeed, Polish conservatives in Kraków and in Warsaw carefully watched the progress of the trial, counting on a harsh verdict to vindicate their own political positions. As one Kraków official wrote to his superior:

> I have the honor to report to your Excellency that those persons arriving here from the Congress Kingdom say that . . . the Warsaw Polish populace asks with great curiosity about the particulars of the Kraków trial against the socialists, describing it as of almost European significance and as carrying great weight in the Polish question, because it is the first trial on Polish lands in which Poles themselves . . . can justify or damn the principles of this consequential and significant theory.
>
> They are concerned there [in Warsaw] that above all this court not find the socialists innocent, for if this occurs, it would give the Russian government not only a cause to begin charging that all of Polish society is receptive to socialism and that, as a result of this, Poles abet nihilist and revolutionary mischief in Russia, but also a justification for those methods of repression used by Russians against Poles.[32]

The apparent collaboration between Austrian and Russian authorities and Polish conservatives upset enough liberal Poles to ensure a fair hearing for the socialists. As Adam Próchnik wrote, "the matter was a dirty one, and it made the same impression at that time."[33] With the two empires obviously ganging up on this tiny group of radical Poles, the liberal court freed Waryński and his co-workers. Through the published trial proceedings and verdict, Waryński spoke to his largest audience ever. The Polish revolutionaries also gained in stature at home in the Congress Kingdom and in Russian revolutionary circles. For the Galician socialist movement, wrote Limanowski, "the trial had enormous significance."[34] It affirmed the advisability of legal propagandistic work as well as indicated a serious breach in the stańczyk hold on Kraków.[35] In addition, Waryński and his colleagues gained one further perspective on legal socialism and on the deep political as well as social and economic differences between Galicia and the Congress Kingdom.

Równość

Expelled from Galicia by the Kraków verdict, Waryński moved in April 1880 to Geneva, where he found an already large and active Polish leftist community. In the last third of the nineteenth century, Switzerland, especially Geneva and Zürich, had superseded Paris as the primary center for the Polish emigration.[36] Young Polish men and women moved to Switzerland in even greater numbers than their Russian counterparts to receive an education and participate in a free cultural and political life. The Polish Communards Miłkowski, Wróblewski, and Mroczkowski organized their political activities among Polish youth in Switzerland. A "Polish Museum" founded by Władysław Plater in Rappersville served as the cultural center and scientific library for thousands of Polish exiles.

Therefore, the Równość group represented only a small fraction of Polish political activities in Switzerland. Even when strengthened by the arrival of Waryński, Mendelson, and Piekarski from Kraków, Równość resembled a loose confederation of like-minded Polish socialists rather than a political organization. In September 1880 the group did prepare a set of membership rules ("Ustawi Cele Stowarzyszenia"), but they were neither formally adopted nor publicized. At that, the Ustawi called only for the spread of the "Brussels Program" throughout the Polish lands and limited the membership to those who were in accord with the program.[37]

The group, best described as an editorial board, functioned reasonably effectively for almost two years and published thirteen issues of *Równość*, which served Polish socialism both as a newspaper and as a theoretical journal. In its former capacity, it reported on events in the Congress Kingdom and Russia, described the activities of the socialist movement in Western Europe, and documented arrests and sentences of comrades in the Congress Kingdom. In the latter capacity, it concentrated on several ideological tasks: (1) to reinterpret the history of Polish insurrections, especially those of 1831 and 1863, (2) to explain the rise of capitalism and demonstrate that it was in a state of imminent collapse, (3) to denounce positivism and constitutionalism, (4) to expose patriotism as a betrayal of the workers' cause, (5) to rouse sympathy for the Russian revolutionaries, and (6) to call for the formation of a Polish workers' party in the Congress Kingdom. The later issues of *Równość* focused increasingly on the latter three tasks as the group became more dogmatically internationalist and, at the same time, professed greater and greater admiration for the Russian movement.[38]

Szymon Diksztajn provided the major historical perspective for the new Polish socialism in his *Równość* series, "The Aims of the Socialists in the Polish Emigration of 1831."[39] Here, Diksztajn concluded that among the socialist groups of the earlier period, "it is impossible to see anything but the usual caste interest."[40] Diksztajn clearly set off what he called the "scientific socialism" of the *Równość* group from the idealism of its predecessors; he wrote, "contemporary socialism has no need to search insecurely for support in idealist [interpretations] of Christianity or gather strength for itself in the fantasy arena of the national spirit, but in the bright light of reality can find a sufficient number of facts to defend its aspirations." Although the socialists of Poland's past could not rise above their own class interests, Diksztajn added, they were partly to be excused, because they had little access to those scientific facts upon which contemporary socialism was based. "The memory of their activities will not die among us," conceded Diksztajn, because of "their clear understanding of the people's needs, the independence of their thought, [and the] courageous pronouncement of their sincere love for the people."[41]

In this same article, Diksztajn predicted that the time was ripe for capitalism to lose its progressive force and "the proletariat to carry out the revolution."[42] This commonly shared belief among the *Równość* group that the last stage of capitalism was at hand appeared repeatedly on the pages of its periodical.

As its downfall comes closer and closer, the capitalist means of production as well as the capitalist structure of society based on economic contradictions grow stronger and stronger. Together with its [capitalism's] growth, poverty increases, together with the growth of poverty, the chasm dividing social classes grows wider, the material dominance of one class over another grows, mutual antagonism of social classes also speeds the final outbreak of the fighting.[43]

Historically, capitalism emerged by capturing the fancy of the Polish *szlachta,* replacing traditional gentry values with its own interests. Capitalism "was able to tie elbow grease with a coat of arms, Catholicism with Jewish gold, Slavic democracy with German industrial enterprise." The *szlachta* became a tool of capitalism as easily as it had once reflected agrarian gentry interests. "Even the finest elements of our democrats . . . never were able to understand properly that the interests of the *szlachta* as a class could never be harnessed to one chariot with the interests of the people — without spilling the blood of the latter."[44]

Just as *Równość* ostensibly exposed the class bias of the *szlachta* democrats, it also attempted to demonstrate that "the whole positivist movement, from the time of its beginning fifteen years ago, does not have a strictly scientific-publicist character, but is at the same time an instrument of the class struggle."[45] Although the socialists realized that they had much to gain from the positivists' call for a constitution, they criticized their liberal opponents for not realizing that a constitution could not alter economic relationships — which were "the most essential facts" and the "bases for any other relationship determining the existence and happiness of the whole society."[46]

If possible, the *Równość* editors would have comfortably continued to dwell on these issues of the history of class interests, the importance of the class struggle, and the future of a working-class uprising. But the ubiquitous and perplexing problem for *Równość* was national rather than class struggle. A perturbed Dłuski wrote of patriotism: "That word is magical among us — but everyone understands it differently. Our entire society in the sense of its nationhood is patriotic — the word electrifies everyone, although it is understood differently."[47] In *Równość*'s most comprehensive article on the national question — "Patriotism and Socialism" — Dłuski launched an attack on patriotism and the national struggle as insignificant and false issues, not worth the faintest consideration until the social question was resolved. "In the view of socialism," Dłuski wrote, "economic inequality is the basic reason for the entire illness of the contemporary social structure. Therefore, first of all, socialism struggles for a radical change of economic relationships."[48]

When the socialist-patriot Limanowski resigned from *Równość,* primarily in protest over Dłuski's article,[49] the editors responded with even more virulent sorties against those "dreamers and pharisees" who would hold off the class struggle in the name of an independent Poland. In the class struggle "there are no compromises, for there can be no common interests between the slave and the master. Under one roof warring parties cannot live, . . . one has no fatherland and the other can have none."[50] Mendelson more gently summarized the conflict between *Równość* and the socialist-patriots: "In conclusion, we beat our breasts and say to ourselves, we are, both you and we, cosmopolitans — but between us there is a basic difference. We separated once and for all from the patriotic program, we want neither a *szlachta* nor a democratic Poland, and not only do we not want it, but we are deeply convinced that a people's liberation struggle for Poland is, at the present, an absurdity."[51]

The *Równość* socialists' antipathy toward Polish patriotism entwined with their sympathy for the Russian revolutionary movement. Long-standing contact with the Russians, an intimate knowledge of Russian revolutionary literature and history, and immediate contacts with the Russian Geneva community also conditioned their positive response to the Russian movement. Most importantly, however, the common sets of political experiences under the Russian autocracy determined the intimacy between revolutionary Poles and Russians in a practical as well as ideological sense. Waryński's career in Lwów and Kraków undoubtedly contributed important aspects to his political philosophy. Yet as a Congress Kingdom revolutionary, his affinities lay more with Zheliabov or Perovskaia than with Limanowski or Wróblewski. *Równość* in turn found more to praise in the Russian struggle than in the socialist patriotic program of Limanowski. "We, Polish socialists, keenly feel and comprehend the heroic struggle that the Russian socialists carry on today against their government . . . with beating hearts we follow its every manifestation, and we heatedly desire the victory of those who write on their standard: struggle to the death with every oppressor and oppression."[52]

In the realm of pure ideology, the *Równość* socialists opposed Narodnaia Volia's Jacobin-style attempts to overthrow the autocracy. At the same time, they condoned the political struggle of the Russian revolutionary movement and clearly distinguished it from the political programs of Polish positivists and socialist-patriots. For the latter groups, the political struggle "is a goal," for the Russians, "a means for further action; for the former it is the alpha and omega of their whole program . . . for the latter it is a minimum action serving only as a prologue to the new, terrible class struggle."[53] *Równość* applauded the assassination of Alexander II, "the hangman," as standing "above any similar expression of revolutionary activity of any other European nation," although the Poles realized that this act had not brought about any changes in the social structure of the empire: "To this time, unfortunately, the [Russian] people have not understood their heroes. But the times must change. Already the urban working class is beginning to turn its attention to the socialist activity of the youth. Gradually, the rural population will follow after them."[54]

Previewing their own later use of terrorism, the Polish socialists analyzed Russian terrorism as a necessary form of struggle in an autocratic system rather than as an ideological element of Russian socialism distinct from the principles of *Równość* and the "Brussels Program." Waryński had stated earlier at the Kraków trial: "Terrorism in Russia is the simple result of persecutions . . . not at all a result of a program. . . . The individual Russian activist . . . has to consume a portion of his strength in the daily struggle against the government, which punishes propagandists with imprisonment and even death."[55] As early as October 1879 the use of terrorism by Warsaw socialists was mentioned in *Równość* by a correspondent from Warsaw. In answer to our peaceful propaganda, the Russian government responds "with the Citadel and murder," the article began: "We do not yet contemplate taking up arms, but we already sense upon us the terrible reality of a state of war."[56]

The Politics of Emigration

The militant tone of *Równość*'s articles was hardly matched by the humble, but certainly not uncomfortable, conditions of life in Switzerland for *Równość*'s editors. Waryński, Diksztajn, Mendelson, Jankowska, and Dłuski lived in a small communal house on the outskirts of Geneva where they shared expenses, held lively sessions on editorial policy, and socialized with other radicals from the Geneva community. The atmosphere of gentility and comradely relations did not, however, survive their two-year period of emigration. Lev Deich and Bolesław

Limanowski, both intimate with the members of the commune, described in their memoirs a number of incidents that illuminate the growing problems of personal and political struggles within the *Równość* group. Jankowska, Dłuski, and especially Mendelson (as the heir of a sizable Warsaw banking fortune) reportedly attempted to use their superior financial positions to influence editorial policy.[57] Mendelson and Erazm Kobylański intended to fight a duel over differences originating in Kobylański's romantic interest in Jankowska.[58] Before the internecine battle broke out, an "impartial" tribunal of Russians, with Plekhanov at its head, decided that the fault was Kobylański's and he was forced to apologize.[59] Diksztajn, the author of the masterful propaganda piece — *Who Lives From What?* — was similarly entraced by the lovely Jankowska; he fell into a state of tragic personal decline in Geneva, drank heavily, and in 1884 committed suicide.[60]

The fact that in the Mendelson-Kobylański quarrel the Polish socialists turned to the Russians for arbitration was symbolic of the growing closeness of the two groups. On the initiative of the *Równość* group, Deich, Zasulich, and Stefanovich — all of Black Partition — even moved their quarters nearer to the Poles so that they could share their daily meals together. Deich noted, "This made for an even greater intimacy with the Polish comrades."[61] Indeed, the richness of Deich's memoirs on the *Równość* commune leads one to assume that the relationships between the Poles and the Black Partition Russians in Geneva were especially friendly and close.

On the broad scope of the Geneva emigration, the most influential Pole among radical youth was Walery Wróblewski, and even he worked closely with the Russian *Nabat* group of Tkachëv and Turski.[62] However, Wróblewski, the "red patriot," wanted no part of *Równość*'s activities. Its doctrinaire antipatriotism and its opposition to the political struggle in Poland contradicted his fundamental principles.[63] Another related segment of the Geneva emigration was the Ukrainian socialist movement, whose most important leaders were Ivan Franko and Mykhailo Drahomanov. Franko exerted an especially important influence on the *Równość* group. At this point a follower of Marx and a proponent of scientific socialism, Franko reinforced the *Równość* Marxist analysis of history and of capitalism and shared *Równość*'s commitment to internationalism. "Political independence," wrote Franko, "means absolutely nothing in view of internal social bondage . . . of what use is it to us to have our own king, if at the same time usurers and capitalists will oppress and exploit us as of old?"[64]

It was the other major figure of the Ukrainian camp, Mykhailo Drahomanov, the liberal *narodnik,* who attained the greater influence in the Geneva radical community. Especially popular among university students, Drahomanov denounced both the Russian and Polish socialists as nationalist oppressors of minorities, infuriating not only Wróblewski and the *Nabat* group, but also the *Równość* group and Black Partition. In fact, it was Drahomanov who first brought the members of Black Partition and *Równość* into alliance. Lev Deich described an evening in the spring of 1880 when "with Plekhanov and Stefanovich, I walked in the university gardens talking about the speech Drahomanov gave at a meeting of émigrés the day before." The Russians, remembered Deich, met Dłuski and Waryński in the gardens, and "Waryński agreed completely" with their critical remarks about Drahomanov. "We decided at that time to form a secret coalition against Drahomanov, in order to strip him of his laurels, to knock him down from the pedestal on which, in our opinion, he unjustifiably stood." A special meeting was held between the Russians and Poles at which Diksztajn and Mendelson were also present. "At all future meetings of the entire emigration, our coalition acted in unanimity."[65]

In 1880 Black Partition was a small and relatively uninfluential group among the Russian émigrés, not to mention its almost complete loss of influence in the empire itself. According to Deich, in fact, the ties between Plekhanov and the Black Partitionists on the one hand and *Równość* on the other provided the Russians a considerable lift "politically and morally."[66] Of even greater ultimate significance to the Russian movement was the influence that the *Równość* group, especially Waryński and Diksztajn, exerted on the ideological transmutations of Black Partition. In part, this was because Plekhanov, according to his wife, had a "special fondness" for Diksztajn and Waryński and thought very highly of the *Równość* effort.[67] In 1880 Plekhanov and Black Partition were still essentially populist; their break with Narodnaia Volia developed primarily over the issue of tactics. Plekhanov still hoped for a compromise with Narodnaia Volia, if not for the actual reunification of the two feuding groups. At this point, both Waryński and Dyksztajn can be called Marxists, at least followers of Marx, which as Deich wrote, "also influenced our [Black Partition's] familiarity with his [Marx's] theory."[68] In addition to theoretical and psychological assistance to the Russians, the *Równość* group also provided valuable practical assistance by transporting Black Partition literature into Russia through their contacts in the Congress Kingdom.[69]

Although the *Równość* group maintained close ties with Black Partition, no firm political alliance was formed.[70] *Równość* acted independently and, despite its sympathy for Plekhanov and friends, also developed close contacts with the increasingly numerous *narodovol'tsy* group and the Bakuninists in Switzerland. Mikhail Zhukovskii, an influential confederate of Bakunin, was on intimate terms with the Poles and the *Równość* commune. Even the suspicious Limanowski recognized that Zhukovskii, the "head of the entire, rather numerous Russian emigration in Geneva," was "a noble person and a sincere friend of the Poles."[71] It was the active struggle that Bakunin and the Russian anarchists carried on against the autocracy that initially attracted the Poles, and it was, in the end, the active struggle of Narodnaia Volia that won the sympathy of most Polish socialists. Kulczycki wrote that at the outset of 1880 almost the entire Polish socialist emigration lined up with Black Partition in its dispute with Narodnaia Volia.[72] In the next two years, however, under the spell of the latter's heroic escapades and "great victories," the Poles' sympathies shifted gradually to the *narodovol'tsy*.[73]

Polish Socialism on the International Stage, 1880

The *Równość* group's first performance on the stage of international socialism took place at their fiftieth anniversary celebration of the November 1830 uprising. For the first time, the West European socialist community was confronted with this new brand of Polish socialism, distinguished by its obtuse and strident internationalism and by its close cooperation with Russian radicals. *Równość* sent out letters of invitation to all the major leaders of European socialism, including Karl Marx, Friedrich Engels, Paul Lafargue, and Friedrich Lessner. Close to five hundred people attended the conference itself. The patriarch of German socialism in Switzerland, Johann Philip Becker, chaired the proceedings; Vera Zasulich of Black Partition served as secretary.[74] Simultaneous meetings to celebrate the anniversary were held in Paris, Rappersville, and elsewhere, sponsored by various patriotic organizations.

These other émigré meetings (characterized somewhat unsympathetically by Borejsza as "monuments to the cult of tradition") focused on the national struggle and played down the social struggle; the *Równość*-sponsored meeting was intended to do quite the opposite.[75] The Polish socialists clearly and unabashedly stated their purpose — to banish forever from the socialist encomium the slogan *"Niech żyje Polska!"* ("Long live Poland") and replace it with "Proletarians of the world, unite." The proceedings of the conference, published in 1881 by *Równość*, similarly aimed to impress upon the Polish working class that "the standard of international social revolution should remain their only standard . . . it is not the independence of the Polish people that is necessary, but the conquering of the means of production."[76] Feliks Kon correctly summarized the tone of the conference: "In its essence it was not a celebration of the fiftieth anniversary of the November uprising, but rather the burial of the slogan of independence."[77]

One after another, Diksztajn, Długi, and Mendelson ascended the podium at the meeting, maligning the *szlachta*-led national uprisings of the past and proselytizing the future of the social revolution in Poland. Długi explained that "owing to a lack of enlightenment, patriotism unfortunately still has credit among the proletariat . . . therefore, citizens, the struggle with patriotism is for us the order of the day. Therefore, we will unceasingly protest against every expression of this deceptive patriotism, in the name of our ideas and in the name of the Polish proletariat."[78]

The anxiously awaited messages from Western socialists unable to attend the fiftieth anniversary conference indicated that not only Poles still cherished patriotism but also that admiration for and advocacy of Polish patriotism remained a cornerstone of Western socialism's political program. The most crushing confirmation of this fact was a letter from London signed by Marx, Engels, Lafargue, and Lessner. In direct contradistinction to the avowed purpose of the *Równość* conference, clearly stated in the invitations and in a private letter from Mendelson to Engels, the giants of international socialism praised the history of the Polish insurrectionary movement, specifically the fighters of 1830–31, and closed their letter with the slogan that *Równość* anathemized — "*Niech żyje Polska!*"[79] At the conference itself, most Western socialists, with the exception of scattered anarchists, agreed with this position. Even letters from Polish comrades inside the empire, from the Gminas, and from a Warsaw workers' circle similarly, though more subtly, bypassed the antipatriotic stand of the conference initiators and bound the national to the social struggle.[80]

Równość did have scattered supporters for its internationalist position among émigré Poles, but more importantly, it had widespread backing from the Russians.[81] Mikhail Zhukovskii (representing the "International Workers' Society"), Petr Kropotkin, and Vera Zasulich took the podium in Geneva in favor of the new internationalism of the Polish movement. Russians and Poles have been bitter enemies for a hundred years, began Zasulich; "only from that moment, when the socialist movement appeared among Poles, did we begin to come close to you — and, as we are now closely tied with several individuals, [Waryński, Dłuski, et al.] so in the future — of this I am convinced — we may, without the least distrust, also be tied to the entire Polish socialist party."[82]

Waryński responded to the sympathetic encouragement of the Russians by addressing his anniversary speech to the "Russian comrades." Before the assembled socialist audience, he delivered his most comprehensive statement on Polish internationalism.[83] In it, he agreed with Zasulich that the failure of normal relations between Russian and Polish revolutionaries "was due to the absence or weak development of socialism in both countries." The emergence of Polish socialism dissolved that mutual distrust, as did the increased magnitude of the Russian revolutionary "heroic struggle against tsarism." Waryński announced that into the place of historical national enmity "will step the proletariat of the whole world, the solidarity of the oppressed in the struggle against the oppressor."[84] It is apparent from Waryński's remarks here and elsewhere that his own internationalism was not based strictly on theory, but on the practical consideration that relations with the highly touted Russian movement improved with the determination of *Równość* to oppose patriotism.

Although it must have been a painful experience for him, Waryński in his speech gently and almost paternally chastised Marx and Engels for their position on the national question.

> Even the creators of the *Communist Manifesto* tie their eternal slogan "Proletarians of the world unite" with another slogan, "Long live Poland!," which can also attract the bourgeoisie and the privileged classes. This worship of and sympathy for Poland, Poland the oppressed and the oppressor, shows that in the views of its defenders, the old political combinations still maintain their meaning. They are gradually losing this significance, and one might expect that shortly they [Marx and Engels] will forget about them.[85]

In the introduction to the proceedings of the conference, sent directly to Marx and Engels in London, Waryński also chided the founders of scientific socialism for paying attention to the émigré Polish heroes while ignoring the needs of the Polish proletariat: "Their [the *szlachta* democrats'] revolutionary fervor, their hot desire for changes in social relations, talked about with such fire in the West, weakened and extinguished in their fatherland. For the Polish people they brought nothing; under their slogans nothing was won for the people."[86]

Despite the cold reception Western socialists gave *Równość*'s anti-patriotism, a number of Waryński's points were incorporated into the final conference resolution. The revolutions of Poland, it stated, had always been initiated by the privileged classes. The "working people" were only "passively" involved, "because it was only the interests of the privileged that was taken into account." Therefore, "the emancipation of labor can take place only by the action of workers." The conferees reached a compromise on the crucial question of patriotism. Stating emphatically that "every political movement should be subordinated to the economic movement," the resolution elsewhere declared that "the liberation of the Polish people can come only with the liberation of all peoples from economic, political, and national oppression."[87]

The Geneva debut of Polish socialism can hardly be considered a smooth or victorious one. *Równość*'s devotion to internationalism and to better relations with the Russian movement, though greeted with approval by the Russians, provoked a bitter debate among European socialists as well as a deafening uproar of protest from the democratic Polish community. *Równość* has shown its true colors, Agaton Giller wrote to Limanowski, and "should be recognized . . . as injurious [to our cause] and published in the interests of the enemies of Poland. He who deprecates the Polish question is neither a sincere revolutionary nor a democrat or socialist."[88] As a result of the conference, Limanowski, E. Kobylański, and M. Brzeziński finally broke with the *Równość* socialists on the national question and formed a completely separate group — Lud Polski ("Polish People"). The conference's stand on nationalism also prompted the democratic community in Switzerland, led by Giller, Miłkowski, and Wróblewski, to halt any further cooperation with *Równość* and to place their moral and financial support behind Limanowski's splinter faction.[89]

Lud Polski and Chur

Limanowski, the 1863 veteran, the follower of Lassalle, and the veteran of a decade of propagandist activity in Galicia, was the architect and central figure of Lud Polski. Although he formally put together the organization in August 1881, Lud Polski, as a related set of socialist and patriotic concepts, existed from the beginnings of the socialist movement in Warsaw in 1877–78. The basic tenets of its program had already been articulated by Wysłouch in his "Notes" on the "Brussels Program." Limanowski's own theoretical work, *Socialism as the Natural Sign of Historical Development* (Lwów, 1879), similarly previewed the official program of Lud Polski. True patriotism, Limanowski explained here, was not the *szlachta* patriotism of the past, but the historical and living patriotism of the people. The "proletariat," as understood by Western socialists, was much too narrow a concept for oppressed Poles. Instead, Limanowski maintained, socialists should carry their propaganda to the entire working population (workers, peasants, and artisans) and then, as well, to the other classes of the enslaved nation. In contrast to *Równość,* Limanowski was also convinced of the advisability of a constitutional struggle. "There, where the people have no voice, the first and natural task is to fight for a general direct vote." Basically then, Limanowski's political philosophy was what he himself classified as "people's socialism," or what he elsewhere called "socialist-patriotism."[90]

The program of Lud Polski — as it was formulated in the Polish socialist patriotic circles in Geneva — derived from the writings of Limanowski.[91] "The fundamental conception for the program came from me," wrote Limanowski in his memoirs: "I said that we should not blindly follow the example of Western socialism and confine the program to industrial workers, but rather to handle matters as begun by our democrats and include in our program the entire working people, both in industry and on the land. This was agreed to without argument. Balicki proposed to give this new organization the name 'Lud Polski' to emphasize this idea."[92] Most significant to the later development of Polish political thought was the quarrel that ensued in these discussions between Limanowski and Balicki over the territorial question. Limanowski did not approve of the name Lud Polski "because I had in mind the old Republic, and therefore not only the Polish people, but also other peoples. . . . I stood fast on the borders of the old Republic, governed on the model of the Swiss federation, giving complete self-determination to each people; Balicki was for an ethnographic Poland."[93] Although irrelevant to the *Równość* program, this dispute became a central problem for Polish political thinking of both the Left and Right during the following decades.

The "Proclamation of the Socialist Group 'Lud Polski'" appeared in programmatic form in August 1881. Although it analyzed the fall of the *szlachta* in terms of the rise of the Polish bourgeoisie and proletariat, it made no references to class struggle. Like Limanowski's work, *Socialism as the Natural Sign,* the program instead pointed out that all classes were united by a "people's patriotism." Similar to both the "Brussels Program" and the programs of Russian socialists, the

"Proclamation" advocated (1) "independent national existence in freely chosen borders" and (2) "the broadest possible autonomy for *gminas* and lands, which would be limited only by their own [freely determined] solidarity."[94]

The *Równość* socialists, now writing for *Przedświt* (Dawn), attacked the program of Lud Polski not so much for its stand on patriotism, which they had already repeatedly criticized, but for its view of socialism, or rather, for its lack of socialism.[95] They mocked Lud Polski's attempt at "individuality" in the European scheme as nothing more than a weak attempt to ignore the entire body of "socioeconomic science," not to mention the history of the proletariat. Socialism, explained the *Równość* group, was above all an "economic pursuit," and denying this, how could Lud Polski call itself socialist? In response to Lud Polski's attempt to unify Prussian, Galician, and Congress Kingdom Polish socialism (on an ethnographic basis or otherwise), Waryński wrote, "I consider [the program] as standing in total opposition to the contemporary socialist movement in our country, and the influence it may bring to bear on that movement [I view] as harmful to its future development."[96]

As might be expected, the conference of the International called for 2 October 1881 in Chur (Switzerland) turned into a full-scale clash between Limanowski, representing Lud Polski, and Waryński, the official representative of "five organized circles from the Grand Duchy of Poznań, the workers' group of Kraków, and the editors of *Przedświt* [the successor of *Równość*]."[97] Sixteen delegates were present at the conference, not including several guests, Dłuski and P. Aksel'rod (who appeared as "Aleksandrovich") among them.[98] Limanowski opened the Polish part of the conference with an unambiguous statement of his fundamental plan — the independence of Poland was the first and foremost concern of Polish socialism. The task of contemporary socialists, he continued, could be linked in a direct line to the radical democratic traditions of émigré Poland.[99] Then it was Waryński's turn to defend the internationalist position of his compatriots. He sketched the unique histories of the three Polish partitions and prognosticated the rapid, though clearly divergent, development of proletarian consciousness in each. Summing up, Waryński directed his remarks to Limanowski: "Polish socialists, like socialists from other lands, cannot extend their hands to the democratic bourgeoisie without the danger of betraying their cardinal principles."[100] In the discussion that followed the Polish speeches, the French socialist B. Malon asked whether the

Polish socialists then had no nationality. Dłuski answered, "it is not a matter of renouncing nationality, but of renouncing the desire for the political reconquest of the old Polish state."[101]

Waryński also introduced and defended a four-point resolution that called for recognition of the predominance of the social question, the irrelevance of the national question, the necessity of organizing on the principle of class warfare, and the renunciation of any cooperation with bourgeois parties.[102] Although this resolution was not accepted fully by the conferees, their final resolution stated, in a formula similar to that used at the Geneva meeting, that "considering that the struggle for liberation is a class and not a national struggle, the congress proceeds to the order of the day over those questions posed by the Polish delegates."[103] For Waryński, this was a partial victory; before the tribunal of international socialism, his exclusive concern for the Polish social question, a unique element in the history of Polish political thought, was vindicated. Limanowski left the meeting bitterly complaining that his formal defeat was the result of personal politics rather than theoretical wisdom. By 1883, wrote Limanowski, "my relations with those past socialists like Waryński, Mendelson, Dłuski, and others were nil."[104]

The cleft in Polish socialism between the internationalism of Waryński and the socialist-patriotism of Limanowski widened into an unbridgeable chasm as a result of Chur, alarming Western socialist circles and prompting last-minute attempts to reconcile the two parties. Kautsky and Bernstein (both of whom had conferred repeatedly with Limanowski at Chur) turned to Engels for advice on how to deal with the intransigent Polish camps.[105] In his responses, Engels apparently saw no reason to alter international socialism's devotion to the cause of an independent Poland. Without mentioning either Limanowski or Waryński by name, he wrote to Kautsky on 7 February 1882:

> The international proletarian movement is possible only among independent peoples — internat(ional) cooperation can occur only among *equals*. . . . As long as Poland is divided and oppressed, it will be impossible in its lands to build a strong soc(ialist) party; other proletar(iat) parties in Germany, etc., will not be able to establish real internat(ional) ties *with any other Poles — except for Poles in emigration.* Every Polish peasant and worker who is aroused from his torpor and begins to take interest in general questions would be hindered by the fact of national oppression. . . . The elimination of this impediment is the fundamental precondition for all healthy and free development.

> Those Polish socialists who do not set forward the freeing of their
> nation as the first point of their program remind me of the German
> socialists who do not aspire first of all to be rid of the measures against
> socialists, [to gain] the introduction of freedom of press, association,
> and assembly. In order to fight, it is above all necessary to have
> ground under your feet, fresh air, light and space.[106]

The considerations that lay behind Marx and Engels's "Long live
Poland!" response to the Geneva meeting were made absolutely clear
by Engels's letters. The giants of international socialism opposed
Polish internationalism and found no logic in an indigenous Polish
workers' movement until the time when Poland was independent.
Waryński would find little support from the Western leadership for a
Congress Kingdom-based, class-oriented workers' party. Engels's
somewhat patronizing view of the backward Polish worker and his
indifference to the efforts of the Polish internationalists must have
increasingly perturbed Waryński and his colleagues, who by now, in
late 1881, were self-proclaimed followers of Marx.[107] At the same time,
Western socialism's patriotic stance fed the Polish internationalists'
determination to seek moral and material support from the Russians,
whose presentation at Chur was sympathetic and encouraging.

More important than the encouragement Waryński received from
the Russians at Chur, or for that matter more important than the
general disapproval with which his ideas were greeted by Western
socialism, was the marked advance of political consciousness displayed by both the Poles and Russians at Chur. In fact, at Chur, it
became apparent that both the Poles and Russians were moving in the
same direction — toward an increasing awareness of the political
struggle. In his proposal to the conference, Waryński spoke of the
necessity of a "mass organization" of the working class based on economic demands. He also offered "complete" support for the "Program
of the Galician Workers' Party," which advocated the use of political
struggle in the name of the working class. Similarly, Waryński more
readily admitted that a terrorist program might be necessary. Still, he
insisted, "it is not for . . . an insurrection that we should prepare, but for
a second revolution by means of propaganda, agitation, and lastly the
organization of our strength on an economic and political basis."[108]

Waryński's emphasis on politics, action, and organization at the
Chur meeting coincided with a new mood among his Black Partition
friends. The assassination of 1 March had not brought about the desired social revolution; the Russians now increasingly looked to
political organization as the crucial missing element. At Chur,

Aksel'rod summarized the differences between Black Partition and Narodnaia Volia and concluded that they were insignificant. Because of the infancy of the Russian workers' movement, continued Aksel'rod, real differences existed not within the Russian movement, but between the western and eastern movements.[109] "As I hear it, at this moment the best elements of Black Partition are ready to unite with Narodnaia Volia," Aksel'rod claimed; "both sides seem to have desisted from several extremes in their practical positions."[110] Although little came of Aksel'rod's hopeful initiative, dreams of an all-empire socialist organization were aroused among Russians and Poles alike.[111]

"To the Russian Comrades"

The Polish socialists of the Congress Kingdom underwent a number of kaleidoscopic changes in Galicia and Geneva. Ideological vacillations, political machinations, and personality conflicts interlocked in shifting patterns that perpetually altered the picture of Polish socialism in exile. However, several reasonably well defined trends can be identified as dominating the period of emigration. First of all, the meaningful contact and cooperation between socialist-patriots and internationalists gradually came to a halt. For the next decade, the socialist-patriots and Lud Polski played a comparatively insignificant role in the development of Congress Kingdom socialism. To be sure, their program was vindicated in the 1890s, when Polish internationalism, with Rosa Luxemburg at its head, was buried under the onslaught of the patriotic movements of the left and right. In the 1880s however, their influence was confined to the emigration, where, supported by Western socialism, they awaited the liberation of the Polish lands. On the other hand, the Polish internationalists in emigration moved even further toward a dogmatic rejection of patriotism and a closer relationship with the Russian movement. Although they more openly considered themselves "Marxists," they also increasingly expressed their independence from the direct authority of Marx and Engels. Finally, during the period of emigration, Waryński and his comrades became more aware of the problems of political action and of building a mass movement. Anarchism no longer answered the question of how to make a revolution. Instead, the internationalists, increasingly frustrated by émigré politics, turned to a Polish workers' party as the focal point for a socialist struggle.

These trends converged at the end of 1881 in the final, in some ways culminating, internationalist document of this period, entitled "To Our Comrade Russian Socialists."[112] The proclamation began with a by this point typical explanation of the foundations of scientific socialism, the nature of economic exploitation, and the state of the workers' movement in the West. Turning to the Russian movement, the document emphasized that the "lack of political freedom is at this time an immensely important question in Russia. . . . Our comrades, the Russian socialists, have taken on the initiative as well as the whole weight of the [political] struggle, as proved by widespread terrorist actions." The proclamation recognized that the Poles could not ignore the important question of political freedom, but insisted again that it had to be separated from the "national question, whose principles have nothing in common with socialism." The document also advocated, for the first time in emigration, a constitutional struggle, though only as a means to help bring organization and consciousness to the working class: "For the realization of these [socialist] goals, political freedom is natural, the lack of which places enormous obstacles before the mass organization of the working class in Russia."

The Poles continued to disagree with Engels's proposition that the only basis for a political struggle was the national question. Instead, socialist parties must be organized according to established geopolitical borders; "a Polish Socialist Party, as a unified whole, cannot exist." The struggle for political freedom in Russia depended on "the cooperation, in the spirit of solidarity, of the organized working masses of the various peoples within the borders of the Russian state." Most significantly, "in relation to the struggle for political freedom . . . to push forward the Polish national independence question can only harm that struggle, and therefore also be detrimental to the interests of the working class."

As an indication of their increasing concern for politics, the *Równość* socialists also included the Polish peasantry in the general liberation movement. Clearly, the proclamation noted, the Polish peasant "with very insignificant and rare exceptions" was always an enemy of uprisings in the name of an independent Poland. When the peasants did rise, the proclamation insisted, it was in the name of economic rather than national freedom. Because peasant emancipation in the partitions was fostered by the governments of the partitions, rather than by their respective privileged classes, the peasants are the "greatest opponents of nationalism." Therefore, the only way to join this numerous segment of the Polish population to the struggle for political freedom would be with "economic demands."

The proclamation concluded with a call for the organization of an all-empire socialist party that would unite the various socialist organizations of the empire's nationalities. This organization would carry on a unified struggle for the political and economic liberation of the empire and would attempt to work out a common program. In essence, then, the Congress Kingdom socialists pledged to cooperate more closely with the Russians, to participate in a struggle for an all-empire constitution, and consented to the use of terrorism as a means in the political struggle.

The proclamation could not and did not venture a more precise description of the Polish socialist party in the Congress Kingdom. It neither outlined the extent of cooperation with the Russians nor indicated how much autonomy the Polish party would maintain. The question of the extent of the party's cooperation with other classes in society, especially with the bourgeoisie, was left open, as was the question of actions to be taken by the party in the constitutional struggle. In fact the entire problem of the kinds of actions the party should undertake was left to the future. Over the next five years, Waryński and other Polish socialists, removed from their splendid isolation in Geneva and directly in contact with the real, rather than theoretical, desires of the Polish proletariat, were forced to find answers to these pressing, unsolved questions under the shadow of the tsarist noose.

VI

The Organization and the Ideology
of the Proletariat

At his trial in Kraków, Waryński attempted to convince the authorities that socialism was an ideology that developed without regard to the particular political circumstances under which it functioned. Only the means of socialist action altered with a change of political systems. However, in the history of the Polish party, like that of other Marxist parties, ideology constantly interacted with environment — ideological changes and tactical alterations were prompted by variations in the political structure of Polish society. In the fall of 1881, when Waryński arrived in Warsaw, the outstanding facts of Polish life that socialism had to confront were the beginnings of severe Russianization in Polish schools and the strength of the positivist slogan of Organic Work. Also crucial to the final program and activities of the socialist party, the Proletariat,[1] was the enormous prestige of the Russian revolutionary movement as well as the existence of a working-class movement already imbued with a measure of political consciousness.

The ideology the Polish socialists developed in Galicia and Switzerland did not simply fade away in face of the political realities in the Congress Kingdom because, in part, it had been purposely developed to confront just these realities. Its Polish formulators had, after all, experienced the brief flowering of workers' socialism in the Congress Kingdom in 1877–78 and had likewise shared the Russian movement's history in the empire's schools and in Geneva. In Lwów and Kraków, and at the conferences of Chur and Geneva, the Polish socialists participated in a form of Western and international socialism. They therefore approached their tasks in the Congress Kingdom armed with an already tempered socialist ideology first formulated in the empire and recast in emigration. Nevertheless, the socialist leaders were forced to approach their first major task in the Congress Kingdom, the formation of an organization, with little help from either their ideology or their experiences. Indeed, totally without precedents, the Polish socialists set out to erect a Marxist party in an autocratic society.

The Building of a Workers' Party

The Poles viewed their experiences and their defeats of 1877–78 as proof that a centralized party was indispensable for any further actions in the Congress Kingdom. Mendelson correctly analyzed the failure of the earliest worker circles as a result of "political conditions" rather than of police persecution. These conspiratorial circles, "taking everything into consideration, could not have lasted very long because of a complete lack of centralization."[2] The problem also resided in the working class, wrote Waryński: "The lack of a feeling of solidarity, disorganization, apathy, incomprehension of the most obvious system of exploitation — this is the sad but unfortunately genuine characteristic of the contemporary Polish working-class proletariat." Therefore, concluded Waryński, "the burning question for us is the *kwestia organizacyjna* [the organization question]." Of course, this organization would not be located "within the traditional borders, not based on ethnographic conditions. We view this as harmful."[3]

Like the proclamation "To Our Comrade Russian Socialists," *Równość* advised that its readers organize an all-empire party, but left the question open how this was to be accomplished, concluding only that the "socialist organization of the masses must be the result of contemporary necessities."[4] Mendelson realized that the difficulties of 1877 were due in part to the fact that "our work was without a tight scheme, without a defined plan in particulars." Still, for the proposed new party, he failed to provide just such a definition of goals and actions. "It is difficult to predict," he wrote, "which means the newly formed organization will use for the daily struggle against the master and the government."[5]

Waryński therefore arrived in Warsaw at the end of 1881 with a burning desire to organize a working-class party (and with the vague blessings of Narodnaia Volia), but without precise instructions from his Geneva backers.[6] He immediately established ties with working-class circles and with Ognisko, a St. Petersburg Polish circle descended from the old Gmina.[7] Waryński once again quickly won the trust of the radical workers, to whom he was known as "Długi," the "tall one." "From the moment of Waryński's arrival in Warsaw," the prosecutor wrote, somewhat overstating his case, "social revolutionary propaganda took on enormous proportions."[8] To be sure, under Waryński's direction, the workers' circles revived and regrouped during the winter of 1881–1882. (They had existed in only nominal form after the destruction of the Gmina and the arrests of spring 1881.)

At the same time, the authorities released many workers and students who had been in prison since 1878–79. Płoski described in his memoirs the depression that many internees felt after their release but also found that some "even more strongly, even more fanatically, loved that idea for which they suffered." Prison, continued Płoski, also served as a "propaganda school." Poorly educated workers, under the tutelage of their intelligentsia comrades in forced confinement, learned "the exact and the deep principles of socialism."[9]

With the indispensable help of his old comrade from 1877 Henryk Dulęba and the university student Kazimierz Puchewicz, Waryński carried the slogans of socialism and workers' organization to all the major industrial enterprises of Warsaw. M. Mańkowski confessed to the police that "Dulęba missed no opportunities to come together with workers for the purpose of propaganda. . . . He constantly came around the factories of Orthwein, Lilpop and Rau, Rudzki, and the Warsaw-Vienna railway workshop. One could always run into him in Praga [the workers' section of Warsaw], he always had brochures and proclamations with him, which he handed out at every meeting."[10] The police apprehensively received reports from all over the city of Warsaw describing meetings, the distribution of literature, and street corner propaganda. The real culprits in this activity, the police perceptively noted, were the socialist "middlemen" between the intelligentsia and the workers, who, like Dulęba and Gostkiewicz, "collected these workers at meetings taking place on the streets, in parks, in pubs and other places, gave these workers brochures and proclamations, and made speeches in which they tried to arouse in the workers and artisans dissatisfaction with their position."[11] Teodor Kallenbrun, Józef Schmaus, and Jan Ptaszyński — all Warsaw workers and socialists — similarly led small workers' groups in various factories, distributing literature and conducting meetings.[12]

Early in April 1882, workers at the Warsaw-Vienna railway workshop walked off the job, precipitating violent clashes at the workshop as well as vociferous worker-management confrontations. Although Dulęba had formed a small circle among the machinists, the role of the socialists in the April disturbances was minimal. Still, the socialists responded in July 1882 with their first leaflet, "Comrades," which belatedly expressed their complete solidarity with the workers' cause. "Four months have passed since our combined efforts of the third of April. . . . We felt as brothers in poverty and degradation." Although the police and management were able to suppress the workers' strike, continued the proclamation, much was learned. "Unity, that is all we need," it concluded, "unity and more unity, and the future and happiness will belong to us. To work then, comrades, for that future! To the struggle for our happiness and that of all those who suffer as we. 'All for one, one for all,' that is our slogan!! "[13]

Propaganda of socialist ideals, agitation for everyday workers' demands, and organization to tie the intelligentsia to the workers' struggle — these were the themes Waryński and his cohorts continued to pursue throughout the summer of 1882. On 15 August, they issued a mimeographed summary of the program of their group entitled "Proclamation of the Workers' Committee of the Social Revolutionary Party Proletariat."[14] On 1 September, the Workers' Committee issued the full text of the program in a proclamation carrying the same title.[15] From this point, wrote Kulczycki, "an entire series of revolutionary proclamations electrified all levels of the working population of Warsaw."[16]

In the fall and winter of 1882–83 socialism spread so quickly among the intelligentsia and working-class circles of the city that Dulęba predicted the revolution would break out in a matter of months.[17] Especially after the arrival of Edmund Płoski and Aleksander Dębski from St. Petersburg in November 1882, Warsaw University and other centers of higher learning became the scenes of constant discussion between positivist and socialist activists.[18] Stanisław Kunicki also arrived in Warsaw from St. Petersburg in the fall of 1882, accepted "immediately" the program of the Proletariat, and was so enthralled by the successes of the organization that he "was almost ready to go at once to the barricades."[19]

The Organization of the Proletariat

The Polish socialists of 1882–83 were no less confident and enthusiastic than those of 1877–78. Now, however, owing both to their practical experience since those first attempts and to their ideological acknowledgment of the necessity for political struggle, they concentrated much more of their efforts on organizational questions. The structure of the Proletariat as conceived primarily by Waryński was based on two coordinate executive organs, a Central Committee and a Workers' Committee.[20] The Workers' Committee, wrote the Warsaw prosecutor, "is composed exclusively of workers and is divided by cities into sections, Warsaw composing only one section."[21] The primary functions of the committee were to carry out socialist propaganda among workers in factories, industrial concerns, and in the countryside, as well as to organize social revolutionary circles. In addition, the Workers' Committee regularly collected money and dues, enforced self-discipline among working-class socialists, and attempted to resolve local conspiratorial problems. The leadership of the Workers' Committee, explained the prosecutor, fell primarily to the "indoctrinated worker-intelligentsia."[22]

The Central Committee (formally constituted in the spring of 1883) was composed exclusively of intelligentsia socialists. "It directs the activities of the Workers' Committee in propaganda and agitation," wrote the prosecutor, "and fulfills those kinds of duties that the Workers' Committee cannot."[23] The authorities maintained as well that the Central Committee's most crucial function was to coordinate political activities with the Executive Committee of Narodnaia Volia. The Central Committee also edited the newspaper *Proletariat,* directed all acts of terrorism, issued proclamations, and supervised the party's printing facilities and treasury. In the indictment of the prosecutor, the socialist intelligentsia — through the Central Committee — was responsible for the conspiratorial activities of the party, and the working-class intelligentsia in the Workers' Committee carried on the daily responsibilities of propaganda and agitation.[24]

Two additional organizational centers of the Proletariat took on greater importance and responsibility in 1885 and 1886, when repeated and widespread arrests paralyzed both the Workers' Committee and the Central Committee. The Section of the Society of the Red Cross, associated with a similar subsection of the International and of Narodnaia Volia, provided material help to exiled and imprisoned socialists and their families. As Płoski confessed to the police, "the Section of the Red Cross as well as the Central and Workers' Committees had their own stocks of books, funds, formularies, and seals."[25] The Drużyna Bojowa ("Fighting Squad"), like the Red Cross, grew out of the Central Committee. As the most conspiratorial of the Proletariat's subsections, the Drużyna was intended to carry out the terrorist decisions of the Central Committee and to provide information on police agents who had infiltrated the party structure.

The successful functioning of the Proletariat depended a great deal more on the personalities involved in the movement than on the structure of its organization. Up until the time of his arrest, Waryński dominated the party through his active involvement in both the Central and Workers' Committees. His personal participation in recruitment at the factories also contributed to his unchallenged and effective leadership of the Proletariat. He "was not content with limiting himself only to contact with workers at meetings," the police wrote, "he got to know them as well in other ways, meeting them in their quarters." Accompanied by Dulęba, "he walked around the factories and there made the acquaintance of workers."[26] In fact, the first "agitational" phase of the Proletariat's history — from the summer of 1882 until his arrest in the fall of 1883 — was stamped by Waryński's energy and skill in dealing with the Warsaw working class. (The second "conspiratorial" phase was dominated by Stanisław Kunicki and lasted from Waryński's arrest until the summer of 1884, when the final "terrorist" phase of the Proletariat under the leadership of Aleksander Dębski, Maria Bohuszewiczówna, and Marian Ulrych led to the party's destruction.)

The initial agitational period under Waryński's leadership is perhaps the most enlightening to the student of Polish socialism because it was the least permeated by paid working-class police agents, mass arrests, and police harassment, all of which increasingly influenced the Proletariat's development. The attempt by the party to subsume its demands to those of Polish labor in order to develop political consciousness in the working class met with a generally positive response all over the Congress Kingdom, even during the conspiratorial and terrorist phases. Waryński himself was the master of the agitational technique. A worker reported to the police that at one socialist meeting "Waryński told the workers that when the tsar arrives in Warsaw, all workers and artisans without exception should rise with their demands, declaring that taxes are too high, that they have no incomes, all should cry out, 'We demand a better life!' The tsar, asserted Waryński, would grant a constitution if the workers refused to live any longer as they did."[27] The prosecutor also noted that the Proletariat successfully simplified its message in oral propaganda among uninitiated workers: "For this purpose, meetings were arranged from time to time in various public places . . . and at the private quarters of workers . . . in a word, through oral propaganda were carried forth those same ideas that were set forth in the printed publications; only here socialist teachings appeared more comprehensible to the simple person."[28] The entire network of representatives from the Central and Workers' Committees was so arranged that the propaganda and agitation functions operated smoothly.

The police remained convinced throughout the period of the Proletariat that the intelligentsia cajoled, misled, and duped the workers into the socialist movement. At the same time they recognized that the socialist members of the working-class intelligentsia were crucial to the recruitment process: "It was difficult for the worker to decline entrance into the party for he took the risk that his more influential colleagues who belonged to the party would cause his release from the factory and he would be without work. To leave [the party] was even more difficult; when Szczepański [a metalworker] wanted to do this, he was threatened with violence."[29] The party itself was caught in an only partly resolved dilemma. On the one hand, it attempted to recruit a mass following; on the other, it had to maintain secrecy and discipline. "The members of one circle did not know those who made up another," wrote the authorities, "the sections were composed only of representatives of a circle and not all of them knew the members of the Workers' Committee. The Central Committee remained separate and not all of the members of the party knew its members." The police found many documents that pointed to the party's attempt to maintain a strong internal organization: blank membership forms, which classified party members by number, section, and circle; lists of particularly offensive factory owners; financial statements of the Red Cross Section; and party dues collection forms.[30]

The determination of Waryński and his associates to form an all-Congress Kingdom party and to secure necessary outside support for the Warsaw movement initiated the spread of Proletariat activities throughout the Congress Kingdom and to Polish centers in European Russia itself. "Płoski and Waryński," concluded the prosecutor, "do not recognize any territorial borders . . . and, only from the point of view of the variety of political conditions, limit their activities for the time being to factory centers in the Congress Kingdom, Lithuania, and the Ukraine."[31] Outside of Warsaw, the Proletariat centered its propaganda and organizational efforts in the Piotrków *guberniia* cities of Łódź, Zgierz, and Tomaszów; the heavy concentration of industrial workers provided a great resource of party manpower and also a more comfortable home for the party's press, away from the central police administration in Warsaw. The Łódź Workers' Committee acted in local Piotrków affairs in the name of the Warsaw Workers' Committee, and in Łódź, the Proletariat successfully organized German and Jewish as well as Polish workers.[32]

The party also spread its message to the smaller industrial towns of Częstochowa, Piotrków, Radom, Żyrardów, Białystok, and Kielce. With the exception of Żyrardów, the linen manufacturing center located close to Warsaw, these smaller cities did not provide fruitful soil for the revolutionary work of the Proletariat. However, they did serve as important centers for attempts by the Proletariat to spread its propaganda to the countryside. Peasants living and working as craftsmen in these towns were often recruited to distribute socialist literature in their home villages.[33]

The necessity to smuggle contraband literature into the Congress Kingdom from abroad forced the Proletariat to concentrate its organizational efforts in several border towns, such as Kalisz and Częstochowa near the Prussian border and Vilna, the center for transporting Russian literature into the Congress Kingdom.[34] The Proletariat branches in these towns also secured transit for socialists fleeing arrest and smuggled new recruits for the party into the Congress Kingdom. The railway system soon became impossibly dangerous for the transportation of illegal literature or revolutionary personnel. Therefore the socialists relied heavily in these areas on local Jews, some of whom were already expert smugglers, for the actual border crossings.[35] The authorities ruefully acknowledged the Proletariat's successes, despite police countermeasures, in the organization of underground contraband routes: "During the previous year [1883] transport from abroad of various pamphlets and socialist brochures was organized on a tremendous scale. In forty-three different cases, the police succeeded in interrupting the spread of these works. Still, at the time of the search at Bardovskii's and at Edmund Osterlof's, one of his comrades, the police found at the former's 1,668 and at the latter's, 8,998 copies of revolutionary publications."[36]

Of major importance to the Proletariat's financial upkeep and recruitment resources was the spread of its organization to the major centers of the Polish population in the empire: Vilna, Kiev, Moscow, St. Petersburg, Riga, Odessa, and Dorpat. The tsarist authorities also noted the presence of Proletariat circles among Poles in the Belorussian towns of Vitebsk and Mogilev.[37] Although many Polish workers and students were recruited into the Proletariat's ranks in these cities, the party's efforts to establish branches in Russia proper were based primarily on material exigencies. One member of the Proletariat's Central Committee was permanently assigned in St. Petersburg to maintain contact with the Executive Committee of Narodnaia Volia and, equally important, to establish good relations with the city's sometimes quite wealthy Polish intelligentsia.[38] Indeed, a substantial portion of the party's funding derived from Polish and Russian radical circles in St. Petersburg and Moscow.[39] Finally, the maintenance of the party's printing facilities in the Congress Kingdom depended on the importation of machinery and printing type from Odessa, Kiev, and Vilna.

In several Russian cities, to be sure, the circles of the Proletariat overlapped with the circles of Narodnaia Volia. In the case of Vilna, it is impossible to determine whether the circle was a branch of the Proletariat or a branch of Narodnaia Volia — it contained Poles, Russians, and Jews and performed services for both parties.[40] Still, it is important to note that the *narodovol'tsy* were especially influential in nonworker, Polish Proletariat circles in Russian cities, a fact that makes the later terrorist struggle of the Proletariat more comprehensible.

The Ideology of the Proletariat

The intellectual tools the Polish socialists brought to bear on the problems of organization and ideology in the Congress Kingdom were, by 1881–82, impressive, varied, and included the works of the prominent socialist thinkers of nineteenth-century Europe. The Proletariat's large and diversified libraries contained numerous works of Marx, Engels, and Lassalle.[41] A wide sample of Russian socialist classics and Russian periodical literature including *Vperëd, Kalendar' "Narodnoi voli,"* and *Na rodine* were available to the Poles as well as five different Polish socialist periodicals and several German social democratic newspapers.[42]

Copies of the Polish socialist newspapers *Praca* (Work) from Lwów, *Robotnik* (Worker) from Kraków, and *Przedświt* from Geneva spread throughout socialist circles in the Congress Kingdom.[43] Jurisdictional dispute over control of *Przedświt* between the émigré community and the Central Committee prompted the Congress Kingdom socialists to publish their own newspaper journal, *Proletariat*. In May 1884 the Geneva socialists also began publishing *Walka Klas* (Class Struggle), which was intended to serve as a monthly informational journal of the Proletariat. When in October 1884 Mendelson rejoined *Przedświt*'s editorial board and the newspaper again recognized the ultimate hegemony of the Central Committee, the Proletariat maintained three official periodicals — *Proletariat, Przedświt,* and *Walka Klas.*[44]

The ideological development and intellectual heritage of the Proletariat can also be traced in at least twenty proclamations issued in the Congress Kingdom from 1882 to 1886 and by over fifty translated socialist works (printed mostly in Geneva).[45] The inspiration for most of these proclamations and a large portion of the translated literature was, quite clearly, the works of Marx and Engels. "There is no doubt," stated an article prepared on Marx for the unpublished sixth number of *Proletariat,* "that Marx is considered the most gifted leader of the internationalist movement and the most noted expert on the social sciences in all of Europe."[46] The police recorded numerous instances of the study of Marx among socialists. In one case, the prosecutor indicted twelve men who had gathered around a table reading the Polish translation of the *Communist Manifesto,* printed in 1882 in Geneva.[47] In the years 1877 to 1881, the Polish socialists had adopted Marx's materialist analysis of history; by 1881–82, Marx became relevant not only to their views of the past but also to their actions of the present and their notions about the future.

Unlike its apolitical and anarchist predecessors, the Proletariat recognized the daily struggle against tsarism as a legitimate aim of socialism. As its program stated:

> in the political field we will strive for the greatest freedom and we will fight with all governments regardless of their nationality so long as we have not completely conquered this freedom. We unequivocally condemn the lack of freedom of conscience, language, assembly, association, speech and press, for these all represent great obstacles to the development of workers' consciousness. Already this causes religious-national hate and fanaticism, already it makes impossible mass propaganda and organization, which is the only means of establishing the foundations of the future organization of the socialist structure.[48]

The socialists advocated the political struggle as a means of easing their organizational efforts and as a source of a direct confrontation with the forces of the Polish bourgeoisie. At the time of the initial 1882 program, the economic struggle against the bourgeoisie was of paramount concern. Yet as the months passed, the Polish socialists increasingly viewed the economic and political struggles as one and the same. As the important Proletariat theorist Tadeusz Rechniewski wrote in "We and the Government," "the struggle with economic oppression is for us at the same time a struggle with the political system that supports it and vice versa. Our blows should be directed against one enemy with two faces."[49] The June 1883 proclamation on the coronation of Alexander III, the first to be signed by the Central Committee and the first addressed to the citizens of the Congress Kingdom as a whole, stated:

> Only the *szlachta* and the bourgeoisie recognize the legitimacy of the contemporary monarchy, realizing that for the defense of their personal interests it commands a million bayonets . . . the coronation completely illustrates these ties. On the one hand stands the tsar, who approves of the capitalists, the great landowners, the upper bureau-

cracy — on the other, the proletariat, the intelligentsia, and the millions of oppressed, the natural enemies of tsarism and capitalism.[50]

We fight the government, Rechniewski wrote, because it "is the defender of the possessing class."[51]

The Proletariat consistently refused to recognize any progressive role the Polish bourgeoisie might have played in the past because, as they saw it, the Russian autocracy and Polish bourgeoisie had an especially strong mutually reinforcing partnership. The maintenance of the autocratic political system was tied directly to the "oppression of the working classes by the capitalists."[52] The socialists also eliminated the possibility of any alliance with the Polish middle class to conquer those constitutional political freedoms that made up their own minimum program. Waryński examined the history of European socialism — that of the Paris Commune in particular — and concluded that cooperation with the bourgeois enemies of the working class would be suicidal for the socialist cause.[53] Rechniewski warned that more political power for the Polish bourgeoisie would mean in the end "even more bayonets to protect private holdings."[54]

The fact that the capitalists and the government were centrally organized to oppress the working class, reasoned the socialists, "leaves us only one effective defense in the struggle against them: the centralization of revolutionary strength and the maintenance of the greatest secrecy."[55] According to the Proletariat, the entire question of the "means" of struggle depended on the extent to which its enemies' forces were centralized. If the government resorted to a great show of force, concluded the newspaper *Proletariat*, then our opposition "must be just as forceful."[56] In similar fashion, the socialists defended their internationalism in juxtaposition to the "cosmopolitanism" of international capital. The working classes understood, the socialists wrote, that "the cosmopolitan bourgeoisie can be defeated only by an international revolution."[57]

Although the invariable position — or at least slogan — of the Proletariat was that the "freeing of the working class can be accomplished only by the workers themselves," the organization of the Proletariat still viewed its function in terms of "directing" the preparations for workers' socialism and "leading" the proletariat into battle. Organization was now all-important, and the "party" in 1881–82 became much more than an association of socialist propagandists: "The times of heroes and leaders have passed, never to return — in their place today stands the organization."[58] Waryński wrote in "We and the Bourgeoisie": "These masses recognize their incapability of carrying out a revolution — they look for people on whom they can rely, to whom they can entrust leadership . . . we can and should acquire that reliance." Polish socialism was now seen in terms of a struggle for the masses in which the party had to prove, wrote Waryński, "that we are the enemies of their oppressors, that we will not back down during the struggle, that we wish that the masses get everything which belongs to them." It is in this context, continued Waryński, and only in this context, that "we reject for the moment jousting with bourgeois parliaments."[59] Later on, the socialists insisted that the proletariat had "already recognized us," and now, in the name of the working class, the party could fulfill its great historical mission.[60]

The impotence and hypocrisy of the Polish bourgeoisie on the one hand and the radicalism of the Polish masses on the other convinced the Proletariat that a unified political struggle for parliamentary democracy could serve only the enemies of socialism. Instead, and in striking contrast to the anarchist conceptions of the 1877–80 socialists, the Proletariat viewed the coming revolution through the prism of Marx's *Communist Manifesto* — "in order to accomplish a social revolution, the proletariat and the organization that will represent its interests should seize political power."[61] Rechniewski concluded that "our cause will be won when the warring socialist party defeats the present-day economic and political organization and takes over its political power. Only then will it be possible to introduce basic reforms." And only then, continued Rechniewski, "would the conditions of political freedom not become a sacrifice to the predominance of the possessing class, but serve exclusively the just development of the people."[62]

For these Polish socialists, the seizure of political power conferred a new and initially shocking positive meaning to the traditionally onerous concept of the state. The creation of a "socialist state" as the immediate goal of the seizure of power is not a concession of defeat, *Przedświt* tried to convince its readers: "The contemporary state is in itself not awful because it is called a state, today's policeman not because he has power, or that he wears a dark blue uniform; the strength of one and the other depends on the fact that they represent a class government, that they are the plenipotentiaries of economic oppression."[63] The Proletariat's final goal still remained the establishment of local *gminas,* but the means to realize the *gmina*-based society had been radically changed. A socialist legal struggle with a bourgeois parliament would come to naught; an all-encompassing social revolution would simply not occur in and of itself. "Rather, the best guarantee for the most complete emancipation of the working class . . . is with a provisional government established by the socialists." Until that time when the district *gmina* would become the basic economic and political unit of society, "at the top, on guard, will be the dictatorial government, enfranchised and supported by the proletariat. *The dictatorship of the proletariat will be the first act of the revolution.*"[64]

The dictatorship of the proletariat, *Walka Klas* admitted, "is not an expression of democracy, but . . . is a necessary act which will have as its goal the encouragement of proletarian action." Its purpose is to protect the proletariat's revolution from the "other already defeated classes."[65] This is not a matter of volunteerism, Waryński later insisted, "We do not stand outside of history, we are subject to its laws." One does not "organize a revolution," he continued, one organizes "for a revolution," which will break out as a natural result of "historical development and social conditions."[66] The Proletariat understood that the revolution was inevitable; the task of the party was to be prepared for it and, in the name of the working class, to see it through to its historically determined conclusion — the socialist society.

The works of Marx and Engels manifestly influenced the Proletariat's concepts of party, revolution, and dictatorship of the proletariat. Also typically Marxist was its blurry picture of the functioning of socialist society after the establishment of the dictatorship. From Waryński's "We and the Bourgeoisie," one can assume that he envisaged the steady growth of local *gminas* under the tutelage of the dictatorial government. The *gminas* would assume more and more societal responsibilities; the socialist government would become redundant and simply fade away.

On the other hand, in "Work Today and in the Future," *Przedświt* described a much more static "people's state" (*ludowe państwo*), which would "regulate the economy after the introduction of common ownership of the means of production and after the introduction of a better economy." The future society depicted in this article was one in which science and rationality would rule centralized economic and administrative institutions. All property and all means of production would be commonly owned, yet "everyone will work for himself and not for a master." The role of the state was to ensure that "work will be carried out only on socially useful items" and that "all will be occupied with productive work."[67] The article intimated, therefore, that the worker would in essence be working neither for himself nor for a master, but for the state, representing, of course, society as a whole.

Here, the Proletariat makes another clean break with its anarchist roots — socialism subordinates individual to social rights as determined by the collective, ordained by history, and manifested in the people's state.

> Man must work collectively and therefore must place his work under collective direction. . . of the independence of the individual person there can be no talk. . . . It is not therefore our plans for the future social system that render the individual dependent on society, this dependence is the result of the evolving social system, of the state of production, which leads us to better social arrangements.[68]

The people's state, according to the socialists, would be governed by all elements of society with the exception of the capitalists and the landowners. Peasants and workers would be united in their common ownership of the farms and factories. Although in the 1883 pamphlet *Who Is a Worker?* the Proletariat recognized only the poor and landless peasants as allies, its official statement on the peasant question — "Manifesto to the Workers on the Land" (and the party's program) — included the entire peasantry, with or without land, into the socialist constellation.[69] The "Manifesto" equated the traditional struggle of peasant against landlord with that of workers against factory owners. "Learn about us," the pamphlet addressed the peasants, "for we are the only ones who will say: the land belongs to those who sow it, factories to those who work in them. Place yourself then in the struggle, and the sooner will come our common victory over the enemies." The chief enemies, the "Manifesto" was quick to point out, were the gentry landowners in league with the tsar.[70]

In the "Manifesto" as well as in other propaganda efforts designed specifically for the peasantry, the socialists were openly in search of political allies and spared the peasants arguments about the materialist bases of history and the dialectics of social change. The party's most impressive attempts to propagandize socialism among the peasants, *Father Simon, a Story* (a year later published as *A Conversation between Two Cronies*) and *Janek Bruzda,* followed a familiar format.[71] Through the voice of a wise but lighthearted peasant who spoke in the vernacular of the common folk, the socialists laid the blame for the difficult economic circumstances of peasants and rural craftsmen on the rich — the same rich who supported and were supported by the government. High prices and exorbitant taxation, all peasant misery in fact, was the result of this evil combination of governors and landlords. Carefully avoiding insulting the national feelings of the peasantry, these works usually concluded with an invocation to the Lord to help those good souls from the cities, known as "socialists," in their holy attempts to save the working people.

The Proletariat managed to spread its "Manifesto" to hundreds of villages throughout the Congress Kingdom and the borderlands (thereby causing undue consternation and mutual recrimination in government circles), but the mostly illiterate and traditional peasantry remained unmoved.[72] The socialists' attempts to awaken the country-side can only be considered an abysmal failure. *Proletariat* wrote, "we must acknowledge that unfortunately very little progress has been made [by our movement] among the people working on the land."[73]

The Proletariat and the National Question

Among the Polish peasantry, the socialists could sidestep the national question; they could not do so, however, in the cities, where the *kwestia narodowa* remained a lively issue. The dogmatic inter-nationalism of the Geneva period could not be propagandized success-fully among the broad cross section of the working class and intelli-gentsia of the Congress Kingdom, whose national consciousness con-tinued to be aroused by the indignities of Russianization. The Prole-tariat's increased attention to the importance of the political struggle similarly dampened, in practice, their earlier obstreperous stand against Polish patriotism.

In the realm of pure theory, however, the most consistent element of the socialists' ideology from the 1878 "Brussels Program" to the pro-gram of the Proletariat was the rejection of the national struggle and of national independence. The program of the Proletariat explicitly stated that the national tradition was harmful to the class struggle because it "deadened in our society class consciousness among the working classes." The workers must be free of these nationalist tradi-tions in order to form a genuine "people's movement."[74] Although the Proletariat dedicated itself to the political struggle against tsarism, *Walka Klas* against emphasized, "we are not concerned about the independence of Poland, from which we do not expect the elimination of social bondage." Besides, it added, "there is no national unity: a deep crevice separates two social classes from each other, their aspira-tions are basically different and they will never be able to agree with each other."[75] Once again, as at Chur and Geneva, the Polish socialists of the Proletariat vehemently criticized the patriotic uprisings of the past and made light of the respect that Western progressive circles still paid to the independence struggle. "Today . . . the old road and slogan,

'Long live Poland!' has entered forever into the archives of crusted and compromised abuses of the national memory."[76]

Rechniewski, in "We and the Government," repeated the socialists' opposition to the nationalist cause but also indicated that they were not indifferent to national indignities: "The social revolution in whose name we struggle will radically do away with all oppression, national-political and moral as well as economic."[77] "We can certainly feel national oppression," wrote Przedświt, but we know that it is only one part of the story and that "at the foundations of this injustice is the suppression of labor. . . . We want equality because from equality comes the elimination of all oppression."[78]

The Proletariat never successfully came to terms with the conundrum of trying to build an internationalist movement among a nationally oppressed people. In theory, it was forced to reject the support of a significant portion of the Polish intelligentsia involved in various forms of the patriotic movement (including Organic Work). "Today," admitted the party's newspaper, "the intelligentsia sphere belongs almost completely to the camp of the privileged class and defends its interests."[79] Yet the Proletariat remained adamant; they saw attempts by the socialists in 1879–80 to compromise with the intelligentsia patriots as the worst manifestations of "opportunism."[80] During the period of the coming revolution, the intelligentsia might be recruited to the banner of the proletariat, but for the time being, "it is our proletariat that is revolutionary; it is exclusively they, and only they."[81] However, the internationalism of the Proletariat roused little enthusiasm among workers themselves. In yet another defensive and pained article on proletarian internationalism entitled "Do the Socialists Hold with Muscovites and Germans?" Przedświt wrote, "It is sad that there are still so many unenlightened in our [working] class, but we can only advise on this matter propaganda and reasonable words. . . . We must all extend our hands and cure stupidity from every quarter."[82]

Some historians sharply criticize the Proletariat — as they do the "Brussels Program" — for its "weighty errors on the national question."[83] Others criticize its "Blanquism" or its narodnik illusions.[84] But most historians conclude that to one extent or another, the program of the Proletariat was Marxist. Arskii even praises the Proletariat for "rejecting elements of nationalism and chauvinism."[85] Kulczycki, Perl, Baumgarten, and Haustein see the Proletariat's internationalism not in terms of a rejection of national existence but as a rejection only of that nationalism historically connected with the szlachta and the bourgeois intelligentsia. As Haustein argues, "the Proletariat displayed a silent patriotism. They certainly recognized the importance of the establishment of an independent Poland but did not openly and clearly explain it and therewith rejected the use of patriotic agitation."[86]

The Proletariat's consistent attacks on patriotism and its seemingly contradictory concern for Polish national survival were, however, not so much a matter of keeping the movement pure and its national feelings unarticulated, as Haustein suggests. Nor was its antipatriotism, as Baumgarten maintains, strictly a matter of distinguishing the movement from the patriotic movement of the past and the contemporaneous patriotism of the Polish intelligentsia. The entire history of the Proletariat, including its views on patriotism, can best be comprehended within the framework of the socialists' ultimate commitment to the political struggle of their party in the Congress Kingdom.

Constant agitation and propaganda in the factories and workshops of Warsaw, Łódź, and other industrial centers brought the Geneva internationalist intelligentsia into direct contact with the real national consciousness of the Polish workers. Nowhere did they attack the most precious elements of that consciousness. They slandered neither Catholicism nor religious belief; they made no propagandistic statements in support of atheism or godlessness. Although they criticized the upper clergy, they did not defame the politics of the Vatican. They bitterly attacked *szlachta* nationalism but not the Polishness of the workers, their language, their culture, or their national solidarity.

Especially in the early stages of the Proletariat movement, the intelligentsia leadership mixed easily with the rank-and-file worker membership. They were able to alter the consciousness of workers in some cases, but they also took on some of the characteristics of their supposed protégés. One of these characteristics was an uncomplicated devotion to the Polish nation. Krzywicki recalled an 1883 discussion among socialists on the national question in which Rechniewski posed the question, "And what do we do in the case of a [national] uprising?" Waryński emphatically answered, "We all go to the forests!" (take up arms).[87] This type of answer from the internationalist who had defied even Marx on the national question reveals, to some extent, the influence that political contact with the working class and with working-class members of the Proletariat had on the party's leadership.

The fact that Marxism served as the ideological foundation for Polish socialism in the period 1882–86 also helps explain the national and political views of the Proletariat. In contradistinction to their earlier preoccupations with Lassalle and the *narodnik* socialist thinkers, the Poles, under the influence of Marx, were able to approach the national question in the flexible terms of the political realities of working-class consciousness. Their appraisal of the diluting properties of the national struggle for working-class solidarity was not a result of any "incorrectness" of theory. In fact, this analysis that an all-Polish socialist national movement would be injurious to the internationalist socialist cause presaged the political developments of the 1890s. That the party itself was obliterated was also not a function of any "incorrectness" of its ideology. Its successes in fact can be attributed to just that ideology. Its ultimate failure lay on the groundwork of its success — advocacy of the political struggle, which, fought against the might of the Russian Empire in the 1880s, was doomed to failure.

VII

The Proletariat among the Polish
Intelligentsia and Working Class

The two groups that made up the bulk of the Proletariat's membership and were the primary targets of the party's propagandistic and
agitational activities were the urban workers and the urban intelligentsia. The urban workers who participated in the party's actions
were employed primarily in the large industrial factories of Warsaw
and Łódź, though a significant percentage were craftsmen and artisans
who toiled in the workshops of the capital. The intelligentsia members
of the Proletariat were predominantly students but included a number
of professionals — lawyers, doctors, and engineers, most of whom had
recently graduated from imperial universities.[1]

The Polish intelligentsia, like its Russian counterpart, was a complex historical phenomenon, difficult to define in consistent socioeconomic or even intellectual terms. The Poles themselves tended to
view the intelligentsia simply as a synonym for the educated classes;
educated workers were called "worker intelligentsia," the *szlachta* in
the countryside the "rural intelligentsia," and the educated Poles of the
cities, the "urban intelligentsia." The task of delimiting the concept of
the Congress Kingdom's intelligentsia of the 1880s is made even more
problematic by the relative lack, especially in comparison to the
Russians, of self-conscious attempts by the Polish intelligentsia to
define its own historical genesis and composition. Therefore, when we
speak here of the "intelligentsia," we mean the urban intelligentsia,
those educated Poles of the 1870s and 1880s who consistently opposed
the contemporary structure of society.

Within the Polish intelligentsia of the 1880s, two movements sometimes intermingled as one: increasing social and political dissatisfaction and the development of the socialist political party Proletariat.
Among the Polish workers, there existed similarly distinct yet inter-
twining processes of, on the one hand, more antagonism toward the
economic and social structure of society and, on the other, an increasing level of participation in the Proletariat. The party's leaders

attempted to resolve the problem of being a political party and a workers' party based on economic interests by merging the two questions into a common ideological platform. Organizationally, however, they acknowledged their dual nature by maintaining two coequal administrative centers, the Central Committee and the Workers' Committee. The extent to which the Proletariat was able to harness to its own movement both the socioeconomic dissatisfaction of the indigenous workers' movement and the sociopolitical demands of the intelligentsia movement.can be measured by its successes and failures in the four major confrontations between these groups'and the ruling class in the period 1882–86: the Buturlin resistance, the Apukhtin affair, the Żyrardów strike, and the Plac Zamkowy demonstration of the unemployed. Although no such confrontations took place in the Piotrków industrial region in these years, the working-class terrorist movement, discussed in the final section of this chapter, can be used to assess the Proletariat's performance in the cities of Łódź, Zgierz, and Tomaszów.

The Intelligentsia and Socialism

As noted in Chapter 3, until the beginning of the 1880s, the intellectual life of Warsaw revolved around positivist discussion circles. Increasingly, however, these circles turned their attention to the new and seemingly more dynamic philosophy of socialism. For example, before entering the ranks of the Proletariat, Maria Bohuszewiczówna conducted just such a circle, or better salon, in her home, where about thirty-five intelligentsia members discussed art, the theater, politics, and the new phenomenon of socialism. "Much time," she wrote, "was occupied with lively arguments, and afterwards singing lasted late into the night."[2] Circles in the universities and high schools were equally harmless and eclectic.

In a matter of a few years this placid picture of positivist discussion groups in the schools and in "society" had changed. By 1882–83, socialism had become *the* topic of discussion at the university and in salons.[3] Although a bitter enemy of socialism, Roman Dmowski nevertheless provided several interesting insights into the growing attraction of socialism for the intelligentsia. "Without a doubt," he wrote, "the most important reason is the moral value of socialism." While every other political movement in the Congress Kingdom and in Europe as a whole was based on selfish interests, he stated, socialism appealed (on false premises, to be sure) to the moral inclinations of intellectuals.[4]

Mieczysław Schmidt, a university student involved in the Proletariat, also spoke of the appeal of socialism's "moral values," though in the context of a generational conflict. "The young people had to find for themselves their own sense of progress, which maintained their individual dignity and feeling of personal worth." He concluded that this moral impulse to socialism derived from the psychological predicament that national oppression forced on Polish youth.[5] Dmowski stated the problem differently: the revolutionary susceptibility of Polish youth was only partly the result of Russianization; it also derived from the mentality of the positivist movement, which was related to the nihilism of the Russian youth of the 1860s by its defiantly critical opposition to society and by its uncompromising materialism.[6] The final reason Dmowski cited for the revolutionary proclivities of Polish youth in the early 1880s was the constant example of the Russian movement, especially the impact of the assassination of Alexander II. S. Koszutski and S. Czekanowski (both of whom were schoolboys in 1881) also noted in their memoirs the deep positive impression made by the events of March.[7]

Undoubtedly, Dmowski's reasoning is sound; the seeming omnipotence of the Russian movement, the desire for a kind of moral divinity among the youth, and the progressive mentality legitimized by the positivists — all help to explain the rapid growth of intelligentsia socialism at the beginning of the 1880s. Leaving aside for the moment the role economic and social changes in the Congress Kingdom played in this development, Dmowski ignored the most obvious reason for the rise of socialism — the increased politicization both of the Russian authorities in the form of Russianization and of the socialist movement in the activities in the Proletariat. Otherwise content to engage in positivist-oriented discussion groups, the intelligentsia was caught in the middle of intensified political, social, and national struggles from which they could not remain aloof. The Proletariat's newspaper was not far from correct when it noted: "The intelligentsia for a long time did not want to recognize that here too an enemy of patriotic principles [socialism] could spread, and maintained that our past protected us from such a 'plague.' But the rapid growth of that 'plague' was thrown in their faces and it became necessary to engage it."[8]

Socialist circles at Warsaw University, established by *kresy* propagandists in 1877–78, now, in 1881–82, commanded a significant student following. From the university, the circles spread to other centers of higher learning in Warsaw — the Veterinary Institute, the women's schools, and even to the gymnasia. Feliks Kon was especially successful in spreading propaganda among older gymnasia students, and he personally recruited dozens of them directly into the socialist movement.[9] At Warsaw University itself, the socialist circles joined together to form a conspiratorial *kasa studencka* ("student treasury"), which also served as the contact point with the Proletariat's Central Committee.[10] Although strictly patriotic circles ceased to hold the interest of the studentry, several circles did engage in both socialist and patriotic activities.[11]

The eclectic ideologies of the student radicals of this period can be seen in the case of the well-known Warsaw University activist, Mieczysław Schmidt. According to the police, Schmidt did not belong to the Proletariat, though he worked on its behalf. He participated in both socialist and patriotic protests, sang patriotic songs, wrote denunciations of Alexander III, and later led a student strike.[12] He also organized a ball to raise funds for the socialist movement. The "Schmidt Ball," as it was called by the police, was attended by several hundred socialist sympathizers, including the leaders of the progressive literary community, and greatly improved the status of socialism among the Warsaw intelligentsia.[13]

Perhaps a more typical sketch of Proletariat influence in the schools can be drawn from the diary and letters found on Aleksander Łopaczyński at the time of his arrest. Łopaczyński was a member of a self-education circle at the Institute of Agronomy and Forestry at Puławy near Lublin. The circle maintained a secret library, which contained brochures of the Proletariat, as well as the writings of Limanowski and Lassalle, examples of positivist literature, including John Stuart Mill, and some patriotic literature. The circle met regularly to discuss the relative merits of socialism, patriotism, and positivism. It collected funds for "student self-help," and it maintained close ties to similar circles in Warsaw. In the fall of 1882, Edmund Płoski came to Puławy to recruit Łopaczyński's and other student circles into the Proletariat movement. Although Płoski denied that his purpose in these meetings was anything more than "scientific," Łopaczyński reported that Płoski in fact had attempted to collect money for the Red Cross, had spoken enthusiastically about the growing Warsaw organization, and had revealed plans to publish a party organ. Although Płoski found no recruits in Puławy, he did manage to secure a number of allies for the Proletariat's program.[14]

The party founded several socialist circles at Warsaw University and at other centers of higher learning in the Congress Kingdom and attempted to infiltrate the existing positivist and patriotic circles. It also sought to organize socialist circles in the army, in the bureaucracy, and in schools all over the empire.[15] Although far from having won over the intelligentsia to socialism, the Proletariat at least made it impossible for them to ignore the new doctrine and at best succeeded in legitimizing its presence among progressive intelligentsia circles.

The growth of socialism in university circles was only one aspect of the heated ideological atmosphere in which the Polish intelligentsia attempted to find its proper role in Poland's future. Bitter and impassioned polemics came from all quarters, and ideological alliances developed between the most unlikely partners. When, for instance, the loyalist editor of *Kraj*, Włodzimierz Spasowicz, attacked the national traditions of Poland in a Warsaw speech, socialist students applauded wildly. Bolesław Prus, the most celebrated literary figure in Warsaw and a well-known progressive, wrote stinging criticisms of the political immaturity of the socialists. Mendelson, Dłuski, and several young socialist students confronted Prus on the streets of Warsaw, and in the ensuing argument one smacked Prus across the face. At a large meeting at the university called to discuss the affair, a brawl almost erupted between the rival camps.[16]

The chasm between the older generation of national-patriots and democrats on the one hand and the young socialists on the other was even wider than that between positivists and socialists. Władysław Wścieklica derided socialism as "laughable" and its "foreign" propagators as "enemies of the people."[17] Dłuski and Piekarski, incensed by Wścieklica's article, attacked him for "not having the slightest idea about the history of the workers' movement and of our economic relations. And of the position of our working class, he has to this day not heard a thing."[18] The patriot and old 1863–64 radical A. Giller wrote to M. Darowski of the possible spread of socialism in the Congress Kingdom: "Socialism as a revolutionary phenomenon has had great fortune in Germany and Muscovy, but I would not like to see it spread to Poland. . . . Its slogan, which is class hatred, could only be injurious. . . . Defend our artisans against socialism."[19] At the opposite end of the political spectrum from the socialists, the conservative triloyalists exerted very little influence on the Congress Kingdom's urban intelligentsia. They discarded socialism as anti-Catholic and therefore incapable of attracting followers in Poland. Under the leadership of the young Wielopolski, these conservatives, based mainly in St. Petersburg, continued to present obsequious, anticonstitutionalist petitions of loyalty to the tsar.[20]

The Apukhtin Affair

Despite the hopes of conservatives and positivists for the peaceful development of Polish society, political struggle spread just as quickly in the Congress Kingdom in 1882–83 as did the "plague" of socialism. Polish and Russian student circles at the Agronomy Institute in Puławy were especially active in resisting efforts at Russianization. The authorities responded with constant police surveillance and the imposition of new school regulations (precursors of the all-Russian University Statutes of 1884).[21] When the school curator Apukhtin arrived in Puławy in March 1883 to oversee the carrying out of the new regulations and the destruction of the "self-education" circles (for which, in part, they were designed), the Puławy students protested, closing down the institute and causing minor violence.[22] In this, the first expression of intelligentsia resistance to the Russian authorities since 1863–64, the result was predictable: dozens of students were arrested and others were expelled from the institute. Some irate Puławy demonstrators managed to avoid detection and made their way to Warsaw.[23]

Warsaw students, similarly seething with anger over the new regulations, now demonstrated in support of their Puławy counterparts. During the second week of April 1883, students shouted down professors in the lectures, forcing the suspension of classes. Large, boisterous meetings were held in university halls, occupied by the students in defiance of the rector.[24] When the university authorities finally threatened the students with military action, the young activists vacated the university grounds and took their demonstration to the streets. After the arrest (on 17 April) of one of their compatriots, the protesting students, now numbering around 200, turned his arrest into a *cause célèbre* and demanded his immediate release.[25]

This time, the authorities moved decisively against the demonstrators, whose numbers were growing at an alarming pace. For the first time in twenty years, regular army soldiers occupied the university and were used to help the gendarmes control and disperse the crowds on the streets. The authorities were convinced as well that they would have to arrest all of the circles' leaders in order to restore peace to Warsaw. It was at this juncture that the Proletariat, temporarily without a printing press, entered the fray by posting several hand-written proclamations entitled "To Everyone!" "We call for as large a gathering as possible tomorrow at 10 in the morning in front of the university building" — signed, the "Workers' Committee of the Social Revolutionary Party 'Proletariat.'"[26] Because of the force of the previous day's police crackdown and the arrest of most student leaders, the meeting was never held.

In an attempt to pacify the demonstrators, Apukhtin called small delegations of the studentry into his office. On one such delegation was the Russian student and self-proclaimed socialist and *narodovolets* Mikhail Zhukovich.[27] Without a word, Zhukovich walked up to Apukhtin and slapped him across the face, prompting his immediate seizure and arrest. The Poles, especially the youthful intelligentsia, made Zhukovich a national hero. The curator of schools, the hated symbol of the Russian domination of Poland, had been rightfully thrashed! The event excited "the whole of Warsaw, the whole country."[28] (In 1885, ten thousand mourners attended Zhukovich's funeral in Lwów.)[29] For their part in the student disturbances of 1883, almost 200 students were suspended from the university.[30] The eight most active student organizers, all socialists or socialist sympathizers, were jailed in St. Petersburg.[31] For his efforts on behalf of "the closer union of the *Privislanskii krai* with the other parts of the empire," Apukhtin received a medal, the Imperial Order of Alexander Nevskii.[32] The socialists participated in the Apukhtin affair not as initiators of a political action but as compatriots in the general escalation of political resentment among the studentry. Schmidt reported that at the height of the disturbances he and Dulęba assembled a bomb, which they intended to send to Apukhtin.[33] The events of April awakened the intelligentsia of Warsaw and the Congress Kingdom from a long slumber of political inertia.

Solidarność: The Polish Economists

The Proletariat's willingness to take part in the political struggle of the intelligentsia against the government was clearly demonstrated by these student disturbances of March and April 1883. The Apukhtin affair was, however, the party's only opportunity to do so during its four-year history. The Proletariat's further political activities involving the educated classes were confined instead to intra-intelligentsia battles, both within the party's own ranks and with the still active positivist movement.

The first signs of internecine struggle within the Proletariat itself erupted during the spring and summer of 1883 precisely over the issue of the party's participation in the political struggle against tsarism. Led by Kazimierz Puchewicz, the son of a Warsaw professor, a small anti-political segment of the party known as Solidarność ("Solidarity") published its own program on 15 April 1883.[34] This program more emphatically underlined the necessity of careful preparatory propaganda among the workers, but it did not depart radically from that of the Proletariat. Like the Proletariat's program, it called for "the complete emancipation of the working class from economic, social, political, and moral oppression." Factories and means of production would, in the end, become the workers' property under collective organization.[35] A 12 March 1883 Solidarność pamphlet, printed at the conclusion of a successful workers' action led by the Proletariat, more distinctly delineated the conflict between Puchewicz's Solidarność and Waryński's Proletariat. In this pamphlet Solidarność did not mention the words *revolution, Poles,* or *Polish.* Instead of calling for an acceleration of the struggle against the government, it pointed to the need for a more comprehensive organization of the workers in industrial factories to bargain for higher wages, health insurance, and better working conditions. Violence was dismissed as counterproductive. The peaceful strike for everyday workers' demands, stated Solidarność, was the only legitimate weapon of the socialist struggle.[36]

Although it attracted barely a handful of followers, Solidarność split with the Proletariat on a fundamental issue, one that had afflicted the Polish movement from its inception — the proper form of action on behalf of the revolution. Puchewicz, a learned devotee of Marx's *Das Kapital,* maintained that the revolution would occur as an inevitable product of the development of capitalism. For the present, the socialists should confine themselves to building a purely workers' organization based on improving the conditions of Polish labor. Puchewicz himself told the police that the reason he left the Proletariat was the party's intention to form a mass movement and to employ terror, both of which he thoroughly disapproved.[37] Płoski, in his confession to the authorities, asserted that at the core of the dispute was the design of the movement rather than the problem of terrorism. Puchewicz advocated a decentralized party structure, said Płoski, more in line "with the innate disinclination of Poles toward centralization."[38]

On the other hand, both Feliks Kon, a member of Solidarność, and the historian R. Arskii later claimed that it was the use of terrorism that prompted the secession of Puchewicz. Z. Heryng offered a personality-oriented explanation: "Waryński and Puchewicz were like fire and water, the antithesis of revolutionary explosiveness and cold circumspection. Both aspired to the same goals, but with very different means."[39] The police also repeatedly emphasized the "intellectual" nature of Solidarność, mindful that its members were almost exclusively students.[40] Żanna Kormanowa, the first historian of Solidarność, centered her analysis of the movement's first splinter group on what she considered to be the more rigorous Marxism of Puchewicz. He was, she wrote, the first Polish social democrat and therefore was able to see that terrorism was nothing more than a heroic mask for the weakness of the movement.[41]

The problem of terrorism was, however, only a symptom of the larger issue of political struggle both against the tsarist government and for the allegiance of Polish workers. In their private discussions, Waryński consistently argued with Puchewicz over the issue of the role of the party in bringing about revolution. "The activities of the party should be in public view," insisted Waryński, in order that the party have "influence on the future revolutionary government." The workers would be won over to the Proletariat only if the party displayed its willingness to confront the government. If the party was afraid to protect itself by the use of any means at hand (including terrorism), then how could it expect the workers to show the courage to revolt?[42] The issue was not then terorrism or the organization's design, nor was it even simply differences in the interpretation of the political struggle. The issue, one that plagues every socialist movement, centered on the concept of the revolution and the role of the party in that revolution.

In September 1883, Puchewicz was arrested, and with his arrest Solidarność fell apart.[43] Its surviving members rejoined the ranks of the Proletariat. The essence of Puchewicz's protest — determinism on the matter of revolution and economism in the workers' struggle — remained alive in the second major battle within the intelligentsia ranks of the Proletariat; this time the opponents of Waryński's view of revolution were even more formidable.

The Legal Marxists and the Vilna Conference

During the winter of 1882–83, when the differences between Puchewicz and Waryński first emerged, another group of Warsaw socialists challenged the Proletariat's concepts of party, revolution, and political action. This group, known as the Krusińszczycy (also discussed in Chapter 3), was led by Stanisław Krusiński, a Marxist dialectician and aesthetician very popular among university students for his wise counsel during the Apukhtin disturbances.[44] The other Marxist intellectuals at the pinnacle of this group were Ludwik Krzywicki, Poland's most prominent nineteenth-century sociologist, and Bronisław Białobłocki, an accomplished literary critic.[45] Under the leadership of this trio, the Poles succeeded in finishing the translation of the first volume of *Das Kapital* in 1884, a project that Diksztajn had begun in 1877–78.[46] Krusiński and his collaborators, though closely tied to the Proletariat, rejected, as did Puchewicz, the political struggle against tsarism. For them, as for the Russians, the question of politics was posed in dichotomous terms — "knowledge or action" and "consciousness or spontaneity."[47] In both cases, they opted for the former.

Like Engels in his letters on the Polish question, the Krusińszczycy argued that socialism was an impossibility within the present autocratic structure and that the intellectuals should therefore concentrate their efforts on propagating Marxism among the intelligentsia and on more thoroughly applying its tenets to Polish conditions. An underground and illegal struggle could only jeopardize both of these efforts. Krusiński, like Puchewicz, respected Waryński's analysis of the national question and indeed sacrificed a portion of his own support, including that of A. Zakrzewski, Z. Straszewicz, and M. Brzeziński, because of this stand.[48] Krusiński's paramount concern was for Marxist scholarship; his ties to the working class were minimal. Krusiński even disagreed with Puchewicz's advocacy of limited "economic" struggle. According to Krusiński and his confederates, the insufficient development of capitalism and workers' consciousness in the Congress Kingdom precluded any revolutionary organization, whether politically or economically based.[49]

Because of Krusiński's valuable intellectual contributions to the Proletariat's cause in the form of articles in the positivist press and propaganda at the university, the leadership of the Proletariat worked smoothly with his group throughout 1882. The schism between them, as in the case of the secession of Solidarność, was provoked by a symbolic issue, this time by the Proletariat's desire to coordinate its activities with those of the Russian movement. As we know from the manifesto "To Our Russian Comrades," published in Geneva with Waryński's approval, the Poles had already expressed their interest in an all-empire Polish socialist party that would cooperate, perhaps even merge, with the Russians. Because of the opposition of Krusiński and Puchewicz, this plank was left out of the Proletariat's program of fall 1882 and was put off to a meeting of Polish socialists to be held in Vilna in January 1883. By the time of the Vilna meeting, Puchewicz had already seceded from the party in spirit and did not attend. Therefore, Waryński and Krusiński as well as Dębski and Płoski represented

Warsaw. From Moscow came L. Janowicz, and from St. Petersburg, representing Ognisko, came Tadeusz Rechniewski and Stanisław Kunicki. The Vilna socialists were represented by L. Rymkiewicz, the Kiev group probably by Zofia Dziankowska, the widow of the 1879 socialist Ludwik Dziankowski.[50]

Unfortunately, no complete text of the Vilna proceedings is available to the historian.[51] In the memoirs of the surviving Vilna conferees themselves, there are only scattered and contradictory accounts of the discussions. The newspaper *Przedświt,* which carried a report on the conference, skewed its presentation because at this point its editors were lobbying for a united Polish party of all three partitions and opposed cooperation with the Russians. Leon Wasilewski, who interviewed several of the surviving participants, concluded — probably correctly — that several meaningless resolutions were discussed. He further suggested that the reason the resolutions were meaningless was that the movement itself had lost its impetus and was in decline.[52] However, the case was quite the opposite. The Proletariat, with Waryński at its head, was at the pinnacle of its prestige and power, and the Vilna meeting served simply as a confirmation of the party's (and Waryński's) attitudes toward revolutionary activities in the Russian Empire. All socialist Poles throughout the empire should work together under the aegis of the Proletariat, and, in turn, the Proletariat should closely cooperate, under certain circumstances even merge, with the Russian party Narodnaia Volia.

At Vilna, the Proletariat also formally elected a Central Committee (which consisted of Waryński, Rechniewski, Kunicki, Dębski, Dulęba, Jentysówna, and Płoski) in order to parallel Narodnaia Volia's party structure, headed up as well by an Executive Committee of intelligentsia and a Workers' Committee. This new committee merely confirmed Waryński's already functional leadership of the Polish party and placed his Warsaw organization at the head of an all-empire Polish socialist movement:

> Should we create separate Polish-Lithuanian and Polish-Belorussian revolutionary parties? [the conferees asked] Unanimously: No. Instead, the Polish, Lithuanian, and Belorussian groups should enter the ranks of a unified Party, active within the borders of a Russian state. . . . Their activities should be two-pronged: on the one hand social revolutionary propaganda and agitation, and on the other, struggle with the Russian government at its very center.[53]

The Vilna meeting therefore affirmed the existing leadership of the Proletariat among Polish socialists in the empire. Now the task was to unify with Narodnaia Volia. "If our talks with it [the Executive Committee of Narodnaia Volia] show that it has the same views as we on revolution, then we will deliver to it the exclusive direction of the political aspect of revolution." During this transferral of leadership, a detailed document would have to be drawn up strictly defining the relationship between the central (Russian) and local (Polish) groups. If the Executive Committee did not fulfill the conditions stipulated by the Proletariat, then "we would relate to it as to a foreign group." The final conference protocol clearly stated that only insofar as Narodnaia Volia would be useful to the Poles could meaningful agreement be reached.[54] On the matters of centralism, terrorism, and internationalism, Waryński's views were similarly upheld in the protocol. The extent to which terrorism and centralization would influence the movement depended on the autocracy's delimitation of the field of battle. On the question of internationalism, the conferees resolved that a revolution could come about only with the "unanimous uprising of the proletariat of the whole world, or at least of the whole of Europe."[55]

At Vilna, Krusiński argued in vain against the Proletariat's concepts of party and revolution, "heatedly debating with the defender of the latter — Waryński." "During these polemics," continued Wasilewski, "it became clear that it would be very difficult for the Krusińszczycy to unite with the Proletariat."[56] In fact, after the Vilna conference, Krusiński abstained from any further political activism and devoted himself exclusively to journalism and scholarship. The Legal Marxists remained in contact and even in sympathy with the Proletariat, though they repeatedly maintained that the party had chosen a false path. *Przedświt* tried to underestimate the differences between the Proletariat and the Krusińszczycy manifested at Vilna and reported that each position "complemented the other."[57] Although Waryński and Krusiński were intransigent ideological opponents, in some ways *Przedświt* was not far from correct. Krusiński and his circle provided an invaluable service to the cause of Polish Marxism by perfecting its ideological content.[58] More importantly in the 1880s, the Krusiński group, by engaging the positivists in a public debate, made socialism (and therefore also the Proletariat) intellectually respectable in progressive public opinion and exposed all levels of the Polish intelligentsia to Marxist theory.

Among the conservative, liberal, patriotic, and socialist camps of the intelligentsia in the early 1880s, the positivist liberal camp reigned supreme. Their supremacy was challenged, however, by the socialists — legally by the Krusińszczycy and illegally by the Proletariat. The Proletariat itself expended little energy in the public campaign against the positivists. Its concern was not the intelligentsia, but the group that according to doctrine would make the socialist revolution — the working class of the Congress Kingdom.

The Buturlin Resistance

On 8 February 1883, shortly after the Vilna meeting of Polish socialists and therefore after the split between Waryński and the splinter groups of Puchewicz and Krusiński, the Warsaw police chief, Nikolai Buturlin, sent a copy of an order to the Warsaw prosecutor, including the following directive:

> 7. On the basis of the resolution in the minutes of the Medical-Police Committee of 4 (16) July 1864, female help in all public and drinking establishments, and all female laborers working at all factories, industrial, and other institutions, should be subjected to medical examination. . . . [Directors of establishments not specifically exempted from this rule] are to send their female help or workers twice a month to the Committee of the Chancellory for medical examination.[59]

This rule, originally conceived during an epidemic of venereal disease during the chaos of the 1863–64 uprising, was announced to the public on 10 February in the *Warsaw Police Gazette,* provoking an uproar of indignation among the Warsaw working-class population. The women workers, already very poorly paid, overworked, and maltreated by factory employers, refused to submit to the new directive, invoked since 1864–65 only for prostitutes.[60]

The Proletariat's leadership — Waryński and Dębski — met with Solidarność's Puchewicz at his home to discuss the directive. Waryński, sensing the agitational value of the issue and, like most of the socialist community, genuinely indignant about its implications, composed a proclamation urging resistance to Buturlin's order.[61] Over the protests of Puchewicz, who objected to the politicization of the issue, the proclamation was posted on 13 February "at various points in Warsaw, on the gates of the entryways of factories, in courtyards, and on the streets."[62] Signed by the "Workers' Committee of the Social Revolutionary Party 'Proletariat,'" it called Buturlin's order an "outrage, such as which the world has not heard." It emphasized that the government was trying to class women workers as prostitutes: "Workers! Don't allow this! Don't withdraw. . . . Fight back. . . . Death is better than disgrace! " The proclamation ended, "If they want a fight — they shall have it."[63]

The police reported that the Warsaw working class reacted for the most part positively to the socialists' proclamation.[64] One woman worker caustically told the authorities that when the leaflet was distributed at the predominantly female Union Tobacco factory, her fellow workers became "indignant" with the police order, "as if, up to this time, nothing had been demanded of them."[65] Not without a touch of bravado, the socialists passed out the proclamations in public places and spoke with workers on the streets, the predictable results of which were the immediate arrests of several street corner propagandists.[66] Still, both because of the threatening reactions of the working populace and because Buturlin initiated his directive without the concurrence of his superiors, acting Governor-General Krudener, in consultation with Minister of Interior Dmitri Tolstoi, rescinded the order on 10 February.

A month later the jubilant Workers' Committee confidently responded:

> Our last proclamation did not pass without effect. . . . The government withdrew in the face of your threatening posture, enraged and ready to defend the workers. . . .
>
> You have won therefore the first case in which you defended the mass of workers. . . . No one except for us spoke for you in this question, no one stood in your defense. We only proclaimed how you must work, and how you are oppressed and are kept in the dark.

The proclamation also warned that the Buturlin struggle was only the first in a long line of necessary confrontations with the government. In order to ensure success, "every factory, every workshop, every store, unite as one in a circle. Form treasuries, in order to help defend those persecuted comrades. . . . Of our help and sympathy you can be sure."[67]

The timely debut of the Proletariat in the Buturlin affair began its history as a working-class party. The withdrawal of Buturlin's order gave the socialists an easy victory. Confident of the success of his formula for political agitation, Waryński proceeded to mock openly the cowardice of the economist Puchewicz and to provoke the final split with the legalist Krusiński. The Proletariat became known through its participation in the Buturlin affair not only among the working class of Warsaw but also in Galicia and the Grand Duchy of Poznań. The *Gazeta Narodowa* (National Gazette) from Lwów wrote that these leaflets of resistance were "printed by some social revolutionary committee of which no one had heard up to this time in Warsaw."[68]

The police only confirmed the Proletariat's image of itself as the organizer of workers' actions; most of the workers involved in this movement, they wrote, "are only tools in the hands of their more enlightened comrades."[69] The extent to which labor's resistance to the Buturlin order was initiated by the Proletariat's proclamation and street corner agitation is impossible to estimate. It is clear that the workers' indignation provoked the Proletariat's agitation and that the resulting combination proved strong enough to force the government's withdrawal of its order. That the workers were far from "the tools" of the Proletariat, however, became evident in the Żyrardów strike of April 1883.

The Żyrardów Strike

The linen-manufacturing Żyrardów Works was one of the largest and most modern factory complexes in the Congress Kingdom. Owned by two Austrians, Dietrich and Hille, and employing over 8,000 workers, the plant maintained comparatively advanced health, education, and insurance programs for its employees. In virtually every area of labor concern, the workers of Żyrardów were significantly better off than their fellow textile workers in the Piotrków industrial towns of Łódź, Zgierz, and Tomaszów.[70] But in 1882–83, owing to an industrywide depression in textiles, the Żyrardów management was forced to lay off numerous workers and to lower the wages of many others. The workers countered by calling for a strike.

The strike began on 23 April 1883, when, after two weeks of working at the lower wage level, about 180 women spinners ignored the threats of the factoryowners and walked off their jobs. On the following day, other sections of the factory were forced to close down or curtail production because of the spinners' action. The weavers also joined the walkout, afraid that they too would be laid off. The strike soon spread to other sections of the factory as the rebelling workers harassed and even violently confronted those Żyrardów laborers who continued to go to work. By Wednesday 24 April, the strike included about 400 workers.[71]

As soon as the spinners walked off the job, the factory management notified the local police who, unable to control the situation, turned to Warsaw for help. After an exchange of telegrams between the Żyrardów and Warsaw authorities, the governor of Warsaw, General

Medem, sent four companies of soldiers and a detachment of Cossacks to quell the disturbances and force the workers to return to the factory. Medem himself arrived on the scene to exert his personal influence to end the strike. When a crowd of workers pressed toward the administration buildings demanding the release of several arrested comrades, the soldiers opened fire, leaving three young workers dead and several wounded.[72]

On the following day, 26 April, the entire factory village of Żyrardów was aroused by the events. One of those fatally wounded was a fifteen-year-old boy. The workers gathered at the factory gates, throwing rocks and breaking windows in the administration quarters. Some workers used the opportunity of the disturbances to terrorize local Jewish shopkeepers. A full-scale rebellion threatened the town. "The uprising has spread to all parts of the factory today," wrote the police. When Medem attempted to speak to the crowds, he was shouted down by the chant, "the tsar forbids shooting at the people." "In Warsaw during the Jewish pogroms, no one shot down the people, but in Żyrardów, when we don't want to work for Germans — they kill our brothers and children."[73] Medem then moved decisively to end the disturbances; a general curfew order was issued (27 April), announcing that anyone found meeting in the streets or hindering workers on the way to the factory "would be immediately arrested and is subject to harsh penalties."[74] Dietrich and Hille, anxious as well to end the strike and get the workers back into the factory, posted on the same day a handwritten notice in which they promised the resumption of the spinners' original pay and a better system of bonuses.[75] Those workers who had been involved in the strike could return without fines, and concessions were made to the weavers. "Tomorrow morning," wrote the factoryowners, "the usual sign of the steam whistle will call [you] to work. He who wishes can return to peaceful work . . . he who is pleased to be an honest worker."[76] The following day, 28 April, less than a week after the strike had broken out, the workers, intimidated by martial law and pleased with their gains, returned to the factory.

Although socialist literature was found on one striking worker and although one Proletariat member (Teodor Łąkowski) was arrested along with the thirty to forty other strike leaders, it is clear that the Proletariat played no role either in the instigation or in the course of the strike.[77] The issue of wages started the disturbance: national enmity, especially against the Cossacks, fed its flames. Throughout 1883 Cossacks remained in Żyrardów, contributing to the rising tensions, which in turn led to a smaller Żyrardów strike in 1884.[78]

The Żyrardów disturbances did not pass unnoticed by the Proletariat. During the Buturlin resistance, the party had served as the partial initiator of a working-class action. In the Żyrardów strike, the working class taught the Proletariat a lesson in strike tactics and especially in the use of factory violence. In an article in the October 1883 issue of *Proletariat* entitled "Work Stoppage and Terror," the party incorporated the positive role of violence into its concept of working-class agitation: "If peaceful work stoppage does not accomplish the goal, then accompanying it must be the punishment of those who are the cause for the respective incidents and the spread of poverty and oppression." The article emphasized that the tactic of work stoppage alone, as in the early days of the Żyrardów strike, would only call forth the soldiers of the doubleheaded eagle and therefore had to be accompanied by violent resistance as well as by individual terrorist acts against the factory management.[79] From the radicalization of the entire factory town of Żyrardów, the Proletariat learned at first hand the positive effects of strikes on the growth of workers' resistance.[80]

In 1883–84 the major issue for Polish labor was increasing unemployment due to the empire-wide depression, especially harsh in textiles, but affecting all branches of industry. In June 1883, when Lilpop and Rau in Warsaw laid off 350 workers and reduced the pay of all the rest, a Workers' Committee functionary, Jan Ptaszyński, led a strike on the Żyrardów model of some two hundred workers. Ptaszyński and several other strike leaders were immediately arrested, but several concessions from the management placated most of the factory's laborers. Finally, the police moved in, halted the disturbances, and the remaining striking workers were released from their jobs.[81] Still, the tactic of strikes had become established socialist ritual and, more important, had become embedded in the steamrolling Polish labor movement as a viable weapon of economic struggle.

The Plac Zamkowy Demonstration

Throughout 1883 and 1884, the working-class population of the Congress Kingdom continued to suffer from hunger and deprivation prompted by the constant layoffs and wage cuts in large industrial enterprises. The textile industries in Łódź, Zduńska Wola, and Kalisz suffered especially heavy financial losses, precipitating untoward misery among an already poverty-stricken working population. In Łódź alone more than 2,000 workers lost their jobs in 1883. In Warsaw, the building trades industry and the metal-manufacturing enterprises were severely curtailed, leaving thousands of workers unemployed and embittered.[82]

The Warsaw police reported more and more instances of worker-management confrontation and violence. Many workers became convinced that "in Warsaw, there will be war." One working-class woman told the police that "my husband has already left work and expects and prepares for the day [of revolt] that will come in the near future."[83] Informers constantly warned the panicky Warsaw police of the "loudly proclaimed dissatisfaction" among Lilpop workers due to their lower wages.[84] The crowds of unemployed in the streets of Warsaw grew so menacing that the Warsaw city and *guberniia* police began to deport all laid-off and unemployed foreign workers, with or without passports, back to their homelands. Rural-born workers who had lost their city domiciles because they were unable to pay rent were similarly escorted back to their villages.[85]

At the outset of the depression, in the spring of 1881, the resentment of impoverished Warsaw workers had turned against Jewish shopowners, owing in part to the anti-Jewish disturbances of that year throughout the borderlands. Because of the steady propagandistic and agitational activities of the Proletariat among the working class and because of the general increase of working-class consciousness, by March 1885 the resentment aroused by lost jobs and low wages was channeled into a mass demonstration of Warsaw's unemployed in front of the governor-general's residence at the Royal Palace.

Throughout February 1885 the police were forced into almost daily street confrontations with groups of itinerant workers. Władysław Wilczyński, himself an unemployed member of the Workers' Committee, and several of his comrades planned to initiate a workers' rebellion among these roaming gangs, prompting, they hoped, a physical attack by the police, which in turn would arouse Warsaw against the government. The leadership of the arrest-ridden Proletariat was not informed of these plans, which in any case ultimately collapsed.[86] At the same time, the Serbian socialist adventurer, Ander Banković, who had engaged in varied revolutionary activities in Russia and in the south of Poland, arrived in Warsaw in search of contact with the Proletariat.[87] Banković met often with Wilczyński and convinced him that a peaceful demonstration would be of greater ultimate agitational benefit than the plan to engage in streetfighting with the police. Using Wilczyński's extensive contacts among the unemployed and at the last moment informing the party leadership (Bohuszewiczówna and Razumiejczyk) of his plans, Banković called a workers' demonstration for 2 March.[88]

The police accounts of the demonstration do not clearly establish either the extent to which Proletariat members initiated the disturbances or the role they played in them. One report unambiguously accused the Proletariat of "leading the workers to a mass demonstration . . . in order to use it for their own purposes."[89] However, the most extensive police accounts emphasized that the demonstration was a spontaneous and even justified (though clearly illegal) protest against the paucity of work in Warsaw. In this latter version of the events of 2 March, the socialists successfully used the demonstration to spread their ideas among the already aroused, susceptible, and semiliterate masses. The source of the dissatisfaction, the police concluded, was the fact that "in the last months many factories in Warsaw either significantly limited their activities or completely closed down."[90]

The unemployed workers had already discussed among themselves various plans to resolve their desperate situation and had concluded that they would demand from the governor "some kind of government work." This proposal was set aside with the hope that in the spring, jobs would open on a new Warsaw sewer project. On 2 March throngs of workers reported to the Koszykowa Market, headquarters of the sewer works, only to find that the work had not yet begun. Angry and frustrated, the rejected workers decided to march to the factories of New Praga where they intended to demand jobs. As the crowd moved through the streets of Warsaw, other unemployed workers joined it. "Several hundred individuals" were now gathered at Konstantynowski Square.[91] Here the workers decided to ask the government for employment. Banković addressed the crowd and convinced them that "their position was so deplorable that the only escape from it was to present a petition to the governor-general with a plea to help the working people, to supply them with some kind of work on the sewer system, or in the construction of the fort." Banković, the police continued, "was easily able to influence the crowds of idle and unemployed workers, the vast majority of whom were quite uneducated."[92]

The crowd then moved several blocks toward Plac Zamkowy to present their petition to the governor-general at his residence. But a cordon of police immediately halted the workers. Banković, at the head of the throng, was arrested. After a brief exchange between the unemployed workers and government officials, the army was called in and the demonstrators were arrested.[93] The official report stated that "all participants in the rally were unarmed and during arrest offered no resistance to the police." "Almost all of the 146 people arrested," the report added somewhat sympathetically, "declared that they had lived for two to seven months without work, pawning and selling their belongings to support themselves and their families." Although the authorities easily controlled the demonstration, it nevertheless caused them a great deal of consternation. The Plac Zamkowy demonstration, wrote an official, "had a completely peaceful character; but in view of such pliability of the working people . . . I fully assume that the present incident was only a trial balloon for the further use of these masses in more serious antigovernment demonstrations."[94]

The party leadership of the Proletariat, though uninvolved in the Plac Zamkowy demonstration itself, issued a proclamation dated 4 March; it appeared on the streets of Warsaw on the 6th and 7th.[95] The proclamation's attitude toward the demonstration was nippy and scolding. After describing the difficult plight of thousands of unemployed workers, the Proletariat wrote: "You turned for help to the government with a petition and what kind of answer did you receive? Did it promise you . . . that you will stop feeling hunger! Oh no! It sent out gendarmes and Cossacks against you and instead of sending you to workshops [sent you] to jail. Isn't that enough proof for you that the government openly takes the side of your capitalist oppressors." The proclamation continued by offering the familiar alternative to fruitless petitions to the government: "We call all our brother workers in the name of human rights, under one banner, under our slogan: 'freedom of the factory and land,' *we call all people of good will to the struggle against the yoke crushing humanity.*"[96]

The Proletariat's appeal to *all Poles* to struggle against the Russian government was the final step in the complete politicization of the socialist movement in the Congress Kingdom. For the Warsaw workers, however, the proclamation represented a step backward. The Central Committee disdained petitions to the government and called the workers to the party's organization; yet it did not offer a viable minimum program to which the masses of workers could respond.[97] By mid-1885, the Proletariat had visibly abandoned the attempt to develop a mass working-class party based on agitational demands. Although members of the Proletariat helped organize and took part in the demonstration, the Central Committee played no role in it and was actually critical of it, indicating that the intelligentsia leadership of the party had veered away from the workers' movement.[98] The Serb Banković, an itinerant socialist adventurer who spoke no Polish and had no following, managed to articulate the needs of Polish labor better than the party that had struggled for three years to gain its confidence.

The Proletariat and the Workers of the Piotrków Industrial Region

The workers of Łódź, Zgierz, and Tomaszów, three of the largest textile centers in the Congress Kingdom, lived under much more severe conditions than their brethren in Warsaw. The Proletariat's attempts to propagandize these workers and draw them into its organization called for agitational techniques different from those employed among the more advanced Warsaw working class. Łódź especially carried the mark of the Proletariat's first propagandistic activities among the city's working class in 1883–85.[99] By the turn of the century, Łódź became the most explosive center of industrial strife in the Russian Empire as well as in all of Eastern Europe.

In the years 1883–84, the industry of Łódź, based exclusively on textiles, suffered more drastic effects of the general European depression than did the more diversified Warsaw industrial region. One-hundred twenty-four textile factories closed down completely; twenty factories of other types halted production. As a result of this industrial catastrophe, about 20 percent of Łódź's workers were left unemployed: with families, about 20,000 out-of-work and impoverished people.[100] Periods of industrial depression generally seem to call forth natural calamities as well, and the years 1883–85 in Łódź were no exception. The miseries of the Łódź, Zgierz, and Tomaszów textile workers were compounded by harsh extremes in the weather, by numerous instances of factory fires, by explosions in the factories, as well as by spontaneous outbursts of workers' dissatisfaction in the form of the destruction of machinery.[101]

The Łódź proletariat, besides being much more destitute than the Warsaw proletariat, consisted mostly of illiterate first-generation workers not far removed from their highly religious peasant origins.[102] Yet, in contrast to peasant-workers in Russia, the Łódź workers had almost completely severed their legal and financial ties to the land. Their internal vibrancy was also hampered by the fact that very few Polish worker-intelligentsia were willing to endure the primitive conditions of the textile industries in the Piotrków region. Instead, the upper stratum of the working class in this region was heavily German, brought to the mills by the primarily German factory managements.[103] Therefore, the Polish workers of Łódź had abysmally little consciousness of social, political, and even economic issues. "The situation in the town," wrote one historian of the Łódź movement, "was not conducive to revolutionary activity. As a result of the crisis [of 1882–83], the workers were quite despondent and apathetic."[104]

Polish socialists began propagandizing among Łódź workers as early as 1878, generally with very limited success.[105] During the period of the Gmina (1880–81), virtually no socialist activities were carried on outside the Warsaw industrial region. This situation changed rapidly with the emergence of the Proletariat; the party's leadership immediately sent experienced working-class agitators to Łódź and Zgierz — among them H. Gostkiewicz, who arrived in Łódź in early 1883 with a mandate to establish the Łódź branch of the Workers' Committee.[106] Gostkiewicz went to work himself in the textile mills, where he gradually built a small following of socialist workers. After organizing several workers' circles, he then moved on to similar activities in Białystok and was replaced by Stanisław Pacanowski as the contact between Warsaw and the growing Łódź Proletariat.[107]

Pacanowski later testified that under orders from Dębski, he arrived in the Piotrków region in December 1883 with "200 copies of *Proletariat* and 300 proclamations for distribution in Łódź and Zgierz."[108] With the assistance of the weaver Franciszek Cobel and the table-maker Wojciech Sławiński, the Proletariat under Pacanowski's leadership managed to organize thirty small workers' circles in Łódź, Zgierz, and Tomaszów, including between 150 and 200 workers.[109] Even when the Warsaw Central Committee was crippled by the arrest of Kunicki and his associates in the winter of 1883–84, the Łódź-Zgierz-Tomaszów organizations continued to expand under the independent leadership of Cobel and Sławiński.[110] The workers' circles, primarily propagandistic in nature, were tied together by the Łódź Workers' Committee, which in late 1884 and the beginning of 1885 acted autonomously and even had its own printing operations.[111]

The introduction of socialism to the Piotrków industrial region can be traced to the frenetic activities of the Proletariat's agents; the fact that it prospered and spread with such alacrity can be attributed to the unique methods the Łódź socialists employed to recruit often illiterate and apolitical workers to the socialist cause.[112] Cobel and Sławiński were particularly adept at combining the religious devotion of the Polish worker with the basic tenets of Proletariat theory, in the process propagating a form of elemental Catholic socialism. It was no accident, Pacanowski testified to the police, that the workers of Łódź and Zgierz "believed in the Central Committee as the Gospel."[113] At a ceremony outside of Zgierz attended by over one hundred workers (May 1885), the socialist Nowacki erected a "high oak cross . . . with an iron crucifix to commemorate the existence and social revolutionary activities of socialist circles in Zgierz."[114]

The social revolutionary question, Sławiński explained to the workers, "began with the birth of Christ. . . . The seeds planted by the first socialist, Christ, multiplied in all parts of the earth and will never die." The government and the church hierarchy conceal the socialist science, the true Christianity, from the people. "That, in reality, forces us now to work for freeloaders, but Christ said that in order that all work together, they should govern themselves and have no dominating ruler."[115] "We don't violate holy laws and scriptures, but live up to them," stated the Proletariat pamphlet *In the Name of Faith and Freedom.* "God himself blesses our undertakings — for the cause, we suffer in his name. Christ, the savior, dying on the cross, endured enormous torment; if we share this torment among thousands — we can bear it." The pamphlet, found on several Tomaszów workers in 1885, concluded with the promise that the Lord would light the heavens with the advent of socialism.[116]

The mixture of hunger, Catholicism, and socialism brought hundreds of Łódź, Zgierz, and Tomaszów workers into the Proletariat movement, providing the groundwork for the explosive labor disturbances of the 1890s. A letter from the imprisoned Zgierz socialist Józef Nowacki to the prosecutor exposes the texture of this Catholic socialism and demonstrates the hardships faced by workers involved in the socialist movement:

A Petition to Your Honor from Your Humble Servant

Prosecutor, please Your Honor, take pity for a moment on a miserable person and hear my Plea. I have already been in jail fourteen months in Łódź, I have been here six months and eleven days only on bread and water. Please, Your Honor that is too harsh a sentence for a living person, may God protect me . . . now I am to be transferred to Warsaw and again imprisoned and I already am out of my mind, Please, Your Honor as there is a one Lord God and Mother of God, know Your Honor that during this time two children of mine died, if all of them I don't know right now, I can no longer hold out. My Merciful God, please your Honor take pity . . . on my fate . . . I beg God and the Mother of God day and night with tears that the highest almighty God full of Grace will grant my Plea. Please, Your Honor, in the name of Christ, take pity on me and hear my plea, for I can go on no longer [*ja już nie mogę*]. Change this harsh sentence, Your Honor, be my savior, Dear God. . . . Your humble servant, Please.[117]

Terrorism in the Piotrków Region

In addition to incorporating the religiosity of the Polish textile worker into its agitational program, the Łódź Workers' Committee successfully played upon the seething hatred of the Polish workers of the Piotrków region for their German foremen and factoryowners. They threatened the most obtusely exploitative bosses and upheld in their statutes, like those of the Warsaw committee, that "in some instances terror is the only means of struggle against political authority, capitalists, and spies."[118] In November 1883 the Zgierz Proletariat singled out the foreman Karol Baume for his "inhuman treatment of workers," for "exploiting workers," and for cheating them of their wages. The handwritten note to Baume ended threateningly, "We summon the accused to abolish the above points immediately."[119] The Łódź Workers' Committee forwarded a series of demands to Ignacy Poznański, the owner of the city's largest textile factory. This notice promised retaliation if workers continued to suffer physical assaults by the management and if socialist workers continued to lose their jobs. The committee warned Poznański: "If your present bearing toward the workers does not change, you will be harshly punished."[120] The Zgierz factoryowner Gustaf Walman was similarly threatened with "harsh punishment" if he persisted in the physical and economic abuse of his workers.[121]

The socialists complemented this fundamentally agitational technique of sending warning notes to factory managements with equally popular assassination attempts on the lives of working-class police informers. The slogan, "For traitors and oppressors we are preparing the dagger!" appeared often in the history of the Proletariat.[122] The Łódź and Zgierz socialists took the slogan quite literally and, with the blessings of the Warsaw organization, twice wounded a police informant, Józef Śremski, and killed another suspected informant, the leader of the Zgierz Proletariat, Franciszek Helszer. Śremski, a textile worker in Zgierz and a member of the local Proletariat organization, aroused the animosity of his comrades when he betrayed three socialists to the police in October 1883. The actual order to kill Śremski was issued by the Central Committee in Warsaw; the assassination was entrusted to the Zgierz Workers' Committee and delegated to the worker Józef Schmaus. On 14 October Schmaus attacked and wounded Śremski with a knife, but before he could complete the murder, he was apprehended by the police.[123]

The first act of party terrorism was applauded for the most part by the workers of Zgierz.[124] Śremski lived in constant fear for his life and was threatened daily by workers both in the factory and at his home. The harassed informant left Zgierz several times, but each time was forced to return because of a lack of funds. Śremski's wife wrote to him in Odessa that he was a marked man, warning him against returning to Zgierz.[125] With the prompting of S. Pacanowski in Łódź and the backing of the Zgierz workers, the Workers' Committee again decided to try to kill Śremski. After receiving approval from Warsaw, the Zgierz committee assigned the second assassination attempt to two young weavers, twenty-year-old Stanisław Bugajski and twenty-four-year-old Kazimierz Tomaszewski.[126] On 26 March 1884, Bugajski recalled in his deposition to the police, "I was arrested in Zgierz for the attempt on the provocateur Śremski. I attacked Śremski on the street and inflicted a wound with a dagger, but, unfortunately, I [only] slightly wounded him."[127]

The atavistic clamor among Zgierz workers for the assassination of Śremski did not cease with this second failure and the resulting arrests. Plans for a third attempt were drawn up under the leadership of Pacanowski in Łódź, Franciszek Helszer in Zgierz, and Kunicki in Warsaw. However, Helszer hesitated. This fateful hesitation, combined with the mysterious arrests of several Zgierz socialist workers, aroused suspicions among the Łódź and Zgierz committees that Helszer himself was a provocateur. Pacanowski and the Zgierz committee reported their doubts to Warsaw, and Kunicki hastily wrote a conclusion to the question on 28 May 1884: "(1) Franciszek Helszer is sentenced to death, (2) the immediate carrying out of the sentence is entrusted to the Workers' Committee of Zgierz."[128]

Apparently, Kunicki had additional motives for condemning Helszer to death.[129] The Warsaw organization had been severely crippled by police surveillance and arrests, and at the same time, the Łódź, Zgierz, and Tomaszów organizations were enjoying a period of rapid expansion. As Pacanowski explained to the police: "He [Kunicki] viewed Łódź, numbering around 50,000 workers, as a center in which all the activities of the party should be concentrated. He intended to move there shortly, form the center for the leadership, and from there issue proclamations and instructions; thus, he tried to sow fear among traitors and at the same time demonstrate the power of the party."[130] These two motives in addition to suspicions about Helszer prompted Kunicki to hand to Pacanowski Helszer's death sentence "together with a dagger, a revolver, and opium, which was to make the killing easier."[131]

Late in the evening of 10 June 1884 one of the conspirators, Teofil

Bloch, escorted the unknowing Helszer to the Zgierz public gardens.[132] Bloch excused himself for a minute to buy cigarettes at a nearby sidewalk store and left Helszer on a park bench. Jan Pietrusiński, a nineteen-year-old weaver, jumped from his appointed hiding place, shot Helszer, and fatally wounded him. The Proletariat's first successful assassination attempt was unanimously cheered by workers' circles in Łódź and Zgierz.[133] Kunicki and Dębski, at that time the leaders of the Warsaw Central Committee, decided to exploit the uproar of approval and issued a two-part proclamation: the first part, a reproduction of the original death sentence, the second, a chilling justification of the deed. "We had a choice, either lose numerous comrades, or render Helszer harmless. We decided on the latter, and Helszer suffered a death that every traitor should and must suffer. . . . Therefore let everyone remember that for those who for any motive will betray us . . . unconditionally awaits death."[134]

The activities of the Proletariat in the Piotrków industrial region were considerably more successful, both in the short and long run, than those among the workers in the Warsaw region. In Łódź, Zgierz, Tomaszów, and other textile centers, the Proletariat created a socialist-oriented workers' movement by merging its goals and actions with those of the local working class. Catholic socialism; threats against factoryowners, managers, and foremen; and the intimidation and even assassination of party unfaithfuls reproduced on a party scale the primitive, violent, hungry, and vengeful existence of the individual Polish textile worker. Although the distance from the central police authorities is often cited as a reason for the success of the Łódź, Zgierz, and Tomaszów organizations, the distance as well from the central *party* organs abetted the growth of the movement in this region. Unperturbed by the "national question" and uninterested in the theoretical arguments about politics, agitation, terrorism, or other typically intelligentsia disputes, the worker-dominated Łódź Proletariat merged its own frustrations and hopes with those of the masses of workers. In doing so it built the foundation for a powerful and dynamic working-class movement closely attuned to the everyday grievances of its participants.

In Warsaw, on the other hand, though considerable gains were made in the factories under the early Proletariat leadership of Waryński and Dulęba, two movements emerged, sometimes intersecting, but for the most part remaining distinct: the labor movement and the party. Quite simply, the Proletariat was unable to harness to its own organization the quickly developing class consciousness of the Warsaw proletariat.

The Buturlin resistance, the Żyrardów strike, and the demonstration at Plac Zamkowy manifested the growing self-awareness of Polish labor in the Warsaw region. In each case, the Proletariat — its intelligentsia leadership and several hundred working-class members — played only peripheral roles in the disturbances. That the Proletariat leaders chided the workers for petitioning the government in the Plac Zamkowy case attests to the growing vanguard mentality of the Central Committee. In fact, the vanguard of the workers' movement was not the Proletariat, but rather the broadly based dissatisfaction and consciousness of dissatisfaction among the urban work force as a whole. The party unquestionably contributed to the advance of this consciousness in the years 1882–86 but in the end could not control it.

VIII

The Proletariat and the Russians

The entire history of the Polish socialist movement, from the initial period of the propagandistic circles in 1877–78 up to the present day, has been dominated (sometimes concurrently and sometimes alternatively) by two overarching factors. The first and most significant is social and economic change in the Polish lands. The second is the Polish movement's relationship to Russian socialism, both in its anti-tsarist and in its Soviet configurations. Between 1882 and 1886, the Russian movement represented by Narodnaia Volia and the Polish movement by the Proletariat, interacted on the basis of physical parity. Although the Russian movement spiritually nourished the Polish founders of the Proletariat from 1876 to 1881, the rapid maturation of Polish socialism based on favorable conditions in the Congress Kingdom transformed the role of the Russian movement from tutor into ally. It can also be convincingly argued that by the end of the 1880s, Russian socialists had become the students of the Polish movement, reversing the situation of the 1870s.

Polish-Russian Revolutionary Relations from Vilna to Paris

The entire year 1883, from the Vilna conference in January to Stanisław Kunicki's trip to Paris in the beginning of 1884, was punctuated by several attempts by the Proletariat and Narodnaia Volia to reach an agreement called for in the final resolution at Vilna. As we have seen, owing to political considerations within the party, there was no mention of the Russians in the Proletariat program of September 1882. The Vilna conference, however, had reaffirmed the consistent desire of Waryński and the Proletariat leadership from the time of their Geneva emigration and "To Our Comrade Russian Socialists" to reach a working agreement with Narodnaia Volia. It was not simply the theoretical demands of internationalism or of a political struggle that prompted Waryński to seek an arrangement with the Russians. The daily exigencies of party life in the Congress Kingdom made some kind of agreement with the *narodovol'tsy* an absolute necessity.

To be sure, extensive cooperation between Russian and Polish revolutionaries already existed; mutual help and mutual sympathy characterized relations between the Proletariat and the Russians from the onset of the Polish movement. When in 1882 and 1883 the number of Polish socialists markedly increased, the Russian and Polish leadership merely attempted to institutionalize the existing cooperation in the hope that with common organization, the common goal of political revolution could be more easily accomplished. The fact that it was Narodnaia Volia that attracted the attention of the Proletariat rather than Black Partition or the later Osvobozhdenie Truda ("Emancipation of Labor") group, both of whose ideologies more closely resembled that of the Poles, attests to the compelling nature of the problem of political struggle within the empire.[1]

In June 1883 the Proletariat appealed to its followers: "define your positions in the struggle we carry on together with the Russians: the time for national separatism is past, and the idea of freedom should unite all of its real friends in common ranks."[2] Beginning in the summer of 1883, the reports of the Warsaw prosecutor incessantly pointed to instances of cooperation between the activists of the Proletariat and the "social revolutionary movement in the empire."[3] When *Przedświt,* in its "national" phase, queried Narodnaia Volia about its stand on the future of Poland, the editorial board of *Vestnik "Narodnoi voli"* accommodatingly replied (August 1883): "We recognize the rights of Poland not from tribal or historical grounds, but because the Polish people want to maintain their national and political independence. What is important for us is only the will of the Polish people — only on this basis do we recognize the historical-national rights of Poland."[4] *Vestnik "Narodnoi voli"* also cheered the publication of *Walka Klas* and the activities of the Polish socialist party, the Proletariat:

> The organization Proletariat, existing all of two years, has already succeeded in capturing a substantial part of the Kingdom, and its Central Committee has already had occasion to demonstrate its strength even by means of terrorist actions. . . . We wish success for the literary brotherhood [*Walka Klas*]. We wish it even more [success] from the feeling that it represents the movement that attempts to place the socialist renascence of Poland on the exclusive foundations of the interests of the working masses, as the *narodovol'tsy* have done in Russia.[5]

Although such statements of mutual support and admiration pervaded the Polish and Russian socialist periodical press throughout

1883, memoirists from both camps recalled that revolutionary Poles and Russians were still wary of one another. Lev Tikhomirov, the leader of the *narodovol'tsy* emigration in Paris and later the famous apostate of Russian populism, wrote that Waryński, simply because he was a Pole, shied away from unifying with the Russians in 1881. Tikhomirov, himself a barely disguised Great Russian chauvinist, also claimed that Waryński was "a person of small stature and not capable enough"[6] and that Mendelson (who in 1883-84 had been in Paris) was prejudiced against the Russians: "Therefore I repeat, a Pole is always a Pole. As for the Muscovites Dębski and Kunicki, all the same, they remained Poles. Nevertheless, it is unquestionable that they were ideologically influenced by the Russians."[7] Turning the tables on Tikhomirov, the Proletariat member Edmund Płoski claimed that the Polish movement was superior to that of the Russians and that the Poles even considered the possibility of subordinating the Russian movement to the Proletariat. According to Płoski, neither Narodnaia Volia nor Black Partition had the talent or brains to exert any influence on Russian factories; it was therefore up to Poles to organize "all workers of the Russian Empire." Our party, Płoski headily asserted, "is not limited by any national or religious boundaries."[8]

To be sure, Waryński's sense of the competence of the Proletariat was much more limited. From the time of his productive Geneva days when he was the constant companion of Black Partition members, Waryński realized the absolute necessity of cooperation with the Russians. In his view, the success of an internationalist and socialist revolution in the Congress Kingdom depended as much on the Russian as on the Polish movement. From the foundation of the Warsaw Proletariat in the fall of 1882, Waryński sought out and maintained contact with prominent revolutionaries in the empire, most of whom belonged to Narodnaia Volia. At the end of 1882, he was especially close to the *narodovol'tsy* Varvara Shchulepnikova and Vera Figner.[9] There is also evidence to suggest that at the end of 1882, during the period of the reorganization of Narodnaia Volia, Figner invited Waryński to become involved in the prestigious Executive Committee.[10]

Waryński himself did not join the momentarily rejuvenated Russian organization, but T. Rechniewski, S. Kunicki, and A. Dębski in St. Petersburg, and L. Janczewski in Moscow served as Proletariat agents in Narodnaia Volia. Thanks primarily to the efforts of these men, considerable sums of money and whole libraries of revolutionary literature made their way from *narodovol'tsy* circles in European Russia to

Warsaw. The Polish *narodovol'tsy* also recruited students in Russia for the Proletariat cause, which was increasingly important as the police began to take the Proletariat seriously and arrest its leadership.[11] Most significantly, as Krzywicki noted, Kunicki, Rechniewski, and Dębski assured that "relations between the *narodovol'tsy* and the Polish revolutionaries were at that time the very best."[12]

Waryński's personal negotiations with the Russians in the fall and winter of 1882–83 are difficult to reconstruct given the sometimes contradictory evidence regarding his movements during this period. From Tikhomirov's letters, it is apparent that Waryński negotiated with the Executive Committee in Switzerland in November 1882, probably as part of his unsuccessful efforts to reinstate *Przedświt* under the direct aegis of the Proletariat.[13] With what can only be described as lukewarm support from Tikhomirov, Waryński proceeded to consolidate his leadership of the party, culminating in the Vilna meeting of January 1883. With the party firmly behind him, Waryński then traveled to St. Petersburg (in the early spring) to find support for his all-empire approach to revolution from Russian *narodovol'tsy* and the Polish colony.[14]

The noted terrorist and socialist conspirator, Sergei Ivanov, described Waryński's mission in St. Petersburg in a series of letters written from the Shlisselburg fortress to P. V. Karpovich at the beginning of the twentieth century. "An enemy of Polish isolationism and narrow Polish patriotism," Ivanov began, "Waryński argued that Polish questions — political, economic, and national — could be settled only by a change in the general regime, and, in the struggle for this, by the Russian revolutionary organization." According to Ivanov, Waryński suggested that a permanent representative of Narodnaia Volia reside in Warsaw and work with the Polish Central Committee for the explicit purpose of creating a unified socialist anti-tsarist force. The representative in Warsaw was (1) "to serve as an intermediary in all relations between both groups" and, more significantly, (2) "to take a supervisory role [*kontrol'noe uchastie*] in the editorship of the paper, *Proletariat*." In essence, this representative was to serve as a *narodovol'tsy* censor. He was, "in case of any contradictions with the general program of Narodnaia Volia, to point them out, offering the corresponding corrections." The third part of Waryński's offer consisted of a proposal to organize in Warsaw the printing operations for the newspaper *Narodnaia volia*.

Ivanov also recalled that he personally spoke with Waryński in St. Petersburg and found him to be the "main proponent of the idea of the merger of the Russian and Polish parties, and not only in the form of a completely equal federation, but also in the sense of some subordination of the Poles to the former during the establishment of general policies of revolutionary action." In the end, Ivanov rejected Waryński's proposal because of the weakness of the *narodovol'tsy* organization and the "duplicity" he saw in the subordination of the stronger Polish to a weaker Russian party. He also objected to Waryński's proposals because he himself had no acquaintances in Warsaw, knew no Polish, and saw little advantage in publishing *Narodnaia volia* in Warsaw.[15]

Waryński's proposals and Ivanov's rejection were a crucial turning point in the history of Proletariat-Narodnaia Volia relations in this period. Waryński's intention to incorporate the Polish into the Russian movement, first broached by "To Our Comrade Russian Socialists" in July 1882 and accepted by the Vilna conferees in January 1883, was informally presented to the Russians in the late spring of 1883. Ivanov's rejection certainly must have forced Waryński and the Poles to rethink their relations with the Russians and formulate another approach to their most significant problem — how to bring about a revolution in the Congress Kingdom. The Waryński-Ivanov talks demonstrated as well that the Poles continued to overestimate the real strength of Narodnaia Volia. Having irreversibly rejected a three-partition solution to the problem of social and political revolution, the Poles realized that they alone could not overthrow the tsarist autocracy. Their only possible ally in the spring and summer of 1883 was Narodnaia Volia, itself crippled and in shreds from the activities of the provocateur Sergei Degaev.

The "Degaevshchina" and Renewed Negotiations

In December 1882, the tsarist authorities arrested numerous *narodovolt'tsy* from the Odessa region, among them Sergei Degaev, the most successful provocateur of nineteenth-century Russian revolutionary history. Within Russian radical circles, Degaev had been a respected and prestigious comrade; as Ashenbrenner wrote, "to us he seemed a very refined, clever, intelligent, resourceful, and enterprising person."[16] The Odessa secret police inspector G. D. Sudeikin nevertheless persuaded the ambitious *narodovolets* not only to help convict his arrested comrades by providing anonymous evidence but also to reenter revolutionary activities as an agent of the secret police. Degaev agreed to recruit new members into Narodnaia Volia, undertake various terrorist activities, and then turn over the participants' names and addresses to Sudeikin.[17] Already severely weakened by the arrests following the assassination of March 1881 and by a dearth of competent leadership, Narodnaia Volia suffered a blinding series of arrests in the first half of 1883 as a result of Degaev's treachery. When in February 1883 his clandestine information led to the imprisonment of Vera Figner, the last of the old party leadership still in Russia, Degaev himself became the chief figure of the *narodovol'tsy* movement inside Russia.

The Paris Executive Committee began to suspect Degaev's involvement with Sudeikin in the early spring of 1883. In May Tikhomirov confronted the provocateur with an ultimatum — either Degaev would assassinate his superior Sudeikin or himself be executed. Further arrests during the summer of 1883, totally paralyzing the Executive Committee's activities in Russia, convinced the party that Sudeikin's assassination had to be quickly arranged. Finally, on 16 December (o.s.), the hesitant double agent Degaev, on the prompting of Narodnaia Volia's emissary German Lopatin, supervised the brutal murder of the secret police inspector.[18] Although the government offered the extraordinary reward of 10,000 rubles for Degaev's capture, he managed to escape to the West with the promised help of Narodnaia Volia.[19]

The "Degaevshchina" is unquestionably central to the history of Narodnaia Volia but is beyond the scope of our considerations here. However, it is also important in that it reflects the integral position of the Polish Proletariat members in the Russian movement during this period. Tadeusz Rechniewski, a close confederate of the Russian Executive Committee in St. Petersburg and a member of the Proletariat's Central Committee, was entrusted with the arrangements for Degaev's escape.[20] Through his contacts in Warsaw and in the Baltic region, Rechniewski (with the help of the *narodovolets* Mikhail Ovchinnikov) supervised the escape of both Degaev and his brother through Riga.

Kunicki's role in the affair was much more mysterious and complex. Degaev had been Kunicki's "big brother" in revolutionary circles; they had been close confederates and intimate friends. The revelations that Degaev was a police agent shook Kunicki, and he assumed a personal responsibility to see that Sudeikin was assassinated.[21] As an agent of the émigré Executive Committee, Kunicki traveled back and forth from Paris to St. Petersburg to help carry out the *narodovol'tsy* verdict on Sudeikin and Degaev. When Degaev completed his obligation and Sudeikin was assassinated, Kunicki met him in Vilna, provided him with a false passport, and with revolver in hand personally escorted Degaev to the awaiting ship.

The close cooperation between the Proletariat members Kunicki and Rechniewski and the émigré Executive Committee in the Degaev affair was matched by their (and Dębski's) intimate relations with all levels of the dispersed organization of Narodnaia Volia in the Russian Empire. Rechniewski was especially well respected by the infant Workers' Section of Narodnaia Volia. The leaders of the Workers' Section, N. M. Flerov and I. I. Popov, read and often discussed the Proletariat's program with him. For his knowledge of socialist theory, Rechniewski was known to these young labor leaders as a "Little Marx."[22] Popov especially can be considered a student of the Polish triumvirate of Rechniewski, Kunicki, and Dębski.[23] The theoretical attraction of the Proletariat for the Workers' Section and the practical services of Kunicki and Rechniewski in the Degaev affair lent Waryński's proposals of the earlier spring considerable credence and support in St. Petersburg *narodovol'tsy* circles.

Partly because of the Degaev affair and its costly results for the Russians the abandoned discussions between Waryński and Ivanov resumed in the fall of 1883. This time it was Narodnaia Volia — represented by Shebalin, Karaulov, Usova, and Iakubovich — that was in search of help from the Poles, Kunicki, Dębski, and Rechniewski.[24] The Degaev affair had convinced the government of the need for greater centralization of the police apparatus.[25] Degaev's betrayals convinced many *narodovol'tsy*, on the other hand, of the desirability of greater decentralization, a cessation of the terrorist struggle, and a more intense propagandistic effort among the Russian working class. The talks of the fall of 1883 therefore had a tone diametrically opposite to that of the Waryński-Ivanov parleys of the earlier spring — decentralization rather than unification was their theme. As Shebalin outlined the course of the discussions:

> At our meetings, no arguments arose over programmatic questions. For us, the Petersburgites, the program of the Executive Committee remained [for the moment] the basis of our activities. Rechniewski, in the name of the Proletariat, without disputing our program set forth the program of the Proletariat. No one took exception to him. The discussion, as well as I can remember, was carried on in the spirit of the exchange of information and opinions. . . . In organizational relations, the hope was expressed for more independence of local groups.[26]

The Proletariat was therefore encouraged to maintain autonomous jurisdiction over revolutionary affairs in the Congress Kingdom. Moreover, the support of the Poles for a less Blanquist, more worker-oriented concept of party activities helped bolster Iakubovich and Shebalin's growing resistance against the Executive Committee's terrorist myopia, which surfaced several months later in the open rebellion of "Young" Narodnaia Volia.

The Workers' Section of Narodnaia Volia anxiously followed the results of these negotiations.[27] As a predominantly labor-oriented group, they pressured the Executive Committee for greater organizational autonomy and a cessation of political terrorism. Some Workers' Section leaders even thought of abandoning Narodnaia Volia for the ideologically more comfortable program of the Proletariat. Three Proletariat workers from Warsaw had already joined the Petersburg section, learned Russian, and became, in Popov's words, "great, splendid propagandists."[28] But a serious divergency surfaced between the Workers' Section and the Proletariat on the question of terror. According to the Workers' Section, the spiraling costs of the program of assassinations, political struggle, and centralization were too high. The socialist movement, especially among the workers, required a breathing spell. The Proletariat countered by stressing the importance of selective acts of economic and political terrorism for the labor movement, gently advising their Russian counterparts that successful propaganda among workers was impossible under the autocracy without measures of self-protection and examples of party courage. "We often discussed economic terror with members of the Proletariat," wrote Popov, "and on this question there was no agreement between us." In any case, he added, "we welcomed the recognition of broad autonomy for the party Proletariat."[29]

While the negotiations between the Russian movement and the Proletariat were being carried on in St. Petersburg, the Paris Executive Committee of Narodnaia Volia exhibited renewed interest in developing institutionalized ties with the Poles. At this point, the Tikhomirov-led committee was fighting for its political life against pressures from dissidents within the home organization for decentralization and the cessation of terrorist activities. "Young" Narodnaia Volia was on the verge of challenging Tikhomirov's program. The increasingly close ties between the Workers' Section and the Proletariat must have also caused the Paris committee some concern. In addition to these factional disputes within Narodnaia Volia, the dynamic growth of the political importance of the Proletariat, which spread beyond the confines of the Congress Kingdom into European Russia, turned the Executive Committee's attention to a Polish alliance.

Russians in the Proletariat — Petr Bardovskii

Rechniewski continued to serve the cause of the Proletariat in Russia itself, but Dębski and Kunicki, as well as dozens of other Polish revolutionaries who had been involved in *narodovol'tsy* activities, emigrated to the Congress Kingdom soon after the Vilna meeting of January 1883.[30] With Waryński's arrest, these "russified" Poles assumed the leadership of the Proletariat, moving it into even closer contact with Narodnaia Volia.[31] "We became russified — that's a fact," wrote Feliks Kon. "But in turn one must not forget that to the same extent and with the same success we 'polonized' the Russian comrades."[32] These polonized Russians exerted a strong influence on the development of the Proletariat and added yet another dimension to the dynamics of Russo-Polish revolutionary relations in this period.

The Russian revolutionary movement in Warsaw revolved around Petr Bardovskii, a justice of the peace and a respected member of Warsaw's Russian colony. One of five brothers eventually convicted of revolutionary activities, Bardovskii, wrote his mother, came from "a very patriarchic, honorable, and completely Russian home."[33] Bardovskii's cellmate in the Tenth Pavilion, M. Mańkowski, recalled that Bardovskii's deepest wish was to travel to Western Europe and there engage in the full-time study of the social sciences and revolutionary literature. Unquestionably, added Mańkowski, Bardovskii would have been a brilliant leader in these fields.[34] The Russian authorities wrote of their horror and of the "great unexpectedness" when the police arrested the "very knowledgeable jurist, Bardovskii."[35] Kon characterized Bardovskii as "a typical representative of the sixties." He was "a nihilist, a reasoner, a liberal, a sympathizer with the revolutionary movement, a justice of the peace in a russified land, yet at the same time a sincere democrat who learned Polish in order to make himself more easily understood to his clients."[36]

Because its owner was absolutely above any suspicion, Bardovskii's residence (which he shared with his common-law wife and socialist Natalia Poll) was quickly turned into the illegal headquarters of the Proletariat. The police reported that Waryński, Kunicki, Dębski, Dulęba, and many others often visited Bardovskii's home, sometimes stayed the night, and held the most important party meetings there. Revolutionary workers were known to gather their thoughts and plan their activities at this impregnable "iron house."[37] Eventually, Bardovskii's home also held most of the Proletariat's library.[38] As Kon put it, Bardovskii's "was the only place where the homeless, illegal conspirators, though for only a short hour, could warm themselves in an atmosphere of a familial hearth, rest themselves from revolutionary questions, breathe the normal peaceful life. At Bardovskii's it was restful, warm, and safe."[39]

Bardovskii himself was a member neither of Narodnaia Volia nor of the Proletariat.[40] Yet his extensive contacts within both groups proved especially valuable in the procurement of supplies for the Poles. He and another justice of the peace, Mikhail Dobrovol'skii, also raised crucial funds for the party's coffers with their Russian Narodnaia Volia contacts Varvara Shchulepnikova, Mikhail Luri, and Zakhar Sokol'skii.[41] It was through these last three as well that Waryński was able to stay in contact with Konstantin Stepurin and the Executive Committee of Narodnaia Volia in St. Petersburg.[42] As an inveterate opponent of Russianization, Bardovskii joined the Warsaw *narodo-vol'tsy* Luri, Ingel'strom, and Sokol'skii in their propagandistic efforts among the Russian occupation army, especially at the Novogeorg'ev-skii Citadel (Dęblin).[43] Together they organized socialist circles within the military (the *militaristy*) and tied these to Stepurin, who at that time directed Narodnaia Volia's efforts in the borderlands. In the course of his organizational activities, Bardovskii personally wrote a fateful proclamation to the Russian soldiers in the Congress Kingdom, urging them to reject their role as agents of Russian despotism and to join forces with the all-Russian revolutionary movement.

> Let us unite therefore against the common enemy. . . . In every company, in every individual military unit, let a separate circle arise, which will aspire to a common goal. These circles should enter into contact with one another and attempt to enter into communication with representatives of the party Narodnaia Volia. . . . Remember the great goal that stands before us — the liberation of the people from century-long enslavement — for the new, better life![44]

Primarily as a result of this proclamation, the Russian authorities sentenced Bardovskii to hang. That he fostered the development of the Proletariat and encouraged its cooperation with Narodnaia Volia in the struggle against the autocracy also contributed to the harsh verdict. Bardovskii's death sentence proved a significant impetus to the on-going negotiations between the Russian and Polish movements. *Przedświt,* in an article about the Russians who had figured prominently in the trial of the Proletariat (Bardovskii, Luri, Sokol'skii, and Ingel'strom), sang a paean to these "heroes" and predicted immense propaganda gains for the common Russo-Polish revolutionary cause from their harsh sentences.

> We recognize with pride that alongside our friends, our Russian comrades are also dying, [men] who do not hesitate even for a moment to bring help to the defenders of the Polish working class. . . . Our goal as well as [that of] the Russian comrades will rightly be to make use of this strong sign of international solidarity, which will provide an abundant harvest when it pervades the Polish as well as Russian working masses and becomes understood by them.[45]

With *narodovol'tsy* active in the Proletariat and Proletariat members active in Narodnaia Volia, the two organizations developed fixed areas of cooperation and a tacit division of labor. The Proletariat confined itself primarily to Polish working-class organization, employing propaganda and agitation as its tactics and selectively using terrorism to maintain party discipline. As an ally in the struggle against the autocracy, it asked for and received technical and material aid from the wealthier and more experienced Russian movement. Jewish *narodovol'tsy* from the Pale served as procurement agents for the rapidly expanding Polish movement.[46] In return, the Proletariat, less dangerous in the eyes of the autocracy, provided the Russians with invaluable agents to carry out illegal tasks of transportation, smuggling, and printing. The party also furnished the Workers' Section with printed materials and even propagandists in the hope of developing an empire-wide labor movement. Meanwhile, the Russian Executive Committee under this informal agreement continued to concentrate its efforts on political terrorism, directed at overthrowing the autocratic government.

Kunicki in Paris: The "General Principles" and the "Confidential Agreement"

As a member of the Proletariat's Central Committee and as an agent of Narodnaia Volia's Executive Committee, Stanisław Kunicki traveled to Paris in January 1884; the Warsaw committee had directed him to regularize relations both with the Polish socialists of *Przedświt* and with Tikhomirov's Executive Committee.[47] With the return of Mendelson to *Przedświt* in January 1884 and the subsequent overruling of Dłuski and Piekarski's concept of a three-partition party, Kunicki had little difficulty in returning *Przedświt* to the fold of the Proletariat.[48] At the same time, he arranged for the publication of the revolutionary journal *Walka Klas,* which was also to be "based on the home organization."[49]

Feliks Kon characterized Kunicki as a "half-Georgian [who], educated in Russia, spoke Polish poorly and in the beginning was completely disoriented . . . in our land."[50] Thanks to his enthusiasm, conspiratorial acumen, and unswerving devotion to the revolutionary cause, Kunicki quickly captured the allegiance of socialist Poles in Warsaw, just as he had in St. Petersburg.[51] After the successful unmasking of Degaev and the assassination of Sudeikin, Kunicki turned his complete attention to ratifying an agreement with the Russians. Before approaching the Executive Committee in Paris, Kunicki worked out a common platform with the editors of *Przedświt* and *Walka Klas.* Although the Polish socialist emigration in Paris was very active in European circles, it held little sway over policy decisions concerning Proletariat activity.[52] Therefore, this platform — the "General Principles" — emanated primarily from Kunicki and the Polish Central Committee's concept of Russo-Polish relations.[53]

As such, the "General Principles" varied little from the Proletariat's previous programs and proclamations. It reaffirmed the party's inveterate opposition to the bourgeoisie and the *szlachta;* it proclaimed the superiority of the working class in the struggle for social revolution; and it saw the two-fisted approach of propaganda and agitation as the fundamental means of struggle. The competence of the party remained limited to those places "where the majority of people speak Polish." The "General Principles" also defended the use of selective political and economic terrorism, which would "not only accelerate the moment of social revolution, but may, in addition, force the government to grant certain concessions, which then would facilitate the organization of social revolutionary cadres." More determinedly Marxist than most Proletariat documents, perhaps because it was completed in Paris under the influence of Mendelson, the "General Principles" completely ignored the peasantry and attacked the government as "one of the largest economic forces in the country, which always defends the interests of the possessing class."

On the matter of relations with the Russians, the "General Principles" rejected the idea of incorporating the Proletariat into the Russian movement, the idea voiced earlier at Geneva, Vilna, and during Waryński's visit to St. Petersburg in the spring of 1883: "The Central Committee remains completely independent of the Executive Committee and, in the sphere of its activities, only it is competent."[54] This statement only reaffirmed the increasing doubts about the benefits of unification expressed by the Proletariat since the disastrous Degaev affair in the fall of 1883. Still, the "General Principles" recognized that the combined and coordinated efforts of the Proletariat and Narodnaia Volia would be necessary to bring down the centralized Russian autocracy. The document therefore proposed an exclusive, bilateral alliance, which would facilitate the exchange of information and aid and would coordinate attacks against the autocracy to the extent that the Poles would initiate no actions without the Russians' consent. The talks between Kunicki and the Russians were not talks about unifying the two parties, *Vestnik "Narodnoi voli"* explained, but talks "about the means to unify the *activities* of the two parties, so far as they related to their common struggle with the common enemy — Russian absolutism."[55]

The Russians responded favorably to the Polish initiative, and on 5 March the Paris Executive Committee announced: "respecting the independence and free development of every people . . . [we] cannot but recognize that the different social conditions in which the Polish and Russian people live do not call for totally identical means of preparatory work of Polish and Russian socialists." At the same time, the Russians expressed their opposition to a merger of Narodnaia Volia and the Proletariat: it would, in their opinion, "do a disservice to the activities of the Russian and Polish socialists, hindering one and the other in the choice of the most appropriate means of organization and struggle for their goals." "Close ties," concluded the Russians, are as much "in the interest of revolution as is 'autonomy.'"[56]

The talks between Kunicki and the Russian socialist emigration, conducted at the end of January and the beginning of February 1884, concluded with the signing of a confidential agreement (*umowa konfidencjonalna*), which reaffirmed the "General Principles" drawn up by the Poles and made provisions for the structural implementation of the alliance. Both parties would have representatives with an advisory voice in the central organization of the other. These representatives were to oversee the mutual material help and active cooperation of the two committees. In general terms, the Proletariat would confine its activities to the Congress Kingdom; its use of terrorism against the central government (beginning with the governor-general and his superiors) would first have to be approved by the Executive Committee.[57] In both cases, the *umowa* simply confirmed ad hoc arrangements already in practice between the Polish and Russian organizations. Each was to maintain autonomous jurisdiction over its own national unit. Narodnaia Volia was responsible for carrying out terrorism against the government and could make alliances with other revolutionary groups only with the concurrence of the Proletariat. The result of over five years of discussions between the Russian and the Polish revolutionary movements reflected, as did the other agreements along the road to the *umowa,* the relative strength and practical needs of the two movements.

The *umowa,* though calling for no concrete changes in the already existing structure of party relations, did confirm an important principle, which had previously been hidden by a mist of internationalist pronouncements. The Poles and the Russians — the Proletariat and Narodnaia Volia — were to remain separate and equal in a combined, but not merged, struggle against the tsarist autocracy. The *umowa* also institutionalized such practical jurisdictional questions as the *narodovol'tsy* predominance in Russian military circles of the Congress Kingdom and Proletariat supervision of the Polish working-class movement in Belystok (Białystok). The socialist leadership of underground Russia officially recognized the ethnic distinctions between its territories and working classes. It anticipated at the same time the necessity of combining forces whenever possible in the face of the centralized police state.

The respective parties represented at the negotiations never ratified the *umowa.*[58] The Warsaw arrests of June and July 1884 weakened the Proletariat to such an extent that it was unable to hold a constituent meeting. On 4 October 1884, German Lopatin was arrested in St. Petersburg, carelessly in possession of a list of party members and circles in the empire, a list that he had painstakingly collected over the previous several months. The result was another series of arrests equal in scope to the Degaev-prompted devastation of the previous year.[59] At this point, wrote Wasilewski, "the matter of the secret agreement finally passed into history."[60] But the police more correctly assessed the meaning of the *umowa* when they concluded that it was "by no means only a paper document": "The Proletariat entered into a brotherly alliance with . . . Narodnaia Volia. The basis of the closeness of the two parties served their common interest and common goal of freeing the working masses from the yoke of capital."[61] The pre-1945 Polish socialist historian, Adam Próchnik, agreed with the police that the document was of great significance but, in his view, a crucial mistake on the part of the Proletariat. With the *umowa,* the Polish party tied its fate to a falling star. The fundamental reason for the demise of the Proletariat, according to Próchnik, was its alliance with the moribund Russian organization. The alliance "was the cornerstone of the politics of the Proletariat," he concluded. "With the removal of this stone, the whole building collapsed."[62]

Other prewar Polish historians of the Proletariat examined the *umowa* within the ubiquitous context of the national struggle and concluded that it was a temporary defeat for the principle of Polish nationhood in the socialist movement.[63] In their view, the agreement was relegated to historical obscurity because Poles and Russians could not rid themselves of "the century-long tradition of hate" and therefore, regardless of their strength, could never agree to a combined struggle.[64] As one might expect, postwar Polish historians look at the *umowa* quite differently, proudly pointing to it as an exemplary event in the history of Russo-Polish revolutionary relations. Especially for contemporary Polish historians, the distinctive aspects of the *umowa* were the Russian guarantee of the independence of the Polish people and the complete autonomy of the Polish party in Polish lands.

In his memoirs, Lev Tikhomirov supported the Polish socialist-patriot's contention that the *umowa* could never have been implemented; the Poles simply did not consider the Russians to be true comrades. To be sure, Tikhomirov wrote, the Poles "paid court" to the *buntovshchiki* (rebels) as long as they could use them, and went along with the Russians as "coreligionists, and nothing more": no friendship, no comradely relations, no mutual sympathy.[65] The attitude of the Plekhanov-led Osvobozhdenie Truda toward the *umowa* was even more critical. For instance, Lev Deich, the long-time friend of the Polish movement, sadly concluded that since Kunicki did not consult with his group in Paris, the Poles were no longer the Marxists they had been under Waryński and the *Równość* group: "This separation of Kunicki and the members of the newly formed Polish paper, *Walka Klas,* from us, the Russian adherents of Marx and Engels, demonstrated that they took the position of our political opponents."[66]

The Proletariat concluded the *umowa* with Narodnaia Volia not because it agreed with the latter's ideology, as Deich asserts, but precisely because they were able to exploit the political flexibility of a Marxist program (in contrast to Deich's group, one might add). For the Proletariat, an alliance with the Russian revolutionary movement was a long-standing political goal. Narodnaia Volia, the only significant Russian revolutionary force inside the empire in the 1880s, was the natural choice and the only choice of a political ally. Although the Proletariat and Narodnaia Volia did share a number of political axioms — including the most important, the inevitability and desirability of revolution — each nevertheless recognized the individuality and autonomy of the other's movement. The maturation of both groups can be seen in their tolerant attitude toward the other's ideological differences, explained in terms of the social and economic peculiarities of those societies in which they operated. The maintenance of Polish autonomy in national and party affairs called for in the *umowa* did not mean that Poles and Russians could never be true allies, as the Pole Kon and the Russian Tikhomirov asserted, but that both parties recognized that the Congress Kingdom and Russia required essentially different revolutionary methods and parties. The extent to which the goals and means of the parties overlapped was the extent to which the alliance was forged.

The Last Stage: Bohuszewiczówna, Ulrych, and Terror

On the afternoon of 28 September 1883 Ludwik Waryński, the founder and the heart of the Proletariat, waited on a Warsaw street corner for his Narodnaia Volia contact, Varvara Shchulepnikova. Impatient at her tardiness, he dropped into a small store to pick up some stamps. Hurrying off to mail a letter, he carelessly left a package filled with revolutionary materials on the store counter. The suspicious clerk opened the package, examined its contents, secured some help, and seized Waryński when he returned with Shchulepnikova to fetch his dangerous treasure. During the brief scuffle that ensued, Shchulepnikova fled and made her way to the Proletariat's headquarters, warning the party of its leader's arrest. But the police moved almost as quickly as Shchulepnikova. In Waryński's apartment, they found an extensive list of Proletariat members as well as addresses of conspiratorial headquarters.[1] In the following days and months, the police were able to track down and arrest several hundred Proletariat leaders and rank and file; by the winter of 1883–84 they had destroyed the original party organization.

The Proletariat Organization: Fall 1883 – Spring 1886

Even with the arrest of Waryński and his comrades, wrote the police, "social revolutionary propaganda not only did not stop but, led by new intelligentsia members, continued with its earlier energy, and every day in different parts of the city, meetings were held."[2] Returning to Warsaw after two years in prison, Stefan Juszczyński wrote that there "had been no hiatus" in the work of the party. "There remained members who continued to carry out propaganda in the workers' circles and formed new ones in Warsaw and in the provinces. The Central and Workers' Committees continued to function as well."[3] When Waryński fell victim to his own carelessness, Kunicki, Dębski, and Rechniewski replaced him. Shortly before his own arrest in July 1884, Kunicki

described the revival of the party in a letter to the imprisoned
Waryński.

> [While you have been in jail] . . . various conditions have changed,
> people have been replaced, you would surely not recognize that which
> remains. The arrests . . . constantly worry us . . . but we don't lose
> energy and everyone remains at their posts, to be sure as long as
> destiny does not force us to share your fate. Our movement, it is pos-
> sible to state boldly, not only has not weakened, but on the contrary,
> having survived a difficult period, gains strength. From among the
> workers, many capable and self-sacrificing people (better than the
> university youth) are joining us. Almost all of our work is based on
> local elements. . . . Issue no. 5 of the *Proletariat* has appeared and
> created a marvelous impression. We have entered into close contact
> with the émigrés — where we established our organ (*Walka Klas* —
> something along the lines of *Vestnik "Narodnoi voli"*). . . . The
> organizations of the workers have been built not only here [Warsaw]
> but also in Łódź, Zgierz, Częstochowa, Piotrków, Radom, Żyrardów,
> and Białystok. Our colonies (St. Petersburg, Moscow, Kiev) also have
> grown significantly. . . . We are very pleased that we have been able to
> stir up and draw to us the local youth. . . . Solidarność will sleep for
> centuries.[4]

After Kunicki and Rechniewski were arrested, the young noblewoman
Maria Bohuszewiczówna held the Proletariat's organization together.
She herself was arrested in September 1885, and the leadership fell to
Marian Ulrych. In the spring of 1886, the police launched a final series
of arrests and could claim with conviction that the Proletariat was no
longer a force to be dealt with.

The Warsaw prosecutor broke down the Proletariat's leadership
into three basic groups: those arrested in 1883 and 1884 (Waryński,
Bardovskii, Kunicki, and Rechniewski), those arrested in 1885 (Bohuszewiczówna, Archangelski, and Felsenhardt), and those arrested in
1886 (Ulrych and Wisłocki). In comparison to the first group, the
prosecutor correctly concluded, the last two groups were disorganized,
less capable of engineering terrorist activities, less in control of the
working-class movement, and less prestigious within Warsaw intelligentsia circles.[5]

To the prosecutor's conclusion should be added a clear distinction
between the Proletariat Waryński led in 1883 and the Proletariat
Kunicki led from the winter of 1883–84 to the fall of 1884. Kunicki left
a strong personal imprint on the party's organization, moving it
toward a structure much more like that of Narodnaia Volia. Unin-

terested in the activities of the Workers' Committee, he allowed it to operate more autonomously, concentrating his energies instead on molding the Fighting Squad into a streamlined terrorist subsection of the Central Committee. With Kunicki's arrest in the summer of 1884 and the dispersal of the Central Committee, two power centers of the Proletariat organization remained — the Fighting Squad under Dębski and Sławiński and the Red Cross section of the Proletariat under Bohuszewiczówna and Rozalia Felsenhardt. By October 1884, however, the authorities succeeded in destroying the Fighting Squad, leaving Dębski no choice but to turn the leadership of the Proletariat over to Bohuszewiczówna and go into exile. Because of the "horrible mass arrests," she wrote, "I had to take into my hands all the threads I was able to grasp. Razumiej[czyk], who up to that point had the same relations to the Proletariat as I — also took up the work, the heavy, almost feverish work."[6]

Under Bohuszewiczówna and her associates J. Razumiejczyk, M. Mancewicz, and R. Felsenhardt, the Central Committee deemphasized the terrorist inclinations of Kunicki and turned once again to the workers' circles as the focal point of the party's activities. Although the Bohuszewiczówna leadership personally favored a limited form of political terrorism, they granted what they considered to be a "necessary concession" to the working classes — namely, the advocacy of factory terrorism.[7] The Bohuszewiczówna committee also maintained the vast Proletariat library and document collection; planned to publish a sixth number of the party newspaper; and issued new charters to the workers' circles, charters that defined both the circles' relationship to one another and to the Central Committee as well as their financial obligations.[8] By March 1885 Bohuszewiczówna had rebuilt the party organization to the extent that, as seen in Chapter 7, it could play a role, albeit a minor one, in the Plac Zamkowy demonstration. At the same time, the Plac Zamkowy events demonstrated that the ties between the workers' circles and the intelligentsia leadership, so carefully nurtured by Waryński and Dulęba, had deteriorated to an alarming extent.

In September 1885, before the sixth number of *Proletariat* could be printed, the police broke up the Bohuszewiczówna organization and arrested its leading participants. "The entire difference between the first and second group [the Waryński-Kunicki and Bohuszewiczówna groups]," wrote the prosecutor, "resided only in the fact that the members of the second were still unable to consolidate as a result of 1883–84 arrests, which had deprived them of their best known and most energetic supporters. Therefore, terrorist activities, which was the characteristic mark of the first group, did not yet occur."[9] The basic supposition behind the prosecutor's statement was accurate; the Bohuszewiczówna group never achieved the organizational strength of the Waryński Proletariat. Nevertheless, the decreased emphasis on terrorism was due more to Bohuszewiczówna's concern for the real work of the party, propaganda, and agitation among the working classes than to the party's weakness.

One of the few members of the "second group" of the Proletariat to escape arrest was Marian Stefan Ulrych.[10] Because the organization had few "gifted, intelligent, and energetic members" still free in the Congress Kingdom, the Proletariat, wrote the prosecutor, "fell immediately under the influence of Ulrych, an energetic person, enlightened and already known for his revolutionary past."[11] The Ulrych group, formed in November 1885, lasted until June 1886, when it too was decimated by police infiltration and its members arrested in association with the attempted assassination of the provocateur Piński.

During the seven months of Ulrych's leadership, the Proletariat was unable to overcome the disorganization and dispersal of its strength caused by repeated police successes. Its attempts to maintain continuity in its propagandistic and agitational efforts among the Congress Kingdom's working class also proved a failure.[12] As a result, Ulrych party members began to lean toward a more Blanquist concept of Proletariat affairs, including an expanded (and desperate) use of political terrorism. It was suggested, for instance, that the guts of the Proletariat movement — the long-standing workers' circles — be severed from the party apparatus, purging all half-propagandized workers in the process. These proposals were made ostensibly to end the infiltration of party ranks by provocateurs, a growing Russian police practice that had successfully decimated the intelligentsia ranks of the Proletariat.[13] After all, Ulrych party members reasoned, workers had proven to be excellent police agents. These plans for the reorganization of the party were stillborn; in April 1886 the Russians arrested Ulrych and several compatriots. Although the workers' circles continued to operate with sporadic vitality, the party survived the April arrests only long enough to assassinate the provocateur Piotr Piński in June 1886. Further arrests following the Piński killing eliminated the Proletariat as a viable underground organization.

The Police and the Proletariat

Beginning in 1878, the Russian government enacted a series of judicial and administrative measures intended to halt the rising number of terrorist assassination attempts on the lives of tsarist officials. "Crimes against the administrative powers" were to be delegated to streamlined judicial districts headed by a prosecutor.[14] In response to the assassination of General Mezentsev, the government also established "military tribunals" in each military district whose function it was to try all politically motivated armed attacks on the civil authorities. The idea behind the military tribunal, wrote Pobedonostsev, was to promote the "quicker and easier" sentencing of political criminals.[15] In these and other acts, the tsarist government expressed far less concern about the spread of socialist ideas among Russian citizens than about catching and prosecuting terrorists and protecting vital government institutions, especially the army and civil bureaucracy, against "nihilist" infiltration.

This antiterrorist policy, also implemented in the Congress Kingdom, facilitated the relatively free development of Polish socialist activities in the years 1878 to 1882. No Russian institutions were threatened; terrorism was not yet a Polish socialist concern. As we have seen in earlier chapters, the Russians certainly arrested pre-Proletariat socialists, broke up discussion groups, and sentenced and sometimes exiled the participants. The socialists in this period also suffered long periods of internment before sentencing, generally one to two years. But their administrative sentences were light, ranging from several months of surveillance to at most six months in jail.[16] For the Russians, dormant Polish patriotism was the main enemy — socialism was only a passing fad with no indigenous roots. The prosecutor's archives are packed with individual cases of Poles cursing the tsar, shouting threats against Russian officials, or singing Polish patriotic songs, all political crimes under the Russian civil code.[17] These cases were treated as thoroughly, and the sentences were just as long, as those of the great majority of socialist cases of the pre-Proletariat period.

With the foundation of the party in 1882 and its subsequent recruitment successes in the ranks of the army and bureaucracy, the authorities' attitude toward Polish socialism noticeably stiffened. For example, the Council of Ministers in St. Petersburg became especially concerned when the reputable Justice of the Peace Petr Bardovskii was arrested and indicted in Warsaw for socialist activities.[18] However, the authorities' view of the Proletariat was only partly shaped by a fear of socialism, terrorism, and a united Russo-Polish "nihilist" movement. Careerism in the police and judicial bureaucracy also motivated certain actions by the authorities against the party and molded the Proletariat's attitude and activities vis-à-vis the Russian bureaucracy. Chief of Police Pavel Belanovskii, Gendarme Major Petr Sekerninskii, and Prosecutor of the Warsaw district Alexander Iankulio were as important to the form and content of Proletariat activities as were many of its own party members.[19] By planting agents and informers in the ranks of the Proletariat,[20] by delaying arrests in the hope of uncovering a more spectacular plot, and by unjustifiably equating the terrorist threat of the Polish party with that of Narodnaia Volia in their reports to the St. Petersburg bureaucracy, these officials exaggerated their own importance and that of their enemy in the hope of rising in the service.[21] Simultaneously, they helped transform the movement into just that kind of "nihilist" specter they conjured up for their superiors.[22]

The authorities also influenced the development of the revolutionary movement by clearly separating, in their minds and in their policies, the intelligentsia from the working-class members of the party, treating the latter as pawns in the hands of the malicious intelligentsia. Members of the intelligentsia were therefore subject to heavier sentences, more undercover surveillance, and more overall police harassment than their working-class comrades. This left the intelligentsia embittered, desperate, and remote from the moderating influence of daily working-class problems. The growing cleft between workers and intelligentsia members of the Proletariat, first exposed by the Plac Zamkowy demonstration and then solidified by the Ulrych proposals, was in part a result of this government practice. The police planted underground provocateurs, usually workers, in the Proletariat organization, fostering intelligentsia mistrust of its working-class members. This in turn encouraged Blanquist conceptions of party organization and, more importantly, the use of terrorism. Terror was inherent in neither the ideology nor the organization of the Proletariat. That it became grafted onto both in this period can be partly attributed to the paranoia and bitterness that resulted from police infiltration.

The Trial of the Proletariat

The Russians began preparing for the trial of the Proletariat members in the fall of 1884 and concluded the indictments in January 1885.[23] The prosecutor of the Warsaw judicial district reached his verdict on the "Question of the 190" on 29 July 1885. Under the provisions of the 1878 laws, the prosecutor served as judge, jury, and attorney for the state; he assessed the evidence, determined the criminal role of each Proletariat member, and recommended administrative sentences to the minister of interior (which were almost always accepted).[24] At the same time, also on the recommendation of the prosecutor, twenty-nine members of the Proletariat were ordered to stand trial before a military court in connection with the 1878 law relating to armed opposition against the authorities.

After extensive preparation and unremitting police interrogation of the members of the Proletariat interned in Warsaw's infamous Tenth Pavilion, Governor-General Gurko called the military tribunal to session on 23 November 1885. The prosecutor's case revolved around linking the Proletariat to Narodnaia Volia, demonstrating its individual members' ties to violent deeds, and proving that the party's raison d'être was the overthrow of the autocracy. The defense denied most of these charges and instead emphasized the Proletariat's apolitical and economic-determinist approach.[25] On 22 December, the tribunal reached its unexpectedly harsh verdict — Bardovskii, Kunicki, Luri, Ossowski, Pietrusiński, and Schmaus were sentenced to hang.[26] Eighteen others, including Waryński, Płoski, and Rechniewski, received the stiff sentences of sixteen years' hard labor.[27]

During the government's preparation of its cases for administrative action and for the military tribunal, many socialists had languished in prison for as long as two and a half years. Waryński contracted pneumonia in Shlisselburg and died in February 1889.[28] Agaton Zagórski went insane in the Tenth Pavilion and, in the process, divulged everything he knew. His confession led to the arrest of the Łódź activist Stanisław Pacanowski, who, intimidated by the specter of Russian prison, effectively destroyed the remaining Proletariat organization by his well-informed revelations.[29] Even Stanisław Kunicki, the courageous *narodovolets* and successor of Waryński, broke down in prison; "I am damaged to the core," he wrote, "and it is hopeless to bring a point home to me."[30] He recovered enough to compose a stirring, defiant letter to his comrades and to suffer the gallows with revolutionary zeal. Most of his comrades likewise endured their imprisonment and exile with honor.[31] Feliks Kon wrote especially moving letters from prison, expressing his renewed commitment to socialism.[32] Even a prison official later admitted his admiration for the courage and dedication of the Proletariat internees.[33]

The major theme throughout the letters of the imprisoned socialists and their testimony in the courtroom was the importance of revolutionary duty. Asked by the tribunal why he sympathized with the assassination of the tsar, Kunicki coolly answered that the tsar's death was necessary to the furtherance of the socialist cause. "You may judge us and convict us," Kunicki concluded his defense summary, "we die with the feeling of a completed obligation."[34] Kon wrote his brother from prison, "I yearn for the world, it is sad to be alone, but to escape from this situation would have meant not having been called by the obligation of action."[35] Much as he had during his Kraków defense, Waryński emphasized before the military tribunal the socialists' obligation to history.[36] "We are not sectarians, nor do we abstract dreams from real life. . . . We look upon the revolution to which we aspire as a result of historical development and social conditions. We foresee it and endeavor to make sure that it does not find us unprepared."[37] Kunicki's impassioned farewell to his comrades in freedom similarly invoked the Muse of history and the century-long struggle for the freedom of the masses as the justification for his own hanging.[38]

The Debate over Proletariat Terrorism

Before the tribunal of military justices assembled in Warsaw on 23 November 1885, the prosecutor accused the "Social Revolutionary Party 'Proletariat'" of murder, of attempted murder, and generally of fostering terrorism within its ranks. In his summary statement, he attributed the Proletariat's use of terrorism to the nefarious influence of its Russian counterpart, Narodnaia Volia. In addition, the tribunal meted out the most severe sentence — death by hanging — not to the leadership of the party responsible for the spread of Marxist propaganda throughout the Congress Kingdom, but to those party members who participated in successful terrorist operations, J. Pietrusiński, M. Ossowski, and S. Kunicki. The members of the Proletariat were therefore on trial primarily for being Polish *narodovol'tsy* and only secondarily for attempting to organize Polish workers and intelligentsia into a revolutionary party.

The prosecutor's argument that the influence of Russian radicalism brought the Poles to terrorism is repeated by most historians of the Proletariat, from Rosa Luxemburg in 1903 to the most recent, Lucjan Blit.[39] Similarly, memoirists from the period blame Proletariat terrorism on the impact of Russian radicalism on the Congress Kingdom. As Feliks Kon wrote, "the formation of a socialist organization in Poland followed to a large extent the example of Russia, from Russia also was taken the form of struggle . . . political terror."[40] In his memoirs, Ludwik Krzywicki suggested that the Poles were by nature opposed to terrorism and that such activities were imported into the

Congress Kingdom by "russified" Poles.[41] Although an admirer of
Ludwik Waryński, the founder and leader of the Proletariat, Krzywicki nevertheless maintained that Waryński was "fundamentally
bewitched by Narodnaia Volia [and] dreamed of terror."[42] Lev Deich,
a leading Russian antiterrorist radical, shared Krzywicki's estimation
of Waryński and, in addition, suggested that the generally positive
response of Poles to the successful *narodovol'tsy* assassination of
Alexander II transformed hundreds of peaceful Polish propagandists
into advocates of terror.[43]

The most thorough contemporary historians of the Proletariat —
the German Ulrich Haustein, the Pole Leon Baumgarten, and the
Soviet T. G. Snytko — agree that Narodnaia Volia had an influence,
but not a primary influence, on the Proletariat's use of terrorism.
Haustein claims that because the Proletariat directed its acts of
terrorism only against party members, these acts "could not be equated
with the deeds of Narodnaia Volia."[44] Baumgarten, on the other hand,
carefully distinguishes between fundamentally propagandistic "economic" terror and "political" terror; the Proletariat, he asserts, viewed
terrorism from the former "economic" perspective, and Narodnaia
Volia used terrorism as a "political" weapon.[45] Snytko, in reference to
Baumgarten's thesis on Polish terrorism, pointedly objects to this distinction. The Poles and Russians viewed terrorism from precisely the
same perspective; revolutionary violence was a necessary retaliatory
measure against persecution of "peaceful propagandists by the tsarist
authorities." "Therefore," Snytko concludes, "the matter had nothing
to do with the recognition by Polish socialists of terror as a *correct*
method of socialist activities in general, but in the recognition of it as a
necessary measure, applicable only in the conditions of Russia."[46]

A resolution of this debate on the role of terrorism in the ideology
and organization of the Proletariat is crucial to the understanding of
the origins, development, and the significance of the movement as a
whole. If one concludes that the members of the Proletariat used terrorism in conscious or even subconscious imitation of their Russian
comrades, then it can be argued that the Proletariat was simply the
Polish wing of Narodnaia Volia. With this view of Proletariat terrorism, it can also be argued, as it is by Kon, Krzywicki, and Rosa
Luxemburg, that the Polish party though purely Marxist at its inception, was led astray, perverted, and subsequently weakened by its
stronger and more prestigious Eastern counterpart. If, on the other
hand, one concludes that Proletariat terrorism was qualitatively different from the Russian brand, as does Haustein, then the Polish

movement itself can be considered a unique revolutionary phenomenon within the Russian Empire, and its downfall can be attributed to
its own deficiencies. Finally, the historiographical arguments over the
"purity" of the Proletariat's Marxism depend to a considerable extent
on Baumgarten's clear distinction between the ostensibly Marxist
"economic" terror of the Proletariat and the populist "political" terror
of Narodnaia Volia.

Terrorism in Theory

The Proletariat formally announced its existence as a Marxist
revolutionary party in the fall of 1882. From that point until its demise
in 1886, its leaders seriously discussed the place of terrorism in its
struggle to organize revolutionary Poles in the Congress Kingdom.[47]
Not until the article "On Assassinations" appeared in *Przedświt* in
June 1884, however, did the Proletariat publicly defend the merits of
terrorism. In "On Assassinations," the Poles reiterated that a conclu-
sive, bloody revolution was the only means to bring about the "liberation of working people." Before this revolution could occur, however,
many minor skirmishes between the forces of the proletariat and those
of capitalism would have to take place. In these skirmishes, *Przedświt*
continued, the party would play the crucial role of efficiently directing
the efforts of the workers, at the same time maintaining the ultimate
vision of a socialist revolution. "While we bravely attack the enemy,"
Przedświt warned, "we must have an organization that understands
the goals before it." The maintenance of the party was therefore a
paramount consideration, and terrorism in *Przedświt's* view was a
legitimate means of party protection.[48] When "On Assassinations"
provoked a flurry of protests on the part of Legal Marxist and
Economist party sympathizers of the Proletariat who claimed that
terrorism hindered the party's propagandistic goals, the underground
newspaper of the Proletariat responded that terrorism not only protected the party against government persecution but also served an
important political function. "No one then can doubt that the terrorist
struggle bears fruit," wrote *Proletariat,* "accelerating the idea of
freedom in our country. . . . It is not terror that stands as an impediment to those wishing to propagandize, but the lack of that wish
[itself]."[49] By the time of the preparations for the sixth and unpublished number of *Proletariat* (1886), the party openly considered terror
an integral part of the socialist struggle: "Terror is the red cape that
drives the bourgeoisie and government wild. They, it goes without

saying, call terror itself only bloody deeds. . . . Let them consider us terrorists! . . . We should recognize that terror is considered the best weapon in our struggle."[50]

The Proletariat's expanded justification of the use of terrorism in the years 1882–86 can be attributed primarily to the escalation of the direct struggle between the government and the socialists during this period. The government increasingly made use of provocateurs and informants to undermine the Proletariat's activities; the party in turn devoted more and more energy to eliminating police spies. After his own arrest on 28 September 1883, Ludwik Waryński wrote to Kunicki and Dębski from prison, encouraging them to "pay attention to traitors, in order that they cause no further damage."[51]

The importance of terrorism to the members of the Proletariat originated as much in their own relationship to the workers of the Congress Kingdom as in their increasingly bitter attitude toward the authorities. During the period 1878–82, the socialists entered into propaganda work with an ebullient faith in the immediacy of social revolution. The formation of the Proletariat followed the recognition in 1881–82 that a political struggle was necessary to hold off government repression of propagandists and to organize the unprepared workers behind the revolution. The socialists soon learned that the authorities would not tolerate any socialist propaganda and, perhaps more importantly, that the workers were not ready to overthrow the social order. The Proletariat further concluded that until the workers became revolutionary the party must persevere and that terror was a legitimate means for maintaining the party. "The question of emancipating the people is not that easily accomplished," admitted *Przedświt*. Socialist propaganda and the "bankruptcy of today's order of things" would, indeed, inevitably bring about the revolution, though it clearly was not just around the bend.[52]

The prosecutor claimed with some justification that especially Stanisław Kunicki, the leader of the Proletariat in 1884, used terrorism to elevate the authority and visibility of the party in this gestation period of the revolution.[53] Nevertheless, the party itself repeatedly insisted that terrorism was of only minor importance in the context of the ultimate struggle. As *Walka Klas* wrote, "Terror as a means we will and at times must use, but a terrorist party we are not and can never be."[54] "On Terror," written on the eve of the party's demise, repudiated the accusation that the Proletariat had become obsessed by terror: "The question arises whether such terror might bring about the revolution. No! Terrorism does not make a revolution . . . one must be ready for everything, one must say from the first that terror is sometimes a very brave means of struggle, but one must never forget that a social revolution will not be the action of individuals but the matter of the whole working class, organized and conscious of its goals."[55] The party's use of terrorism therefore did not indicate, as some historians have suggested, that the Proletariat abandoned its Marxist position on revolution. It did indicate that a revolutionary Marxist party under an authoritarian monarchy such as the Russian autocracy would necessarily make certain tactical changes to adjust both to the political realities of confronting police action and to the complexities of organizing a relatively young working class.

Terrorism in Practice

As we saw in Chapter 7, the Proletariat's use of terrorism in the Piotrków industrial region followed a distinct pattern. On the initiative of local workers' committees and with the approval of the Central Committee, often semiliterate and generally young working-class party members were recruited to carry out assassinations. The victims — Helszer and Śremski — were party members suspected of complicity with the police. The party followed the assassination attempts with explanations, and the deeds were generally applauded by the working population of the textile centers. Although the party orally and in notes threatened the lives of the most obstreperous factory-owners and foremen, the socialists carried out no known terrorist acts against them.

The pattern of revolutionary violence in the Warsaw region was roughly similar. It is difficult, however, to gauge the reactions to the assassinations among Warsaw workers' circles since they were socially and economically more diverse than the textile workers of the Piotrków region. Although the Warsaw Proletariat threatened to kill two party members suspected of treachery — Leonard Gzowski and Napoleon Mehle[56] — the only assassinations to take place were those of a tram conductor, Michał Skrzypczyński, in August 1884 and the police provocateur Piotr Piński (Piotrowski) in July 1886.

Aleksander Dębski recalled that the workers themselves demanded the death of Skrzypczyński. They, "in view of the obvious treachery, naturally called for the removal of the traitor Skrzypczyński . . . who was the reason for [Henryk] Dulęba's arrest. All Warsaw knew and loved Dulęba. The workers point-blank desired that the traitor be sentenced to death."[57] On 3 August 1884 the Fighting Squad, the organization created by Kunicki and Dębski to carry out Warsaw terrorist acts, passed sentence on Skrzypczyński, and the matter was entrusted to S. Gładysz, P. Dąbrowski, and M. Ossowski. On 7 August "at 11:30 in the evening a youth [Ossowski] approached Michał Skrzypczyński, . . . and under the pretext of lighting a cigarette, fatally stabbed him in the stomach, as a result of which Skrzypczyński died on 26 August."[58] On the day of the alleged traitor's death, a printed proclamation appeared on the streets of Warsaw signed by the Central Committee: "In the struggle we carry on with the Russian government, the most tyrannical and autocratic in Europe, we have been forced to call upon violent measures, corresponding to those the government uses against us." After explaining that Skrzypczyński was sentenced to death for his treachery, the proclamation concluded, "We continue to announce that no traitor or informer will escape the death sentence."[59]

The assassination attempt on Piotr Piński proved to be the final terrorist act of the Proletariat. After Marian Ulrych revived the party in the beginning of 1886, he and his immediate comrades were arrested in March and April owing to the information delivered by Piński to the police. After several months of hiding, the few remaining party functionaries decided to carry out the long-prepared sentence on Piński.[60] (Several other assassinations were planned as well; the police discovered a number of printed form proclamations announcing the death of traitor "blank" on "blank" day, 1886.)[61] The party assigned the Piński assassination to the workers Wiktor Hipszer and Władysław Kowalewski. On 1 July 1886 Kowalewski shot Piński three times, wounding him seriously but not fatally.[62] The authorities hanged Kowalewski (4 September 1886) for his part in the assassination attempt. The Russian government, unusually severe in its punishment of the entire Ulrych group, exiled Hipszer to Sakhalin for life.[63]

More significant to the general problem of terrorism in the Proletariat than these terrorist attempts on the lives of alleged traitors were the discussions within party circles about politically motivated terrorism. The Proletariat carried out no major "political" assassinations, and Haustein is thus correct in differentiating its defensive use of terrorism in party circles from Narodnaia Volia's "political" terrorism.[64] Yet considerable evidence suggests that the Proletariat at least contemplated political assassinations of major government figures. If in fact it did not assassinate them only because the party could not muster the resources to do so, then it would be difficult to dissociate completely their view of terrorism from that of the Russian party. Bolesław Sławiński and Stanisław Kunicki, for instance, excitedly discussed the prospect of assassinating the governor-general of the Congress Kingdom, I. V. Gurko.[65] The Proletariat also considered assassinating its more direct persecutors — Prosecutor Iankulio and the Gendarme Colonel Sekerninskii.[66]

Even before his arrest, Waryński was reported to have been positively inclined toward an assassination attempt on the life of the tsar. "Whether this thought was in passing or whether it was a permanent objective," wrote B. Jędrzejowski, Waryński's biographer, "we do not know."[67] After Waryński's arrest and with the new leadership cf Kunicki, the Proletariat genuinely favored the assassination of the tsar. At a large meeting in early 1884, the leaders of the party and of the workers' circles raised "the question of the necessity of the tsar's assassination and the benefits that would accrue from it. Kunicki was of the opinion that this act was necessary and positive, because through the arousal of fear one could count on concession."[68]

Kunicki's and Waryński's favorable reactions to the question of assassinating Alexander III do not necessarily indicate that they wanted the Proletariat to do it. In fact, two weeks before his arrest, Kunicki informed Pacanowski that the Executive Committee of Narodnaia Volia would once again assassinate the tsar.[69] The Okhrana did report, however, that after the arrests of 1884, the remaining Proletariat leaders drew up definite plans to assassinate the tsar in Warsaw.[70] In this connection, the authorities found on Maria Bohuszewiczówna two printed copies of the following manifesto to the tsar, entitled "Milostivyi Gosudar'" and signed by the Central Committee: "The Workers' Committee calls for the completion of your death sentence, resolved by the above-named committee as a result of your inhumane treatment of workers; therefore, we warn you that if you do not change your course of action, then despite [our] aversion to shedding blood, we will be forced to agree with this extreme [action]."[71] The recent research of a senior Polish party historian, Żanna Kormanowa, in the archives of a Dutch envoy in Warsaw corroborates scattered evidence that the Proletariat planned, at least, to assassinate Alexander III at his coronation as King of Poland in Warsaw.[72] Although Leon Baumgarten skillfully debunks the reliability of this Dutch source in his review of Kormanowa's work,[73] the question remains: did the Proletariat not carry out political assassinations because this conflicted with their ideological views of terrorism, did it simply not have the resources to carry out such actions, or did assassination somehow conflict with its status as a working-class party?

Polish Terrorism and the Russians

Although many historians argue that the Russians introduced terrorism into the Polish movement, the actual history of Proletariat terrorism indicates otherwise. First of all, the assassinations in Łódź and Zgierz, immensely popular among the local workers, were planned and carried out by non-"Russianized" Polish workers. Similarly, though the Warsaw organization was led by Poles who for the most part had been schooled in Russia, the actual "terrorists" in the Warsaw region were local workers. Jan Krzesławski, in his biography of Piotr Dąbrowski, the artisan assassin of the police agent Skrzypczyński, noted that the use of terrorism as a political weapon was far from unknown to the Polish working people. "The principles of political terror, to which the Proletariat paid homage, could not discourage him [Dąbrowski], but rather attracted [him]. In Warsaw artisan circles terror was unusually popular. From among the artisans were recruited the perpetrators of the attempts on the Grand Prince Konstantin Nikolaevich, on Lüders, on Wielopolski, and very many other so-called daggermen [*sztyletnicy*]."[74]

The Polish working class's acceptance of terror independent of Russian influence was matched by the Polish radical intelligentsia's openness to the possible use of terrorism. The initial Proletariat program included among its political measures: "We will punish spies, traitors, and in general those who from personal motives betray the cause."[75] In November 1883 the Proletariat clearly warned its opponents of an all-out terrorist struggle. "Comrades . . . do not forget — that over our corpses, socialism marches to triumph. . . . To arrests and investigations we answer from our side with doubled energy and carefulness — for traitors and oppressors we are drawing our daggers."[76]

Almost from the Proletariat's beginning in 1882, its leaders carried guns and knives with them in their trips around Warsaw from meeting to meeting. In July 1884, in a Warsaw milk bar, the police intercepted one such meeting among Aleksander Dębski, Bronisław Sławiński, and Ludwik Janowicz. When the police attempted to arrest them, the three drew their guns, fired at the police, and ran.[77] With the bravado typical of many Proletariat leaders, Dębski described the incident: "Our shots caused a sensation, it was the first shot fired after the 1863 revolution, the shots of revolutionaries in the very center of Warsaw."[78] It was with this same bravado and inflated confidence in violent resistance that Dębski, among others, called for the organization "of a special secret committee to carry on the terrorist struggle with the government."[79] Feliks Kon, an early opponent of direct violent attacks on the government, later planned to blow up the offices of the Warsaw prosecutor with the help of Sławiński and Kunicki.[80] Kon himself recalled that the plan was given up because the group's inexperience with explosive devices had already caused several accidental explosions in the laboratory.[81] Other Proletariat bombing targets included the offices of the factoryowners Poznański in Łódź and Walman in Zgierz.[82]

Waryński, often dissociated by historians from the terrorism of the Proletariat, rapidly accepted the terrorist necessities of the socialist struggle in the Congress Kingdom and was responsible, according to the police, for the importation of "ten revolvers of the bulldog type."[83] "We will kill all spies and traitors," Waryński was reported to have said at a meeting.[84] The police reported that the members of the Proletariat were in general admirably outfitted with the weapons of a terrorist struggle: they had "revolvers, daggers, brass knuckles, poisons. Several members carried weapons on themselves."[85] In fact, by 1884 the terrorist struggle had reached the point where the Proletariat assigned assassinations to a separate group, the Fighting Squad. The Squad, wrote the prosecutor:

> was made up primarily of workers and artisans . . . who either themselves undertook the carrying out of terrorist actions (Kmiecik, Gostkiewicz); or other members of the group (Formiński, Sieroszewski) searched out those people (Mańkowski, Gładysz, Dąbrowski, Ossowski, Trzeszkowski), who as a result of a taste for laziness were ready for easy money, and at any provocation to fall (with a knife in hand) on the accused man.[85]

Although these men were not the apolitical, throat-slitting vagabonds that the prosecutor described, their activities grew so intense that the tenor of the organization shifted toward terrorist activities and away from propagandistic work. In mid-1885 the leadership of Bohuszewiczówna had returned the major effort to propaganda among the working class; but now the government marked the Proletariat as "terrorist" and therefore moved decisively to crush its remaining members.

In a letter of 1924 to V. Burtsev, Kacpar Turski, the first Polish socialist terrorist and the co-editor of *Nabat,* praised Burtsev's recently published memoirs, but also protested against his treatment of

Russian terrorism: "Speaking only of terror, you lead the readers and the future historians of the Russian revolution to an error by attributing to Narodnaia Volia, Stepniak, and others the initiation of the idea of terror. This is completely false and misleading. Drahomanov was a hundred percent correct when he wrote that the idea of terrorism came from daily action [*vyshla iz raboty*]."[87] The Polish terrorists — Kunicki, Schmaus, Pietrusiński, and others — should be examined in the same context as their Russian counterparts, that is, as products of the political structure of the Russian Empire. That Polish terrorism was indeed generally confined to party self-defense and "factory terror" attests not to any basic ideological difference with Narodnaia Volia, though those differences did exist, but to the fact that the Poles' party apparatus, methods, and goals derived from the growing class consciousness among Polish workers in the Congress Kingdom. Although the Proletariat leaders became increasingly concerned with their private duel with the Warsaw police and judicial authorities, this kind of party structure and party work among Polish workers militated against the use of direct political terrorism, a method, on the other hand, well suited to the political goals and social isolation of Narodnaia Volia within the Russian Empire.

X

Epilogue: The Years of Transition in Polish Politics, 1886–87

In the spring and summer of 1886, the tsarist authorities successfully destroyed the already severely weakened central organization of the Proletariat. The government *Chronicle* of the revolutionary movement noted about the year 1886 in the Congress Kingdom: "Socialist propaganda among the workers in Warsaw in this year was less fruitful than in the previous years; only two circles (the tailors and the locksmiths) functioned; on the other hand, the workers' organizations in the provinces — in Zgierz, Tomaszów, and Łódź — grew very rapidly."[1] Therefore, although 1886 saw the demise of the Proletariat, it did not spell the end of working-class socialism in the Congress Kingdom. Rather it began as a genuinely autonomous element of the Polish labor movement. Herein resides the main contribution of the Proletariat — through the party's efforts, a socialist class consciousness was indelibly imprinted onto the Polish workers' movement. With the party destroyed and in shambles in mid-1886, Ludwik Kulczycki was still able to write that it was "difficult to find a worker or artisan who had not heard of the Proletariat, [the party] that defended the interests of the working classes, that struggled with the possessing class and government, and to which belonged socialists."[2] In 1890 socialism among the Congress Kingdom workers was widespread enough to organize a May first demonstration of about 8,000 workers. In 1892 the famous Łódź strike involved over 20,000 workers and provoked large-scale street battles between workers and the authorities.[3]

The Proletariat therefore fulfilled its historical mission well. Its propaganda and agitation found receptive ground among Polish workers suffering the repercussions of the great surge of Congress Kingdom industrialization in the 1870s and the depression of the 1880s. That the strength of the intelligentsia-led Proletariat dissipated while socialism advanced within the working class can only partly be attributed to what the Russian authorities called "strong measures taken against the members of the Proletariat."[4] Of equal importance to the fate of socialism among educated Poles was their inner questioning of its validity as a form of political struggle. As we have seen, beginning in 1877–78, socialists launched a successful attack on the intellectual predominance of Warsaw Positivism to the extent that, by 1881–82, socialism had won over a substantial portion of Polish educated youth. Now, in 1886–87, Polish socialism, especially in its internationalist and Marxist form, was faced by the new political and intellectual challenge of modern Polish nationalism.

Much like the dialectical force of socialism's assault on positivism, the force of modern nationalism swept aside socialist ideology by the early 1890s, in the process incorporating some of its tenets and destroying others. As in the origins of the positivist and socialist movements, the emergence of modern Polish nationalism can be tied to concrete social and economic developments in the Congress Kingdom: in the case of nationalism, to the maturation both of the lower middle class in the towns and of a politically conscious peasantry in the countryside. The impact of these processes can be traced to the end of the 1880s when intelligentsia interest and action shifted from the arena of international socialism and the Proletariat to various forms of nationalism.

The Proletariat in 1886–87

Languishing in his prison cell in St. Petersburg, Ludwik Waryński justifiably worried about the fate of the party he had so painstakingly helped to organize. Two basic dangers threatened the party, he confided to a prison comrade: the first was the tendency of émigré party leaders to favor tactics used in Western parties, entertaining even the idea of serving as a parliamentary opposition; the second, a more significant and immediate danger, was "patriotism," which threatened the party from the outside as well as divided the movement from within.[5]

Waryński's observations were uncannily astute; part of the reason the Proletariat fell was that by 1885 the leading figures of the party (Mendelson, Jankowska, and Dębski) were living in Paris and thus out of touch with the problems of the movement. As the struggle in the Congress Kingdom turned gradually to a direct and bloody confrontation between the socialists and the police, the émigrés increasingly and irrelevantly proclaimed the merits of Western-style agitation. The "class struggle," wrote *Przedświt,* "does not only mean the bloody fight in the future, but rather the struggle that unites the workers by any means against their enemies."[6] Not until the spring of 1887, a full year after the fall of the remnants of the Proletariat, did the émigrés recognize the futility of a semilegal struggle in the Congress Kingdom.[7] Also, by the beginning of 1887, the once decidedly internationalist *Walka Klas* reopened the discussion of socialist-patriotism: the elimination of class distinctions must go hand in hand with an "intelligible and sensible idea of national honor."[8]

While the émigré Proletariat continued to discuss the problems of legalism and patriotism in its press, the movement at home suffered from unremitting arrests and searches. From Warsaw, "B.T.G." wrote to Paris in July 1886: "Here, we again have arrests. It is the yearly tribute our organization must pay to the contemporary order of things."[9] Although the imprisoned socialists optimistically viewed the future of the revolutionary movement in the Congress Kingdom, they also wrote to their "Dear Comrades" in 1886 that even though the government certainly was never on the side of the socialists, the Proletariat's increased political involvement "means, to be sure, that they will persecute us even more."[10] Increased police surveillance of the party did not entirely halt the flow of new young intelligentsia members into its ranks but did reduce it to a trickle.[11] Publication of revolutionary and socialist manifestos ceased, organizational activities stopped, and terrorism disappeared; the movement, in short, expired.[12]

The Appearance of "New Patriotism"

For twenty years, from 1865 to 1885, materialism in its positivist and socialist forms engaged the loyalty of the Polish intelligentsia. To be sure, patriotism had not simply vanished — the indignities of Russianization made sure of that. Still, in the view of the educated public of the Congress Kingdom, patriotism remained a tainted and outmoded political formula in the face of the seemingly more dynamic theories of positivism and socialism. The powerful force of nationalism emerging at the end of the 1880s was not simply the continuation of a Polish patriotism that had lain low for twenty years, waiting for the right moment to reemerge. In its early and "democratic" stage Polish nationalism was a genuinely new ideological force, which, though tracing its ancestry to the patriotic past, was nevertheless born in the socialist and positivist struggles of the late 1870s and 1880s.

The ideologues of this new force in Polish political history — Bolesław Wysłouch, Zygmunt Balicki, J. S. Potocki (Marian Bohusz), and Jan Popławski arrived at their nationalism from the training grounds of the socialist struggle.[13] From their socialist past, these nationalists derived their ultimate devotion to the *lud* — the people — as well as their distrust of liberalism and constitutionalism in its Warsaw Positivist form. From the positivists they borrowed the concept of the "social organism" and the organic view of history, rejecting in the process, also like the positivists, the legitimacy of class conflict. The nationalists added to this formula a strong populist element — devotion to the peasantry, suspicion of the intelligentsia, and ambivalence toward the benefits of industrialization. Stanisław Czekanowski, typical of this new generation of patriots, admitted that he was an eclectic; he rejected the class struggle in socialism but sympathized with socialism as a form of "national solidarity with the interests of the whole standing above those of individuals."[14]

As in the case of socialism, the new patriotism began its struggle for intellectual acceptance on the pages of the positivist press with the articles of Marian Bohusz in *Przegląd Tygodniowy* and Jan Popławski in *Prawda*. Beginning in 1885, Bohusz wrote for *Przegląd* a series of articles devoted to the Polish peasantry and peasant *gmina* in which he advocated the formation of agricultural credit unions and the extension of the *gmina*'s juridical prerogatives.[15] But Jan Popławski's articles in *Prawda* were of greater ultimate consequence to the development of Polish nationalism. In a series entitled "Social Life," Popławski (the one-time Szymański conspirator) attempted to define what he himself termed the "new patriotism."[16] In his view, the old patriotism was the property of the gentry. Like *szlachta* democracy, it "was never the natural expression of the enlightened aspirations of the lower classes." In contrast to this class-exclusive patriotism of the past, Popławski announced the existence of a "contemporary patriotism, perhaps better — a natural [patriotism]." The patriotism of the past served "the narrow interests" of the gentry; the new patriotism is "progressive, conquering, and creating new values." The patriotism of the past is rapidly losing its strength and relevance; the new patriotism "conserves [its resources] for a future day."[17]

In an implicit criticism of positivism, Popławski accused the intelligentsia of having isolated itself from the Polish people as a whole and, more specifically, from the masses of Polish peasants, in whose hands rested the real future of Poland. At the same time, he discarded the socialists because they opposed the modest, though beneficial, program of Organic Work, which he defined as "work toward the development of its [the people's] intellectual, moral, and material strength."[18] Popławski also took up the positivists' cry that socialists only provided ammunition for "our grey-horsed conservatives" who conjure up the specter of nihilism to stop the tide of liberalism and national progress.[19] Popławski also hinted at a further motif of modern Polish nationalist thought — anti-Semitism. Too much land, he complained, was falling "into the hands of elements spiritually and tribally foreign to us" as a result of the gradual dissolution of large gentry estates.[20] Aleksander Świętochowski, the editor of *Prawda* and the leading publicist of Warsaw Positivism, recognized the dangerous aspects of this "new patriotism," the by-product of what he called an "ethic of egoism," as unscientific as it was impractical. When materialism and positivism were bringing about such basic transformations in the intellectual and economic life of the Congress Kingdom, when society was acquainted with "the theory of Marx and the unfinished chain of its practical results," he wondered aloud, how could there still be those who yielded to slogans of patriotism. In his earlier criticisms of socialism, Świętochowski expressed an implicit fear of the masses of workers; he now responded to Popławski's "new patriotism" with a warning against arousing the lethargic Polish peasantry. The masses of peasants have no idea about the benefits of materialism, wrote Świętochowski, and they too quickly learn the principles of the glorification of power. Herein, concluded Świętochowski, "reside the bases of the corruption of our century."[21]

Głos and Przegląd Społeczny

The year 1886 also marked the appearance of two new periodicals directed to the problems of political and social action in the Congress Kingdom: *Głos* (Voice), edited by J. S. Potocki (Marian Bohusz), and *Przegląd Społeczny* (Social Review), edited by Bolesław Wysłouch. The founders of and contributors to these periodicals represented a broad cross section of progressive intelligentsia who were dissatisfied with both the positivist liberals and the socialist revolutionaries. They were considerably more patriotic, more concerned with the peasantry, and more "tribal" (anti-Semitic and anti-Russian) in their approach than either the positivists or socialists. Although they did not reject completely the concept of class struggle as posed by the socialists, they tended to see it in the rather oversimplified terms of conflict between two civilizations — that of the privileged and enlightened Poles versus that of the broad masses of peasants, workers, and artisans. These publicists expressed their solidarity with the latter, the masses, in which they discovered the "new patriotism," the real Poland, forecast by Popławski in *Prawda*.

The program of *Głos* appeared as the "Prospekt" (Prospectus) in its first issue (1886) and proclaimed the intention of the new patriots "to subordinate the interests of separate classes to . . . the interests of the *lud.*"[22] Stefan Żeromski, the talented Polish positivist writer and journalist, commented on the controversial "Prospekt": "*Głos* has begun to babble naively. It calls itself a progressive journal. . . . Lovely, wonderful, magnificent. What have they shown to this point? Not one fact — where the interests of separate classes will be subordinated to the interests of the people. They've done nothing."[23] In his indignation over a program without a party and a platform without a means to implement it, Żeromski overlooked the importance of the appearance of *Głos*. In itself, Potocki's "Prospekt" was a powerful criticism of both the positivists' and the socialists' inability to garner the forces of the nation behind them. The demoralized atmosphere of the Congress Kingdom's political and social life in 1886, wrote Potocki, was proof enough of this fact.

> After numerous difficult trials, our society has entered a state of weakness and apathy, in which the awakening of a new intellectual force has become indispensable. All around us we see confused ideas and beliefs, the fall of old programs and of slogans of domestic politics, a lack of clear examples of goals for societal development. . . . Yet, stirred by a love of country, we cannot close our eyes to its defeats and contemporary weaknesses, and all the more intensely we will search there, where a vital strength is concealed, where exist the seeds of a new harvest.

The seeds of the future Poland, Potocki claimed, were embedded in the Polish masses, the true Polish nation, though not necessarily in the Polish state. "We will begin our struggle not over the existence of an independent state, but over the life of the tribe, a struggle that all the reserves of the people must join." The duty of the intelligentsia, then, was "to recognize the *lud* as the most important element of the national community." Although he took his pen name "Bohusz" from his friend Maria Bohuszewiczówna, the leader of the Proletariat in 1886, Potocki disengaged his new movement both from the socialists and from the positivists: "We will support on the one hand any endeavor that has as its goal the liberation of labor, but on the other, we declare war with the apostles of cosmopolitan socialism, who do not remember that our people have their own perception of happiness and will not allow themselves to be dragged along by abstract formulas from foreign sources."

Potocki left open the possibility that *Głos* and the positivists might work together, because, after all, they were both for "knowledge and progress." But he firmly rejected what he saw as the "caste or class exclusiveness" in the positivist camp. He also affirmed *Głos's* positivist-style concern for economic improvement and advocated "the greatest accumulation of national wealth in all areas of production, as well as its normal distribution." On the other hand, in stark contradistinction to the positivists, he was not at all impressed with "the ideal of capitalism." Unlike both the positivist and socialist programs, the "Prospekt" argued that religion had beneficial effects on the life of the masses. "It does not hurt us to recognize the powerful force of religious feeling in the lives of the people," Potocki wrote; religion exerts a strong "moral influence" among the folk and is held in high esteem by them.[24]

Catholic, democratic, patriotic, and peasantist, the core of the *Głos* world view can be best classified as a form of Polish populism, less socialist and antiindustrial than its Russian relative of the 1870s and 1880s, but considerably more nationalistic. The *Głos* column "Our Periodicals" described it thus:

> National consciousness must be based on the feelings of the masses, who have no historical tradition. . . . The Polish *lud* [nevertheless] preserved their nationality more strongly than did the educated classes. Without a historical tradition, the *lud* have a tribal feeling, a love of the land on which they grew up. . . . To awaken the minds of the *lud*, to fortify their strength, to guarantee them land — this is the task of contemporary patriotism, the task of the intelligentsia.[25]

On the question of the role of the intelligentsia, *Głos* can be considered a bridge between the democratic traditions, socialism, positivism, and socialist-patriotism of the 1880s and the Dmowskiite nationalism of the 1890s.[26]

The extent to which this populist-nationalism of the "new patriotism" can be linked to the later, vituperative National Democracy of Roman Dmowski is *Głos's* attitude toward the Congress Kingdom's Jewish population. In a two-part article entitled "Anti-Semitism and the Jewish Question," *Głos* reveals a major dilemma of the "new patriots" — its schizophrenic, that is democratic and racist approach to the Jewish problem. "Jews should have the same rights as other citizens," *Głos* announced, "which would have the even better effect of facilitating their freely chosen emigration." One must remember, it added, that the Jewish problem is only a symptom of the deeper ills of the social and economic order. Yet Jews "specialize in certain forms of oppression, and from among them are recruited the majority of its representatives." The state should not make laws against Jews, but against usurers; of course, among the latter, "Jews compose 99 out of 100."[27]

The anti-Semitic aspect of the "new patriotism" was evident as well in *Głos*'s ruminations on the problem of national assimilation. Although there is no way of knowing the results of such "tribal assimilation," *Głos* maintained, it is inadvisable to encourage it. The masses would never consider it, and assimilation among the educated classes "we would forthrightly call harmful and dangerous to our national growth." There was already too great a difference between gentry and peasant, capitalist and employee. These differences would be minuscule in comparison to racial differences. Under contemporary conditions, then, the only thing to do, stated *Głos,* democratically to be sure, was "to aspire toward a civic assimilation," to attempt "to teach the Jews to be members of our society, Poles of semitic origin and Hebrew faith." "In the sphere of tribal and religious relations we see no other way out." Everything would work out reasonably well "if these new citizens tie themselves to us in an alliance of conscious aspirations."[28]

In 1886, as Potocki was establishing *Głos,* Bolesław Wysłouch, the socialist critic of the "Brussels Program" and co-leader of Limanowski's socialist patriotic Lud Polski, founded the Lwów periodical *Przegląd Społeczny.* Although *Głos* developed from the democratic, "organic" views of the positivist press and combined this with the "new patriotism," *Przegląd* owed its intellectual origins primarily to the socialist movement. In *Przegląd,* Wysłouch meshed the "new patriotism" with a revolutionary commitment to the political struggle against the autocracy. *Przegląd* also incorporated many elements of both Proletariat and populist ideology; Plekhanov, Debagorii-Mokrievich, Kazimierz Dłuski, Ivan Franko, Limanowski, and other prominent socialists wrote articles for its first issue.[29] Still, it was not a socialist periodical; rather, as Kulczycki wrote, it was "an expression of a new social-political trend, a manifestation of the dissatisfaction with the existing state of affairs in the Polish lands."[30]

Wysłouch's program in *Przegląd* never became much clearer than Kulczycki's "general dissatisfaction," in part because the Austrian authorities closed down the carefully censored periodical within six months of its foundation. The goal of *Przegląd,* as stated in the first number of 1886, was "to develop programmatic courses" and to formulate "a contemporary program of activity" based on an umbrella concept of "sociopolitical reorganization." The "ideal structure" to which the periodical referred was never defined.[31] In fact, neither

Przegląd nor *Głos* can be said to have advocated a specific political program, though especially the latter worked closely with the Liga Polska (Polish League) in the Congress Kingdom.[32] Still, Wysłouch made it clear enough in his journal that the interests of the Polish nation and the Polish peasantry were one and the same, thus supporting the historian Peter Brock's assertion that *Przegląd* and Wysłouch established "the ideological foundations upon which the building of the future peasant movement arose."[33] More importantly, *Przegląd,* together with *Głos,* challenged the positivists' and socialists' fundamental assumptions about Polish society and found willing converts among the Polish intelligentsia.

Miłkowski's Rzecz, Liga Polska, and Zet

The political program of the new Polish patriotism vaguely broached by *Głos* and *Przegląd Społeczny* crystallized around a pamphlet published in 1887 in Paris by the respected radical democrat and patriot Zygmunt Miłkowski (T. T. Jeż). The *Rzecz o obronie czynnej i skarbie narodowym (On Active Defense and a National Treasury),* written during the preparations for organizing Liga Polska in Switzerland, reiterated Miłkowski's commitment to the careful preparation of an eventual insurrection and the collection of funds for a Polish national treasury. Miłkowski designed this new formulation of his views as a kind of "vade mecum, by which the Polish public could find signposts to direct them through the difficult conditions in the fatherland."[34] In turn, the Congress Kingdom's intelligentsia greeted the pamphlet with an unexpected uproar of approval.[35] The Russian police, increasingly worried about the explosion of patriotic activity in 1887 and 1888, soberly noted that the *Rzecz* noticeably influenced "the mood of Poles both abroad and in the empire."[36] Żeromski, who had been so irritated by *Głos*'s vagueness, now wrote in his diary: "In my opinion Jeż's brochure is the manifesto of the president of the dispersed Polish republic. I welcomed it, loved it, agreed with it. . . . To distribute the brochure as widely as possible, to begin collecting contributions from cellars and attics, to affirm life wherever possible — this is today's task. To die for one's country and independence when its time comes is the task for later."[37]

In his attack on the positivists' passivity in the face of German and Russian assaults on Polish nationhood, Miłkowski revived the idea of a Polish uprising under the rubric of "active defense." Poles should put together a national treasury, carry out moral and educational propaganda among the *lud,* especially in the countryside, and perhaps even engage in the selected use of terrorism.[38] "Active defense" called as well for a national organization that would prepare systematically and above all rationally for the propitious moment when a democratic Poland could rise and seize its freedom. Nothing, insisted Miłkowski, should be left to chance.

It should be noted that Miłkowski did not dissociate himself completely from the patriotism of the past as did Wysłouch and to a greater extent Popławski, Balicki, and Potocki. Instead, he maintained that the socialists and the positivists, as well as repressive tsarist policies, had emasculated but had not wiped out the Polish patriotic movement. Patriotism only "quieted down, but did not abdicate."[40] While the enthusiastic reception of Miłkowski's *Rzecz* indicated a swell of "new patriotism" in the Congress Kingdom, Miłkowski himself represented one of the few solid links between modern Polish nationalism and the democratic *szlachta* patriotism of the Communards and the 1863 generation.

In the autumn of 1887 the organization that Miłkowski had called for in the *Rzecz* was formed in Switzerland under the name "Liga Polska" (Polish League). The Liga's program, also authored by Miłkowski, reiterated the basic tenets of the *Rzecz:* Poles should assemble their financial and moral resources for the purpose of preparing a national uprising; the independence movement could and should not count on outside intervention; therefore, the Liga itself must have a strong and disciplined organization. In addition, the future Poland can exist only as a democratic republic with a just social structure based on the broad masses of the population.[41] The socialist historian Ludwik Kulczycki attacked Jeż for not defining what he meant by "a just social structure," but he admitted, at the same time, that the program repeatedly emphasized the centrality of social justice for the masses.[42]

Shortly after its foundation, the Liga Polska established contacts with Wysłouch of *Przegląd Społeczny,* the Głosites, and Warsaw student circles. In the winter of 1887–88, mainly as the result of the organizational work of the *Przegląd* associate and socialist Zygmunt Balicki, the student youth formed their own group "Związek Młodzieży Polskiej" (Union of Polish Youth), known as "Zet." While the Liga Polska remained primarily an émigré organization of radical democratic patriots, Zet became the central focus of the socially radical, patriotic struggle in the Congress Kingdom itself. The student group maintained a tight-knit secret organization on the masonic model. At the same time, its stated aims and goals were as general and ill-defined as those of its parent Liga Polska.[43] Zet's program announced that it "aspires to an independent Poland and stands on the basis of political, national, and social justice." "The struggle with Germanization and Russianization," it continued, "is not only formally but also spiritually a canon of the Union." Zet hoped to create a new and morally pure "type of Pole." These purified Poles would "inoculate" into the academic youth and into the masses the "highest principles of nationhood."[44]

Zet and Liga Polska were primarily patriotic organizations whose goals revolved around the desire to construct a democratic Poland based on the broad masses of the Polish peasantry. In 1886-87 both organizations vacillated between a form of peasant socialism and radical democracy. In January 1888 Zet formally incorporated itself into the Liga Polska and gradually lost both its socialist content and membership. The young biology student and son of a Warsaw stonemason, Roman Dmowski (with the help of Balicki and Popławski), strengthened the nationalist content of the "new patriotism" and moved it even further from its democratic origins. In 1893, as a result of a "coup" by young Warsaw activists, the Liga Polska became Liga Narodowa (National League), which in turn institutionalized modern Polish nationalism.

Socialism and the "New Patriotism"

Among the intelligentsia of the Congress Kingdom, the Proletariat's socialism was overwhelmed by the combined effects of *Głos, Przegląd Społeczny,* the *Rzecz,* Liga Polska, and Zet. The dynamic, peasant-oriented, democratic nationalism of Miłkowski, Balicki, and Wysłouch proved more compelling than Waryński's Marxism and internationalism. Even in the socialist movement itself, the Proletariat's ideology fell victim to the new forces of nationalism. The party's successor groups — the "Second Proletariat" (1887-88), and the Związek Polskich Robotników (Union of Polish Workers, 1890-91) — were considerably weaker and more oriented toward economism and, in the case of the Second Proletariat, toward patriotism than the Proletariat itself had been.[45] There was a "clearly distinguishable" ideological discontinuity between the first and second Proletariat, according to the German historian of Polish socialism, Ulrich Haustein; the second Proletariat "did not leave patriotism to the bourgeoisie, in fact, it even attempted to rescue love of Fatherland from bourgeois misuse."[46] The historian of National Democracy, Władysław Pobóg-Malinowski, also pointed to the profound "ideological evolution" that the socialist movement experienced — from "doctrinal internationalism to the recognition and practical application of the slogan of the struggle for independence."[47]

Under the influence of the nationalist consensus of the 1890s, even the surviving members of the Proletariat denounced the party's internationalist past and vilified the program of Rosa Luxemburg's Social Democratic Party of the Kingdom of Poland and Lithuania (SDKPiL). It is interesting to note in this context that few members of the Proletariat went on to be Marxist internationalists in the 1890s; when political at all, they aligned themselves mostly with patriotic parties of the left and right rather than with the SDKPiL, the party with the greatest ideological affinity to the Proletariat.[48] For example, Aleksander Dębski , in a letter to a friend in 1896, assailed the Proletariat for not raising the flag of the national struggle in order to mobilize the masses of workers around the socialist movement. "Today, however," Dębski wrote, "the Polish socialist party [PPS] to which we belong derives from the desire of the Polish working class to place as the most immediate of its goals, the formation of an independent Polish republic. We think that in such a republic, our proletariat, earlier than in other circumstances, can receive the opportunity to take power in its own hands for the introduction of a socialist order."[49]

The ideological transformation from internationalism to nationalism in the socialist movement, which began in 1886-87, was completed with the foundation of the Polish Socialist Party (PPS) in 1892. Józef Piłsudski, the leader of the PPS and with Dmowski the co-architect of the second Polish republic, reportedly portrayed his own personal ideological development in terms of having stepped "off the red tram at the stop of independence."[50] As a consequence of the "fashion of socialism," wrote Piłsudski, he became a follower of the Proletariat in 1884. All of his Vilna comrades who went on to become members of a wide range of political movements "for a shorter or longer time" were socialists. Indeed, he added, "no one from the most intelligent and energetic of my colleagues avoided passing through a socialist phase in their development."[51]

The Proletariat therefore served a dual historical function. It was, to be sure, the first Polish Marxist party and as such the predecessor of the SDKPiL, the Communist Party of Poland (KPP), and the contemporary Polish United Workers' Party, the PZPR. But it was also the entry point — Piłsudski's "red tram" of the 1880s — for hundreds of Poles who jumped into the arena of political activity and opposition. From Piłsudski on the left to Popławski and Balicki on the right, modern Polish nationalism was born on the skirts of Polish socialism. PPS historians tend to view this question quite differently: patriotism endured the interruption of "cosmopolitan" socialism and "revived" rather than emerged at the end of the 1880s and in the 1890s in all Polish political movements.

The decidedly antipatriotic mood of the 1870s and early 1880s did not come to an end, however, because patriotism revived, as these historians suggest. The "new patriotism" announced by Popławski, institutionalized by Balicki and Miłkowski in Zet and Liga Polska, and formulated by Potocki in *Głos,* by Wysłouch in *Przegląd Społeczny,* and Miłkowski in *Rzecz,* was more a new Polish political phenomenon than a revival of an old one. Unquestionably, aspects of the radical democracy of the 1830–63 generation were present. Limanowski's Lud Polski also served as an important source of the patriotic upsurge. Yet the "new patriots" consciously and unconsciously referred not to the teachings of the past but to the formation of a genuinely unique Polish political front — a combination of the progressive intelligentsia and the broad masses of the people — in an attempt to foster (by their active politics) the spiritual and material well-being of the nation, at the core of which was the peasantry.

The ingredients of this political front derived not so much from the pre-1863 patriotism as from positivism and socialism. From Warsaw Positivism the new patriots learned of Darwin and organic theories of social development. Dmowski's own nationalism was partly based on a vulgarized Darwinian concept of the Polish tribe, locked in a deathly struggle with the Germans and Russians. From the positivists the "new patriots" adopted the superiority of a "rational" approach to political affairs. They rejected emotionalism, romanticism, and messianism, all of which thoroughly pervaded patriotic theories of the left and right in the pre-1863 era. Miłkowski's *Rzecz* especially insisted that though the Poles should prepare for an insurrection, the plans should be prepared rationally and carried out almost scientifically. No insurrection would be encouraged that might fail. In fact, "rationalism" was so strongly imbued in the nationalist movement by the "new patriotism" that the later National Democracy, in the name of political realism, participated in the Russian Duma and fought against the 1905 revolution in the Congress Kingdom.

The "new patriots" derived their most important political concept — "active defense" — from the middle ground between the positivists' Organic Work, which in their view was too passive, and the Proletariat's terrorism, which was too dangerous. During the ascendance of the Proletariat, Balicki, Popławski, Wysłouch, and other leaders of the national movement operated on the peripheries of the party. They participated in the Gminas, maintained ties to workers' circles, and protested at Puławy and at Warsaw University against Apukhtin. The Proletariat itself provided an example for the "new patriots" of how to build an organization. Agitation, "active defense," and even terrorism in the Proletariat inspired similar approaches by the "new patriots" to the problem of political action with the goal of revolution. The patriots built an underground party, engaged in legal and illegal activities, and undertook defensive measures to build the national (as opposed to social) consciousness of the *lud*.

Originally aroused by economic exploitation and social injustice in the Congress Kingdom, the Proletariat evolved into a political organization shaped by the direct struggle against the autocracy. Its propaganda and agitation, the demonstrations, the shootings, the strikes, and the hangings of the early 1880s awakened the political consciousness of the Polish intelligentsia from a fifteen-year slumber to a mentality of struggle. The new struggle of the post-Proletariat generation was the national struggle, Pole against Russian, German, and Austrian. In this sense, then, the social struggle brought the Proletariat to a political struggle, which in turn brought the "new patriots" to a national struggle. The national struggle of Pole versus partitioner was not devoid of its social components, and this too can be partly attributed to the strength of socialism in the early 1880s. Wysłouch's peasant nationalism with its unmistakable agrarian socialist elements served as the foundation for the future peasant parties of Poland. Although in general the "new patriots" concentrated on the improvement of the material and spiritual well-being of the peasant class, they also, especially through Zet, engaged the urban workers in the regeneration of the *lud*.

The socialists therefore awoke the Congress Kingdom to political action. The Polish intelligentsia responded with a flurry of activity in 1886–87 that laid the foundations for modern Polish political parties. Herein resides part of the enormous success and significance of the Proletariat. Its crucial failing was its inability to restrict the political struggle to social issues and survive. The social issues faded from the consciousness of the Polish intelligentsia, the political struggle remained, and the new and more vital force of nationalism took center stage.

Appendix

A Collective Biography of Polish Socialists and a Suggestion on the Role of Social Change in the Development of Polish Marxism

The purpose of this appendix is to use numbers to broaden the historian's understanding of the origins of Polish Marxism in the years 1878 to 1886. As we have seen, it was during these years that Polish propagandists first carried the message of socialism to workers in the Congress Kingdom, culminating in the formation of Poland's first Marxist party, the Proletariat, 1882–86. The historian of the Proletariat is tempted to describe the development of Polish Marxism in terms of a biography of its leading spirit, Ludwik Waryński. My intention here is to use the tools of the biographer on the widest possible spectrum of Congress Kingdom socialist activists during this period.

The following statistical material on the biographies of 622 socialists involved in the revolutionary movement in the Congress Kingdom from 1878 to 1886 was compiled from the arrest and trial lists of the Warsaw prosecutor.[1] Because the data sources were of uneven quality, no claim to absolute accuracy can be made. Still, this group of 622 does represent the approximate number of those Congress Kingdom socialists either arrested or indicted in absentia for political activities in these years.[2]

Biographical data were collected in thirty different categories for each revolutionary. Within the various categories, variables ranged from two (sex) to sixty-nine (occupation). The number of categories in which information was available on each revolutionary averaged between 65 percent and 85 percent of the total. Sometimes contradictory information was found. In these cases, the variable was chosen from the most reliable source of information. With the use of a computer and the program "Standard Package for the Social Sciences," each category was coded according to specific variables, and variables were cross-tabulated with other variables. Some of the most interesting and most important results of these straightforward tabulations are included in this statistical appendix. The first section of the appendix presents information on the background of the 622 revolutionaries. The second section analyzes the various distinct revolutionary circles during the period and provides information on their particular comparative biographies. Each section is broken down first by categories (Roman numerals) and then by selected variables that enlighten these categories (alphabetic letters).

This kind of statistical comparative biography can serve as a legitimate *supplement* to traditional scholarly analysis and comparative historical reflection. It should be emphasized, however, that in no case can these data be used as statistical proofs of particular historical arguments. Whenever both possible and useful, data on the Polish movement are compared in the Notes to the appropriate cases of the Russian Empire, the Congress Kingdom, and the Russian revolutionary movement.

The essay is divided into two parts for the purpose of presenting a cross section of ways in which the compiled data can be used. The first part consists of a general collective biography of the 622 revolutionaries and explores several categories of variables that are either particularly enlightening about the nature of the Polish socialist movement in this period or demonstrate the extent of the validity of several commonly accepted historiographical generalizations about this group. The second part of the essay attempts to construct a hypothesis about the role of social change in the formation and development of the Polish movement by comparing its collective biography with that of the Russian movement.

Statistical Portrait

The socialists arrested between 1878 and 1886 were overwhelmingly male (89 percent), of Polish descent (84 percent), and Catholic (88 percent). According to judicial records, there were thirty-eight Jews in the movement (or about 7 percent of all the revolutionaries), a relatively small number given the large Jewish population of the Congress Kingdom (12 percent). Germans and Russians were even more insignificant in the ranks of Congress Kingdom socialism (Tables 2–4).

Ninety-four percent of the revolutionaries held Russian citizenship, 30 percent were born in Warsaw *guberniia,* and 20 percent were born in the city of Warsaw itself. A surprisingly large number (41 percent) were born in the countryside. Although 66 percent of the revolutionaries came from the ten *gubernii* of the Congress Kingdom, 28 percent were born in the Russian *gubernii* of the empire. The largest group of Russian-born revolutionaries (18 percent of the total) came from the *kresy,* the western borderlands of the Russian Empire. If one compares several variables of the socialists born in the *gubernii* of the borderlands and those born in the Congress Kingdom, it is apparent that the group from the *kresy* is distinguished by its much higher noble composition (81 percent as compared to 20 percent). It was also a more literate group (98 percent/85 percent), included more women (20 percent/9 percent), and had a greater percentage of university, technological, and agricultural school graduates (59 percent/29 percent). Interesting in this latter context is the higher percentage of *kresy*-born graduates of technological and agricultural schools (30 percent/5 percent) (Tables 2, 17–18, 20–24).

The frequent historiographical generalizations about the important role of Germans, Russians, and Jews in the movement are thus clearly exaggerated. On the other hand, the hypothesis that the socialist movement in the Congress Kingdom was initiated by Russian-born Poles is corroborated by statistics that demonstrate the 1878 Warsaw circles consisted of thirty-five members (49 percent) born either in the western or southwestern borderlands *gubernii* of European Russia and thirty members (42 percent) born in the Congress Kingdom itself. At the same time, the Proletariat was numerically dominated by activists born in the Congress Kingdom. Of the original Waryński Proletariat of 1882–84, only 24 percent were from the *kresy* and 63 percent were from the Congress Kingdom. By the last stage of the Proletariat (under Marian Ulrych, 1885–86), the component of *kresy*-born activists dwindled to 11 percent of the total. In the Łódź-Zgierz-Tomaszów group of the Proletariat, which dominated the socialist movement in the mid-1880s, only one out of the thirty-nine members whose birthplaces were recorded were born outside of the Congress Kingdom. Numerically, the Congress Kingdom movement in the years 1878 to 1886 became increasingly worker, increasingly Polish-Catholic, and increasingly made up of activists born in the Congress Kingdom (Tables 39–42).

The Polish movement shared the generally youthful quality of other European revolutionary movements. The largest number of Polish socialists were between the ages of twenty and twenty-four at the time of their arrests (196 altogether, or 36 percent of the total). The mean age upon arrest was twenty-six, and over 60 percent of the Polish group was between twenty-one and thirty years of age (Table 26).

The literacy rate of the movement was predictably high — 88 percent. Fifty-nine percent, or twenty-six revolutionaries, were categorized by the judiciary as semiliterate and 7 percent as illiterate. Of those revolutionaries who had some kind of formal schooling, 28 percent attended the university and 18 percent attended a technological or agricultural institute. The third largest category of "highest level of education attained" was elementary education, including 12 percent of the sample. The most common university faculties attended by revolutionaries were the medical (38 percent) and the law faculties (28 percent). Out of the total of 622 socialists, 41 (7 percent) attended one of the five Warsaw gymnasia, and 59 or 10 percent attended Warsaw University. Thirteen (2 percent) attended the Institute of Technology in St. Petersburg and 17 (3 percent) attended the Medical-Surgery Academy in the same city (Tables 25, 27, 30, 31).

As for the group's origin by estates, 46 percent were listed as *meshchane* or townspeople. Thirty-nine percent were listed as nobles and 15 percent as peasants. The most common occupational category was that of student (140, or 23 percent of the known group). A remarkably large number were locksmiths (*slesar', ślusarz* — 58, or 10 percent) and cabinetmakers (*stoliar, stolarz* — 49, or 8 percent). According to my own somewhat arbitrary division of various occupations into broader categories of work, 117 revolutionaries (20 percent of the total of 622) belonged to the metalworking industrial workforce while 56, or 9 percent, were textile industry laborers. Together, then, what might be called the industrial proletariat made up 29 percent of the group, 27 percent were students, and 23 percent can be classified as artisans (Tables 13, 32, 36).

Out of 183 noblemen and women in the movement whose occupations were recorded, 44 (24 percent) were engaged in working-class occupations. The largest number of these, 23 (13 percent), were employed in metalworking industries. Thirty-two percent of all the locksmiths arrested in this period were nobles, 15 percent of the carpenters, 40 percent of the bronzeworkers, and even 24 percent of the common laborers (Tables 15, 35).

The locksmiths, as the group of workers with the highest percentage of noble-born, also had the lowest percentage of workers born in the Congress Kingdom (74 percent). In part, this accounts as well for the higher rate of literacy among the metalworkers (82 percent) than among the textile workers (72 percent) or common laborers (53 percent). Of the 367 members of the Proletariat from 1882-86, most (61 percent) were workers and artisans. Textile workers played only a very minor role in the Warsaw based organization (about 4 percent), but in the Łódź-Zgierz-Tomaszów organization, more than 50 percent were textile workers. Concomitantly, the Łódź-Zgierz-Tomaszów organization had the lowest literacy rate of any of the other revolutionary organizations (Tables 33, 37, 46, 41).

The involvement of the sixty-seven women in the movement is also illuminated by the collective biography. The women were 62 percent noble (males, 36 percent). The women were more literate (97 percent/ 87 percent), and a higher percentage of women were born in non-Congress Kingdom *gubernii.* Although the percentage of students in both gender groups was approximately the same, the percentages in the workers' groups were notably different. Fifteen percent of the women involved (versus 4 percent of the men) can be classified as unskilled — primarily day laborers. Similarly, 13 percent of the women (9 percent of the men) worked in the textile industry. No women (22 percent of the men) were employed in metal industries; only 4 percent of the women versus 25 percent of the men fall into the artisan category. In the three numerically highest variables of occupation, the women's jobs also diverged from the men's. Fifteen women were teachers, twelve were students, and seven were seamstresses. (The highest male variables were students — 140, locksmiths — 58, and cabinetmakers — 49) (Tables 10-12, 22, 34).

In order to be more specific, I broke down the particular involvement of socialists in this period into as many different groups as I could justify historically (twenty-one in all). Clearly, many revolutionaries played some role in more than one of these groups. I then assembled these groups under broader headings: the Warsaw socialist circles, 1878-80 (201 individuals); the Polish socialists associated in some way with the Russian revolutionary movement (43); the Gmina movement among Polish students in imperial universities (91), and the Proletariat itself (367) (Tables 38, 44).

Of the 574 socialists whose sentences could be identified, 225 were imprisoned, 146 were sent into exile, and 26 were condemned to hard labor, mostly on the island of Sakhalin. Five members of the Proletariat were executed by hanging, and 106 were eventually released from detention on minor charges. It is interesting to note that lighter sentences were meted out to illiterate revolutionaries, most often peasants and workers, both because of their lesser involvement in the movement and because the police assumed, sometimes incorrectly, that they were less involved. Twenty-nine percent of all arrested illiterates were released on minor charges (Tables 55, 57).

Data are also available on the subsequent political (or nonpolitical) fate of 194 of the 1878–86 socialists. Fifty died in exile, in jail, by execution, or suicide. Sixteen eventually made Siberia their home. Twenty-one became involved in PPS activities and nine in the National Democratic movement; but only three became members of the Marxist internationalist SDKPiL. Eventually, 11 did join the Communist Party of the Soviet Union, and 20 became involved in émigre socialist politics. If various political fates are grouped into the broad categories of socialist (Communist, labor, and socialist politics) and nonsocialist (liberals, conservatives, reactionaries, and apoliticals), the majority (116 out of 194) remained active in socialist politics and the minority (36) can be classified as apostates. These apostates, as one might suspect, came primarily from the student-intelligentsia ranks (Tables 50–54).

Social Change in the Polish and Russian Revolutionary Movements

If the collective biography of this sample of 622 Polish socialists in 1878–86 is compared with published statistics on the Russian revolutionary movement of the same approximate period, the crucial role of social change in an analysis of the development of both movements becomes apparent. By estate the Polish movement included a higher percentage of peasants than the Russian (15 percent to 9 percent), a lower percentage of nobility (39 percent to 49 percent), and almost double the percentage of townspeople (*meshchane* — primarily workers) (46 percent to 29 percent). In this context, it should be emphasized that the category of priests' sons, which makes up 39 percent of the Russian movement, did not exist for the Polish movement. In the 1870s in the Russian movement, the percentage of peasants and priests' sons was higher than from 1876 to 1886 and the percentage of nobles and townspeople lower (Table 13).

In terms of occupation at the time of arrest, the proportion of students was much lower in the Polish than in the Russian movement (27 percent to 44 percent) and the proportion of workers and artisans higher (30 percent workers to 14 percent, 23.3 percent artisans to 17 percent). In addition, the Russian movement included by profession 5 percent peasants; the Polish movement had less than 2 percent peasants. Therefore, one can conclude that the Polish movement was almost 60 percent workers of some type, the Russian about 36 percent (Table 36).

As for the change of social status of the individual revolutionary, one finds that among Congress Kingdom revolutionaries there is far greater movement of both nobles and peasants into the working class than among Russian revolutionaries. In the Congress Kingdom, 15 percent of the revolutionaries were of peasant origin — those whose occupation was peasant was 1.5 percent. In Russia, on the other hand, those whose estate was peasant was 9 percent and those whose occupation was peasant was 5 percent. Of the Congress Kingdom's 15 percent revolutionaries of peasant estate, 76 percent entered the working class (Tables 13–15).

Statistics on the downward mobility of Russian noble revolutionaries into the working class are more difficult to isolate. Since there were almost no active priests in the Russian movement, assuming that priests' sons split evenly between the student and professional population and that peasants who did not remain peasants went into the working-class population, then most of the Russian movement's noble estate, which constituted 49 percent of the total, would have had to have been either student or professional, indicating no rapid downward mobility. For the Polish movement the statistics are more precise. Of the 39 percent noble estate, 24 percent earned their living as workers. Over half of these worked in the more highly mechanized metal and machinebuilding industry, and another third worked as skilled artisans (Table 15).

In order to place the identifiable elements of social change within the revolutionary movements into a broader historical perspective, it is necessary to review briefly several aspects of social change in Russia and the Congress Kingdom following the Russian emancipation of 1861 and the Polish emancipation (uwłaszczenie) of 1864. Although industrialization proceeded at an accelerated pace in both areas during the period 1860–80, the social changes that normally occurred in the European pattern of industrialization were skewed by the decidedly political considerations of both Russian and Polish emancipation edicts. Those who promulgated the Russian emancipation were determined to maintain social stability; the result was a series of laws that effectively blocked what might be called "modernizing" social change. As a result, Russian nobles, peasants, and artisans generally retained their noble or peasant status through the first spurt of Russian industrialization, 1856–86. The Polish emancipation, on the other hand, was issued with different political considerations in mind. The 1863 rebellion had convinced the St. Petersburg authorities that political stability in the Congress Kingdom was dependent on social change — the disenfranchisement of the unreliable Polish nobility and the strengthening of the middle level and momentarily politically inert Polish peasant. The Polish emancipation therefore encouraged rather than hindered modernizing social changes. With the onset of industrialization (and, indeed, partly as its cause), Polish nobles, poor peasants, and artisans became permanent members of the industrial workforce.

The causal relationship between these social changes in the Congress Kingdom and the lack of similar social changes in Russia and the ideologies, Marxist and populist, of their respective revolutionary parties is corroborated to some extent by the individual biographies of Polish and Russian revolutionaries of this period. Comparing the estates of individual revolutionaries with their occupations, we have seen that in the Polish movement significant numbers of noble-born and peasant-born Poles became worker-revolutionaries; but that in Russia revolutionaries were not subject to drastic changes in social class. (Unfortunately, these statistics cannot indicate how many Polish and Russian artisans became workers.) I would cautiously suggest that the class consciousness stimulated in individual members of the Polish working class by social changes in the Congress Kingdom encouraged the development of a party based on the "class-conscious" working-class revolutionary ideology of Marxism. The influx of peasants into the permanent ranks of the urban working class — greatest in the Łódź region — increased that class's insurrectionary potential. The change of status from urban artisans to urban industrial workers, most common in Warsaw, increased factory tensions. And, most importantly perhaps, the movement of educated nobles into the working class increased that group's political and social consciousness.

Because Russian society and Russian revolutionaries were generally not subject to these modernizing social changes from 1861 to 1886, class consciousness remained underdeveloped. Instead, social consciousness and a desire for revolution, not by and for a class but by and for society as a whole, dominated revolutionary thinking in Russia and was reflected in the populist ideologies of the movement — *narodnik, narodovol'tsy,* and "young" *narodovol'tsy* of the 1870s and 1880s.

The large group of Polish noble-born worker-revolutionaries was also crucial to the successful struggle waged by the Proletariat. These noble-born workers brought the industrial workers together with the intelligentsia in an organizational as well as ideological sense. In

Russia, on the other hand, a physical and intellectual chasm separated workers and the intelligentsia to the extent that the economic struggle of the former and the political struggle of the latter did not converge in the 1880s. This chasm continued to be a structural impediment to the formation of a viable Marxist party in Russia. The noble-born workers of the Congress Kingdom, created by social changes prompted by industrialization and emancipation, socially and intellectually expressed the convergence of the economic and political struggles and in this sense encouraged the acceptance of Marxism in the Polish revolutionary tradition.

SECTION I

Polish Revolutionaries, 1878–1886:
A General Portrait

I. Revolutionaries related by blood or marriage to other revolutionaries[3]

		(Absolute Frequency)	(Adjusted Frequency Percentage)
Table 1	616/622	A.F.	A.F.%
	Related	130	21.1
	Unrelated	486	78.9

II. Official citizenship of revolutionaries[4]

Table 2	552/622	A.F.	A.F.%
	Prussian	13	2.4
	Austrian	14	2.5
	Russian	519	94.0
	Other	6	1.1

III. Religion of revolutionaries

Table 3 552/622	A.F.	A.F.%
Catholic	485	87.9
Protestant	7	1.3
Jewish	38	6.9
Orthodox	22	4.0

IV. Nationality of revolutionaries[5]

Table 4 530/622	A.F.	A.F.%
Pole	446	84.2
Russian	16	3.0
Lithuanian	9	1.7
Jew	38	7.2
German	12	2.3
Ukrainian	2	0.4
Belorussian	3	0.6
Other	4	0.8

A. Nationality by estate[6]

Table 5 449/530

	Peasant	Noble	Town
Pole	55 — 14.5%	159 — 41.8%	166 — 43.7%
Russian	—	10 — 90.9%	1 — 9.1%
Jew	—	3 — 8.8%	31 — 91.2%
German	1 — 10.0%	1 — 10.0%	8 — 80.0%

B. Nationality by literacy[7]

Table 6 463/530

	Literate	Semiliterate	Illiterate
Pole	341 — 88.6%	19 — 4.9%	25 — 6.5%
Russian	14 — 3.3%	1 — 6.7%	—
Jew	38 — 100.0%	—	—
German	7 — 87.5%	1 — 12.5%	—

C. Nationality by job category[8]

Table 7 510/530

	Unskilled	Industrial Proletariat Metals	Industrial Proletariat Textiles
Pole	19 — 4.4%	90 — 20.9%	36 — 8.4%
Russian	—	1 — 6.3%	—
Jew	—	1 — 2.9%	2 — 5.7%
German	—	6 — 50.0%	1 — 8.3%

	Student	Artisan	Professional
Pole	96 — 22.3%	121 — 28.1%	39 — 9.1%
Russian	7 — 43.8%	1 — 6.3%	6 — 37.5%
Jew	22 — 66.9%	1 — 2.9%	6 — 17.1%
German	—	2 — 16.7%	3 — 25.0%

D. Nationality by highest level of education

Table 8 307/530

	University	Technological/ Agricultural	Gymnasium	Real School
Pole	61 — 24.5%	34 — 13.7%	23 — 9.2%	14 — 5.6%
Russian	4 — 33.3%	5 — 41.7%	1 — 16.7%	1 — 8.3%
Jew	15 — 46.9%	7 — 21.9%	1 — 3.1%	4 — 12.5%

V. Sex of revolutionaries[9]

Table 9	622/622	A.F.	A.F.%
	Male	555	89.2
	Female	67	10.8

A. Sex by estate

Table 10 495/622

	Peasant	Noble	Town
Male	73 — 16.7%	156 — 35.7%	208 — 47.6%
Female	2 — 3.4%	36 — 62.1%	20 — 34.5%

B. Sex by literacy

Table 11 535/622

	Literate	Semiliterate	Illiterate
Male	416 — 87.2%	26 — 5.5%	35 — 7.3%
Female	56 — 96.6%	—	2 — 3.4%

C. Sex by job category

Table 12 597/622

	Unskilled	I. P. Metals	I. P. Textiles
Male	22 — 4.1%	117 — 21.6%	49 — 9.0%
Female	8 — 14.5%	—	7 — 12.7%

	Student	Artisan
Male	143 — 26.4%	137 — 25.3%
Female	15 — 27.3%	2 — 3.6%

VI. Estate of revolutionaries[10]

Table 13 495/622

	A.F.	A.F.%
Peasant	75	15.2
Noble	192	38.8
Town	228	46.1

A. Estate by literacy

Table 14 405/495

	Literate	Semiliterate	Illiterate
Peasant	35 — 54.7%	10 — 15.6%	19 — 29.7%
Noble	185 — 100.0%	—	—
Town	174 — 89.2%	9 — 4.6%	12 — 6.2%

B. Estate by work categories

Table 15 477/495

	Unskilled	I. P. Metals	I. P. Textiles
Peasant	9 — 12.5%	21 — 29.2%	5 — 6.9%
Noble	2 — 1.1%	23 — 12.6%	2 — 1.1%
Town	13 — 5.9%	60 — 27.0%	25 — 11.3%

	Student	Artisan
Peasant	5 — 6.9%	20 — 27.8%
Noble	88 — 48.1%	17 — 9.3%
Town	27 — 12.2%	75 — 33.8%

C. Estate by relations among revolutionaries

Table 16 492/495

	Related	Unrelated
Peasant	13 — 17.3%	62 — 82.7%
Noble	62 — 32.6%	128 — 67.4%
Town	46 — 20.3%	181 — 33.8%

VII. *Guberniia* born[11]

Table 17	A.F.	A.F.%
Warsaw	131	30.3
Grodno	16	3.7
Piotrków	36	8.3
Siedlce	19	4.4
Vilna	12	2.8
Minsk	18	4.2
Kiev	14	3.2
Łomża	24	5.5
Suwałki	10	2.3
Podolia	12	2.8
Płock	16	3.7
Radom	12	2.8
Kovno	18	4.2
Kalisz	24	5.5

VIII. Area born[12]

Table 18 454/622	A.F.	A.F.%
Congress Kingdom	298	65.6
Western *gubernii*	82	18.1
Prussian Poland	17	3.7
Austrian Poland	10	2.2
Baltic *gubernii*	2	0.4
SW Russian *gubernii*	28	6.2
Other Russian *gubernii*	17	3.7

A. Area born by relations among revolutionaries

Table 19 453/454

	Related	Unrelated
Congress Kingdom	62 — 20.9%	235 — 79.1%
Western *gubernii*	30 — 36.6%	52 — 63.4%
SW *gubernii*	9 — 32.1%	19 — 67.9%

B. Area born by literacy[13]

Table 20 419/454

	Literate	Semiliterate	Illiterate
Congress Kingdom	232 — 85.3%	18 — 6.6%	22 — 8.1%
Western *gubernii*	79 — 97.5%	1 — 1.2%	1 — 1.2%
SW *gubernii*	28 — 100%	—	—
Other *gubernii*	16 — 100%	—	—
Prussian Poland	13 — 92.9%	1 — 7.1%	—

C. Area born by estate[14]

Table 21 418/454

	Peasant	Noble	Town
Congress Kingdom	59 — 20.8%	59 — 20.8%	166 — 58.5%
Western gubernii	3 — 3.9%	62 — 80.5%	12 — 15.6%
SW gubernii	—	23 — 88.5%	3 — 11.5%
Other Russian gubernii	—	12 — 80.0%	3 — 20.0%
Prussian Poland	2 — 14.3%	3 — 21.4%	9 — 64.3%

D. Area born by sex

Table 22 454/454

	Male	Female
Congress Kingdom	276 — 92.6%	22 — 7.4%
Western gubernii	66 — 80.5%	16 — 19.5%
SW gubernii	21 — 75.0%	7 — 25.0%
Other Russian gubernii	12 — 70.6%	5 — 29.4%
Prussian Poland	16 — 94.1%	1 — 5.9%

E. Area born by highest level of education

Table 23 287/454

	Univ.	Tech./Ag.	Gymnas.	Women's
Congress Kingdom	40—23.4%	9— 5.3%	22—12.9%	2— 1.2%
Western gubernii	19—29.7%	19—29.7%	4— 6.3%	9—14.1%
SW gubernii	13—52.0%	4—16.0%	2— 8.0%	2— 8.0%
Other gubernii	5—35.6%	4—28.6%	1— 7.1%	—

IX. Town born of revolutionaries[15]

Table 24 390/622	A.F.	A.F.%
Warsaw	77	19.7
Poznań	8	2.1
Zgierz	5	1.3
Kraków	5	1.3
Vilna	11	2.8
Country-born	159	40.8
Other towns	125	32.0

X. Literacy of revolutionaries[16]

Table 25 535/622	A.F.	A.F.%
Literate	472	88.2
Semiliterate	26	4.9
Illiterate	37	6.9

XI. Age of revolutionaries[17]

Table 26 549/622	A.F.	A.F.%
15–19	85	15.5
20–24	196	35.7
25–29	144	26.2
30–34	76	13.8
35–39	39	7.2
40 and over	46	8.4

XII. Highest level of education of revolutionaries[18]

Table 27 338/622

	A.F.	A.F.%
University	95	28.1
Tech. or ag. school	59	17.5
Real school	22	6.5
Gymnasium	31	9.2
Private school	13	3.8
Women's school	21	6.2
Peasant school	9	2.7
Sunday craft school	22	6.5
Trade school	11	3.3
Parish school	3	0.9
Elementary school	41	12.1

A. Highest level of education by estate

Table 28 296/338

	Peasant	Noble	Town
University	4 — 4.9%	56 — 69.1%	21 — 25.9%
Tech. or ag. school	2 — 5.0%	30 — 75.0%	8 — 20.0%
Gymnasium	1 — 3.3%	20 — 66.7%	9 — 30.0%
Women's school	—	19 — 100%	—
Peasant school	1 — 11.1%	—	8 — 88.9%
Sunday craft	6 — 24.0%	5 — 23.8%	10 — 47.6%
Elementary	9 — 27.5%	4 — 10.0%	27 — 67.5%

B. Highest level of education by work categories

Table 29 332/338

	Unskilled	I. P. Metals	I. P. Textiles
University	—	—	—
Tech. or ag. school	—	—	—
Real school	—	4 — 19.0%	—
Gymnasium	—	10 — 33.3%	—
Private	—	1 — 7.7%	1 — 7.7%
Women's school	—	—	—
Peasant school	—	3 — 33.3%	—

	Professional	Student	Artisan
University	15 — 16.0%	74 — 78.7%	—
Tech. or ag. school	8 — 13.6%	47 — 79.7%	—
Real school	7 — 33.3%	7 — 33.3%	2 — 9.5%
Gymnasium	6 — 20.0%	5 — 16.7%	8 — 26.7%
Private	4 — 30.8%	3 — 23.1%	—
Women's school	6 — 30.0%	12 — 60.0%	1 — 5.0%
Peasant school	—	—	6 — 66.7%

XIII. Schools attended by revolutionaries[19]

Table 30 245/622

	A.F.	(Relative Frequency Percentage) R.F.%
Warsaw gymnasia 1–5	41	6.5
Institute of Technology, St. Petersburg	13	2.1
Medical-Surgery Academy, St. Petersburg	17	2.7
Warsaw University	59	9.5
Kiev University	11	1.8
St. Petersburg University	13	2.1
Warsaw Sunday Craft School	16	2.6
Warsaw Veterinary Academy	16	2.6
St. Petersburg Women's Medical Course	9	1.4
Institute of Communications, St. Petersburg	9	1.4
Warsaw Elementary School	9	1.4

XIV. University branch of revolutionaries[20]

Table 31 63/622	A.F.	A.F.%
Law	19	27.9
Medicine	26	38.2
Humanities	9	13.2
Auditor	14	20.6

XV. Jobs and professions[21]

Table 32 601/622	A.F.	A.F.%
Student	140	23.3
Shoemaker	32	5.3
Weaver	28	4.7
Bronzeworker	11	1.8
Cabinetmaker	49	8.2
Typesetter	11	1.8
Locksmith	58	9.7
Teacher	23	3.7
Pupil	12	2.0
Carpenter	17	2.8
Blacksmith	12	2.0
Common laborer	30	5.0
Latheturner	10	1.7

A. Jobs and professions by area born

Table 33 442/601

	Cong. King.	*West. Gub.*	*Pruss. Pol.*
Shoemaker – 29	25 — 86.2%	—	1 — 3.4%
Student – 94	36 — 38.3%	39 — 41.5%	—
Weaver – 17	17 — 100%	—	—
Cabinetmaker – 41	34 — 82.9%	1 — 2.4%	4 — 9.8%
Locksmith – 46	34 — 73.9%	5 — 10.9%	3 — 6.5%
Teacher – 18	8 — 44.4%	2 — 11.1%	—
Carpenter – 13	11 — 84.6%	—	2 — 15.4%
Blacksmith – 12	11 — 91.7%	—	1 — 8.3%

	SW Gub.	*Other Gub.*
Shoemaker – 29	—	2 — 6.9%
Student – 94	13 — 13.8%	6 — 6.4%
Weaver – 17	—	—
Cabinetmaker – 41	—	—
Locksmith – 46	3 — 12.0%	—
Teacher – 18	4 — 22.2%	3 — 16.7%
Carpenter – 13	—	—
Blacksmith – 12	—	—

B. Jobs by professions by sex[22]

Table 34 601/601

	Male	*Female*
Student – 140	128 — 91.4%	12 — 8.6%
Bookbinder – 3	1 — 33.3%	2 — 66.7%
Teacher – 23	8 — 34.8%	15 — 65.2%
Seamstress – 7	—	7 — 100%
Common laborer – 30	25 — 83.3%	5 — 16.7%
Washerwoman – 2	—	2 — 100%
Flower seller – 2	—	2 — 100%
Housewife – 5	—	5 — 100%
Absolvent (graduate) – 10	8 — 80.0%	2 — 20.0%

C. Jobs and professions by estate

Table 35 481/601

	Peasant	Noble	Town
Shoemaker – 29	7 — 24.1%	4 — 13.8%	18 — 62.1%
Student – 106	6 — 5.7%	77 — 72.6%	23 — 21.7%
Weaver – 19	4 — 21.1%	—	15 — 78.9%
Bronzeworker–10	2 — 20.0%	4 — 40.0%	4 — 40.0%
Ironworker – 7	—	—	7 — 100%
Cabinetmaker–39	8 — 20.5%	4 — 10.3%	27 — 69.2%
Locksmith – 53	10 — 18.9%	17 — 32.1%	26 — 49.1%
Teacher – 20	—	15 — 75.0%	5 — 25.0%
Accountant – 7	—	4 — 57.1%	3 — 42.9%
Pupil – 10	—	5 — 50.0%	5 — 50.0%
Carpenter – 13	1 — 7.7%	2 — 15.4%	10 — 76.9%
Blacksmith – 13	6 — 54.4%	—	5 — 45.5%
Engineer – 7	—	7 — 100%	—
Common laborer – 21	5 — 23.8%	5 — 23.8%	11 — 52.4%
Latheturner – 9	—	1 — 11.1%	8 — 88.9%
Tinsmith – 7	6 — 85.7%	—	1 — 14.3%

XVI. General categories of work[23]

Table 36 597/622	A.F.	A.F.%
Unskilled labor	30	5.0
Industrial proletariat metals	117	19.6
Industrial proletariat textiles	56	9.4
Student	158	26.5
Professional	59	9.9
Landowner	4	0.7
Professional revolutionary	8	1.3
Artisan	139	23.3
Bureaucrat and office worker	7	1.2
Other	17	2.8
Businessman	2	0.3

A. Work categories by literacy

Table 37 518/597

	Literate	Semiliterate	Illiterate
Unskilled 19/30	10 — 52.6%	1 — 5.3%	8 — 42.1%
Industrial proletariat metals 85/117	70 — 82.4%	8 — 9.4%	7 — 8.2%
Industrial proletariat textiles 47/56	34 — 72.3%	7 — 14.9%	6 — 12.8%
Student 155/158	155 — 100%	—	—
Artisan 120/139	103 — 85.8%	8 — 6.7%	9 — 7.5%

SECTION II

Polish Revolutionaries 1878–1887:
Groups, Sentences, and Fates

I. Particular circles of involvement of revolutionaries[24]

Table 38 617/622	A.F.	R.F.%
Warsaw socialist circles 1878–1879	98	15.8
Warsaw socialist circles 1879–1880	104	16.7
Socialist circles – Switzerland	11	1.8
Zemlia i Volia	14	2.3
Narodnaia Volia	28	4.5
Warsaw Gmina	44	7.1
St. Petersburg Gmina	18	2.9
Moscow Gmina	7	1.1
Vilna Gmina	5	0.8
Kiev Gmina	7	0.1
Szymański conspiracy	2	0.3
Kraków trial	11	1.8
Proletariat 1882–1884	181	29.1
Proletariat 1884–1885	56	9.0
Proletariat 1886	48	7.7
Łódź-Zgierz-Tomaszów Proletariat	90	14.5
Solidarność	25	4.0
Apuchtinada	6	1.0
Plac Zamkowy demonstration	3	0.5
Lud Polski	2	0.3
Black Partition	1	0.2

A. Revolutionary circles by estate

Table 39 — A.F.%

	Peasant	Noble	Town
Socialist circles Warsaw 1878 84/98	7 — 8.3%	49 — 58.3%	28 — 33.3%
Socialist circles Warsaw 1879–1880 98/104	13 — 13.3%	39 — 39.8%	46 — 46.9%
Socialist circles Switzerland 7/11	—	5 — 71.4%	2 — 28.6%
Zemlia i Volia 13/14	1 — 7.7%	9 — 69.2%	3 — 23.1%
Narodnaia Volia 23/28	1 — 4.3%	19 — 82.6%	3 — 13.0%
Warsaw Gmina 43/44	9 — 20.9%	12 — 27.9%	22 — 51.2%
St. Petersburg Gmina 11/18	1 — 9.1%	10 — 90.9%	—
Solidarność 22/25	3 — 13.6%	7 — 31.8%	12 — 54.5%
Proletariat 1882–1884 Waryński 142/181	23 — 16.2%	56 — 36.6%	67 — 47.2%
Proletariat 1884–1885 Bohuszewiczówna 50/56	11 — 22.0%	18 — 36.09%	21 — 42.0%
Proletariat 1885–1886 Ulrych 44/48	6 — 13.6%	11 — 25.0%	27 — 61.4%
Łódź-Zgierz-Tomaszów Proletariat 45/90	10 — 22.2%	2 — 4.4%	33 — 73.3%

B. Revolutionary circles by job category

Table 40 — A.F.%

	Unskilled	I. P. Metals	I. P. Textiles	Student	Prof.	Prof. Rev.	Artisan
Socialist circles Warsaw 1878 91/98	7 — 7.7%	21 — 23.0%	1 — 1.9%	41 — 45.0%	7 — 7.7%	6 — 6.7%	4 — 4.4%
Socialist circles Warsaw 1879–1880 103/104	3 — 2.9%	19 — 18.4%	1 — 1.0%	24 — 23.3%	11 — 10.7%	—	42 — 40.8%
Socialist circles Switzerland 10/11	—	—	—	4 — 40.0%	—	5 — 90.0%	1 — 10.0%
Zemlia i Volia 12/14	—	—	—	10 — 83.3%	1 — 8.3%	—	1 — 8.3%
Narodnaia Volia 26/28	—	1 — 3.8%	—	13 — 63.9%	8 — 30.8%	1 — 3.8%	3 — 11.5%
Warsaw Gmina 43/44	2 — 4.8%	16 — 38.0%	—	5 — 11.6%	4 — 9.3%	—	13 — 20.2%

Table 40 (cont.)

	Unskilled	I. P. Metals	I. P. Textiles	Student	Prof.	Prof. Rev.	Artisan
St. Petersburg Gmina 17/18	—	—	—	14 — 82.4%	2 — 28.6%	—	—
Solidarność 24/25	2 — 8.3%	13 — 54.2%	—	4 — 16.7%	2 — 8.3%	—	3 — 12.5%
Proletariat 1882–1884 174/181 Waryński	8 — 4.6%	38 — 21.8%	7 — 4.0%	43 — 24.7%	20 — 11.5%	1 — 0.6%	41 — 23.6%
Proletariat 1885–1886 53/56 Bohuszewiczówna	3 — 5.7%	9 — 17.0%	2 — 3.8%	17 — 32.1%	8 — 15.1%	—	13 — 24.5%
Proletariat 1885–1886 48/48 Ulrych	—	12 — 25.0%	2 — 4.2%	3 — 6.3%	5 — 10.4%	—	24 — 50.0%
Łódź-Zgierz-Tomaszów Proletariat 89/90	9 — 10.1%	5 — 5.6%	46 — 51.7%	2 — 2.2%	—	—	24 — 27.0%

C. Revolutionary circles by literacy

Table 41 — A.F.%

	Literate	Semiliterate	Illiterate
Socialist circles Warsaw 1878 73/98	73 — 100%	—	—
Socialist circles Warsaw 1879–1880 96/104	86 — 89.6%	2 — 2.1%	8 — 8.0%
Socialist circles Switzerland 9/11	9 — 100%	—	—
Zemlia i Volia 14/14	14 — 100%	—	—
Narodnaia Volia 28/28	28 — 100%	—	—
Warsaw Gmina 33/44	28 — 84.8%	2 — 6.1%	3 — 9.1%
St. Petersburg Gmina 18/18	18 — 100%	—	—
Solidarność 24/25	20 — 83.3%	1 — 4.2%	3 — 12.5%
Proletariat 1882–1884 Waryński 169/181	145 — 85.8%	10 — 5.9%	14 — 8.3%
Proletariat 1884–1885 Bohuszewiczówna 51/56	46 — 90.2%	4 — 7.8%	1 — 2.0%
Proletariat 1885–1886 Ulrych 45/48	42 — 93.3%	—	3 — 6.7%
Łódź-Zgierz-Tomaszów Proletariat 70/90	49 — 70%	10 — 13.3%	11 — 15.7%

D. Revolutionary circles by area born

Table 42 — A.F.%

	C.K.	West. gub.	Pruss. Pol.	SW gub.	Other Russ. gub.
Socialist circles Warsaw 1878 72/98	30 — 41.7%	25 — 34.7%	2 — 2.8%	10 — 13.9%	3 — 4.2%
Socialist circles Warsaw 1879–1880 91/104	65 — 71.4%	9 — 9.9%	8 — 8.8%	6 — 6.6%	2 — 2.2%
Socialist circles Switzerland 7/11	3 — 42.9%	2 — 28.6%		2 — 28.6%	
Zemlia i Volia 12/14	1 — 8.3%	8 — 66.7%		2 — 16.6%	1 — 8.3%
Narodnaia Volia 20/28	5 — 25%	8 — 40%		3 — 15%	4 — 20%
Warsaw Gmina 35/44	30 — 85.7%	2 — 5.7%	1 — 2.9%	1 — 2.9%	1 — 2.9%
St. Petersburg Gmina 7/18	—	4 — 57.1%		2 — 28.6%	1 — 14.2%
Solidarność 24/25	20 — 83.8%	2 — 8.3%	1 — 4.2%	—	—
Proletariat 1882–1884 Waryński 145/181	92 — 63.4%	29 — 20%	5 — 3.4%	6 — 4.1%	8 — 5.5%
Proletariat 1884–1885 Bohuszewiczówna 48/56	37 — 77.1%	8 — 16.7%	1 — 2.1%		2 — 4.2%
Proletariat 1885–1886 Ulrych 44/48	35 — 79.5%	4 — 9.1%	1 — 2.3%	1 — 2.3%	1 — 2.3%
Łódź-Zgierz-Tomaszów Proletariat 39/90	37 — 94.9%	1 — 2.6%		—	—

E. Revolutionary circles by school attended

Table 43 — R.F.%

	Wars. Gymn. 1–5	Inst. Tech.	Med.-Surg. Acad.	Wars. Univ.	Kiev Univ.	SPb. Univ.
Socialist circles Warsaw, 1878–79	10 — 10.2%	4 — 4.1%	10 — 10.2%	21 — 21.4%	2 — 2.0%	1 — 1.0%
Socialist circles 1879–1880	12 — 11.5%	3 — 2.9%	2 — 1.9%	10 — 9.6%	1 — 1.0%	2 — 1.9%
Zemlia i Volia	—	2 — 14.3%	3 — 21.4%	—	2 — 14.3%	2 — 14.3%
Narodnaia Volia	5 — 17.9%	1 — 3.6%	1 — 3.6%	3 — 10.7%	1 — 3.6%	5 — 17.9%
Warsaw Gmina	1 — 2.3%	—	—	2 — 4.6%	1 — 2.3%	1 — 2.3%
St. Petersburg Gmina	—	4 — 22.2%	3 — 16.7%	—	1 — 5.6%	3 — 16.7%
Solidarność	7 — 28.0%	—	—	5 — 20.0%	—	—
Proletariat 1882–84	12 — 6.6%	2 — 1.1%	—	14 — 7.8%	—	4 — 2.2%
Proletariat 1884–85	8 — 14.3%	—	—	13 — 23.2%	—	—
Proletariat 1885–86	2 — 4.2%	—	—	2 — 4.2%	—	—
Łódź-Zgierz-Tomaszów Proletariat	1 — 1.1%	—	—	1 — 1.1%	—	—

Table 43 (cont.)

	Wars. Sund. Craft	*Wars. Vet. Acad.*	*SPb. Women's Med.*	*SPb. Inst. of Comm.*	*Warsaw Elem.*
Socialist circles 1878–79		3 — 3.1%	2 — 2.0%	2 — 2.0%	—
Socialist circles 1879–80	5 — 4.8%	2 — 1.9%	1 — 1.0%	1 — 1.0%	1 — 1.0%
Zemlia i Volia			1 — 7.1%	1 — 7.1%	—
Narodnaia Volia			1 — 3.6%	1 — 3.6%	—
Warsaw Gmina	2 — 4.6%		—	1 — 2.3%	5 — 11.4%
St. Petersburg Gmina			4 — 22.2%	1 — 5.6%	—
Solidarność			—	—	—
Proletariat 1882–84	4 — 2.2%	10 — 5.6%	2 — 1.1%	4 — 2.2%	1 — 0.6%
Proletariat 1884–85	1 — 1.8%	1 — 1.8%	—	—	2 — 3.6%
Proletariat 1885–86	5 — 10.4%	2 — 4.2%	—	—	3 — 6.3%
Łódź-Zgierz-Tomaszów Proletariat	1 — 1.1%		—	—	—

F. Grouped revolutionary circles by highest level of education

Table 44 — A.F.%

	Socialist Circles 1878–80 133/201	Russian Movement 32/43	Gminists 65/91	Proletariat 167/367
University	43 — 32.3%	15 — 46.9%	21 — 32.2%	37 — 22.2%
Tech./ag. school	25 — 18.8%	6 — 18.8%	15 — 23.1%	22 — 13.2%
Real school	3 — 2.3%	2 — 6.3%	2 — 3.1%	18 — 10.8%
Gymnasium	16 — 12.0%	1 — 3.1%	2 — 3.1%	15 — 9.0%
Private school	4 — 3.0%	1 — 3.1%	2 — 3.1%	8 — 4.8%
Women's school	5 — 3.8%	6 — 18.8%	8 — 12.3%	8 — 4.8%
Peasant school	7 — 5.3%	—	2 — 3.1%	4 — 2.4%
Sunday craft school	10 — 7.5%	—	3 — 4.6%	11 — 6.6%
Trade school	1 — 0.8%	1 — 3.1%	1 — 1.5%	10 — 6.0%
Home schooling	2 — 1.5%	—	1 — 1.5%	9 — 5.4%
Parish school	—	—	—	3 — 1.8%
Elementary school	17 — 12.8%	—	8 — 12.3%	22 — 13.2%

G. Grouped revolutionary circles by literacy

Table 45 — A.F.%

	Literate	Semiliterate	Illiterate
Socialist circles 1878–1880 168/201	158 — 94%	2 — 1.2%	8 — 4.8%
Russian movement 43/43	43 — 100%	—	—
Gminists 77/91	72 — 93.5%	2 — 2.6%	3 — 3.9%
Proletariat 327/367	274 — 83.8%	24 — 7.3%	29 — 8.9%

H. Grouped revolutionary circles by job category

Table 46 — A.F.%

	Unskilled	I. P. Metals	I. P. Textiles	Student
Socialist circles 1878–1880 193/201	10 — 5.2%	40 — 20.7%	2 — 1.0%	64 — 33.2%
Russian movement 39/43	—	1 — 0.7%	—	24 — 61.5%
Gminists 86/91	2 — 2.3%	16 — 18.6%	—	35 — 40.7%
Proletariat 356/367	19 — 5.3%	64 — 18.0%	55 — 15.4%	63 — 18.0%

	Prof.	Prof. Rev.	Artisan
Socialist circles 1878–1880	18 — 9.3%	6 — 3.1%	46 — 23.8%
Russian movement	9 — 23.1%	2 — 5.1%	3 — 7.7%
Gminists	9 — 10.5%	5 — 5.8%	14 — 16.3%
Proletariat	33 — 9.3%	1 — 0.3%	99 — 27.8%

I. Grouped revolutionary circles by estates

Table 47 — A.F.%

	Peasant	Noble	Town
Socialist circles 1870–1880 199/201	20 — 10.1%	87 — 43.7%	74 — 37.1%
Russian movement 37/43	2 — 5.4%	29 — 78.3%	6 — 16.2%
Gminists 74/91	10 — 13.5%	40 — 54.1%	24 — 32.4%
Proletariat 276/367	49 — 17.8%	83 — 36.1%	144 — 52.2%

J. Grouped revolutionary circles by nationality

Table 48 — A.F.%

	Pole	Russian	Lithuanian	Jew	German	Belorussian	Ukrainian
Socialist circles 1878–1880 174/201	148 — 85.1%	5 — 2.9%	2 — 1.1%	13 — 7.5%	4 — 2.3%	—	2 — 1.1%
Russian movement 36/43	22 — 61.1%	7 — 19.4%	2 — 5.5%	5 — 13.8%	—	—	—
Gminists 81/91	75 — 92.6%	—	3 — 3.7%	3 — 3.7%	—	—	—
Proletariat 314/367	260 — 82.8%	12 — 3.8%	5 — 1.6%	23 — 7.3%	8 — 2.5%	3 — 10.0%	—

K. Grouped revolutionary circles by fate

Table 49 — A.F.%

	Głos	Ludowiec	SDKPiL	PPS-L	PPS	N.-D.	Nonpolit.
Socialist circles 1878–1880 80/201	5 — 6.3%	1 — 1.3%	1 — 1.3%	2 — 2.5%	7 — 8.8%	6 — 6.3%	11 — 13.8%
Russian movement 33/43	2 — 6.1%	—	1 — 3.0%	2 — 6.1%	1 — 3.0%	2 — 6.1%	5 — 15.2%
Gminists 42/91	—	1 — 2.4%	1 — 2.4%	2 — 4.8%	4 — 9.6%	2 — 4.8%	7 — 16.8%
Proletariat 127/367	1 — 0.8%	2 — 1.6%	2 — 1.6%	4 — 3.1%	14 — 11.0%	3 — 2.4%	8 — 6.3%

	C.P. USSR	Socialist Abroad	S.D. Russ.	Liberal	Siberian Settler	Pol. Labor Movement	Died in Jail, Exile, Suicide or Execution
Socialist circles 1878–1880	2 — 2.5%	7 — 8.8%	2 — 2.5%	10 — 12.5%	4 — 5.0%	3 — 3.8%	20 — 25.0%
Russian movement	1 — 3.0%	4 — 12.1%	4 — 12.1%	3 — 9.1%	—		3 — 24.2%
Gminists	2 — 4.8%	5 — 11.9%	—	8 — 19.0%	3 — 7.1%		7 — 16.8%
Proletariat	10 — 7.9%	12 — 9.4%	5 — 3.9%	4 — 3.1%	14 — 11.0%	15 — 11.8%	33 — 26.0%

II. Fate of revolutionaries[25]

Table 50 194/622

	A.F.	R.F.%
Died in exile, jail, execution, suicide	50	8.0
Głos	6	1.0
Ludowcy	4	0.6
SDKPiL	3	0.5
PPS Left	6	1.0
PPS	21	3.4
National Democrat	9	1.4
Nonpolitical	23	3.7
Pilsudski	5	0.8
C.P. Poland	1	0.2
C.P. USSR	11	1.8
Socialist abroad	20	3.2
Nonpolitical émigré	3	0.5
Social Democrat Russia	9	1.4
Liberal	20	3.2
Siberian settler	16	2.6
Polish labor movement	17	2.7
Zionist	1	0.2
Social Revolutionary Russia	1	0.2

A. Grouped fate of revolutionaries by nationality

Table 51 — A.F.%

	Pole	Russian	Jew	German
Future socialists 116/132 Labor movement, socialism, Communism	91 — 78.4%	6 — 5.2%	12 — 10.3%	1 — 0.9%
Future nonsocialists 34/36 Liberals, reactionaries, apoliticals	29 — 85.3%	—	5 — 14.7%	—

B. Grouped fate by literacy

Table 52 — A.F.%

	Literate	Semiliterate	Illiterate
Future socialists 115/132	105 — 91.3%	5 — 4.3%	5 — 4.3%
Future nonsocialists 35/36	35 — 100%	—	—

C. Grouped fate by estate

Table 53 — A.F.%

	Peasant	Noble	Town
Future socialists 102/132	12 — 14.4%	54 — 52.9%	36 — 35.3%
Future nonsocialists 33/36	—	25 — 75.8%	8 — 24.2%

D. Grouped fate by job category

Table 54 — A.F.%

	Unskilled	I. P. Metals	I. P. Textiles	Student
Future socialists 128/132	1 — 0.8%	18 — 14.1%	13 — 10.2%	44 — 34.4%
Future nonsocialists 36/36	—	—	—	20 — 55.6%

	Prof.	Prof. Rev.	Artisan
Future socialists	13 — 14.1%	6 — 4.7%	24 — 18.8%
Future nonsocialists	12 — 33.3%	4 — 11.1%	—

III. Sentences of revolutionaries[26]

Table 55 574/622

	A.F.	*R.F.%*
Placed under surveillance	43	6.9
Jail and prison	225	36.2
Exile	146	23.5
Hard labor	26	4.2
Death	5	0.8
Reprimand — release	34	5.5
Release and preventive arrest	72	11.4
Escaped arrest	15	2.4
Other	26	4.2

A. Sentence category by estate

Table 56 — A.F.%

	Peasant	*Noble*	*Town*
Placed under surveillance 33/43	2 — 6.1%	24 — 72.7%	7 — 21.2%
Jailed 192/225	28 — 14.6%	60 — 30.3%	104 — 52.5%
Exiled 117/146	17 — 14.5%	50 — 42.7%	50 — 42.7%
Hard labor 23/26	6 — 26.1%	11 — 47.8%	6 — 26.1%
Executed 4/5	—	3 — 75.0%	1 — 25.0%
Reprimanded 29/34	5 — 17.2%	8 — 27.6%	16 — 55.2%
Released and preventive arrest 58/72	17 — 29.3%	9 — 11.5%	32 — 55.2%

B. Sentence category by literacy

Table 57 — A.F.%

	Literate	*Semiliterate*	*Illiterate*
Placed under surveillance 35/41	35 — 100%	—	—
Jailed 192/225	166 — 86.5%	12 — 6.3%	14 — 7.3%
Exiled 140/146	123 — 87.9%	9 — 6.4%	8 — 5.7%
Hard labor 24/26	21 — 87.5%	1 — 4.2%	2 — 8.3%
Executed 4/5	4 — 100.%	—	—
Released and preventive arrest 58/72	47 — 74.6%	5 — 7.9%	11 — 17.5%
Reprimanded 18/34	16 — 88.9%	—	2 — 11.1%

C. Sentence category by job category

Table 58 — A.F.%

	Unskilled	I. P. Metals	I. P. Textiles	Student	Prof.	Artisan
Placed under surveillance 41/43	—	3 — 7.3%	5 — 12.2%	19 — 46.3%	8 — 19.5%	4 — 9.8%
Jailed 221/225	10 — 4.5%	61 — 27.6%	22 — 100%	31 — 14.0%	15 — 6.8%	67 — 30.3%
Exiled 138/146	2 — 1.4%	20 — 14.5%	15 — 10.9%	43 — 31.2%	23 — 16.7%	31 — 22.5%
Hard labor 25/26	—	4 — 16.0%	3 — 12.0%	8 — 32.0%	1 — 0.8%	6 — 24.0%
Executed 5/5	—	1 — 20.0%	1 — 20.0%	1 — 20.0%	1 — 20.0%	1 — 20.0%
Reprimanded 29/34	7 — 24.1%	5 — 17.2%	1 — 3.4%	1 — 3.4%	—	13 — 44.8%
Released and preventive arrest 70/72	10 — 14.2%	17 — 24.2%	6 — 8.6%	16 — 22.9%	3 — 4.3%	11 — 15.7%

Notes

Abbreviations used in the Notes for Archival and Periodical Sources:

AGAD   Archiwum Główne Akt Dawnych
AM   Archiwum Mikrofilmów
AZHP   Archiwum Zakładu Historii Partii
DKGW   "Delo" Kancelaria Gubernatora Warszawskiego
DP   Departament Politsii
GOT   *Gruppa "Osvobozhdenie truda": Iz arkhivov G. V. Plekhanova, V. I. Zasulicha i L. G. Deicha*
HI   Hoover Institution Archives
KL   *Krasnaia letopis'*
KS   *Katorga i ssylka*
KRRP   *Kronika Ruchu Rewolucyjnego w Polsce*
PT   *Przegląd Tygodniowy*
PWIS   Prokurator Warszawskiej Izby Sądowej
TsGAOR   Tsentral'nyi Gosudarstvennyi Arkhiv Oktiabr'skoi Revoliutsii i Sotsialisticheskogo Stroitel'stva
TsGIA SSSR   Tsentral'nyi Gosudarstvennyi Istoricheskii Arkhiv
WGZŻ   Warszawski Gubernialny Zarząd Żandarmeri
ZPW   *Z Pola Walki*

Chapter 1. The Background

1. W. A. Day, *The Russian Government in Poland; with a Narrative of the Polish Insurrection of 1863* (London, 1867), p. 6.

2. Adam and Lidia Ciołkosz reject the concept of "utopian socialism" as well as that of "scientific socialism." They prefer to use the term *romantic socialism.* L. and A. Ciołkoszowie, *Zarys dziejów socjalizmu polskiego,* vol. I (London, 1966), p. 3. Contemporary PPR historians refer to these men most often as "radical democrats," stressing the Marxist character of the word *socialism. Radykalni demokraci polscy: Wybór pism i dokumentów, 1863–1875,* ed. F. Romaniukowa (Warsaw, 1960).

3. A. Próchnik, *Ku Polsce socjalistycznej: Dzieje polskiej myśli socjalistycznej* (Warsaw, 1936), p. 3.

4. Ludwik Kulczycki claims that Polish utopian socialism was also unique in that it formed no experimental communes and remained "purely abstract." M. Mazowiecki [L. Kulczycki], *Historia polskiego ruchu socjalistycznego w zaborze rosyjskim* (Kraków, 1903), p. 7. However, several Polish communal experiments were carried on in England. See P. Brock, *Z dziejów wielkiej emigracji w Anglii* (Warsaw, 1958).

5. S. Diksztajn and W. Jodko-Narkiewicz, *Polski socjalizm utopijny i na emigracji — dwie rozprawy* (Kraków, 1904), pp. 99-100.

6. The essence of the Gromada program is in Brock, *Z dziejów emigracji,* pp. 99-100. The Gromada broke with the T.D.P. in 1835; see W. Łukasiewicz and W. Lewandowski, eds., *Postępowa publicystyka emigracyjna 1831-1846, Wybór źródeł* (Wrocław, 1961), p. 257. See also the proclamation, "Lud Polski gromada rewolucyjna na Londyn do Polaków, 23 Maja 1858," photocopy in AZHP, zespół 2, teczka 1. This proclamation reiterates the familiar theme of the utopian socialists' devotion to national independence.

7. Veto (W. Studnicki), *Dwadzieścia lat walki proletariatu polskiego* (Lwów, 1899), p. 3.

8. Ciołkoszowie, *Zarys,* vol. I, p. 494.

9. See J. Buszko, *Narodziny ruchu socjalistycznego na ziemiach polskich* (Kraków, 1967), pp. 33-34.

10. S. Walczak, "Rola genewskiego ośrodka emigracyjnego polskich socjalistów w kształtowaniu się świadomości socjalistycznej w kraju," reprint from *Ze Skarbca Kultury,* no. 7 (Wrocław, 1955), pp. 58-59. Buszko, *Narodziny,* p. 30. Wróblewski's correspondence with Marx and Engels is in J. Borejsza, *W kręgu wielkich wygnańców, 1848-1895* (Warsaw, 1963).

11. Engels to Wróblewski, 4 Dec. 1875, Borejsza, *W kręgu,* pp. 270-271.

12. See especially Karl Marx, *Manuscripte über die polnische Frage* (1863-1864) (Gravenhage, 1961), p. 93. Here Marx advocated Polish independence for typically geopolitical reasons, "the emergence of Poland . . . is the denial of Russia's candidacy for world domination."

13. For the tremendous influence of these works on Polish youth, see Ludwik Kulczycki's memoirs, *Dokoła mego życia,* AZHP special collections, typed copy, p. 7. The handwritten original is in the Polish National Library in Warsaw.

14. L. Chrzanowski, *O dążeniach i polityce Moskwy oraz o potrzebie stanowczego powstrzymania jej zaborczych działań* (Kraków, 1866), p. 5. Jan Kucharzewski, in his classic seven volume work, *Od białego caratu do czerwonego* (Warsaw, 1923-25), claims that all Russians, even in the revolutionary movement, wanted to truncate Poland and suppress the Poles. The book is available in an abridged translation, J. Kucharzewski, *The Origins of Modern Russia* (New York, 1948).

15. A. L. Pogodin, *Istoriia pol'skogo naroda v XIX veke* (Moscow, 1915), pp. 205-206.

16. Ibid., pp. 210-211. The Soviet historian T. G. Snytko dates the concept

of "Privislanskii krai" to 1866, but the term did not come into common official usage until the reign of Alexander III. T. G. Snytko, *Russkoe narodnichestvo i pol'skoe obshchestvennoe dvizhenie, 1865–1881 gg.* (Moscow, 1969), p. 30. The Russians also used both *Privislinskii* and *Privislianskii.* We will use the term commonly used by Poles until World War I — *Kongresówka* or *Congress Kingdom,* rather than the more official "Kingdom of Poland."

17. The archives of the St. Petersburg censorship committee are packed with picayune objections of Russian censors to the use of words in the loyalist newspaper *Kraj.* The Polish word "kolonia" (colony) could not be used for Petersburg Poles because it indicated that "Russians of Polish descent" (Poles) did not think of the Russian autocracy as "their state." TsGIA SSSR, f. 777, op. 3, 1. 8. The Ministry of Interior also informed the St. Petersburg committee to watch out for the proper use of official greetings. Poles arriving in the capital from Warsaw should be introduced with "I am happy to present" (meant for citizens of the Russian homeland) rather than "I have the honor to present" (meant for foreigners). Ibid., 1. 131.

18. Quoted in Kucharzewski, *Origins,* p. 352.

19. Ibid., p. 353.

20. Quoted in Snytko, *Russkoe narodnichestvo,* p. 33.

21. P. A. Zaionchkovskii, *Rossiiskoe samoderzhavie v kontse XIX stoletiia (politicheskaia reaktsiia 80-kh-nachala 90-kh godov)* (Moscow, 1970), p. 59.

22. Gurko was governor-general from 1883 to 1894 and Apukhtin curator from 1879 to 1897. They were friends and close collaborators. Stanisław Czekanowski recalled many highly uncomplimentary stories that circulated around Warsaw about Gurko, Apukhtin, and Gurko's infamous Polonophobe consort, Maria Andreevna. S. Czekanowski, *W domu niewoli, 1879–1888,* memoirs written in 1943–44, reworked and typed January, 1953, Manuskripta Institute Ossoliniani, 13258, Warsaw University Library, pp. 60–61.

23. *Pis'ma Pobedonostseva k Aleksandru III* (Moscow, 1925), pp. 386–388.

24. *Dnevnik gosudarstvennogo sekretar'ia A. A. Polovtsova,* vol. I (Moscow, 1966), p. 383.

25. Quoted in Zaionchkovskii, *Rossiiskoe samoderzhavie,* p. 120. It was often reported that Gurko even made Polish deaf-mutes communicate in Russian. A. L. Pogodin, *Istoriia,* p. 217.

26. For a good biographical sketch of Apukhtin, see J. Krzesławski (J. Cynarski), "Spoliczkowanie Apuchtina," *KRRP,* no. 3(15) (1938), pp. 129–130. Apukhtin was widely known as a reactionary in the Russian school system before his Warsaw experience. P. A. Zaionchkovskii, *Krizis samoderzhaviia na rubezhe 1870–1880-kh godov* (Moscow, 1964), pp. 64–65.

27. Czekanowski, *W domu niewoli,* p. 2.

28. J. Offenberg, *Stan umysłów wśród młodzieży akademickiej Universytetu Warszawskiego w latach 1885–1890 (Ze wspomnień kresowca)* (Warsaw, 1929), p. 8.

29. R. Skrzycki (Roman Dmowski), *Młodzież polska w zaborze rosyjskim* (Lwów, 1896), reprint from *Przegląd Wszechpolski,* vol. I (1896), pp. 16–17.

Chapter 2: *The Industrialization of the Congress Kingdom and the Formation of the Polish Working Class, 1864–1885*

1. For theories of modernization, see W. Rostow, *The Stages of Economic Growth* (Cambridge, 1964), pp. 6–8, and the critiques of his schema by A. Gershenkron and R. Aron: A. Gershenkron, *Europe in the Russian Mirror: Four Lectures in Economic History* (Cambridge, 1970), p. 103; R. Aron, *The Industrial Society: Three Essays on Ideology and Development* (New York, 1967), pp. 29–35. Gershenkron's framework for modernization maintains that the more backward a country, the more its "industrial history is shot through with substitutions of all kinds." Gershenkron, *Lectures,* p. 104. "Substitutions," variations from patterns of industrialization in more advanced countries, depend not only on "the degree of backwardness" but also on political factors. Therefore, when considering the modernization of the Congress Kingdom, significant "substitutions" result from the lack of an independent Polish administration in the Congress Kingdom. See also C. Black, *The Dynamics of Modernization* (New York, 1967), pp. 95–128.

2. Rosa Luxemburg, *Die industrielle Entwicklung Polens* (Leipzig, 1898), pp. 90–91. "There is not the least doubt," concluded Ianzhul, "that if the history of the contemporary Congress Kingdom had gone by a different route and if the acts of the Congress of Vienna had not tied the fate of the Kingdom to that of Russia — contemporary Poland would possess neither a Łódź nor a Sosnowiec." I. I. Janżułł, *Przemysł fabryczny w Królestwie Polskim* (St. Petersburg, 1887), p. 84.

3. See, for instance, J. Łukasiewicz, *Przewrót techniczny w przemyśle Królestwa Polskiego 1852–1886* (Warsaw, 1963), pp. 387–388.

4. K. Marks and F. Engels, *Manifest komunistyczny* (Warsaw, 1948), intro. F. Engels, p. 25.

5. By 1902 Łódź and Warsaw ranked third and fifth in the entire empire according to the size of urban worker population.

City	No. of Enterprises	No. of Workers
St. Petersburg	488	129,000
Moscow	918	105,300
Łódź	475	62,000
Riga	287	40,000
Warsaw	426	32,900

A. V. Pogozhev, *Uchet chislennosti i sostava rabochikh v Rossii: Materialy po statistike truda* (St. Petersburg, 1906), p. 63. A. G. Rashin claims that Pogozhev's figures are too low: *Formirovanie rabochego klassa Rossii* (Moscow, 1958), p. 76.

6. According to the 1897 all-empire census, the Congress Kingdom,

though containing 7.5 percent of the empire's total population and 0.5 percent of the empire's total area, accounted for 12.9 percent of the empire's "workers and servants" category. In 1897 the density of the Congress Kingdom was 84.28 per square *verst;* in European Russia, the density was 22.09 per square *verst.* European Russia was 12.9 percent urban — the Congress Kingdom was 23 percent urban. It is interesting to note, however, that Piotrków and Warsaw *gubernii* were less urban than their Russian counterparts, St. Petersburg and Moscow *gubernii:* 43.8 percent in Warsaw, 36.4 percent in Piotrków, 46.7 percent in Moscow, and 67.3 percent in St. Petersburg. *Obshchii svod po imperii: Rezul'tatov razrabotki dannykh pervoi vseobshchii perepisi naseleniia, proizvedennoi 28 ianvaria 1897* (St. Petersburg, 1905), vol. I, part 1, p. 1; vol. I, part 2, pp. 6, 10. See also Rashin, *Formirovanie rabochego klassa Rossii,* p. 176.

7. This line also connected the Russian and Prussian border from Dorohuska near the Russian border through Lublin, Dęblin, Warsaw, and Mława to the Prussian border.

8. Figures for railway building in the Congress Kingdom are in S. A. Kempner, *Rozwój gospodarczy Polski od rozbiorów do niepodległości* (Warsaw, 1924), pp. 98–100; Łukasiewicz, *Przewrót techniczny,* p. 303; *Historia Polski,* vol. III, part 1, ed. by Ż. Kormanowa and I. Pietrzak-Pawłowska (Warsaw, 1967), pp. 398–400.

9. *Historia Polski,* vol. III, part 1, p. 400.

10. Kempner, *Rozwój gospodarczy,* p. 98.

11. Ibid., p. 98. Liashchenko correctly emphasizes that railway building in Russia in the 1860s and 1870s affected the economy differently from the railway building of the 1890s. In the former case, "it occurred almost exclusively by the direct transplanting of foreign techniques and by the importation of locomotives, cars, and rails from abroad." The growth of "domestic ferrous metallurgy and machine building" of the 1890s, which supported and profited from this later Russian railway building, occurred in the Congress Kingdom in the 1880s. P. I. Liashchenko, *History of the National Economy of Russia to the 1917 Revolution* (New York, 1949), pp. 423–424. See also P. A. Khromov, *Ekonomicheskoe razvitie Rossii v XIX–XX vekakh, 1800–1917* (Moscow, 1950), pp. 88–89, 211.

12. S. Kieniewicz, *The Emancipation of the Polish Peasantry* (Chicago, 1969), p. 182. It should be remembered, however, that the Poles continued to export grain to Western Europe through Gdańsk and that this remained the largest portion of Congress Kingdom export to the West. Still, an increasing percentage of grain production was consumed domestically owing to the rapidly expanding nonagrarian population. *Historia Polski,* vol. III, part 1, p. 404.

13. See Kempner, *Rozwój gospodarczy,* p. 86, and B. Budkiewiczówna, *Ruch robotniczy w Królestwie Polskim w latach 1870–1890* (Minsk, 1934), p. 11. For Russian industry in the 1850s, see W. L. Blackwell, *The Beginnings of Russian Industrialization* (Princeton, 1968).

246   THE HISTORY OF THE PROLETARIAT

14. *Historia Polski,* vol. III, part 1, p. 403.

15. The higher tariffs were a result of a new policy to collect import duty on the gold standard, which raised the real rates about 50 percent. A. Wóycicki, *Dzieje robotników przemysłowych w Polsce* (Warsaw, 1929), p. 192; Kempner, *Rozwój gospodarczy,* p. 102; Łukasiewicz, *Przewrót techniczny,* p. 305. For the official Russian view of the 1877 tariff, see Ministerstvo Finansov, *Fabrichno-zavodskaia promyshlennost',* 2nd ed. (St. Petersburg, 1896), pp. 550–551. Rosa Luxemburg in her *Die industrielle Entwicklung Polens,* p. 9, is convinced that this is the most important single factor of Polish industrialization.

16. Wóycicki, *Dzieje,* p. 197. I. I. Ianzhul, one of Russia's first and most prolific factory inspectors and later professor at Moscow University, after spending "a rather long time" in Kalisz inspecting its "Polish, or more precisely, German" clothing factories, noticed that most of the raw materials for these "superb" plants easily crossed the border from Prussia as contraband. *Vospominaniia I. I. Ianzhula o perezhitom i vidennom v 1864–1909 gg.,* vol. I (St. Petersburg, 1910), p. 307. The new regulations "not only brought about the immediate founding of many new enterprises," writes Luxemburg, "but also caused the moving of a whole string of German factories from Saxony and Silesia to the western part of Poland [Congress Kingdom]." Luxemburg, *Die industrielle Entwicklung,* p. 16.

17. The most important were Schön in Sosnowiec (1870), Schmelzer in Myszków (1883), Hüffer in Łódź (1880), Heldner in Łódź (1883), and Kürzl in Zgierz (1884). It should be noted, however, that these new factories only reinforced the already pervasive influence of foreign, mostly German, capital in Polish industry. At an exhibition of Congress Kingdom industry in St. Petersburg in 1870, of more than 200 exhibitors, 131 had foreign names. An additional 30 exhibitors had Jewish names, and 42 had Polish-Catholic names. These last belonged primarily to agricultural firms and small industries. Wóycicki, *Dzieje,* pp. 197–205. See also Luxemburg, *Die industrielle Entwicklung,* p. 16; and W. Kula, *Historia gospodarcza Polski 1864–1918* (Warsaw, 1947), p. 33.

18. In Łódź alone from 1877 to 1879, the worth of textile production increased from 4.6 to 34.8 million rubles. Łukasiewicz, *Przewrót techniczny,* pp. 205–350. M. Tugan-Baranovskii justifiably warns that tariffs are as much a result of particular economic factors as a cause: *Statisticheskie itogi promyshlennogo razvitiia Rossii* (St. Petersburg, 1898), p. 18. On the politics of tariff assessments, see Zaionchkovskii, *Rossiiskoe samoderzhavie v kontse XIX stoletiia* (Moscow, 1970), p. 431, and Luxemburg, *Die industrielle Entwicklung,* pp. 76–77.

19. Among the largest bankers were prominent members of the assimilated Jewish community: L. Kronenberg, J. Bloch, J. Natanson, and H. and P. Wawelberg. For the history and importance of the Bank of Poland and Minister of Finance Lubecki in the pre-1863 period, see T. Rutowski, *W sprawie przemysłu krajowego* (Kraków, 1883), p. 246; E. Boss, *Sprawa robot-*

nicza w Królestwie Polskim w okresie paskiewiczowskim, 1831–1855 (Warsaw, 1931), pp. 16–17. For the post-1863 period, see Wóycicki, *Dzieje,* pp. 192–193.

Rutowski considers the banks of supreme importance in the industrialization of the Congress Kingdom, *W sprawie przemysłu,* p. 45. Kempner, *Rozwój gospodarczy,* p. 92.

20. W. Kula, *Historia gospodarcza,* p. 33.

21. Janżułł (Ianzhul), *Przemysł fabryczny,* p. 1.

22. This export to Russia and to the Far East is crucial in Rosa Luxemburg's argument that the Congress Kingdom formed a natural economic component of the Russian Empire. See her doctoral dissertation and book: Luxemburg, *Die industrielle Entwicklung Polens,* pp. 6, 90–91.

23. Janżułł, *Przemysł,* p. 80; *Historia Polski,* vol. III, part 1, p. 403; Wóycicki, *Dzieje,* p. 192.

24. Łukasiewicz, *Przewrót techniczny,* p. 308; Snytko, *Russkoe narodnichestvo i pol'skoe obshchestvennoe dvizhenie, 1865–1881 gg.* (Moscow, 1969), p. 39. By the mid-1880s almost all the Żyrardów linen and half of the entire Congress Kingdom wool production was exported to Russia. Polish metal products, on the other hand, were almost exclusively consumed by the booming local industrial economy. The industrially potent Piotrków *guberniia,* including the textile centers of Łódź, Zgierz, and Tomaszów, accounted for two-thirds of all Congress Kingdom exports to Russia (1897). Janżułł, *Przemysł,* pp. 53–54. *Historia Polski,* vol. III, part 1, p. 403.

25. Janżułł, *Przemysł,* p. 1. Ianzhul, an expert on Russian factory conditions, was commissioned by Minister of Finance Bunge to investigate how the growth of Polish industrial competition affected the Russian market. *Vospominaniia I. I. Ianzhula,* vol. II, p. 102.

26. Ibid., p. 103. Wóycicki adds that through Odessa and Kharkov, Polish products for the first time reached the Near East, the Balkans, the Ottoman Empire, and North Africa. Wóycicki, *Dzieje,* p. 192.

27. Janżułł, *Przemysł,* pp. 6–7. Poznanskii estimated that in 1878 factory income was 150 million rubles and agriculture income 250 million. I. Poznanskii, *Istoricheskii ocherk ekonomicheskogo polozheniia Pol'shi* (St. Petersburg, 1875), p. 43.

28. Łukasiewicz, *Przewrót techniczny,* p. 205. Rutowski, *W sprawie przemysłu,* p. 53.

29. Warsaw dominated the metal industry, having thirty-two of the industry's sixty-two factories, including the two largest, "Rudzki and Company" and "Lilpop, Rau and Lowenstein." The latter, the largest in the Congress Kingdom, was incorporated in 1873 after having operated as a family factory since 1818. Wóycicki, *Dzieje,* p. 202; Budkiewiczówna, *Ruch robotniczy,* p. 10.

30. J. Buszko, *Narodziny ruchu socjalistycznego na ziemiach polskich* (Kraków, 1967), p. 37.

31. Łukasiewicz, *Przewrót techniczny,* p. 255. According to various statistics, in 1857 the machine-building industry did not figure at all into Congress

Kingdom industrial production. In 1872, the value of its output was 2 million rubles and in 1877, 6.7 million rubles. Budkiewiczówna, *Ruch robotniczy,* p. 10.

32. A. Gershenkron, "The Rate of Industrial Growth in Russia since 1885," *Journal of Economic History,* Supplement 7 (1947), pp. 144–174; (N. D. Kondrat'ev) Kon'iunkturnyi Institut, *Ekonomicheskii biulleten',* vol. V (2) (1926), pp. 17–21; R. W. Goldsmith, "The Economic Growth of Tsarist Russia 1860–1913," *Economic Development and Cultural Change,* vol. IX (1961), pp. 441–475. Gershenkron admits that estimating Russian industrial growth prior to 1885 is "very uncertain indeed" but nevertheless offers 3.5 percent as the annual growth rate figure for the years 1862–1882. "The Rate of Industrial Growth," p. 145. Goldsmith, also working from Kondrat'ev's index, comes up with the figure of about 5 percent for the same period. Goldsmith, "The Economic Growth," p. 465. Gershenkron estimates a growth rate of 8 to 9 percent for the 1890s (p. 150); Goldsmith emphasizes more continuity between the 1880s and 1890s, estimating the growth rate as 7 to 8 percent for the 1890s. (p. 465). My own calculations, using the figures for industrial growth cited in the sources of the following note, support Goldsmith's conclusions that the rate of Russian industrial growth between 1865 and 1885 is much more profound (I would estimate 6 to 7 percent) than assessed by Gershenkron or the general historiography of the period.

33. The Russian figures are taken from Liashchenko, *History,* pp. 530, 628, 630; Tugan-Baranovskii, *Statisticheskie itogi,* pp. 3, 18; V. I. Lenin, *The Development of Capitalism in Russia* (Moscow, 1956), pp. 528, 535, 661; Ministerstvo Finansov, *Fabrichno-zavodskaia promyshlennost',* pp. 370–371. The Polish figures are taken from Janżułł, *Przemysł,* pp. 4–6, and corroborated by Rutowski, *W sprawie przemysłu,* p. 241; "Z kraju i o kraju," *Równość,* no. 3 (1879), p. 29; Łukasiewicz, *Przewrót techniczny,* pp. 193, 199, 303, 309; S. Koszutski, *Rozwój ekonomiczny Królestwa Polskiego w ostatnim 30-leciu 1870–1900* (Warsaw, 1901), p. 298; Wóycicki, *Dzieje,* p. 216; Kempner, *Rozwój gospodarczy,* p. 95; L. Grosfeld, *Z dziejów kapitalizmu w Polsce* (Warsaw, 1948), p. 22.

34. Compare figures on these factors in Polish industrialization with similar figures on Russia in A. G. Rashin, *Naselenie Rossii za 100 let (1811–1913): Statisticheskie ocherki* (Moscow, 1956), pp. 98, 114–115; Lenin, *Development of Capitalism,* pp. 609–614; Rashin, *Formirovanie rabochego klassa,* pp. 12–13, 112–114, 354; Tugan-Baranovskii, *Statisticheskie itogi,* p. 3; M. Tugan-Baranovskii, *Geschichte der russischen Fabrik* (Berlin, 1900), p. 339; Pogozhev, *Uchet chislennosti,* pp. 20–21, 28–29, 35–37; Khromov, *Ekonomicheskoe razvitie Rossii,* p. 27.

35. Janżułł, *Przemysł,* p. 6. Here Ianzhul gives figures for the number of machines per textile factory in 1877 and in 1886. Luxemburg claims that the number of machines per factory was about the same, but that the Poles had more equipment per employee. Russian industry also employed more women, which she maintains cut down worker productivity. R. Luxemburg, *Die industrielle Entwicklung,* pp. 52–54.

36. These conditions in the Congress Kingdom in the 1840s persisted in Galicia through the last half of the nineteenth century. In 1880 Galicia had 26.9 percent of the Austrian Empire's population and 26.1 percent of its land space, but it had less than 4 percent of the empire's large industry and 9 percent of all industrial factories and shops. Buszko, *Narodziny*, p. 40. See J. Durko, "Klasa robotnicza," *ZPW*, no. 1–2 (1963), pp. 51–54, for statistics on the worker population of Galicia and Prussian Poland in the 1880s.

37. Janżułł, *Przemysł*, pp. 6–7.

38. In the pre-Crimean war period, around 250,000 foreign craftsmen emigrated to the Congress Kingdom; in the post-1863 period, around 10,000 craftsmen and their families emigrated. Janżułł, *Przemysł*, p. 19. Boss, *Sprawa robotnicza*, pp. 21–22. The heaviest emigration occurred between 1818 and 1828.

39. Janżułł, *Przemysł*, pp. 6–7.

40. Productivity per worker in the Congress Kingdom and European Russia, 1860–1890

Congress Kingdom	European Russia
1864 — 640 rubles/worker	1863 — 691
1870 — 915	1870 — 894
1875 — 1137	1875 — 870
1880 — 1443	1879 — 1123
1887 — 1538	1886 — 1366

The Russian statistics are from Lenin, *Development of Capitalism*, p. 661, and are generally corroborated by Załęski, *Statystyka porównawcza*, p. 246, and Liashchenko, *History*, p. 526. The Polish statistics are from Łukasiewicz, *Przewrót techniczny*, p. 309, and are corroborated by Załęski, *Statystyka porównawcza*, p. 246. The figure for 1887 in the Congress Kingdom is taken from several other sources. Łukasiewicz only traces these developments to 1880. Khromov, who also compiles figures for the individual output of the Russian worker, though from Lenin's statistics on thirty-four industries, comes up with approximately the same conclusions, including a drop in production per worker from 1870 to 1875. Khromov, *Ekonomicheskoe razvitie*, p. 181.

41. Łukasiewicz, *Przewrót techniczny*, pp. 306, 307, 384. *Historia Polski*, vol. III, part 1, p. 402. Over 50 percent of all steam-driven machinery was imported from abroad. Lenin lamented that, unfortunately, steam engine use in Russia "did not make very rapid progress." Lenin, *Development of Capitalism*, p. 513. According to Lenin, the Congress Kingdom's superiority in steam-driven machines continued unabated to the point where in 1892 the Congress Kingdom possessed 24 percent of the empire's entire steam horsepower capacity. In fact, in 1892, Piotrków *guberniia* led all others in the empire in steam-power capacity. Lenin, *Development*, pp. 556–557.

42. According to Pogozhev, 31.8 percent of St. Petersburg *gub.* factories, 31.3 percent of Moscow *gub.* factories, 24.7 percent of Warsaw *gub.* and 11.7 percent of Piotrków *gub.* factories up to 1903 were built before 1870. Pogo-

zhev, *Uchet chislennosti,* pp. 75–76. Rashin breaks these figures down by industrial sector, *Formirovanie,* pp. 38–39. According to a study of 166 factories in the Congress Kingdom by Rutkowski, 18 percent were built before 1850, 11 percent between 1850 and 1860, 13 percent between 1860 and 1870, 31 percent between 1871 and 1880, and 27 percent between 1881 and 1888. J. Rutkowski, *Historia gospodarcza Polski,* vol. II (Poznań, 1950), p. 245. See also Janżułł, *Przemysł,* pp. 48–49.

43. O. Crisp, *Studies in the Russian Economy before 1914* (London, 1976), p. 41.

44. Ministerstvo Finansov, *Fabrichno-zavodskaia promyshlennost',* p. 151.

45. *Historia Polski,* vol. III, part 1, p. 406; Załęski, *Statystyka porównawcza,* p. 246; Kempner, *Rozwój gospodarczy,* p. 94; F. Sulimierski, "Notatka statystyczna," *Ognisko* (Warsaw, 1882), p. 61.

46. In 1872 the Congress Kingdom was already 16.21 percent urban; Warsaw *guberniia* was 34.04 percent urban. There were thirty-two towns with populations of over 5,000. Kempner, *Rozwój gospodarczy,* p. 95. Jews outnumbered Poles in the urban population of the Congress Kingdom four to three in 1877. This phenomenon was more pronounced in the less industrialized towns of Suwałki, Łomża, and Siedlce *gubernii,* where Jews outnumbered Poles four to one and five to one. "St.," "Droga wyjścia," *Prawda,* no. 14 (1882), pp. 157–158.

47. *Historia Polski,* vol. III, part 1, p. 406.

48. Ibid., p. 407. Budkiewiczówna, *Ruch robotniczy,* p. 11. Founded by the Frenchman Phillippe Girard, the factory after 1857 was run by the Austrians Helle and Dietrich. During this period, "Żyrardów monopolized almost the entire manufacturing of linens in the Congress Kingdom." Wóycicki, *Dzieje,* p. 199.

49. *History of Poland,* eds. A. Gieysztor, S. Kieniewicz (Warsaw, 1968), p. 309; Wóycicki, *Dzieje,* p. 216; Załęski, *Statystyka porównawcza,* p. 246; Koszutski, *Rozwój ekonomiczny,* p. 40; "Z materiałów statystycznych Królestwa Polskiego," *Nowiny,* no. 117 (1878), pp. 2–3; L. Grosfeld, *Z dziejów,* pp. 25–26.

50. *Historia Polski,* vol. III, part 1, p. 408. Meloch and Grosfeld estimated that in 1870 there was one worker for every ninety-five inhabitants, in 1882 one for every sixty-two inhabitants, and in 1897 one for every thirty-seven inhabitants. Meloch, *Ruch strajkowy,* pp. 4–5; Grosfeld, *Z dziejów,* p. 26. Kelles-Krauz wrote that in the 1890s in the Congress Kingdom there were twenty-four workers per thousand population, and in Russia's central industrial region only twelve per thousand. K. Kelles-Krauz, *Pisma wybrane,* vol. II (Warsaw, 1962), p. 110. According to Durko's estimates, derived from official sources in the 1880s, 1 percent of the Russian, 1.5 percent of the Congress Kingdom, and 16 percent of Germany's population were workers. Workers in large-scale industry, according to Durko, made up 0.3 percent of Russia's population, 0.7 percent of the Congress Kingdom's population, and 3.5 percent of Germany's

population. J. Durko, "Klasa robotnicza w dobie działalności Proletariatu," *ZPW*, nos. 1–2 (1963), p. 56.

51. Łukasiewicz, *Przewrót techniczny*, pp. 72, 175, 309; Buszko, *Narodziny ruchu*, p. 37. In the years 1869–1879, the value of cotton mill production in the Congress Kingdom grew by four times.

52. Łukasiewicz, *Przewrót techniczny*, p. 309.

53. V. V. Sviatlovskii, *Fabrichnyi rabochii: Issledovanie zdorov'ia russkogo fabrichnogo rabochego. Sanitarnoe polozhenie fabrichnogo rabochego v Privislianskom krai i v Malorussii* (Warsaw, 1889), p. 22. Sviatlovskii was factory inspector in Warsaw from 1886 to 1888.

54. Łukasiewicz, *Przewrót techniczny*, pp. 175–176.

55. Ibid., p. 255; Budkiewiczówna, *Ruch robotniczy*, p. 10.

56. In 1879 Łódź had 530 institutions with 16,500 workers producing a value of 37 million rubles; Warsaw had 307 institutions with 14,300 workers producing a value of 27.2 million rubles. By 1885 Łódź employed 23,000 workers who produced a value of 40 million rubles; Warsaw had 15,000 workers producing a value of 29 million rubles. Łukasiewicz, *Przewrót techniczny*, pp. 309–310, 385.

56A. The observations and statistics on the Polish emancipation are taken from: G. T. Robinson, *Rural Russia under the Old Regime* (Berkeley, 1957), p. 85; S. Kieniewicz, *The Emancipation of the Polish Peasantry* (Chicago, 1969); *Historia Polski*, vol. III, part 1, pp. 374–377; Kempner, *Rozwój gospodarczy*, p. 103; V. Studnitskii (W. Studnicki), *Pol'sha v politicheskom otnoshenii ot razdelov do nashikh dnei* (St. Petersburg, 1908), p. 91; M. Mazowiecki (Kulczycki), *Historia ruchu socjalistycznego w zaborze rosyjskim* (Kraków, 1903), p. 12.

According to these sources, the amount of land in peasant hands increased by 28 percent between 1864 and 1872. The emancipation created many small peasant landowners. Before the reform, 339,000 peasants were landless; after it, 220,000 were landless. As a result of the emancipation small holdings quadrupled. This situation did not last long, since a family could not be supported by these small holdings. By 1891 the number of landless peasants increased to 850,000. After the emancipation, landless peasants were 3.5 percent of all peasants; in 1891 they had increased to 13.2 percent. The largest portion of the land remained in large holdings: in 1872 about 54 percent of all cultivated land in the Congress Kingdom. Kieniewicz concludes that between 1870 and 1899 the percentage of small holdings, under three *morgi* or four acres, fell from 21.8 percent to 15 percent, middle-sized holdings rose from 40.6 percent to 44.5 percent, and large holdings, over 15 *morgi*, rose from 37.6 percent to 40.5 percent.

57. In 1873 personal and hereditary *szlachta* made up 11 percent of Warsaw's population, six times that of the percentage for the entire Congress Kingdom. By 1882, however, the *szlachta* population had declined to 3.5 percent of the city's total. W. Załęski, *Statystyka porównawcza*, p. 2; *Rezultaty spisu jednodniowego ludności miasta Warszawy 1881*, part 3 (Warsaw, 1885), pp.

31-35. According to the positivist periodical *Atheneum*, "proletarianized" *szlachta* were now counted as *"meshchane"* (predominantly workers). Based on police statistics, *Atheneum* printed the following table and concluded that the *szlachta* were entering the *meshchane* and traders categories:

	1878	1879	Difference
Traders	34,000	40,000	+6,000
Artisans	38,000	43,000	+5,000
Meshchane	194,000	211,000	+17,000
Szlachta	19,000	17,000	-2,000

"Kronika miesięczna," *Atheneum*, vol. IV (1879), pp. 183-184. T. Łepkowski notes that even before 1864 Warsaw *szlachta* were entering the urban workforce: *Początki klasy robotniczej Warszawy* (Warsaw, 1956), p. 190. L. Kulczycki estimates that 300,000 lower *szlachta* entered the workforce between 1863 and the late 1880s: *Dokoła mego życia*, unpublished manuscript, AZHP, p. 93. Among the young members of the *szlachta*, the technical schools of the railways were popular means of entering the workforce. W. Sieroszewski, *Pamiętniki: Wspomnienia* (Kraków, 1959), p. 118. On *szlachta* entrance into the urban middle class, see J. Żurawicki, "Z problematyki formowania się intelligencji warszawskiej i jej świadomości w końcu XIX w.," *Warszawa popowstaniowa*, vol. II, book 1 (Warsaw, 1968), pp. 158-196.

58. It has been estimated that about 25,000 artisans became factory workers in the 1870s and 1880s. *Historia Polski*, vol. III, part 1, p. 401. Wóycicki estimated that from 1871 to 1880 "several thousand" small artisan shops folded and their employees entered the factory labor forces. *Dzieje*, p. 232. See also N. Gąsiorowska, *Kształtowanie się klasy robotniczej* (Warsaw, 1955), pp. 7-8. Nevertheless, the number of artisans continued to increase as did the value of their production — though at rates less than those of industrial workers. The type of artisan shop was also changing, owing to the competition of industry. Kempner, *Rozwój gospodarczy*, pp. 86, 101; "Kronika miesięczna," *Atheneum*, vol. IV (1879), p. 184; (L. Waryński), "Czy jest u nas kwestia robotnica?" *Równość*, no. 8-9 (1880), p. 17.

59. On Russian artisan-workers, see Tugan-Baranovskii, *Geschichte der russischen Fabrik*, pp. 526-588, and Lenin, *The Development of Capitalism*, p. 661.

60. K. Grünberg and C. Kozłowski, *Historia polskiego ruchu robotniczego 1864-1918* (Warsaw, 1962), p. 42; E. Boss, *Sprawa robotnicza*, p. 60; Mazowiecki (Kulczycki), *Historia*, p. 13. In *Dokoła mego życia*, p. 94, Kulczycki argues that those artisans who did not enter the factory workforce after 1864 formed the petty bourgeoisie. Their social-political consciousness faded just as their patriotic and especially Catholic consciousness grew.

61. Łepkowski, *Początki*, p. 132; *Vospominaniia I. I. Ianzhula*, p. 117. The Polish peasant-worker was geographically much more stable than his Russian counterpart. While he generally more often traveled beyond his home *guber-*

niia to find work in the first place, he also usually stayed at this destination. "Worker-nomads" did exist in the Congress Kingdom (though less than in Russia); these were usually confined to the Łódź-Zgierz-Tomaszów region. The vast majority of Warsaw's peasant population remained in Warsaw. "Przegląd statystyczny," *PT*, no. 51 (1883), p. 641; *Rezultaty spisu jednodniowego* ... *1881*, part 3, pp. 31–34. For migration patterns and ties to the land see: R. Luxemburg, *Die industrielle Entwicklung*, p. 47; Tugan-Baranovskii, *Fabrik*, p. 525; Zelnick, "The Peasant and the Factory," *The Peasant*, p. 187; Robinson, *Rural Russia*, p. 108; Rashin, *Formirovanie*, pp. 411–412; and *Historia Polski*, vol. III, part 1, p. 409.

From a sample of 200 Warsaw workers born in the 1850s through the 1870s, Anna Żarnowska concludes that at the end of the 1870s and beginning of the 1880s (and even more at the end of the 1880s and beginning of the 1890s), recruits for the factories and workshops of Warsaw were drawn from the peasantry. Three-quarters of her sample came from outside of Warsaw; about half of these came directly from the villages. Of thirty-four Łódź workers, only 15 percent were born in Łódź, and over 65 percent were direct recruits from villages. "Z badań nad składem klasy robotniczej w Królestwie Polskim w latach 1870–1914," *Polska klasa robotnicza*, vol. IV (Warsaw, 1973), p. 103. On the high percentage of peasants in the Łódź workforce see: K. Groniowski, "Udział robotników okręgu łódzkiego w emigracji do Brazylii w 1890 r.," *Polska klasa robotnicza*, vol. III, p. 206; Ihnatowicz, *Przemysł łódzki*, pp. 80–89; and G. Missalowa, *Studia nad powstaniem łódzkiego okręgu przemysłowego*, vol. II (Łódź, 1964), p. 77.

62. A year is computed on the basis of 288 days, a day on twelve hours. Ia. T. Mikhailovskii [a former chief factory inspector] "O zarabotnoi plate i prodolzhitel'nosti rabochego vremeni na russkikh fabrikakh i zavodakh," Ministerstvo Finansov, *Fabrichno-zavodskaia promyshlennost' i torgovlia Rossii*, 2nd ed. (St. Petersburg, 1896), p. 465. "S. Bienias," "Rezultaty spisu jednodniowego w Warszawy," *Prawda*, no. 31 (1884), p. 363; *Równość*, no. 3 (1879), p. 30. Here *Równość* estimates the average worker's wage in Warsaw in 1879 at 252 rubles 52 kopeks a year.

63. Ibid. V. S. Pankratova, "Iz deiatel'nosti sredi rabochikh v 1880–1884 gg.," *Byloe*, no. 3 (1906), p. 247. The average wage of some advanced metalworkers was 60–70 rubles a month in the 1880s, or around 750 rubles a year. Mikhailovskii's appendix categorizes wage earning in the empire according to the major industrial professions. Generally, the textile workers earned half the amount of metalworkers and machine-building workers, 160 rubles to 330 rubles a year. Mikhailovskii, "O zarabotnoi plate," pp. 481–492.

64. Women's work was often the same as the men's. Budkiewiczówna writes, "The average wage of a male worker at Poznański factory in Łódź was 8 rubles a week [which was quite respectable], but there were in the whole factory 87 male weavers in the years 1884–1887, actually they were masters, and besides that over 1,000 women worked as weavers, and they, even on the average, did not earn over 4 rubles a week." Budkiewiczówna, *Ruch robot-*

niczy, p. 5. According to another source, the average male wage in the Congress Kingdom in 1880 was 17 rubles a month, 204 rubles a year. The average female wage was 9 rubles 75 kopeks a month, slightly more than one-half the male wage. M. Meloch, *Ruch strajkowy*, p. 5.

65. Mikhailovskii, *Fabrichno-zavodskaia promyshlennost'*, p. 471.

66. *Równość*, no. 3 (1879), pp. 30–31.

67. Ibid.

68. Mikhailovskii, *Fabrichno-zavodskaia promyshlennost'*, p. 469.

69. "Uwagi," *Kwartalnik Historyczny*, p. 949.

70. Twenty-nine out of 209 strikes and workers' uprisings from 1870 to 1879 were caused directly by the issue of penalties. *Rabochee dvizhenie semidesiatykh godov: Sbornik arkhivnykh dokumentov*, ed. E. A. Korol'chuk (Moscow, 1934), p. 17. Although Inspector Mikhailovskii claimed that the factory stores benefited the workers and were generously run, the Morozov and the Żyrardów strikes demonstrate that both in Russia and the Congress Kingdom, the factory store was a hated symbol of the workers' oppression. Mikhailovskii, *Fabrichno-zavodskaia promyshlennost'*, p. 470. "Uwagi," *Kwartalnik Historyczny*, p. 947.

71. Mikhailovskii, *Fabrichno-zavodskaia promyshlennost'*, p. 472.

72. For skilled ironworkers the situation was better. They earned 345 rubles a year and spent 170 rubles for staples. "Uwagi," *Kwartalnik Historyczny*, p. 949.

73. *Vospominaniia I. I. Ianzhula*, p. 116.

74. Luxemburg, *Die industrielle Entwicklung*, p. 45. It should be added that night work was also rare in the Baltic and St. Petersburg regions. Mikhailovskii, *Fabrichno-zavodskaia promyshlennost'*, p. 479.

75. V. V. Sviatlovskii, *Fabrichnyi rabochii* (Warsaw, 1889), pp. 39–40. "Uwagi," *Kwartalnik Historyczny*, p. 951.

76. Mikhailovskii, *Fabrichno-zavodskaia promyshlennost'*, pp. 479–480.

77. Ibid., p. 478. Factory legislation of 1882, 1884, and 1890 supposedly forbade labor of children under twelve and limited those of ages twelve to fifteen to an eight-hour day.

78. Budkiewiczówna, *Ruch robotniczy*, p. 6.

79. See Mikhailovskii, *Fabrichno-zavodskaia promyshlennost'*, p. 471.

80. *Vospominaniia I. I. Ianzhula*, p. 116.

81. Sviatlovskii, *Fabrichnyi rabochii*, pp. 110, 120, 179. Emphasis in original.

82. "Drobne warsztaty," *Równość*, no. 1 (1880), pp. 5–8. See also W. Sieroszewski, *Pamiętniki: Wspomnienia* (Kraków, 1959), pp. 103–111, for an excellent description of workshop life.

83. "From the director of the Department of Trade and Manufacture to Baron N. N. Medem, 29 September 1883," AGAD, DKGW, 1883, no. 301, ll. 1–2.

84. "Report of the Łowicz uezd nachal'nik, 16 November 1883," AGAD, DKGW, 1883, no. 301, ll. 11–15.

85. AGAD, DKGW, 1883, no. 301, ll. 47–48.

86. "Report of representative Ermakov, April 1884," in ibid., ll. 49–54.
87. "Doklad varshavskogo gubernatora, Jan. 1882, no. 8," AGAD, DKGW, referat 1, 1882, no. 64, ll. 1–2. This report was part of an investigation of anti-Jewish disturbances in Warsaw in December 1881. The governor recommended setting up homes for destitute children and charitable institutions to feed the hungry.
88. A copy of this letter was sent by the gendarme nachal'nik of Błońsk *uezd* to the nachal'nik of Warsaw *guberniia* recommending investigation. AGAD, DKGW, referat 1, 1880, no. 172, ll. 2–3.
89. *Rezultaty spisu jednodniowego ludności miasta Warszawy 1882,* part 2 (Warsaw, 1884), pp. 69–75.
90. J. Heurich, *Jak robotnicy u nas mieszkają: A jak mieszkać mogą i powinni* (Warsaw, 1873), p. 10.
91. Ibid., pp. 9, 23–24.
92. Sviatlovskii, *Fabrichnyi rabochii,* p. 86.
93. Ibid., p. 215.
94. Ibid., p. 83.
95. "Z kraju," *Głos,* no. 10 (1886), p. 152.
96. Quoted in Luxemburg, *Die industrielle Entwicklung,* p. 47.
97. "Uwagi," *Kwartalnik Historyczny,* p. 949.
98. *Rezultaty spisu jednodniowego,* part 2, pp. 50–51. Polish workers were sometimes bilingual in Polish and in Russian. Some spoke Polish but could read and write only Russian. Handwritten confessions of revolutionaries, workers, and intelligentsia alike were sometimes in Polish, sometimes in Russian. In Warsaw workshops, reported Sieroszewski, workers bantered in half-Russian, half-Polish. Sieroszewski, *Pamiętniki,* p. 108. A list of seventeen workers involved in an investigation of Żyrardów socialist workers indicated that all spoke Russian. AGAD, DKGW, referat 1, 1883, no. 122, ll. 125–129.
99. For literacy rates among Russians, see Rashin, *Formirovanie rabochego klassa,* p. 586–590.
100. R. Luxemburg, *Pamięci "Proletariatu"* (Warsaw, 1922), pp. 6–8.
101. Ibid., p. 58. She also concluded that the "development of the social democratic movement in the Congress Kingdom would be permanently guaranteed only when Russian socialism also stood on social democratic foundations." Ibid., pp. 58–59.
102. Amerykanin (J. Uziembło), "Wielki proces krakowski," *ZPW* (London, 1904), p. 51.
103. *Rabochee dvizhenie v Rossii,* ed. A. El'nitskii (Moscow, 1925), p. 229.
104. The Chancellory goes on to recommend the reestablishment of a secret Imperial Commission in Warsaw to investigate socialist propaganda among workers and undertake measures to "protect" workers against it. Quoted in Meloch, *Ruch strajkowy,* pp. 12–13.
105. *Khronika sotsialisticheskogo dvizheniia v Rossii 1878–1887: Ofitsial'nyi otchet* (Moscow, 1906), p. 33.
106. Łukasiewicz concludes that the Congress Kingdom underwent the

industrial revolution about seventy-five years after England, but that England took fifty-five years to complete it while Poland took only twenty years. Łukasiewicz, *Przewrót techniczny,* pp. 386–387, Tugan-Baranovskii concludes that Russia of the 1890s was about fifty years behind England and forty years behind France. Tugan-Baranovskii, *Die russische Fabrik,* p. 514. George Rudé appends to the process of industrial revolution, the transition of the "crowd" from self-employed to wage earners. This occurred in France in the 1840s, in England in the 1850s, and, one might speculate, in the Congress Kingdom in the early 1880s and in Russia in the late 1890s. See G. Rudé, *The Crowd in the French Revolution* (Oxford, 1959), pp. 238–239.

107.

		Empire	
year	no. of disturbances		workers
1885	73		29,077
1886	53		6,593
1887	88		29,844
1888	45		17,411
1889	42		39,591
1890	39		12,394
1891	40		29,074
1892	45		51,865
Totals	425		215,849

	Congress Kingdom		*Percent of Polish Workers*
	no. of disturbances	workers	
1885	6	382	1%
1886	5	905	14%
1887	4	340	1%
1888	11	9,850	57%
1889	2	2,870	7%
1890	7	10,000	84%
1891	30	25,541	88%
1892	9	35,000	67%
	74 (17%)	85,287	40%

Compiled from A. M. Pankratova, "Vstupitel'naia stat'ia," *Rabochee dvizhenie v Rossii v XIX veke,* vol. III, part 1 (Moscow, 1952), pp. 72, 79; and from F. Tych, "Narodziny masowego ruchu klasy robotniczej w Królestwie Polskim," *Polska klasa robotnicza,* vol. II (Warsaw, 1971), p. 41. Pankratova, in compiling her statistics for the empire, may well have missed some Polish labor disturbances.

108. See p. 305 (n. 5) and p. 307 (n. 3).

Chapter 3. Warsaw Positivism and the Origins of Polish Marxism

1. The only work that explores some of the ideological ties between Warsaw Positivism and Polish Marxism is Alina Molska's monograph, *Model ustroju socjalistycznego w polskiej myśli marksistowskiej lat 1878–1886* (Warsaw, 1965). For a full discussion of the historiography of Organic Work and Warsaw Positivism, see S. A. Blejwas, "Organic Work as a Problem in Polish Historiography," *Surabu Kenkyu (Slavic Studies)*, The Slavic Institute, Sapporo, Japan, no. 19, pp. 191–205.

2. For a complete discussion of the origins of Warsaw Positivism and the early history of Organic Work see B. Skarga, *Narodziny pozytywizmu polskiego, 1831–1864* (Warsaw, 1964). Also of interest is her analysis of positivism's increasing sophistication: *Z historii filozofii pozytywistycznej w Polsce; ciągłość i przemiany* (Wrocław, 1972).

3. The most important of these associations included the temperance societies, the Poznań Bazar (a clearinghouse of Polish culture and commerce), the "Society for the Promotion of Education" in Galicia, the Kasa im. Mianowskiego (which supported Polish learning), the "Agricultural Society," and the "Land Credit Association." Zamoyski's publication *Rocznik gospodarstwa krajowego (Yearbook of the National Economy)* was an especially important focus of the self-improvement movement.

4. See A. Bromke, *Poland's Politics: Idealism vs. Realism* (Cambridge, 1967), for an analysis of these alternative directions of Polish political thought in the twentieth century.

5. U. Haustein, *Sozialismus und nationale Frage in Polen: Die Entwicklung der sozialistischen Bewegung in Kongress Polen von 1875 bis 1900 unter besonderer Berücksichtungen der Polnischen Sozialistischen Partei (PPS)* (Köln, 1969), p. 10.

6. Stańczyk was a fabled court jester of King Sigismund I. His feigned stupidity led him successfully through exploits reminiscent of Til Eulenspiegel. In 1869, a pamphlet *Teka Stańczyka* appeared, which satirized the conspiratorial approach to the Polish question in Galicia. Thereafter the Galician conservative camp became known as the stańczycy.

7. W. Feldman, *Dzieje polskiej myśli politycznej w okresie porozbiorowym*, vol. II (Kraków, 1918), p. 215.

8. A. Świętochowski, *Wspomnienia* (Wrocław, 1966), p. 76.

9. L. Buchner, *Force and Matter* (London, 1870), p. xix.

10. Ibid., p. 256.

11. J. S. Mill, *Auguste Comte and Positivism* (London, 1891), p. 6.

12. See D. G. Charlton, *Positivist Thought in France during the Second Empire* (Oxford, 1959), p. 50; I. S. Kon, *Die Geschichtsphilosophie des 20 Jahrhunderts*, vol. I (Berlin, 1964), p. 49; R. G. Collingwood, *The Idea of History* (Oxford, 1946), p. 128.

13. There is no doubt, wrote Ludwik Kulczycki, "that the possibility of a gradual peaceful development of Russo-Polish relations was founded on the analogy of the transformation that had taken place between the peoples of Galicia and Austria." L. Kulczycki, *Dokoła mego życia,* Maszynopsis AZHP. (Special Collections), p. 26.

14. Feldman, *Dzieje,* vol. II, p. 249.

15. F. Kon, *Narodziny wieku: Wspomnienia* (Warsaw, 1969), p. 23. The Szkoła Główna served as the main university of Warsaw between 1862 and 1869. Other talented alumni of the school included prominent figures of nineteenth-century Polish cultural and intellectual life: P. Chmielowski, B. Prus, H. Sienkiewicz, A. Kraushar, W. Przyborowski, J. Ochoworowicz, and A. Dygasiński.

16. Feldman, *Dzieje,* vol. II, p. 214.

17. Quoted in T. G. Snytko, *Russkoe narodnichestvo i pol'skoe obshchestvennoe dvizhenie 1865-1881 gg.* (Moscow, 1969), p. 46.

18. *Prawda,* no. 1 (1881), p. 1.

19. Scriptor (Erazm Piltz), *Nasze stronnictwa skrajne* (Kraków, 1903), p. 5.

20. *Atheneum,* no. 11 (1878), p. 409.

21. Ibid., pp. 432, 417.

22. *PT,* no. 31 (1881), pp. 373-375.

23. "Nowoczesny dopływ antysemityzmu," *Prawda,* no. 32 (1883), pp. 373-374. In the fall of 1878, a long series of articles in *Nowiny* sympathetically "explained" Jewish culture and history to the Polish public.

24. A. Wiślicki, "Zadanie intelligencyi naszej," *PT,* no. 51 (1880), pp. 605-608; ibid., no. 52 (1880), pp. 617-619. "M.," "Czego nam trzeba?" *PT,* no. 34 (1881), pp. 409-411; ibid., no. 35 (1881), pp. 426-428. A. Wiślicki, "Bez wodzów," *PT,* no. 36 (1881), pp. 433-436.

25. *PT,* no. 34 (1881), p. 411.

26. *PT,* no. 35 (1881), p. 427.

27. Ibid., p. 428.

28. *PT,* no. 36 (1881), p. 436.

29. *PT,* no. 52 (1880), p. 618.

30. *PT,* no. 51 (1880), p. 605.

31. *PT,* no. 52 (1880), p. 616.

32. Ibid., p. 619. This message appeared frequently in the positivist press. In F. Łagowski's "Literatura dla ludu," *Atheneum,* no. 15 (1879), pp. 584-601, the matter was one of fulfilling the moral obligation of the intelligentsia "to their younger half-brothers."

33. *PT,* no. 56 (1880), p. 619.

34. *PT,* no. 52 (1880), p. 618.

35. *Prawda,* no. 14 (1882), p. 158.

36. *Prawda,* no. 39 (1883), p. 462.

37. *Prawda,* no. 1 (1881), p. 4.

38. *Atheneum*, no. 9 (1878), p. 385. Prus (Aleksander Głowacki) expressed his views in his *Atheneum* column, "Kronika miesięczna."

39. *Prawda*, no. 39 (1883), pp. 461-462.

40. *Atheneum*, no. 9 (1878), p. 385.

41. See for instance, *Atheneum*, no. 12 (1878), pp. 585-601.

42. *Atheneum*, no. 11 (1879), pp. 196-197.

43. *Nowiny*, no. 102 (1878), p. 3.

44. *Nowiny*, no. 81 (1878), pp. 3-4.

45. *Atheneum*, no. 13 (1879), pp. 411-413. See also *PT*, no. 11 (1885), pp. 124-125.

46. *Prawda*, no. 32 (1883), p. 379. Emphasis added. See A. Złotnicki, "Prawa fabryczne i położenie robotników w zachodniej Europie," *Prawda*, nos. 28-32 (1883).

47. *Prawda*, no. 39 (1883), p. 461.

48. *Atheneum*, no. 2 (1880), p. 403.

49. *Atheneum*, no. 2 (1880), p. 403.

50. *Prawda*, no. 9 (1885), p. 103.

51. *Prawda*, no. 10 (1885), pp. 102-113.

52. *Atheneum*, no. 2 (1880), p. 402.

53. Ibid., pp. 397-398.

54. A. Świętochowski, "Wskazanie polityczne," in *Ognisko: Książka wydana dla uczczenia 25-letniej pracy T. T. Jeża* (Warsaw, 1882), p. 51.

55. Ibid., p. 54.

56. See the favorable obituary of Governor-General P. Albedynskii in *Prawda*, no. 23 (1883), pp. 267-268.

57. F. Perl (Res), *Dzieje ruchu socjalistycznego w zaborze rosyjskim* (Warsaw, 1958), p. 46.

58. Kulczycki, *Dokoła mego życia*, Maszynopis AZHP, p. 225.

59. Świętochowski described the literary "gymnastics" he and his colleagues performed in order to avoid Russian censorship of articles on even the most general topics of European nationalism. Świętochowski, *Wspomnienia*, p. 77.

60. Kulczycki, *Dokoła mego życia*, p. 35.

61. R. Skrzycki [Roman Dmowski], *Młodzież polska w zaborze rosyjskim* (Lwów, 1896), pp. 38-39. Reprinted from *Przegląd Wszechpolski*, vol. I, 1896.

62. Ibid., p. 15.

63. J. Offenburg, *Stań umysłów wśród młodzieży akademickiej Uniwersytetu Warszawskiego w latach 1885-1890 (Ze wspomnień kresowca)* (Warsaw, 1929), p. 14. See also D. Wawrzykowska-Wierciochowa, ed., *Pamiętnik — Maria Bohuszewiczówna*, introduction Ż. Kormanowa (Wrocław, 1955), p. 30; M. Schmidt, *Wspomnienia młodzieży z przed 50-ciu lat* (Warsaw, 1929), p. 13; K. Pietkiewicz, "Michał Mancewicz i jego czasy," *Niepodległość*, vol. 3 (1931), p. 28.

64. Skrzycki [Dmowski], *Młodzież polska*, pp. 46, 54.

65. S. Koszutski, *Walka młodzieży polskiej o wielkie ideały: Wspomnienia*

z czasów gimnazjalnych i uniwersyteckich (1881-1900) (Warsaw, 1928), p. 11.
S. Czekanowski, *W domu niewoli, 1879-1888*, memoirs written in 1943-1944, reworked and typed Jan., 1953, Manuskripta Institute Ossoliniani, 13258, Warsaw University Library, p. 36. Skrzycki [Dmowski], *Młodzież polska*, p. 60.

66. Skrzycki [Dmowski], *Młodzież polska*, p. 54.

67. *Prawda*, no. 12 (1883), p. 134. See also "Z powodu drugiego tomu 'Kapitału' Marksa," *Prawda*, no. 38 (1885), p. 45.

68. "Teorya wartości Marksa," *Prawda*, no. 41 (1885), p. 488. See also "Germanizacja naszego przemysłu," *Prawda*, no. 42 (1885), p. 577.

69. "Apage satanas!" *Prawda*, no. 30 (1884), p. 251.

70. "Dla dzieci pracujących," *Prawda*, no. 31 (1884), p. 40.

71. "Nowy organ w Anglii," *Prawda*, no. 40 (1884), p. 40.

72. *Atheneum*, vol. III (1879), p. 195.

73. *Nowiny* was particularly well informed on the German social democratic movement. It printed the entire copy of German special measures against the socialists. *Nowiny*, no. 118 (1878), pp. 2-3. It also published transcripts of trials of Russian socialists, among them the trial of Soloviev. *Nowiny*, no. 159, no. 164 (1879). *Prawda* generally quoted Russian press articles on the revolutionary movement. See for instance *Prawda*, no. 34 (1884), p. 404.

74. *Prawda*, no. 11, no. 13 (1880).

75. *Prawda*, no. 14 (1882), pp. 167-168.

76. *PT*, no. 43 (1881), pp. 533-534.

77. "Nash put'," in "Archiwum Bardowskiego," *ZPW*, no. 1 (9) (1960), p. 93.

78. *Prawda*, no. 9 (1881), p. 97.

79. *Prawda*, no. 30 (1884), p. 350.

80. *Prawda*, no. 20 (1882), pp. 229-230.

81. *Prawda*, no. 25 (1884), p. 289.

82. *Prawda*, no. 8 (1881), p. 94.

83. *Prawda*, no. 9 (1881), p. 97.

84. *Prawda*, no. 21 (1885), p. 242.

85. See "Gospodarka wsteczników," *Prawda*, no. 36 (1884), pp. 421-423; (A. J. Cohn), "Kłamstwa socjalizmu," *Prawda*, no. 43, no. 45 (1885); (L. Gumplowicz), "Kommunizm, socjalizm i antysemityzm," *Prawda*, no. 45 (1883), pp. 530-531; (A. Świętochowski, "Nić czerwona," *Prawda*, no. 36 (1883), p. 401.

86. *Nowiny*, no. 110 (1878), p. 1.

87. See "Społeczne kierunki w teoryi i w życiu," *Prawda*, no. 40 (1883), p. 473.

88. Socialists since the late 1870s had written while in emigration for the positivist press. E. Przewóski, K. Sosnowski, A. Złotnicki, S. Diksztajn, and B. Limanowski were the most important contributors. They submitted articles

almost exclusively for the purpose of earning a living. "Socialists wrote," Ludwik Krzywicki recalled, "but did not write about socialism," Krzywicki, *Wspomnienia,* vol. II, p. 137. Both Limanowski (a leading socialist) and Świętochowski note that in this period, 1879–1882, the positivists tolerated socialists but not socialism. B. Limanowski, *Pamiętniki (1870–1907),* vol. II (Warsaw, 1955), p. 185; Świętochowski, *Wspomnienia,* pp. 77–78.

89. On Krusiński, see T. Kowalik's introduction to *Stanisław Krusiński: Pisma zebrane* (Warsaw, 1958). Oskar Lange wrote that "as a theorist of historical materialism, Krzywicki stands on a par with Kautsky, Plekhanov, Mehring." O. Lange, "Ludwik Krzywicki — Theorist of Historical Materialism," *Papers in Economics and Sociology* (Warsaw, 1970), p. 59.

90. Even Kowalik, who thinks of Krusiński as the Polish Plekhanov and has earned considerable animosity among his colleagues for this view, admits that Krusiński "did not duly appreciate the level of development of the Polish working class." Kowalik, "Wstęp," in *Krusiński: Pisma zebrane,* p. xi. For hostile reviews of his book, see especially L. Baumgarten, "'Odkrywczość' więcej niż wątpliwa," *ZPW,* no. 3 (1958), pp. 92–93.

91. Under the leadership of Krusiński, the first volume of *Das Kapital* was fully translated into Polish in 1884, a project that Szymon Diksztajn had begun in 1877–1878. The precise history of *Das Kapital*'s Polish translation is a matter of considerable dispute. See Baumgarten, *Dzieje,* pp. 105–106; Ż. Korman(owa), "Kazimierz Puchewicz i 'Solidarność,'" *Niepodległość,* vol. XIV (1939), p. 6; L. Krzywicki, *Wspomnienia,* vol. II, p. 133. See also the Krzywicki-Engels correspondence in J. W. Borejsza, *W kręgu wielkich wygnańców 1848–1895* (Warsaw, 1963), pp. 336–338.

92. The formal split occurred at a Vilna conference in January 1883. See Chapter 7, pp. 133–137.

93. "Za kulisami," *PT,* no. 36 (1883), p. 40.

94. "Za kulisami," *PT,* no. 52 (1883), p. 682.

95. "Zniżenie ideału," *PT,* no. 7 (1884), pp. 77–79. See also Białobłocki's "Nadprodukcya intelligencji," *PT,* no. 21 (1884), p. 249; and Krzywicki's "Ziemianie o mieszczanach," *PT,* no. 18 (1883), pp. 218–219.

96. Krzywicki wrote that Zakrzewski "was a sincere *ludowiec* [populist], and remained so until the end, a *ludowiec* free from the doctrine and from the one-dimensionality of the Russian *narodniki,* although unquestionably that current . . . influenced him and determined the final formation of his views." Krzywicki, *Wspomnienia,* vol. II, p. 187.

97. "Polemika," *PT,* no. 29 (1883), p. 360.

98. "O program T. T. Jeża," *PT,* no. 10, p. 117.

99. *PT,* no. 15 (1883), p. 178.

100. *PT,* no. 15 (1883), p. 178.

101. "Polemika," *PT,* no. 21 (1883), pp. 263–264.

102. "Polemika," *PT,* no. 30 (1883), p. 371.

103. "Polemika," *PT,* no. 29 (1883), p. 360.

104. "Polemika," *PT,* no. 33, no. 34 (1883). See also his "Nowiny contra Schäffle," *PT,* no. 7 (1883), pp. 89–90, and "Mała własność rolna," *PT,* no. 4, no. 5 (1883).

Chapter 4. *Polish Socialism in Russian Schools and in the Congress Kingdom, 1876–1881*

1. L. Krzywicki, *Wspomnienia,* vol. II (Warsaw, 1957), p. 12.

2. Ibid., p. 63. Lev Deich (Deutsch, Dejcz) wrote that "the most gifted representatives of the Polish socialist movement in the second half of the seventies came not from the Congress Kingdom, but mostly from the Ukraine and St. Petersburg." L. Dejcz, "Pionerzy ruchu socjalistycznego w Królestwie Polskim," *ZPW,* no. 9–10 (1930), p. 37. This statement is supported by numerous other memoirists. See J. Chmielewski, "Pierwsze lata korporacji studentów Polaków w Kijowie," *Niepodległość,* vol. XIX (1939), p. 111; Kulczycki, *Dokoła mego życia,* p. 12; and L. Wasilewski, "Walka o postulat niepodległości w polskim obozie socjalistycznym," *Niepodległość,* vol. X (1934), p. 3. See Appendix: tables 17, 18, pp. 213–214.

3. H. Truszkowski, "Z dalekiej przeszłości (Wspomnienia o Waryńskim)," *KRRP,* no. 1 (5) (1936), p. 45. E. Brzeziński, "Wspomnienia z mego życia," *Niepodległość,* vol. IV (1931), p. 54. Krzywicki, *Wspomnienia,* vol. II, p. 63.

4. B. A. Jędrzejowski, "Ludwik Waryński," *Światło,* no. 7 (1899), p. 98. In a mediocre, though the best to date, biography of Ludwik Waryński, Leon Wudzki asserts that Waryński in his last years at the gymnasium (1873–74) was at least familiar with socialist propaganda. L. Wudzki, *O Ludwiku Waryńskim* (Warsaw, 1956), p. 12. For a recent popular biography of Waryński, see J. Targalski, *Ludwik Waryński: Próba życia* (Warsaw, 1976). There is great difficulty assessing the involvement of Waryński in activities not explored by the police. Memoirists frequently contradict each other. Brzeziński, "Wspomnienia," p. 46, recalls that Biała Cerkiew (Belaia Tserkov) gymnasium was a hot bed of Polish national resentment against Russians, while Truszkowski, "Z przeszłości," p. 45, reports that the school was a comfortable home of Polish liberalism.

5. Educated Poles from the Congress Kingdom often sought professional careers in Russia proper — a movement that reached its height in the 1870s. Z. Łukawski, *Polacy w rosyjskim ruchu socjaldemokratycznym w latach 1883–1893* (Kraków, 1970), p. 21. See Appendix: table 30, p. 218; table 31, p. 219; table 36, p. 221.

6. Law, with its mixture of history, economics, and a "bit of philosophy," especially attracted Polish "theorists and dreamers." Płoski, *Wspomnienia: Czasy uniwersyteckie* (Płock, 1938), p. 3.

7. Ibid., p. 4. Chmielewski, "Pierwsze lata," p. 111, writes that graduates of gymnasia in Lithuania did not have the right to attend the Warsaw University and therefore most often went to Kiev and Dorpat, the nearest imperial universities.

8. See pp. 308-309 (n. 19).

9. N. A. Borodin, "Pervye glavy: Idealy i deistvitel'nost'," galley proofs, HI, Nicolaevsky Archives, no. 168, folder 5, p. 7.

10. Płoski, *Wspomnienia*, pp. 7-8.

11. E. Pekarskii, "Otryvki iz vospominanii," *KS*, no. 4(11) (1924), p. 79.

12. K. Dłuski, "Wspomnienia z trzech lat (1875-1878)," *Niepodległość*, vol. I (1930), p. 222.

13. Płoski, *Wspomnienia*, p. 6.

14. Dłuski, "Wspomnienia," p. 223. Stempowski wrote that Lavrov and Lassalle were his first introductions to socialist thinking. Stempowski, *Pamiętniki 1870-1914* (Wrocław, 1953), p. 84.

15. Wudzki, *O Waryńskim*, p. 13.

16. Dłuski, "Wspomnienia," p. 223. On the importance of Russian literature, see Veto (W. Studnicki), *Dwadzieścia lat*, p. 7.

17. Iu. Z. Polevoi, *Zarozhdenie marksizma v Rossii 1883-1894 gg.* (Moscow, 1959), pp. 129-130. See also L. Schapiro, *Rationalism and Nationalism in Russian Nineteenth Century Political Thought* (New Haven-London, 1967), pp. 130-131. The first Russian translation of *Das Kapital*, vol. I, appeared in St. Petersburg in April 1872. Polevoi, *Zarozhdenie*, p. 129. See Z. Heryng, "W zaraniu socjalizmu polskiego," *Niepodległość*, vol. III (1931), p. 53.

18. "Prilozhenie k protokoly osmotra Vladimira Butkiewicza," AGAD, PWIS, 1879, no. 347, l. 203. For a picture of small Polish circles in St. Petersburg, see the letters of Ludwik Straszewicz, AGAD, PWIS, 1885, 1021, ll. 103-129.

19. Russian translation of a letter from Maria Krivtsova to Stanisław Ptak, Moscow, 8 August (o.s.), AGAD, PWIS, 1879, 347, l. 229.

20. Płoski, *Wspomnienia*, pp. 8-9. Waryński was also expelled from the Institute of Technology for a similarly vague involvement.

21. The friend was Aleksander Więckowski, a Polish member of Zemlia i Volia. Heryng, "W zaraniu," p. 56. Erazm Kobylański was also noted for his participation in the Kazan demonstration. He was expelled from the Institute of Technology the same year, 1876. AGAD, PWIS, 1879, 346, ll. 239-240.

22. Płoski, *Wspomnienia*, pp. 5-6, 10.

23. Stempowski, *Pamiętniki*, p. 50. *Pamiętnik — Maria Bohuszewiczówna* (Wrocław, 1955), p. 14.

24. Kucharzewski, *Origins*, p. 257.

25. Kon, *Narodziny*, pp. 14-15.

26. E. Haecker, *Historia socjalizmu w Galicji i na Śląsku*, vol. I (Kraków, 1933), p. 134. Walczak, *Rola genewskiego ośrodka*, pp. 32-33.

27. Płoski, *Wspomnienia*, p. 14. See Dłuski, *Wspomnienia*, pp. 222-233, and I. Wołkowiczer, *Początki socjalistycznego ruchu robotniczego w Królestwie Polskim* (Warsaw, 1955), pp. 28-29, for contacts of these groups with groups in Warsaw. This circle was founded by L. Waryński, E. Kobylański, B. Wysłouch, A. Więckowski, and E. Brzeziński (all of the Institute of Tech-

nology) and Jan Hłasko and Bolesław Mondszajn of the Medical-Surgery Academy. See Wudzki, *O Waryńskim,* pp. 14–15; and AGAD, WGZŻ, no. 3, l. 95.

28. Heryng, "W zaraniu," p. 52.

29. Ibid., p. 60.

30. *Kółka socjalistyczne, Gminy i Wielki Proletariat: Procesy polityczne 1878–1888: Żródła,* ed. Leon Baumgarten (Warsaw, 1966), p. 213. Rodziewicz, when arrested in Warsaw in the spring of 1881, confessed, causing the arrest of many other confederates.

31. A. Dębski, "Wspomnienia Kunickiego i Bardowskiego," *ZPW: Zbiór materiałów tyczących się polskiego ruchu socjalistycznego* (London, 1904), p. 81.

32. Very little is known of the activities of the Vilna, Kiev, and Moscow Gminas. In the case of the Kiev Gmina, Snytko explains that this was due to unclear distinctions between the Kiev Gmina and other local revolutionary groups. Snytko, *Russkoe narodnichestvo,* p. 347. As for the Moscow Gmina, he claims the small number of Gmina adherents was due to direct participation of Poles in the Russian movement. Ibid., p. 345. See *Kółka* for the respective prosecutors' conclusions on the Vilna Gmina, pp. 244–247, the Kiev Gmina, pp. 271–282, and the Moscow Gmina, pp. 284–296. The major documents of the St. Petersburg Gmina are also in *Kółka,* pp. 248–268.

33. *Khronika sotsialisticheskogo dvizheniia v Rossii, 1878–1887: Ofitsial'nyi otchet* (Moscow, 1906), p. 197. Snytko agrees with this official opinion, *Russkoe narodnichestvo,* p. 346. Płoski claims that Hłasko was the "pope" of the St. Petersburg Gmina but that he maintained no relations with the Russians. Instead Hłasko maintained close ties with the Polish emigration, especially with Wróblewski, and attempted to combine efforts with Lavrov in London. Hłasko also led the Gminists' unsuccessful efforts to found a newspaper. See "Smirnov to Idel'son, 11 June 1876," in *Lavrov,* vol. II, ed. Sapir, pp. 296–297. Płoski also names Józef Czerniewski as the "contact man" — a fact he discovered by accident when he met Zheliabov in Czerniewski's flat at the end of 1880. Płoski, *Wspomnienia,* p. 16. Snytko in fact names Czerniewski and Bohuszewicz as either members of, or close to, Narodnaia Volia. S. S. Volk, *Narodnaia volia, 1879–1882* (Moscow–Leningrad, 1966), p. 404, claims that Wilczyński was the Gmina representative to Narodnaia Volia.

34. Volk, *Narodnaia volia,* pp. 407–408.

35. B. Szapiro (Besem), *Tadeusz Rechniewski* (Warsaw, 1957), pp. 16–17, emphasizes the all-Polish character of the Gmina. Baumgarten is of the opposite opinion; the raison d'être of the St. Petersburg Gmina as well as its only goal was to help the Russians. L. Baumgarten, *Dzieje Wielkiego Proletariatu* (Warsaw, 1968), p. 22.

36. Szapiro, *Rechniewski,* p. 16.

37. AGAD, PWIS, 1884, 977, ll. 78–79.

38. For contacts between socialist Poles in Moscow and Warsaw universities, see AGAD, PWIS, 1879, 347, l. 253. See also *Kółka,* pp. 206–244, for an intricate tracing of Polish socialist ties throughout the empire.

39. AGAD, PWIS, 1885, 1021, l. 89.

40. *Kółka,* pp. 213-219.

41. *Khronika,* p. 197. In January 1881, as the government reported, the Warsaw Gmina met with other Gmina representatives to broach the question of workers' circles. "Sprawa Gminy socjalistów polskich w Kijowie, 1880 — Wniosek," *ZPW,* no. 2 (1927), p. 140.

42. *Kółka,* p. 256. Baumgarten claims here that the program was written by Z. and T. Balicki, K. Sosnowski, J. Hłasko, and J. Czerniewski. Volk says that Czerniewski wrote the program after that of Black Partition. Volk, *Narodnaia volia,* p. 404.

43. Perl states that this document along with the earlier "Odezwa socjalistów polskich, wystosowana do Józefa Ignacego Kraszewskiego z powodu jubileuszu prac jego na polu literackim," written primarily by J. Uziembło, characterized a general "return to patriotism" among Polish socialists in 1880. Perl, *Dzieje,* p. 129. For the "Odezwa" see ibid., pp. 500-504, and AZHP, 305, I, 1.

44. "Ot Gminy . . ." *Narodnaia volia,* no. 4 (1880), in *Literatura partii "Narodnoi voli,"* ed. B. Bazilevskii.

45. Baumgarten, *Dzieje,* p. 22. In this instance, as in many others, Baumgarten overweighs the role of Narodnaia Volia. One might surmise that the reason for this is his thorough familiarity with the Russian police and judicial archives, in which officials tended to see the involvement and influence of Narodnaia Volia in every revolutionary occurrence.

46. Snytko, *Russkoe narodnichestvo,* p. 311.

47. This difference is reflected as well in their approach to political action. The Kiev prosecutor reports a quarrel between the Warsaw and Kiev Gminas, "the first advocated agitation, whereas the second advocated propaganda." "Sprawy Gminy w Kijowie," *ZPW,* p. 140.

48. Dłuski, "Wspomnienia," p. 223.

49. See Appendix, table 49, p. 234.

50. The extent of Polish involvement in the Russian movement has become a major issue of socialist historiography. See T. G. Snytko, "K voprosu o vzaimootnosheniiakh i sviaziakh narodnichestva s pol'skim sotsial'no-revoliutsionnym dvizheniem v kontse 70-kh — nachale 80-kh godov XIX v." *Revoliutsionnaia Rossiia i revoliutsionnaia Pol'sha [vtoraia polovina XIX v.]* (Moscow, 1967), p. 314; and I. S. Miller, "Nekotorye obshchie problemy istorii russko-pol'skikh revoliutsionnykh sviazei," *Sviazi revoliutsionerov Rossii i Pol'shi XIX — nachala XX v.* (Moscow, 1968), p. 18. Miller adds an historiographical "key" to contemporary Soviet research on the Polish movement. In his view, earlier Soviet historians unjustly denigrated the progressive role of the "national liberation" movements among the empire's oppressed peoples. Ibid. See also L. Bazylow, *Działalność narodnictwa rosyjskiego w latach 1878-1881* (Wrocław, 1960), pp. 238-239; and Snytko, *Russkoe narodnichestvo,* p. 13.

51. L. Dmochowski and five or six other Poles participated in the "v narod" movement. See K. Pietkiewicz, "Leon Dmochowski w kółku 'Dołguszyń-

ców,'" *Niepodległość,* vol. II (1930), p. 164. See also W. Śliwowska, "Udział Polaków w rewolucynym ruchu narodnickim lat siedemdziesiatych XIX stulecia," *Z dziejów współpracy rewolucyjnej Polaków i Rosjan w drugiej polowie XIX wieku* (Wrocław, 1956), pp. 225–285. Together, Śliwowska and Wawrykowa name about fifty *narodnik* Poles.

52. Więckowski was the most influential Pole in Zemlia i Volia. He was an editor of *Nachalo* and a gifted propagandizer of young Polish students. Heryng, "W zaraniu," pp. 53–54. Krzywicki, *Wspomnienia,* vol. II, p. 72. In a letter to Boris Nicolaevsky, A. Zundelevich wrote, "In my view the main organizer of the foundation and operation of this magazine [*Nachalo*] was Więckowski, who under the name of 'Pan' had excellent relations with several members of Zemlia i Volia . . . I consider him in close contact with the Polish socialists." Zundelevich to Nicolaevsky, 25 January 1923, HI, Nicolaevsky Archives, box 35, folder Z.

53. Ludwik Kobylański was a noted terrorist who participated in the Soloviev attempt and in the Kropotkin assassination. See V. D. Novitskii, *Iz vospominanii zhandarma* (Leningrad, 1929), pp. 106–107; Krzywicki, *Wspomnienia,* vol. II, p. 63; Dejcz, "Pionerzy," p. 67. He later received money from Narodnaia Volia and worked with both Goldenberg and Kwiatkowski. *Arkhiv "Zemli i voli" i "Narodnoi voli"* (Moscow, 1932), pp. 132, 235, 240, 249, 344. See also *Svod ukazanii, dannykh nekotorymi iz arestovannykh po delam o gosudarstvennykh prestupleniiakh* (May 1880).

54. M. Wawrykowa, *Rewolucyjne narodnictwo w latach siedemdziesiątych XIX w.* (Warsaw, 1963), pp. 10–11. She claims here that Evgenii Zaslavskii, the first leader of the Southern Workers' Society, was probably a Pole. She further claims that the Poles in the group, Jan Rybicki and Witalis Mroczkowski, had ties with Warsaw. The attempt to set up the International in Odessa took place in 1872, as recorded in Odessa police files. B. Itenberg, *Iuzhnorossiiskii soiuz rabochikh — pervaia proletarskaia organizatsiia v Rossii* (Moscow, 1954), p. 21. For Poles in the Kiev movement, see AGAD, PWIS, 1879, 348, l. 7. For those in Vilna and Riga, see AGAD, PWIS, 1879, 349, l. 460.

55. Dłuski, *Wspomnienia,* p. 16.

56. Łukawski, *Polacy w rosyjskim ruchu,* p. 135.

57. See Chmielewski, "Pierwsze lata," p. 111; and Z. Heryng, "X-ty Pawilon przed 50-ciu laty," *Niepodległość,* vol. I (1930), p. 75.

58. Heryng, "W zaraniu," p. 59. On this period of Balicki's career, see Haecker, *Historiia,* pp. 285–288.

59. Krzywicki, *Wspomnienia,* vol. II, pp. 164–166. Of course, along with the Russian styles, the *kresy* youth brought to the Congress Kingdom intellectual styles, which often meant the complete libraries of Russian leftist literature. Ibid., p. 165.

60. Snytko, *Russkoe narodnichestvo,* pp. 140–141.

61. Bazylow writes, "It would be necessary to read through many hundreds if not thousands of pages of *Katorga i ssylka* in order to encounter the rather

valueless and insignificant citations of Polish involvement." *Działność narodnictwa,* pp. 238–239.

62. Snytko, *Russkoe narodnichestvo,* p. 161.
63. "E. P.," "Hryniewiecki," *Światło,* no. 15 (1902), p. 81.
64. Dłuski, *Wspomnienia,* p. 11.
65. *Bohaterowie "Proletariatu"* (Warsaw, 1906), p. 26.
66. Krzywicki, *Wspomnienia,* vol. II, p. 44.
67. Ibid., p. 166.
68. Snytko, *Russkoe narodnichestvo,* p. 375.
69. B. S. Itenberg, *Dvizhenie revoliutsionnogo narodnichestva: Narodnicheskie kruzhki i "khozhdenie v narod" v 70-kh godov XIX v.* (Moscow, 1965), p. 3.
70. *Arkhiv "Zemli i voli" i "Narodnoi voli,"* pp. 53–54.
71. For the first draft of second program, see ibid., p. 55, and for final draft see ibid., p. 59.
72. L. Tikhomirov, *Nachalo i kontsy: Liberaly i terroristy* (Moscow, 1890), pp. 29–30.
73. AGAD, PWIS, 1884, 977, l. 9. See also Próchnik, "Ideologia Proletariatu," p. 1; *Bohaterowie,* p. 3. W. Jodko-Narkiewicz dates the beginnings from 1877. *Geschichte der socialistischen Bewegung in Polen* (Zürich, 1895), p. 2.
74. AGAD, PWIS, 1884, 977, l. 9. Warsaw Prosecutor Pleve came to the same conclusions in an 1879 report, *Procesy polityczne w Królestwie Polskiem: Materiały do historii ruchu rewolucyjnego w Król. Polskim, 1878–1879* (Kraków, 1907), p. 12.
75. Waryński left Lilpop for the Institut Rolniczo-Leśny in Puławy in October 1877 when he was threatened by the draft. Leaving Puławy a few months later, he went underground under the name Jan Buch. He continued to work in a metalworking shop that he founded with a few socialist cohorts. K. Dłuski, "Ludwik Waryński," *ZPW* (London, 1904), p. 47.
76. Krzywicki, *Wspomnienia,* vol. II, p. 38.
77. Dłuski, "Wspomnienia," p. 227. See also Krzywicki, *Wspomnienia,* vol. II, pp. 13–14.
78. Heryng, "W zaraniu," p. 49.
79. Of the 201 socialists (excluding Gminists) associated by the police with the Congress Kingdom movement from 1878–1880, 87 (43.3 percent) were of noble origin, 74 (36.8 percent) of the urban class (*meshchane*) origin, 20 (10 percent) of peasant origin, and 20 (10 percent) of unknown origin. Of the 183 known noblemen and women who participated in Congress Kingdom socialism from 1878–1886, a total of 44 (24.1 percent) were engaged in working-class occupations, the largest number, 23 (12.6 percent) in metalworks and shops. The largest portion of noble-born socialists were students, 88 (48.1 percent). See Appendix: table 47, p. 232; table 15, p. 213.
80. Sieroszewski, *Pamiętniki,* pp. 93–103, 140. T. Rechniewski, "Henryk Dulęba," *Kuźnia* (1914), pp. 28–29.

81. Other 1878 propagandists from the southwest region included Waryński, Ludwik and Kazimierz Kobylański, Fillipina Płaskowicka, and Maria Hildt. From the northwest region came B. Mondszajn, K. Daniłowicz, M. Akimov, P. Abramowicz, and J. Hłasko. *Procesy polityczne,* pp. 12–13.

82. Dłuski, "Wspomnienia," pp. 223–224. The same meeting is reported in Krzywicki, *Wspomnienia,* vol. II, p. 19. Krzywicki says these meetings were constantly held and had "several tens" of participants.

83. See Ż. Kormanowa, "Z pierwszego pokolenia walczących: Przyczynek do działalności braci Józefa i Kazimierza Pławińskich," *KRRP,* vol. III (1936), pp. 193–196.

84. Dłuski, "Wspomnienia," pp. 224–225.

85. *Procesy polityczne,* p. 14. Especially Dłuski and Hildt, wrote the Department of Police, were crucial in forming "in a very short time" "a social revolutionary circle among Warsaw University students." TsGAOR, f. 102, DP-V, d. 2104, 1882, l. 2.

86. Snytko inconclusively claims that indeed a "Warsaw social revolutionary organization was born at the end of 1877." *Russkoe narodnichestvo,* p. 253.

87. Jodko-Narkiewicz calls it a mixture of "Volkstümlichkeit, Anarchie und Sozialismus," *Geschichte,* p. 5.

88. HI, Okhrana Archives, folder 12A, index no. XIV, "Polish Revolutionaries," p. 1.

89. Kulczycki, *Dokoła mego życia,* AZHP manuscript, pp. 14–15.

90. Kulczycki, in ibid., states that Miłkowski personally told him this in their 1887 conversations. See also, Mazowiecki [Kulczycki], *Historia,* pp. 21–23.

91. Limanowski suggests that the inspiration for the National Government came from Agaton Giller, the 1863 insurrectionist. B. Limanowski, *Pamiętniki (1870–1907)* (Warsaw, 1958), p. 196. Szymański asked for Limanowski's cooperation in Lwów in 1877. Ibid., p. 195.

92. Szymański was both an "unenthusiastic" participant in student socialist circles in the fall of 1877 and worked with Świętochowski on the positivist *Przegląd Tygodniowy* (1878). Dłuski, "Wspomnienia," p. 230; Świętochowski, *Wspomnienia,* p. 90. Perl claims that Szymański and the socialists were "unmitigated enemies": *Dzieje,* p. 64. It is likely, however, that Szymański maintained contacts with the Warsaw University socialist circles as indicated in official documents. AGAD, PWIS, 1879, 345, ll. 34–35. "Diary of Wiśniewski," in ibid., l. 159. *Procesy polityczne,* p. 71. Russian police reports suggest that Szymański was also committed to an eventual "federal state" composed of Slavic peoples. TsGAOR, f. 102, DP-III, d. 1566, 1883, l. 1.

93. Ibid., pp. 3–5. See also AGAD, PWIS, 1878, 220.

94. AGAD, PWIS, 1878, 218, l. 109. The police arrested 50 suspects.

95. Snytko, *Russkoe narodnichestvo,* pp. 105–106; Kulczycki, *Dokoła mego życia,* p. 16.

96. Feldman, *Historia,* p. 174.

97. AGAD, PWIS, 1878, 218, l. 110.

98. AGAD, PWIS, 1878, 219, l. 241. For Miński's papers, see ibid., ll. 231-249.

99. AGAD, PWIS, 1878, 218, l. 107. For Szymański's entire confession, see AGAD, PWIS, 1878, 219, ll. 15-29.

100. Sieroszewski writes of the deep impression the Szymański arrests made on the patriotic intelligentsia and working class: *Pamiętniki,* p. 135.

101. Novitskii, *Vospominanii zhandarma,* pp. 146-147. Beginning in March 1878, wrote the Russian police, the gradual process of the merging of intelligentsia and workers' circles was completed, prompting the rapid growth of an organizational structure of five circles with fifteen members apiece. TsGAOR, f. 102, DP-V, d. 2104, 1882, l. 2.

102. Próchnik, "Ideologia," p. 2.

103. Dłuski, "Waryński," *ZPW* (London, 1904), p. 46.

104. Dłuski, "Wspomnienia," p. 233.

105. *Procesy polityczne,* p. 17. Heryng is very critical of this "unheard-of naivete" and calls the 1878 socialists "grown-up children": "W zaraniu," p. 61.

106. AGAD, PWIS, 1879, 345, ll. 158-159.

107. J. Uziembło, "Wspomnienia," *Przedświt,* no. 5 (1902), p. 162.

108. W. Sieroszewski, "O świcie," *ZPW* (London, 1904), p. 41.

109. For accounts of these first meetings, see AGAD, WGZŻ, 1878, no. 3. These documents contain the confessions of Redlich (ibid., ll. 47-49) and Tomaszewski (ibid., ll. 58-63), as well as a list of materials found in Waryński's and Tomaszewski's flat. Ibid., l. 41.

110. "Tomaszewski's confession," AGAD, WGZŻ, 1878, no. 3, l. 61.

111. J. Uziembło, "Filipina Płaskowicka," *Światło,* no. 16 (1902), p. 127. See also L. Waryński, "Filipina Płaskowicka: Życiorys," *Przedświt,* no. 3 (1881), p. 4, no. 6-7 (1881), pp. 3-4.

112. AGAD, PWIS, 1879, 347, l. 12.

113. Brzeziński, "Wspomnienia," *Niepodległość,* vol. IV, p. 216.

114. Sieroszewski, *Pamiętniki,* p. 151.

115. Dłuski, "Waryński," *ZPW* (London, 1904), p. 47. It has been estimated that six thousand copies were smuggled into the Congress Kingdom from Leipzig in 1878-1879. R. Grünberg and Cz. Kozłowski, *Historia polskiego ruchu robotniczego, 1864-1918* (Warsaw, 1962), p. 47; *Procesy polityczne,* pp. 86-87. See Perl, *Dzieje,* pp. 67-70, for a complete list; see *Procesy polityczne,* pp. 81-82, for the prosecutor's comments on the most numerous: F. Lassalle, *Kapitał i praca;* W. Różałowski, *Żywot Generała Dąbrowskiego;* and S. Dyksztajn, *Opowiadanie starego gospodarza.*

116. *Bohaterowie,* p. 5. Mazowiecki [Kulczycki], *Historia,* p. 21. Dłuski says there were 400 members, "Wspomnienia," p. 228.

117. AGAD, PWIS, 1879, 346, ll. 250-251. For Rogalski's role, see ibid., 345, ll. 200-205.

118. AGAD, PWIS, 1879, 345, ll. 43-44.

119. AGAD, PWIS, 1879, 346, ll. 95-96.

120. The arrests were made largely on the basis of Tomaszewski's and Redlich's confessions in the Tenth Pavilion of the Warsaw Citadel. Płaskowicka wrote to her mother from this prison that the loneliness and mental anguish which resulted in Tomaszewski's confession was being fought by all prisoners, and that they were now even more determined not to reveal further evidence. AGAD, PWIS, 1879, 348, l. 28.

121. *Procesy polityczne,* p. 87. Sometimes, though rarely, this group was described by the authorities as "social democratic." AGAD, PWIS, 1879, 349, l. 1.

122. A. Dębski, "Stanisław Kunicki," *Światło,* no. 5 (1899), p. 3.

123. AGAD, PWIS, 1879, 345, l. 82. See Dziankowski's notes entitled "Mikhailov, Martinov, Chernyshevskii, Zemlia i Volia," in ibid., ll. 119–120. Some socialists, like Wiśniewski, advocated a total if temporary capitulation to the growth of industry. "Only a change in economic conditions," he writes in his diary, "can lead to that which the agitators wish to attain by means of propaganda." AGAD, PWIS, 1879, 345, l. 161.

124. AGAD, PWIS, 1880, 472, ll. 39–40.

125. This handwritten document found in the homes of Rogalski and Paszke was probably written by J. Uziembło, A. Więckowski, and L. Dziankowski. The prosecutor considers it a programmatic statement passed "hand to hand": *Procesy,* p. 86. A Russian translation of the document is in AGAD, PWIS, 1879, 345, ll. 78–81.

126. Ibid., l. 80.

127. Ibid., ll. 79, 81.

128. Dłuski, "Waryński," *ZPW* (London, 1904), p. 47.

129. Sieroszewski, *Pamiętniki,* p. 158.

130. Ibid., p. 157.

131. AGAD, PWIS, 1879, 345, l. 73.

132. *Procesy polityczne,* p. 88.

133. AGAD, PWIS, 1879, 345, l. 179. This particular handwritten document found on Sidorek and translated into Russian contains a very sophisticated indictment of ties between Polish capitalists and the Russian authorities. Ibid., ll. 176–180.

134. For some of these circles, see AGAD, PWIS, 1879, 346, l. 215; 1879, 302, l. 12; 1879, 346, l. 184.

135. Contacts were also maintained between Polish workers' circles in the empire. Krzywicki reported that T. Wróblewski was the main contact between Warsaw and St. Petersburg workers. Russian working-class leaders also had contact with Poles. Krzywicki, *Wspomnienia,* vol. II, p. 92.

136. The police found in Dziankowski's home along with numerous other Russian pamphlets and works: *Rabotnik* from St. Petersburg (1875); Chernyshevskii's *Chto delat'* (1876); *Obshchina;* and Herzen's history of the Paris Commune. AGAD PWIS, 1879, 345, ll. 119–123. At Piechowski's, the police found a library of over two hundred different titles, sixty-eight of which were Russian — including the complete works of Chernyshevskii, Herzen, and

Drahomanov. AGAD, PWIS, 1880, 472, ll. 8–41. For financial relations between St. Petersburg and Warsaw, see AGAD, PWIS, 1879, 345, l. 345.

137. Ibid., ll. 120–121.

138. The police found at Rymkiewicz's and Czarkowski's 17 copies of "Co to jest Socjalizm?" printed in Leipzig, 1878. Ibid., ll. 143–156.

139. *Procesy polityczne,* p. 69.

140. AGAD, PWIS, 1879, 345, ll. 29–31. Here the prosecutor accuses Więckowski of "maintaining ties between Warsaw socialists and their comrades from the other parts of Russia."

141. V. I. Nevskii, *Ot "Zemli i voli" k gruppe "Osvobozhdenie truda"* (Moscow, 1930), pp. 137–138. Some historians assert that Obnorskii was a Pole: see Snytko, *Russkoe narodnichestvo,* pp. 329–330. Plekhanov recalled an address from the Warsaw workers to the Northern Workers' Circle, but Wołkowiczer finds no trace of such an address in the Russian archives. Wołkowiczer, *Początki,* p. 162.

142. L. Plokhotskii [L. Wasilewski], *Vzaimnyia otnosheniia pol'skikh i russkikh sotsialistov* (London, 1902), p. 6.

143. No mention of this visit is contained in the police or judicial archives, casting doubt on its significance. The first mentions of the visit are in Plokhotskii (Wasilewski), *Vzaimnyia otnosheniia,* p. 5, and Amerykanin [J. Uziembło], "Wspomnienia z 1878 g.," *ZPW* (London, 1904), p. 61. Snytko, Mazowiecki [Kulczycki], and Wołkowiczer accept Uziembło's version.

144. Mazowiecki [Kulczycki] concludes from conversations with socialists of this period that such a proposal was never voiced. *Historia,* p. 38.

145. Amerykanin [Uziembło], "Wspomnienia," *ZPW* (London, 1904), p. 61. Wasilewski (Plokhotskii) argues that even at the end of 1877, Polish socialists began the attempt to reach an agreement with the Russians. The negotiations were unsuccessful, not without considerable irritation on the part of the Russians, who thought the Warsaw Poles were causing harm to the movement by drawing Poles away from the movement's ranks throughout the empire. Plokhotskii [Wasilewski], *Vzaimnyia otnosheniia,* p. 4.

146. *Procesy polityczne,* pp. 83–84. Lavrov, through Uziembło, also maintained ties with these Poles on federative bases, "for each group operates fully independently and is independent in its socialist goals." See the handwritten proposal written by the Lavrists at the end of 1878, "Proekt ustav druzhestvennoi federatsii mezhdu russkim kruzhkom sotsialistov-propagandistov v Parizhe i pol'skoi federatsii sotsial'no-revoliutsionnoi propagandy v Varshave," in E. K. Zhigunov and E. V. Rashkovskii, "Iz istorii russko-pol'skikh revoliutsionnykh sviazei, 1878–1880 gg.," *Obshchestvennoi dvizhenie v poreformennoi Rossii (sbornik statei k 80-letiiu so dnia rozhdeniia B. P. Koz'mina)* (Moscow, 1965), p. 277.

147. See S. Giza, "Do biografii Józefa Beutha," *Niepodległość,* vol. XV (1937), pp. 400–403. For the official Russian view, see *Khronika,* p. 97. The killing of Beuth must have been a great shock for Governor-General Kotzebue who had maintained, even against Ministry of Interior pressure, that the

matter of Polish socialists be handled in local and quiet fashion. *Khronika,* pp. 34–35.

148. The three numbers totaled about twenty pages. AZHP, AM, *Głos Więźnia,* no. 1–3 (1879). About 15 handwritten copies were passed around in prison and smuggled out, some even reaching Kraków. AZHP, Materiały procesu krakowskiego, sygn. 5/II/1, dodatek do *Czas,* p. 28. See Heryng, "X-Pawilon," pp. 60–61, Ż. Kormanowa, "Pławińscy," p. 195; and Wołkowiczer, *Początki,* p. 133.

149. AGAD, PWIS, 1879, 348, l. 43.

150. Of the total number of socialists involved in activities from 1878–1886 (622), at least 130 (21 percent) were related in one way or another to a fellow socialist. This tendency was especially marked among noble-born revolutionaries; 62 or 33 percent of all noble-born revolutionaries were related to another. See Appendix: table 1, p. 209; table 16, p. 213.

151. AGAD, PWIS, 1879, 348, ll. 28–44, contains many of these letters. Cesaryna Wojnarowska's sister cared for her immense socialist library. Klementyna Płaskowicka, Filipina's sister, smuggled *Głos Więżnia* out of prison.

152. AGAD, PWIS, 1879, 347, l. 33.

153. The prosecutor's reports on Poznański's circle are in *Kółka,* pp. 138–206. AGAD, PWIS, 1880, 473, ll. 409–410. Here appears Poznański's handwritten confession (in Russian), March 1880.

154. Ibid.

155. Krzywicki, *Wspomnienia,* vol. II, pp. 87–88. The police report a Poznański circle meeting, "every Sunday or every ten days." AGAD, PWIS, 1880, 473, l. 341.

156. The police report that he also gave needy families of arrested workers financial help. AGAD, PWIS, 1880, 472, ll. 331, 537.

157. "Piechowski papers" in ibid., l. 37.

158. AZHP, Materiały procesu krakowskiego, sygn. 5/II/2, "Listy znalezione przy rewizji u Ludwika Straszewicza i do niego w toku śledztwa nadeszłe," portfolio (teka) 45, no. VI, pp. 12–13.

159. Ibid., p. 12.

160. See AGAD, PWIS, 1880, 472, l. 349, for Żyrardów agitation. See also ibid., l. 71; AGAD, PWIS, 1880, 473, l. 419, l. 537, for other new workers' circles.

161. "Testimony of Piotr Riabin," AGAD, PWIS, 1880, 472, ll. 286–287.

162. The reaction against internationalism in the Poznański era, writes Mazowiecki [Kulczycki], "only to a small extent filtered down to the workers, who were incapable of intellectually grasping it." *Historia,* p. 39.

163. AGAD, PWIS, 1880, 473, ll. 336–338.

164. Krzywicki, *Wspomnienia,* vol. II, p. 110.

165. For the development of the "Brussels Program," see Chapter 5, pp. 81–84.

166. (Wysłouch papers), AGAD, PWIS, 1880, 472, l. 165.

167. The full Russian transcription of the notes is in ibid., ll. 19–24.

168. See a handwritten document by Wysłouch entitled, "Regulations of an Industrial Society," ibid., ll. 176–182.

169. "Kółko Socjalistów Polskich z Kongresówki — 29 November 1880," *Sprawozdanie z międzynarodowego zebrania zwołanego w 50-letnią rocznicę listopadowego powstania przed redakcyję "Równości"* w Genewie (Geneva, 1881), pp. 11–13.

170. "Kółko Socjalistów Polskich spod zaboru Moskiewskiego, November 1880," *Sprawozdanie,* p. 8.

171. "Robotnicy polscy pod panowaniem Cara, (November 1880)," *Sprawozdanie,* pp. 9–10.

172. *Arkhiv "Zemli i voli" i "Narodnoi voli,"* pp. 322–323.

Chapter 5. *The Development of the Ideology of Polish Socialism in Galicia and Switzerland, 1878–1881*

1. Quoted in Wudzki, *O Waryńskim,* pp. 66–67.

2. The "Brussels Program" also appeared in proclamation form in Geneva, October 1879. AZHP, AM, 1349, "Program Socjalistów Polskich, Bruksela, 1878."

3. Uziembło's memoirs provide a personal history of the program. He maintains that his program was the first and that it showed "how closely the first Polish socialists tied patriotism to socialism." J. Uziembło, "Wspomnienia," *Przedświt,* no. 5 (1902), p. 164. Zhigunov, Rashkovskii, "Iz istorii," pp. 277–293, claim that Lavrov, through Uziembło, had great influence on the program and also that Waryński was clearly a patriot. The precise history of the development of the "Brussels Program" and the "Principles" is one which occupies all the major early historians of this period of Polish socialism, Perl, Kulczycki, and Wołkowiczer. The last, in *Początki,* pp. 101–110, provides a textual analysis of the two programs, presenting them side by side. Of contemporary historians, Haustein, *Sozialismus,* pp. 20–24, and Snytko, *Russkoe narodnichestvo,* pp. 291–302, provide the most complete historiography of the programs. The best summation of the history of the "Brussels Program" is in Alina Molska, *Pierwsze pokolenie marksistów polskich, 1878–1886,* vol. II (Warsaw, 1962), note 1, pp. 687–693. The original text was written by Waryński and Dziankowski among others in May and June 1878. After Waryński left Warsaw and Dziankowski was arrested, Uziembło and A. Więckowski altered the program which appeared in several slightly different copies under the title, "Principles." They then sent this program to Geneva where Stanisław Mendelson and Kazimierz Dłuski, upon consultation with their Russian colleagues, including Lavrov and Zhukovskii, once again altered the text and printed it in *Równość* under the name, "Brussels Program." The "Principles," also called the "Warsaw Program" and the "Lwów Program," has attracted great historical attention. It is clear, however, that Waryński, the central figure of early Polish socialism, sided with the "Brussels" version.

4. *Równość*, no. 1 (1879), pp. 3–4.

5. "Only those people who don't understand our program call it utopian," wrote *Równość*. "Nasz program," *Równość*, no. 6–7 (1880), p. 14.

6. "Nasz program," *Równość*, no. 5 (1880), p. 9.

7. "Nasz program," *Równość*, no. 6–7 (1880), p. 16.

8. Ibid., p. 3.

9. "Nasz program," *Równość*, no. 5 (1880), pp. 10–11.

10. "Nasz program," *Równość*, no. 2 (1879), p. 20, no. 6–7 (1880), pp. 4–5.

11. See A. Schaff, *Narodziny i rozwój filozofii marksistowskiej* (Warsaw, 1950), pp. 279–280.

12. E. Haecker, *Historia socjalizmu w Galicji*, p. 105. For an excellent English-language treatment of the rise of Galician socialism, see John-Paul Himka, "Polish and Ukrainian Socialism: Austria, 1867–1890," Ph.D. Dissertation (University of Michigan, 1977).

13. The title of Limanowski's doctoral dissertation was "The Sociology of Auguste Comte." For a brief biography of Limanowski, see K. Czachowski, "Szermierz wolności (Bolesław Limanowski)," *Niepodległość*, vol. II (1930), pp. 193–213.

14. Workers' socialism in Lwów and Kraków continued throughout the 1880s to be trade-union based. The "Program of Galician Socialists," altered to the "Program of Polish Socialists of Eastern Galicia, Lwów [January 1881]" [15 pages], was gradualist and Lassallean. See Limanowski, *Pamiętniki (1870–1907)*, p. 266, for the negative reaction of Ukrainian socialists to the program. *Robotnik*, the most radical Galician socialist newspaper, printed in Kraków in 1883, typically wrote that the "principles of socialism need time and the realization of certain conditions." *Robotnik*, no. 4 (1883), p. 1.

15. The police intercepted a series of letters between Mendelson and Waryński ("Lipski") that indicated the latter came to Lwów to set up a socialist organization. TsGAOR, f. 102, DP-III, d. 527, 1884, ll. 2–4.

16. Limanowski, *Pamiętniki (1870–1907)*, p. 181.

17. See E. Hornowa, *Ukraiński obóz postępowy i jego współpraca z polską lewicą społeczną w Galicji, 1876–1895* (Wrocław, 1968), p. 76. Hornowa here tends to underestimate both Waryński's conflict with the Lwów socialists and the Ukrainian-Polish socialist conflicts.

18. *Bohaterowie*, p. 6.

19. J. Uziembło, "Wielki proces krakowski," *ZPW* (1904), p. 94.

20. Haecker, *Historia*, p. 165. It is more likely that Waryński, like Diksztajn, simply did not find common cause with Limanowski's brand of socialism. Diksztajn was invited to Lwów in 1878 to begin a socialist newspaper. He declined this kind of cooperation with Limanowski because the latter's socialism was "on the one hand too pompous and on the other, too limited." AZHP, Materiały procesu krakowskiego, 1880, *Czas* dodatek, z. 1, p. 21.

21. Uziembło, "Wielki process krakowski," *ZPW*, p. 93.

22. See a letter from Jan Ulinowicz in Kraków to Stanisław Ptak dated 30 July (1879). AGAD, PWIS, 1879, 347, ll. 145–147.

23. S. Mikołajski, "Pierwszy posiew socjalizmu w Galicji (Wspomnienia z procesu Ludwika Waryńskiego i 34 spólników w Krakowie, 1878–1880 r.)," *Niepodległość*, vol. XII (1935), p. 348.

24. Russian copy of a letter from Jan Witort to E. Bervi (Flerovskii), 6 June 1879 (o.s.). AGAD, PWIS, 1880, 460, ll. 11–12.

25. Ibid. Waryński's success at Kraków was actually very limited. See *Krakowski komisarz policji na służbie carskiego wywiadu*, ed. L. Baumgarten (Kraków, 1967), p. 8. TsGAOR, f. 102, DP-III, d. 527, 1884, l. 2.

26. *Czas*, the conservative Kraków newspaper, carried as a supplement (*dodatek*) a full report of the trial. This trial coverage is in AZHP, Materiały procesu krakowskiego, 1880, *Czas* dodatki, zeszyt 1–5, and contains 298 pages of trial proceedings and commentary.

27. Haecker asserts that even Warsaw Prosecutor Pleve went to Kraków, "at the head of a whole company of Russian gendarmerie and together with them, ruled the Kraków police and the Kraków courts, as if in his own office...." Haecker claims that several German agents from Poznań and Berlin were also in Kraków for the trial. Haecker, *Historia*, p. 182. Próchnik maintains that it is impossible to establish the presence of Pleve in Kraków, but there is no question that Russian police agents had enthusiastic support from the Polish dominated administration of Kraków. A. Próchnik, "Z dziejów wywiadu rosyjskiego i wzajemnych usług rządów zaborczych (Na marginesie procesu krakowskiego)," *Niepodległość*, vol. VII (1933), pp. 187, 194. This cooperation continued throughout the 1880s. See *Krakowski komisarz* and *Khronika*, p. 35. The Kraków and Warsaw police constantly exchanged letters during the trial. See AGAD, PWIS, 1879, 345. From Kraków, the Russians received all names and addresses from Warsaw found on the Kraków group (ibid., ll. 22–23), and much of this evidence helped in the conviction of Warsaw socialists (ibid., l. 72).

28. AZHP, Materiały procesu krakowskiego, 1880, zeszyt 2, pp. 63, 66–68.

29. Ibid., pp. 68–69.

30. Ibid., p. 75.

31. Ibid., zeszyt 5, p. 293. See ibid., pp. 293–296, for similar reactions from private and public Polish sources.

32. Quoted in Mikołajski, "Pierwszy posiew socjalizmu," pp. 359–360.

33. Próchnik, "Z dziejów wywiadu," p. 186.

34. Limanowski, *Pamiętniki (1870–1907)*, p. 243. See also Haecker, *Historia*, pp. 220–225; Wudzki, *O Waryńskim*, p. 79; Brzeziński, "Wspomnienia," *Niepodległość*, vol. IV, p. 212; and Uziembło, "Proces krakowski," *ZPW*, p. 93. See *Arkhiv "Zemli i voli" i "Narodnoi voli,"* pp. 187–188, for Russian commentary on the trial.

35. This gain in socialist popularity in Galicia did not go unnoticed by Austrian Minister of Interior Taafe who was in Kraków for the trial. As a

partial result of the indictment, Taafe encouraged the passing of the Austrian antisocialist laws of 1884. See the document "Vorkehrungen gegen die Ausbreitung nihilistischer und sozialistischer Bestrebungen, 6 April 1879," in M. Sobolewski, "Dwa dokumenty w sprawie krakowskiego procesu Ludwika Waryńskiego," *Zeszyty Naukowe Universytetu Jagiellońskiego,* no. 2 (1955), pp. 127–128.

36. J. Borejsza, *W kręgu wielkich wygnańców, 1848–1895* (Warsaw, 1963), p. 131.

37. "Papiery M. Koturnickiego (Erazm Kobylański)," *KRRP,* no. 1 (17) (1939), p. 50.

38. Numerous reasons can be cited for this dogmatic internationalism, none of which are satisfactory in themselves: (1) lack of contact with intelligentsia and workers' circles at home which more acutely felt national oppression, (2) increased contact with internationalists, especially the Russians, in Geneva, (3) the formation of a socialist patriotic camp under Limanowski necessitating a struggle not only against right wing (stańczyk) patriotism, patriotism of the middle (positivism), but now patriotism on the left.

39. "Dążenia socjalistyczne na emigracji polskiej 1831 roku," *Równość,* no. 5, no. 6–7, no. 8–9 (1880).

40. "Dążenia," *Równość,* no. 5, p. 23.

41. "Dążenia," *Równość,* no. 8–9, pp. 31–32.

42. Ibid., p. 32.

43. *Równość,* no. 1 (1879), p. 11.

44. *Równość,* no. 10–11 (1880), pp. 4–5.

45. W. Rewaza [Mendelson], "Co robić?" *Równość,* no. 3–4 (1881), pp. 28–29. See [K. Dłuski], "Echa," *Równość,* no. 1, no. 2, no. 3 (1879), for the socialist critique of positivism.

46. "Z kraju i o kraju — socjaliści polscy wobec konstytucji," *Równość,* no. 1 (1879), p. 18.

47. "Echa," *Równość,* no. 1 (1879), pp. 45–46.

48. K. Dłuski, "Patriotyzm i socjalizm," *Równość,* no. 2 (1879), pp. 7–8.

49. Limanowski wrote that even in the preparation of the first number of *Równość* quarrels existed "but they didn't contain a sharp character." He was infuriated by Dłuski's article in the second number and threatened to leave the editorial board because of it. Limanowski compromised "in order not to provide ammunition against those accused of socialism in the contemporaneous trial in Kraków," but insisted that Dłuski sign the article so that it would not reflect an editorial policy. "But my relationship with the editors," he wrote, "was already strained, my further cooperation was only nominal and, when the [Kraków] trial ended, I finally withdrew." Limanowski, *Pamiętniki (1870–1907),* pp. 242–243.

50. *Równość,* no. 5 (1880), pp. 4–5.

51. [S. Mendelson], Editorial article, *Równość,* no. (1880), p. 5.

52. "Naszym 'Patriotom'," *Równość,* no. 5 (1880), pp. 4–5. A long informational article by Lev Deich on the Russian movement likewise appeared in *Równość:* "Szkic ruchu socjalistycznego w Rosji (1871–1880)," *Równość,* no.

10–11, no. 12 (1880). For Waryński's pro-Russian messages to the Western press, see TsGAOR, f. 102, DP-III, d. 527, 1884, ll. 4–6.

53. "Po zamachu," *Równość*, no. 5–6 (1881), p. 58.

54. "13 Marca," *Równość*, no. 5–6 (1881), p. 45.

55. "Sprawa Krakowska," *Równość*, no. 8–9 (1880), p. 66.

56. "Korespondencja z Warszawy," *Równość*, no. 1 (1879), p. 30.

57. Lev Deich calls this group, "the firm of Mendelson and company." Dejcz, "Pionerzy," pp. 50–51. Mendelson's large and steady income from his banker father certainly helped more than hindered the socialist cause. Limanowski also reported, however, that because Mendelson financed the commune, he often took a paternal attitude towards its inhabitants. Brzeziński, drawn into the commune after his activities in Vienna, remembers it as a happy and lively place. Brzeziński, "Wspomnienia," *Niepodległość*, vol. IV, p. 219. For a biography of S. Mendelson, see T. Rechniewski, "Stanisław Mendelson," *Kuźnia*, 1913.

58. Originally Kobylański and Jankowska were to play a "couple" in a socialist ruse. Kobylański took the disguise seriously, and convinced of Jankowska's affections, did not want to let her go to Mendelson, her future husband.

59. The tribunal consisted of the representatives of Black Partition, Plekhanov and his wife, Deich, Zasulich, and Stefanovich as well as Kravchinskii and Morozov from Narodnaia Volia. Dejcz, "Pionerzy," pp. 47–48. The incident is revealing in that Waryński turned to the Russians for advice and not to other Poles. Limanowski was irate that the commune did not consult his choices for arbiters, the non-*Równość* Polish socialists, E. Przewóski and L. Straszewicz. Limanowski, *Pamiętniki (1870–1907)*, pp. 255–256.

60. Diksztajn was a passionate devotee of Western and Russian revolutionary thought, and especially that of Marx and Lavrov. In Geneva, however, he "began to drink heavily and completely disintegrated morally." Krzywicki, *Wspomnienia*, vol. II, p. 256. He shut himself in a room and wrote long love letters to Jankowska. He also wrote sometimes incoherent suicide notes. "Already in 1878 came to me the persistent thoughts of suicide." Ibid., p. 256. The last note read, "It would be better to die on the barricades, but that is difficult — it is better to die a feeling person." Ibid., p. 260. These notes, "Zwierzenia przedśmiertne," are in ibid., pp. 256–260. Diksztajn's major work *Kto z czego żyje* ("Who lives from what") is a masterpiece of translating Marxist theory of surplus value into layman's terms. Under the name of "Jan Młot," it first appeared in Warsaw in 1881, in the first of seven Russian editions in 1885, and was translated into several other languages.

61. Dejcz, "Pionerzy," p. 46.

62. Borejsza says that the other Geneva leader, Z. Miłkowski (T. T. Jeż), lost much of his influence due to his diminishing concern for social change. Borejsza, *W kręgu*, pp. 134–135.

63. Limanowski, *Pamiętniki (1870–1907)*, pp. 216, 223–224. Borejsza, *W kręgu*, pp. 134–135.

64. I. Franko, *Co to jest Socjalizm?* (Leipzig, 1878), pp. 14–15. Franko later

abandoned his earlier Marxism; see J. Himka, "Polish and Ukrainian Socialism," pp. 359–371.
65. Dejcz, "Pionerzy," pp. 43–44.
66. Ibid., p. 45.
67. Quoted in I. N. Kurbatowa, "J. W. Plechanow a polski ruch robotniczy," *ZPW*, no. 3(7)(1959), p. 4. Waryński probably met Plekhanov as early as 1875 in St. Petersburg. "L.M.L.," "V. N. Ignatov," *GOT*, vol. III, p. 125.
68. Dejcz, "Pionerzy," p. 46. Deich recorded a heated conversation between Russian and Polish socialists concerning the publication of V. P. Vorontsov's ("V.V.") famous study, *The Fate of Capitalism in Russia*, which ostensibly showed that capitalism had no future in Russia. Both Waryński and Diksztajn, remembered Deich, rejected every aspect of this book. L. Deich, "Pis'mo Plekhanovym," *GOT*, vol. II, p. 218.
69. For the entire question of *Równość*'s influence on Black Partition see ibid., pp. 41–46. It is interesting in this context that Deich was arrested in Germany for transporting Polish socialist literature to Wrocław (Breslau) and Leipzig. See also Łukawski, *Polacy w rosyjskim ruchu*, p. 98.
70. Brzeziński, "Wspomnienia," *Niepodległość*, vol. IV, p. 220.
71. Limanowski, *Pamiętniki (1870–1907)*, pp. 218–219. During Krzywicki's stay in Geneva in 1884, he met Zhukovskii twice at the printing home of *Przedświt*, *Równość*'s successor. Krzywicki, *Wspomnienia*, vol. II, p. 251.
72. The exception was Stanisław Mendelson who still leaned towards anarchism. Mazowiecki (Kulczycki), *Historia*, p. 41.
73. Ibid. See Volk, *Narodnaia volia*, pp. 410–411, for the ties of the *narodovol'tsy* to *Równość*.
74. The idea for the conference came from *Równość* and "The Society for Mutual Help," led by Miłkowski. Supposedly, the Miłkowski group was to share the program with *Równość*, which never occurred. Limanowski reports that since he agreed neither with the "Society" nor with *Równość*, he stayed away from the conference preparations. Limanowski, *Pamiętniki (1870–1907)*, pp. 256–257. His speech at the conference, he readily admits, "had little effect." Ibid., p. 228.
75. Borejsza, *W kręgu*, p. 151.
76. *Sprawozdanie z międzynarodowego zebrania zwołanego w 50-letnią rocznicę listopadowego powstania przez redakcyję "Rowności" w Genewie* (Geneva, 1881), pp. III–IV.
77. Kon, *Narodziny*, p. 19. Diksztajn said as much in his speech at the conference: "We are gathered . . . not to celebrate the 29th of November uprising . . . not in the defense of the principles for which the soldiers of the thirties fought, but in order to present a catechism of our ideals." *Sprawozdanie*, p. 52.
78. Ibid., pp. 50–51.
79. Ibid., pp. 30–32. Haecker says that Marx and Engels were unhappy with the Polish "internationalists" and sympathized rather with Limanowski. Haecker, *Historia*, pp. 260–261.
80. *Sprawozdanie*, pp. 7–13.

81. W. Piekarski, A. Złotnicki, S. Padlewski, and O. Lubbeck sent a telegram from Rappersville, "Down with Old Poland, long live the country's workers' organizations." Ibid., p. 16. From Brzeziński and Truszkowski in Bern, "Long live the International, Long live the Polish proletariat." Ibid., p. 17.

82. *Sprawozdanie*, pp. 71–72. Kropotkin echoed the theme of traditional Russian socialist mistrust of Poles and he specifically mentioned the ties of *Równość* and Black Partition as a positive expression of a new era of revolutionary relations. Borejsza, *W kręgu*, p. 142.

83. Jędrzejowski wrote, "We find in it [Waryński's speech] all the weak aspects of Waryński's views." Jędrzejowski, "Waryński," *Światło*, p. 109. Waryński and *Równość* are similarly criticized for their "paramount [*kapitalny*] error on the national question." Borejsza, *W kręgu*, p. 153. Snytko likewise joins the chorus of criticism against their "incorrect position in this [the national] question." Snytko, *Russkoe narodnichestvo*, p. 312.

84. *Sprawozdanie*, pp. 82–83.

85. Ibid., p. 81.

86. Ibid., pp. v–vi.

87. Ibid., pp. 5–6.

88. Quoted in Limanowski, *Pamiętniki (1870–1907)*, pp. 256–257.

89. See Borejsza, *W kręgu*, p. 158, for Wróblewski's position.

90. B. Limanowski, *Socjalizm jako konieczny objaw dziejowego rozwoju* (Lwów, 1879), pp. 61, 63, 66.

91. Other members of Lud Polski were E. Kobylański, Z. Balicki, A. Zawadzki, J. Uziembło, and K. Sosnowski.

92. Limanowski, *Pamiętniki (1870–1907)*, p. 268. Brock indicates that the name was consciously taken from the 1835 Portsmouth organization of soldier peasants, "Lud Polski." Brock, *W zaraniu ruchu ludowego* (London, 1956), p. 19.

93. Limanowski, *Pamiętniki (1870–1907)*, p. 268. One historian finds the views of Lud Polski to be similar to those of the "bourgeois-nationalistic" Liga Polska. N. N. Pukhlov, *Iz istorii pol'skoi sotsial-demokraticheskoi partii (1893–1904 gg.)* (Moscow, 1968), p. 49. Balicki's views of an ethnographic Poland were indeed carried forward to the Liga Polska. Limanowski's views, at least as he portrays them in his memoirs, are much more akin to Piłsudski's. For other evaluations of Lud Polski see Snytko, *Russkoe narodnichestvo*, pp. 409–410; Jodko-Narkiewicz, *Geschichte*, pp. 59–62; Veto (Studnicki), *Dwadzieścia lat*, p. 10.

94. *Przedświt*, no. 3 (1881), p. 2.

95. "Z powodu odezwy stow. soc. 'Lud Polski,'" *Przedświt*, no. 3, no. 6–7 (1881), no. 8 (1882).

96. "Z powodu," *Przedświt*, no. 3 (1881), pp. 2–3.

97. That circles in the Congress Kingdom were not represented at this conference is indicative of the weak and chaotic organization of socialism in Poland following the arrests of 1880.

98. Limanowski in *Pamiętniki (1870–1907)*, pp. 270–271, lists the delegates. He also claims that in the hall before the opening meeting, "Dłuski and Waryński approached me, proposing to present, in some ways, a common platform. I said that it seemed to me this would be impossible, because there was so great a difference in our views on the political struggle in the Polish question." Ibid., p. 270.

99. "Sprawozdanie delegowanych z krajów Polskich," *Przedświt*, no. 5 (1881), p. 3. For Limanowski's view of the conference proceedings, see *Pamiętniki (1870–1907)*, pp. 271–272, and his highly censored report in the positivist *Przegląd Tygodniowy*, no. 43 (1881), p. 544.

100. "Sprawozdanie," *Przedświt*, p. 3. Dłuski later spoke for Waryński because the discussions were conducted in French.

101. Ibid., p. 7. Here Waryński states that the accusations against him for denying Polish nationality were too absurd to consider. Limanowski, *Pamiętniki (1870–1907)*, p. 271.

102. "Sprawozdanie," *Przedświt*, p. 5.

103. Ibid., p. 6. *Przedświt* reports that this resolution was favored by the majority of delegates.

104. Jędrzejowski states that "neither the views of one or of the other Polish delegate were denied." *Bohaterowie*, p. 15. Limanowski, however, conceded formal defeat: "In general, I was convinced that when those same people who in private discussions acknowledged my correctness came to vote, most took on the views of my opponents rather than mine; for with them they lived a comradely life; they drank, socialized and danced together; in all this I did not take part because I didn't have the financial means." Limanowski, *Pamiętniki (1870–1907)*, pp. 272, 318.

105. Borejsza, *W kręgu*, p. 160. Marx by this time was fatally ill.

106. Engels to Kautsky, 7 Feb. 1882, Borejsza, *W kręgu*, p. 161. Emphasis in original.

107. Waryński and Diksztajn authored a note in the name of *Równość* to the anathemized Jan Most, leader of the anarchist faction of the International. This visible sign of their irritation with established West European socialism was prompted by a meeting of the anarchists in London in July 1881. Sent without the consent and knowledge of Dłuski, Mendelson, Jankowska, and Piekarski, the letter prompted this group to leave the editorial board and to begin their own paper, *Przedświt*. Waryński and Diksztajn soon recanted their move and joined *Przedświt*, for without Mendelson's financial backing, the publishing of *Równość* was impossible. *Przedświt* operated as did *Równość* and was still based on the "Brussels Program." *Przedświt*, no. 1 (1881), p. 1. Mendelson and Piekarski explained in "Koniecznie wyjaśnienia" that they could not agree with separatism in the internationalist movement and therefore broke with *Równość*. Indicating a growing devotion to political questions among *Równość*, they added as well that they recognized "political agitation, as a means for the struggle and the organization of the masses." *Przedświt*, no. 1 (1881), p. 3. Kon claims that Waryński and Diksztajn sent the letter to Most

because they sympathized with anarchism. *Narodziny,* p. 142. Snytko suggests that the letter was simply a "mistake," which the two soon realized. *Russkoe narodnichestvo,* p. 409. See also Mazowecki (Kulczycki), *Historia,* p. 40.

108. "Sprawozdanie," *Przedświt,* no. 6–7 (1881), pp. 5–7.

109. Ibid., p. 4.

110. "Mezhdunarodnyi kongress v Khur'e," *Narodnia volia,* no. 7 (1881), in *Literatura partii "Narodnoi voli,"* p. 466.

111. Lev Tikhomirov attacked Aksel'rod's speech saying that Narodnaia Volia was neither a socialist nor a politically radical group, but simply *narodovol'tsy.* Socialists, Tikhomirov continued, ignored politics and radicals leave aside the social question. Plekhanov discusses this criticism and Aksel'rod's presentation at Chur in G. V. Plekhanov, "Sotsializm i politicheskaia bor'ba," *Sochineniia,* vol. I (Geneva, 1905), p. 144. Anna Korba recalled that Tikhomirov's hostile reaction to Aksel'rod's Chur speech gained support for Black Partition, and was significant in the foundation of Emancipation of Labor. A. P. Pribyleva-Korba, *"Narodnaia volia," vospominaniia o 1870–1880-kh gg.* (Moscow, 1926), p. 53.

112. *Przedświt,* no. 6–7 (1881), p. 1. The document was dated 3 November 1881 and was signed by "The earlier members of 'Równość' and the editors of the socialist periodical 'Przedświt'." The authorship of the document has not been established. Kulczycki writes that he learned from his friends that Długski and Mendelson initiated the document; Waryński and Diksztajn agreed with it; and only Jankowska was opposed to it. Mazowecki [Kulczycki], *Historia,* p. 43. Deich agrees that Waryński had little to do with the document. He also writes, "we three Black Partitionists [Deich, Zasulich, and Plekhanov] agreed completely with their proposition after we had discussed point by point their proclamation to the Russian comrades. To the project were added certain corrections and completions, [proposed] actually by Plekhanov, and they were accepted by everyone." "Pionerzy," p. 554. Deich elsewhere adds that both he and "George" actually encouraged the Poles to unify with Narodnaia Volia. L. Deich, "Iz kariiskikh tetradei," *GOT,* vol. I, p. 139. If this is in fact the case, then the document is very significant in demonstrating that still in late 1881, even after the Chur conference, Black Partition hoped to reunify the Russian movement by using the Poles as mediators.

Chapter 6. *The Organization and the Ideology of the Proletariat*

1. Because of later Polish Proletariat parties, this first Marxist party is often called in the literature the "Great" or "Wielki Proletariat."

2. W. Rewaza [Mendelson], "Co robić?" *Równość,* no. 3–4 (1881), p. 30.

3. [L. Waryński], "Czy jest u nas kwestia robotnicza," *Równość,* no. 8–9 (1880), p. 27.

4. Editorial article, *Równość,* no. 3–4 (1881), p. 27.

5. "Co robić?" *Równość,* pp. 27, 29.

6. Deich claims that Waryński's return to Warsaw was paid by the Execu-

tive Committee and that he met with Tikhomirov and Oshanina, Narodnaia Volia's representatives in Paris, before returning to Warsaw. Narodnaia Volia supposedly wanted to subordinate the Poles to its movement and therefore no agreement was reached. Dejcz, "Pionerzy," pp. 55–57. Elsewhere Deich writes that Waryński's frustrations with émigré politics led him to seek ties with the action-oriented Narodnaia Volia in Russia. L. Deich, "Iz kariiskikh tetradei," *GOT*, vol. IV, p. 140. Krzywicki asserts, in the same vein, that Waryński intended to establish a section of Narodnaia Volia in Warsaw. Krzywicki, *Wspomnienia*, vol. II, p. 49. Volk says that Waryński stopped in Moscow to negotiate with Narodnaia Volia, *Narodnaia volia*, p. 44.

7. AGAD, PWIS, 1884, 977, ll. 27–28. After the fall of St. Petersburg Gmina, Polish socialists regrouped into the "Polish-Lithuanian Social Revolutionary Party," led by a "Secret Council." This council also was known as "Ognisko" and included Kunicki, Rechniewski, Płoski, Zagórski, and Dębski. According to the police, Ognisko was closely tied to the activities of Narodnaia Volia. Ibid., ll. 76, 89. See also Volk, *Narodnaia volia*, pp. 412–413, 416; Snytko, *Russkoe narodnichestvo*, pp. 349–350; Płoski, *Wspomnienia*, p. 20.

8. AGAD, PWIS, 1884, 977, l. 28.

9. Płoski, *Wspomnienia*, p. 17.

10. AGAD, PWIS, 1884, 977, l. 91.

11. AGAD, PWIS, 1884, 974, l. 86.

12. For Kallenbrun's activities see AGAD, PWIS, 1883, 966, ll. 127–128. For Schmaus's see AGAD, PWIS, 1883, 864, l. 103.

13. "Towarzysze," AZHP, 305/I, 1.

14. "Odezwa Komitetu Robotniczego Part. Soc.-Rew. 'Proletariat,'" Warsaw, 1882, in ibid.

15. "Odezwa Komitetu Robotniczego Part. Soc.-Rew. 'Proletariat,'" Warsaw, 1882 [Sept. 1], ibid. Also in *Przedświt*, no. 4 (1882), pp. 1–2.

16. Mazowiecki [Kulczycki], *Historia*, p. 65.

17. Krzywicki, *Wspomnienia*, vol. II, p. 9.

18. Płoski began self-education circles among positivist students and introduced them to socialist materials. For a report by one of these students to the police, see AGAD, PWIS, 1883, 918A, l. 278. Płoski was one of those socialists who later confessed to the police. Aleksandra Jentysówna wrote to the Central Committee from the Tenth Pavilion, "With sadness I must add that Edmund Płoski did not hold up as he should have — during one of the reports on me, his statement was used — through this I know for sure that he said a great deal — if everything and if commanded — I don't know." "Archiwum Bardowskiego," *ZPW*, no. 1 (1960), pp. 123–124.

19. AGAD, PWIS, 1884, 977, l. 33.

20. Three lengthy descriptions of the organization of the Proletariat based primarily on the confessions of members are in AGAD, PWIS, 1884, 966; ibid., 970; ibid., 980. Baumgarten in *Dzieje*, p. 211, diagrams the organizational structure of Proletariat. His diagram emphasizes the leadership of the Central Committee over the Workers' Committee. The above police and judiciary reports indicate, however, that the two committees provided a dual

leadership whose efficacy depended on the personalities in control. In 1883 the two power centers operated smoothly together under Waryński's leadership.

21. AGAD, PWIS, 1884, 966, 1. 134.
22. Ibid., 966, 1. 134; 977, ll. 13–14.
23. Ibid., 966, 1. 134.
24. Ibid., 980, 1. 293; 977, ll. 13–14.
25. Ibid., 977, 1. 14. See "Krasnaia Krest," *Byloe*, no. 3 (1906), p. 282; Snytko, *Russkoe narodnichestvo*, p. 232.
26. AGAD, PWIS, 1884, 966, ll. 29–30.
27. Ibid., 1. 29.
28. Ibid., 976, ll. 12–13. For reports of individual agents on several circle meetings see ibid., 966, zapiska 8, ll. 155–159.
29. Ibid., 977, 1. 22.
30. Ibid., 976, ll. 5–7.
31. Ibid., 977, 1. 12.
32. Ibid., 974, 1. 81. For aspects of the problems of maintaining a printing center, see ibid., 966, ll. 138–141, 157; 1885, 1051, 1. 37. For Piotrków activities see AGAD, PWIS, 1884, 977, 1. 14; AGAD, PWIS, 1883, 866, 1. 83.
33. AGAD, WGZŻ, 1883, no. 7. "Archiwum Bardowskiego," *ZPW*, p. 134. Kon describes his frustrations in Belystok (Białystok) in *Narodziny wieku*, p. 72. For literature in peasant villages, see AGAD, PWIS, 1883, 906, 1. 1, ll. 14–15; 911, 1. 3; 870.
34. The imported literature was generally stamped, "Agentura Książkowa Proletariat." AGAD, PWIS, 1884, 974, 1. 74. For the role of Kalisz, Częstochowa, and Vilna, see also AGAD, PWIS, 1884, 966, 1. 12; 1882, 7736, ll. 15–19; 1883, 880.
35. Contacts with these smugglers were often facilitated by Jewish *narodovol'tsy* in Vilna, Minsk, and Grodno. TsGIA, SSSR, f. 1405, op. 85, d. 10807, ll. 159–160. For train smuggling, see AGAD, PWIS, 1883, 899; 1888, 1507.
36. *Khronika*, p. 269.
37. Volk says of Odessa, Vitebsk, Mogilev, Riga, and Vilna: "in the majority of cases these circles were made up almost exclusively of worker-Poles." Volk, *Narodnaia volia*, pp. 420–421.
38. At various times this function was fulfilled by Kunicki, Rechniewski, and Dębski. AGAD, PWIS, 1884, 977, 1. 13.
39. For contacts between the Proletariat and the Polish intelligentsia in these cities, see ibid., ll. 12–13; 1884, 980, 1. 256; Novitskii, *Iz vospominanii zhandarma*, pp. 18–19. For the same purposes, a small section of the Proletariat was maintained in Kraków. AGAD, PWIS, 1884, 980, 1. 249. Baumgarten reproduces a police map of all the Proletariat contacts and agents throughout Europe in *Dzieje*, p. 336.
40. Baumgarten prefers to call the Vilna branch of the Proletariat an affiliate of Narodnaia Volia and suggests that the Proletariat was not really interested in spreading its organization to empire cities, but rather using these circles to increase its contact with Narodnaia Volia. *Kółka*, p. 366.
41. Numerous Marxist works, from "Kwestionariusz robotniczy" in 1880 to

"Marks contra Michajłowski" in 1886, were translated in this period. For a list see Borejsza, *W kręgu,* pp. 168–169.

42. See Schmaus's library in AGAD, PWIS, 1884, 966, ll. 30–32.

43. The police in a 57-page report describe the spread of *Przedświt* in the Congress Kingdom. AGAD, PWIS, 1883, 864. For the spread of *Praca* and *Robotnik,* see AGAD, PWIS, 1884, 933, which contains numerous confiscated numbers of these papers.

44. *Proletariat* appeared in four numbers in the fall of 1883, and the last number appeared in May 1884. A sixth number was planned, but the police arrested the editors and confiscated the materials. The May number, Kon says, appeared in three thousand copies: *Narodziny,* p. 45. The dispute with *Przedświt* was founded as well on the fact that Dłuski, Piekarski, and Diksztajn, its editors, had gravitated toward a three-partition Polish party concept. *Walka Klas* was edited by Mendelson, Diksztajn, Jankowska, Wojnarowski, and Kunicki. Dłuski and Piekarski, who did not agree to the close ties with the Russians, did not join the editorial board.

45. The largest collection of the proclamations are in AZHP, 305/I, 1, and are listed in Żanna Korman[owa], "Odezwy Proletariatu," *Niepodległość,* vol. XIV (1936). The list of translated titles are in a brochure "Wydawnictwa socjalistyczne w języku polskim" (Geneva) in AGAD, PWIS, 1884, 1933, l. 23.

46. "Karl Marks," [in Russian], "Archiwum Bardowskiego," *ZPW,* no. 1 (1960), p. 100.

47. AGAD, PWIS, 1884, 974, l. 66.

48. "Odezwa Komitetu Robotniczego Partyi Soc.-Rew. 'Proletariat'" (Warsaw, 1882). Program of the Proletariat, AZHP, 305/I, 1, p. 10.

49. [T. Rechniewski], "My i rząd," *Proletariat: Organ międzynarodowej, socjalno-rewolucyjnej partii (Warsaw, 1883–1884),* no. 4 (1883): reprinting (Warsaw, 1957), p. 46. The program of the Proletariat stated "in our struggle we will mostly have in mind private economic relations." Program of the Proletariat, AZHP, 305/I, 1, p. 12.

50. "Obywatele," AZHP, 305/I, 1.

51. "My i rząd," *Proletariat,* p. 45.

52. "Odezwa," 6 August 1884, in AGAD, PWIS, 1887, 1283, l. 20.

53. [L. Waryński], "My i burżuazja," *Proletariat,* no. 3 (1883), p. 29.

54. "My i rząd," *Proletariat,* p. 45.

55. *Proletariat,* p. 5.

56. "My i rząd," *Proletariat,* p. 63.

57. "Material dla vstupitel'noi stati," "Archiwum Bardowskiego," *ZPW* (1960), p. 109.

58. *Proletariat,* no. 3 (1883), p. 2, p. 33.

59. "My i burżuazja," *Proletariat,* p. 31.

60. *Proletariat,* no. 1 (1883), p. 2.

61. "Paris, 1884," *Walka Klas,* no. 2 (1884), p. 6.

62. "My i rząd," *Proletariat,* p. 46.

63. "Dlaczego my nie jesteśmy anarchistami," *Przedświt,* no. 6, 7, 8 (1886), p. 4.

64. "My i burżuazja," *Proletariat*, p. 31. Emphasis in the original.

65. "Paris, 1884," *Walka Klas*, no. 2 (1884), p. 7.

66. "Sprawozdanie z procesu," *ZPW: Książeczka pierwsza*, ed. T. Rechniewski (Geneva, 1886), pp. 152–153.

67. "Praca dziś i w przyszłości," *Przedświt*, no. 8 (1884), p. 1.

68. "Dlaczego nie jesteśmy anarchistami," *Przedświt*, p. 4.

69. "Kto jest robotnikiem," 1881, in AGAD, PWIS, 1884, 933, ll. 24–31 (includes 7 copies). "Manifest do pracujących na roli" (Warsaw, 1883), in AZHP, 305/I, 1. The concurrent Lithuanian proclamation "Manipestas Artojams" is also in ibid.

70. "Manifest do pracujących na roli" (Warsaw, 1883), in ibid.

71. Tomek Kujawczyk, "Ojciec Szymon; Opowiadanie" (Warsaw, 1882). "Rozmowa dwu kumotrów" (Kraków, 1883). "Adam z pod Krakowa," *Janek Bruzda* (Geneva, 1884).

72. Up to several thousand pages of intricate prosecutor, governor-general, and even Ministry of Justice reports exist on the spread of the "Manifesto." See especially AGAD, PWIS, 1883: 866, 869, 877, 886, 888, 891, 894, 896, and 906.

73. "Ze wsi," *Proletariat*, no. 1 (1883), p. 9.

74. Program of the Proletariat, "Odezwa, 1882," AZHP, 305/I, 1, p. 3, p. 7.

75. "My i patrioci," *Walka Klas*, no. 3 (1884), p. 3.

76. "Nowe hasło," *Proletariat*, no. 2 (1883), p. 16.

77. T. Rechniewski, "My i rząd," *Proletariat*, p. 64.

78. "Dlaczego chcemy równości," *Przedświt*, no. 2 (1885), p. 2.

79. "Nowe hasło," *Proletariat*, p. 17.

80. *Proletariat*, no. 1 (1883), pp. 3–4.

81. "Nowe hasło," *Proletariat*, p. 17.

82. "Czy socjaliści trzymają z Moskalami i z Niemcami," *Przedświt*, no. 4 (1885), pp. 4–5.

83. Żanna Kormanowa, "Wstęp," *Proletariat*, p. xvii. See also Wudzki, *O Waryńskim*, p. 142.

84. Zhigunov, "Iz istorii," p. 275.

85. Arskii, "Iz istorii," *KL*, p. 50.

86. Haustein, *Sozialismus und nationale Frage*, p. 51. See also L. Baumgarten, "Na marginesie reedycji pisma 'Proletariat' (kilka sprostowań i uzupełnień)," *ZPW*, no. 3 (1958), pp. 259–260.

87. Krzywicki, *Wspomnienia*, vol. II, note 6, p. 609.

Chapter 7. *The Proletariat among the Polish Intelligentsia and Working Class*

1. See Appendix: tables 44–47, pp. 231–232.

2. *Pamiętnik — Bohuszewiczówna*, p. 30.

3. K. Pietkiewicz, "Michał Mancewicz i jego czasy," *Niepodległość*, vol. III (1931), p. 28.

4. Skrzycki [Dmowski], *Młodzież polska*, pp. 46, 54.

5. M. Schmidt, *Wspomnienia młodzieży z przed 50-ciu latu* (Warsaw, 1929), p. 13.

6. Skrzycki [Dmowski], *Młodzież polska*, pp. 53–54.

7. Skrzycki [Dmowski], *Młodzież polska*, p. 54. S. Koszutski, *Walka młodzieży polskiej o wielkie ideały: wspomnienie z czasów gimnazjalnych i uniwersyteckich (1881–1900)* (Warsaw, 1928), p. 11. S. Czekanowski, *W domu niewoli*, p. 36.

8. *Proletariat*, no. 1 (1883), p. 3.

9. Report of 30 September 1883 (o.s.), AGAD, WGZŻ, no. 5. See also Czekanowski, *W domu niewoli*, pp. 34–35. AGAD, PWIS, 1884, 966, l. 116; 1883, 885, l. 1. At this time Kon was in the sixth class of the gymnasium. Kon, *Narodziny*, pp. 11–12.

10. Offenburg, *Stan umysłów*, p. 9. Pietkiewicz, "Mancewicz," *Niepodległość*, p. 229.

11. The police wrote that the patriotic party "does not represent at this time a great danger." AGAD, PWIS, 1884, 966, zapiska 5, l. 156.

12. See AGAD, PWIS, 1884, 988, l. 29; 1888, 1012, l. 15. For the fate of Schmidt see AGAD, DKGW, 1885, 122.

13. *Pamiętnik — Bohuszewiczówna*, note 26, pp. 40–41.

14. AGAD, PWIS, 1883, 918A, ll. 4–5, 13–23.

15. For army circles see AGAD, PWIS, 1884, 977, l. 19. For influence of the Proletariat on Kiev studentry, see Chmielewski, "Pierwsze lata," *Niepodległość*, p. 114. For direct Proletariat action among the studentry, see AGAD, PWIS, 1887, 1002; Długi, "Wspomnienia," *Niepodległość*, p. 226.

16. *Procesy polityczne*, p. 70. See also Świętochowski, *Wspomnienia*, pp. 78–79. Here Świętochowski writes, "Prus took the assault very tragically, it remained for his entire life a painful trauma."

17. W. Wścieklica, "Rojenia socjalistów polskich wobec nauki ich mistrza," *Ognisko* (Warsaw, 1882), pp. 107, 114.

18. K. Długi, W. Piekarski, "Mistrz Wścieklica i spółka" (Geneva, 1883), in Molska, *Pierwsze pokolenie*, vol. II, p. 654.

19. "A. Giller to M. Darowski, 14 October 1881," W. Piekarski: *Listy z więzienia (1879)* (Wrocław, 1953), p. 8.

20. It is interesting that these Polish loyalist deputations were often shunned by the tsar. Feldman, *Dzieje*, p. 221. For conservative Polish views on the emergence of socialism see the antisocialist brochure, *Propaganda socjalistyczna między ludem wiejskim* (Kraków, 1879), and "B. P.," *Ocherki Privislian'ia* (Moscow, 1897), pp. 25–26.

21. Tolstoi and Delianov initiated the educational counter-reforms which increased tensions in all learning centers in the empire, and especially in Warsaw. For the background of the university laws of 1884, see G. I. Shchetinina, "Universitetskii vopros 1870–1880-kh gg. i ustav 1884 g.," Dissertation abstract (Moscow, 1965), p. 11. Łukawski, *Polacy w rosyjskim ruchu*, p. 14.

22. "Zajścia w Puławach," *Przedświt*, no. 15 (1883), pp. 2–3.

23. The Puławy students wrote a proclamation asking for the solidarity of the Warsaw University students: "Ostatnie wiadomości," *Przedświt*, no. 15 (1883), p. 4.

24. Czekanowski wrote that he saw, "a crowd of students moving, gesticulating excitedly. I heard the uproar of their talking; sticking our heads out the window we saw a movement of police and gendarmes on horses and maybe even soldiers." Czekanowski, *W domu niewoli,* p. 58.

25. Krzesławski, "Spoliczkowanie Apuchtina," *KRRP,* no. 1 (1934), pp. 5–10. See also the pamphlet "Szczegóły o rozruchach w Warszawie" in TsGIA, f. 1410, op. 1, 436, ll. 11–15. This *delo* also contains an unfortunately damaged mimeographed, handwritten proclamation in Russian describing the events of the student strike. Ibid., l. 9.

26. Krzesławski, "Spoliczkowanie," p. 10.

27. Limanowski later met Zhukovich in Geneva and said that he "spoke Polish well, though he was Orthodox and considered himself a Russian." Limanowski, *Pamiętniki (1870–1907),* p. 317. Krzesławski doubts that at that time Zhukovich was an actual member of Narodnaia Volia. Krzesławski, "Spoliczkowanie," *KRRP,* no. 3 (1939), p. 161.

28. Czekanowski, *W domu niewoli,* p. 59.

29. Krzesławski, "Spoliczkowanie," *KRRP,* no. 3 (1939), p. 162.

30. The names of 199 students implicated in the affair are recorded in TsGAOR, f. 102, DP-V, 1883, d. 3903, ll. 2–6. The *delo* also contains considerable biographical information on the demonstrators. Ibid., ll. 15–176.

31. Among a list of the 34 most dangerous students compiled by the university authorities were included L. Krzywicki, S. Barański, K. Pławiński, and other socialists. Krzesławski, "Spoliczkowanie," *KRRP,* no. 1 (1939), pp. 12–13.

32. Zaionchkovskii, *Rossiiskoe samoderzhavie,* p. 118.

33. Schmidt, "Wspomnienia," p. 27.

34. For a biography of Puchewicz, see "Kazimierz Puchewicz," *Walka Klas,* no. 7 (1884), pp. 9–10. Puchewicz's first involvement was in the propaganda efforts among workers in 1878–1879. AGAD, PWIS, 1879, 346, ll. 158–159.

35. The prosecutor wrote that "from the point of view of goals and aspirations contained in the program [of Solidarność] as well as from the point of view of the activities of that party, at the core of the matter, it is identical with the party Proletariat." AGAD, PWIS, 1884, 977, l. 15. TsGIA, SSSR, f. 1405, op. 83, d. 11116, l. 5.

36. *Przedświt,* no. 24 (1883), pp. 1–2.

37. AGAD, PWIS, 1884, 977, l. 15.

38. Ibid.

39. Heryng, "X-ty Pawilon," *Niepodległość,* p. 73. Kon, *Narodziny,* p. 32; R. Arskii, "Iz istorii 'Proletariat'," *KL,* p. 61. L. Wasilewski claims that it was Waryński's specific intention to use terror if police chief Buturlin did not accede to the demands of the workers which caused Puchewicz to leave the party. L. Vasilevskii (Plokhotskii), "Polskaia s.-r. partiia 'Proletariat' 1882–1886," *Byloe,* no. 4 (1906), p. 206.

40. AGAD, PWIS, 1884, 966, ll. 136–137.

41. Ż. Korman[owa], "Kazimierz Puchewicz i 'Solidarność,'" *Niepodległość,* vol. 19 (1939), p. 7. A. Molska in "Wstęp," *Pierwsze pokolenie,* vol. I, p. xix, agrees that Solidarność was "social democratic" and the Proletariat "social revolutionary." Kulczycki in this vein called Solidarność a forerunner of the SDKPiL. Mazowiecki, [Kulczycki] *Historia,* p. 70.

42. AGAD, PWIS, 1884, 966, zapiska 5, l. 156. See also ibid., 974, ll. 71–72.

43. AGAD, PWIS, 1883, 871; 1884, 966, l. 43.

44. T. Kowalik, the editor of Krusiński's works and a great admirer of Krusiński, wrote that it was mainly due to Krusiński's efforts that the student disturbances of April came about. Kowalik, "Wstęp," *Stanisław Krusiński: Pisma zebrane* (Warsaw, 1958), p. xii.

45. Oskar Lange writes that to Krzywicki, "historical materialism in Poland owes its synthetic approach, the confrontation of theory with extremely rich factual material, and extensive application to sociology, ethnology and the history of culture. . . . As a theorist of historical materialism, Krzywicki stands on a par with Kautsky, Plekhanov, Mehring." O. Lange, "Ludwik Krzywicki — Theorist of Historical Materialism," *Papers in Economics and Sociology* (Warsaw, 1970), p. 59.

46. The participation of Waryński and Puchewicz in the translations remains a matter of considerable dispute. See Baumgarten, *Dzieje,* pp. 105–106; Korman[owa], "Kaz. Puchewicz," *Niepodległość,* p. 6; Krzywicki, *Wspomnienia,* vol. II, p. 133. Krzywicki names here K. Pławiński, J. Siemaszko, and M. Brzeziński as the other participants. Krzywicki was at this time already planning for the translation of volume II. See the Krzywicki-Engels correspondence in Borejsza, *W kręgu,* pp. 336–338.

47. Krusiński was a great admirer of Plekhanov and of Black Partition, though he had little respect for the revolutionary potential of the peasantry.

48. Krzywicki, *Wspomnienia,* vol. II, p. 139.

49. Even Kowalik, who seriously exaggerates Krusiński's role in the 1882–1885 period, writes that the Krusińszczycy "did not duly appreciate the level of development of the Polish working class." Kowalik, "Wstęp," *Krusiński,* p. xi.

50. Mazowiecki [Kulczycki], *Historia,* p. 63. Baumgarten, *Dzieje,* p. 144.

51. *Przedświt* leaves out any mention of cooperation with the Russians in its report on Vilna, *Przedświt,* no. 17 (1883), p. 1. Baumgarten found in the Russian archives what he thinks is a Russian transcription of the original Vilna protocol. *Dzieje,* pp. 150–151. See also A. Dębski, "Wspomnienie o Kunickim i Bardowskim," *ZPW* (London, 1904), pp. 83–84.

52. Plokhotskii [L. Wasilewski], "Iz istorii," *Byloe,* p. 204.

53. *Przedświt,* no. 17 (1883), p. 1.

54. Quoted in Baumgarten, *Dzieje,* pp. 150–151.

55. *Przedświt,* no. 17 (1883), p. 1.

56. Plokhotskii [L. Wasilewski], "Iz istorii," *Byloe,* p. 203.

57. *Przedświt,* no. 10 (1883), p. 3.

58. Kowalik bitterly denies accusations that Krusiński was a "revisionist"

and overcompensates by making out of him the father of Polish Marxism and out of the Proletariat a group of renegade revolutionaries who were insensitive to theoretical problems. Kowalik, "Wstęp," *Krusiński*. Baumgarten, in his fascinating review of Kowalik's book, scorns Kowalik's thesis of the role of Krusiński in Polish socialist history, unjustifiably degrading Krusiński in the process. L. Baumgarten, "'Odkrywczość' więcej niż wątpliwa," *ZPW*, no. 3 (1960), pp. 60–69. Although Alina Molska sides with Baumgarten in his reviews, she calls Krusiński (as well as Puchewicz) a "social democrat" more than a "social-revolutionary." A. Molska, "Wstęp," *Pierwsze pokolenie*, vol. I, p. xxvi. Kowalik's arguments follow the lines of those of the prewar socialist historian, A. Próchnik, *Ku Polsce*, p. 11.

59. "Prikaz po varshavskoi politsii," AGAD, PWIS, 1884, 964, l. 19.

60. For the background of the incident, see *Gazeta Narodowa* from Lwów, 8 March 1883: AGAD, PWIS, 1884, 964, ll. 59–60.

61. This prompted an open split with Puchewicz who formed Solidarność at this time. Upon Puchewicz's objections to this political action, Waryński was reported to have said, "You do what you wish and I will do what I wish." "In that case," said Puchewicz, "give me what belongs to Solidarność." This consisted of a printing press and a sum of money. The lack of printing facilities severely hindered the Proletariat in the spring of 1883. See Baumgarten, *Dzieje*, pp. 159–160. Kon wrote that Waryński even advocated assassinating Buturlin if the law was carried out: *Narodziny*, pp. 30–31.

62. AGAD, PWIS, 1884, 964, l. 27. Copies of the proclamation were even transported to outlying areas of Warsaw. AGAD, PWIS, 1884, 933, ll. 32–45 (includes 14 copies of the proclamation).

63. "Robotnicy Obywatele," AZHP, 305, I, 1.

64. AGAD, PWIS, 1884, 964, ll. 51–54.

65. Ibid., l. 54.

66. Ibid., l. 27.

67. "Robotnice!" AZHP, 305, I, 1. Also in *Przedświt*, no. 15 (1883), p. 1.

68. *Gazeta Narodowa*, Lwów, no. 54 (1883), in AGAD, PWIS, 1884, 964, ll. 59–60.

69. AGAD, PWIS, 1884, 977, l. 160.

70. For a history of Żyrardów, see I. Wołkowiczer, "Strajk żyrardowski," *ZPW*, no. 2 (1927), p. 67.

71. AGAD, DKGW, referat 1, 1883, 122, ll. 4–8.

72. Ibid.

73. Ibid., l. 18.

74. "Obiavlenie-Obwieszczenie," AGAD, DKGW, referat 1, 1883, 122, ll. 20–21.

75. M. Meloch, "Ruch strajkowy w Królestwie Polskim 1870–1886," *Studia historyczne* (Warsaw, 1958), p. 170.

76. "Robotnicy," AGAD, DKWG, referat 1, 1883, 122, ll. 23–25.

77. AGAD, DKGW, Referat 1, 1883, 122, l. 142. Thirty-four names are listed in ibid., ll. 32–33. The police recommended the expulsion of fifteen

dangerous workers from Warsaw. A. Eisert was in possession of socialist literature. Ibid., l. 26. Thirty-nine workers, their backgrounds, and their factory conduct reports are listed in ibid., ll. 112-118. The Warsaw police chief wrote that the August 1884 strike "was called by socialist circles in Warsaw . . . they [the socialists] lead them [the workers] with threats of economic struggle against the employer." Ibid., l. 142.

78. On 21 and 22 August 1884, a brief strike of 200 workers was suppressed by police and a new factory-hired armed force. Żyrardów became a leading strike center in Polish labor history. AGAD, DKGW, referat 1, 1883, 122, ll. 138a, 154.

79. "Bezrobocie i terror," *Proletariat,* no. 2 (1883), p. 21.

80. Several thousand workers attended the funeral of the slain strikers. "Robotnik" [Dukaczewski], "Z dziejów ruchu robotniczego w Żyrardowie," *Przedświt,* no. 6 (1902), p. 219.

81. For the Lilpop strike, see AGAD, DKGW, referat 1, 1883, 168, ll. 1-2; AGAD, PWIS, 1884, 977, ll. 94-95. M. Meloch, "Ruch strajkowy w Królestwie Polskim w latach 1870-1886," reprint from *Przegląd Socjologiczny,* vol. V (1937), p. 30. Ptaszyński was a typical working-class leader; he was a member of the *szlachta,* attended military school in St. Petersburg, became a metalworker, and joined the Proletariat.

82. Meloch, "Ruch strajkowy," p. 24.

83. AGAD, PWIS, 1884, 966, zapiska 1, l. 152.

84. Ibid., zapiska 2, l. 153.

85. AGAD, DKGW, refera. 1, 1885, 265.

86. Baumgarten, *Dzieje,* p. 561.

87. For the career of Banković, see I. Oczak, "Działalność serbskiego rewolucjonisty Andra Bankowicza w Polsce w latach 1885-1886. *ZPW,* no. 3 (1959), pp. 56-63. Among other materials found on Banković was a German manuscript which he had authored on "the conditions of workers in several Moscow factories." TsGAOR, f. 102, op. 168, d. 8 (1884), l. 66.

88. Baumgarten establishes the initiatory role of Wilczyński and Banković from several reliable sources. *Dzieje,* pp. 563-564.

89. AGAD, PWIS, 1884, 976, ll. 1-2. AGAD, PWIS, 1885, 1082, ll. 9,

90. This latter report from the office of the Warsaw chief of police at first called the event a disturbance (*besporiadok*), then they crossed this out and wrote in demonstration (*manifestatsiia*). Similarly they at first said of Banković that "he can be considered one of the members . . . of the Proletariat." This was likewise crossed out and instead they wrote that there "is some evidence, though to this time insufficiently established, that he can be considered a member of . . . the Proletariat." Ibid., l. 60. The change of attitude reflected in the alterations in these reports can be attributed perhaps to extensive police questioning of the 146 arrested.

91. The account of events is paraphrased from both versions: AGAD, PWIS, 1884, 976, ll. 1-2; and AGAD, PWIS, 1885, 1082, ll. 9, 59-61.

92. Various reports indicate that Banković spoke in broken French. Gost-

kiewicz remembered that he spoke in a Slavic mix of Russian and Serbian. H. Gostkiewicz, "Wspomnienia proletariatczyka," *ZPW*, no. 2 (1927), p. 44.

93. AGAD, PWIS, 1885, 1082, ll. 21–44, lists the names and employment of all 146 arrested.

94. AGAD, PWIS, 1885, 1082, l. 60.

95. The police report that the initiative for the proclamation came from Michał Mancewicz who approached Bohuszewiczówna about the idea. Gabriel Oleszkiewicz also participated in drawing up the document. AGAD, PWIS, 1884, 976, l. 24.

96. "Odezwa do robotników" (Warsaw, 4 March 1885), AZHP, 305, I, 1. Emphasis added.

97. The editorial article in no. 10, 11, 12 (1885) of *Walka Klas*, p. 4, similarly criticized the party's "Odezwa" for insufficiently articulating minimum demands for the workers. See also: G. Lur'e, "Manifestatsiia bezrabotnykh v Varshave," *KS*, no. 10 (1931), pp. 60–81. Meloch, "Ruch strajkowy," p. 33.

98. Both Bohuszewiczówna and Mancewicz were at the demonstration, but easily avoided arrest and did not participate in the proceedings.

99. See Adam Próchnik's classic study, "Bunt łódzki w roku 1892," in *Studia i szkice* (Warsaw, 1962), pp. 329–495.

100. E. Ajnenkiel, "Wydawnictwa i druki Proletariatu w Łodzi," reprint from *Prace Polonistyczne*, vol. II (1953), p. 275 (AZHP, AM, no. 1308). Paweł Korzec estimates the number of unemployed and their families at 30,000. "Dwa bunty łódzkie (1861, 1892)," *Z dziejów ruchu robotniczego w Łodzi* (Łódź, 1967), p. 45. "Łódź," *Proletariat*, no. 1 (1883), p. 8.

101. Ajnenkiel, "Wydawnictwa," p. 275; R. Arskii, "Iz istorii," *KL*, p. 58.

102. Korzec, "Dwa bunty," *Z dziejów*, p. 45. In 1897, Łódź's population was 61 percent illiterate, a much lower literacy rate than Warsaw's working-class population alone.

103. Though some of these workers were originally German social democrats, they had few, if any, organizations in Łódź and had nothing to do with the Proletariat. Gostkiewicz, "Wspomnienia," *ZPW*, p. 44. The prosecutor disagrees and, indulging in scapegoatism, blames the growth of socialism in this area partly on the German's familiarity with socialist ideas and willingness to participate in "secret social revolutionary circles." *Kółka*, p. 826. This original "wniosek" is contained in AGAD, PWIS, 1886, 1282, ll. 69–100, but is illegible. Baumgarten in *Kółka* translates the Minister of Justice's copy from TsGIA, f. 1405. Jewish workers at this time composed the lowest stratum and were not yet involved in socialist activities. See M. Kaufman, "Początki roboty żydowskiej PPS," *Niepodległość*, vol. VII (1933), p. 336; Kon, *Narodziny*, p. 69. On the other hand, the distinguished German historian of Poland, Georg Strobel, argues that Jews and especially Germans played an important role in the Łódź Proletariat. *Die Partei Rosa Luxemburgs, Lenin und die SPD* (Wiesbaden, 1974), pp. 45–48.

104. I. Hałas, "Powstanie i rozwój zorganizowanego ruchu robotniczego w Łodzi," *Z dziejów ruchu robotniczego w Łodzi* (Łódź, 1967), p. 93.

105. AGAD, PWIS, 1879, 320, ll. 1–11. Ibid., 346, l. 45.

106. Gostkiewicz, "Wspomnienia," *ZPW,* p. 44.

107. Pacanowski was an "enthusiastic supporter of the cause" and a "determined terrorist." Very much under the influence of Kunicki, Pacanowski confessed everything upon arrest. See A. Dębski, *Zajścia,* p. 11.

108. "Zeznanie Pacanowskiego (Tłumaczenie oryginalnych protokołów żandarmskich)," *ZPW* (London, 1904), p. 218.

109. *Khronika,* p. 285. Baumgarten is unjustifiably skeptical of the government figures on the number of circles and size of the southern Proletariat: *Kółka,* footnote 47, p. 855 and footnote 48, p. 856. The number of actual Proletariat members was probably smaller than the government figures, the number of sympathizers probably greater. Cobel wrote numerous semiliterate descriptions of Łódź working-class poverty and grief. AGAD, PWIS, 1887, 1284, l. 13.

110. The following reports of the prosecutor document the rapid increase of socialist propaganda in Łódź, Zgierz, and Tomaszów in 1883-1886. AGAD, PWIS, 1883, 896, ll. 1-200; 1884, 966, ll. 53-57; 1885, 1028, ll. 10-15; 1887, 1282, l. 1.

111. S. Bugajski, "Autobiografia," *ZPW,* no. 4 (1927), p. 13; "Zeznanie Pacanowskiego," *ZPW* (London, 1904), p. 233.

112. One should also remember that the southern district was distant from the administrative police center of the Congress Kingdom and generally avoided mass police interference. Similarly, the lack of intelligentsia leadership in the south led the authorities to believe that no imminent danger was posed in these areas.

113. "Zeznanie Pacanowskiego," *ZPW* (London, 1904), p. 232.

114. *Kółka,* p. 843.

115. Ibid., p. 857.

116. TsGAOR, f. 102, op. 168, d. 9 (1885), l. 219.

117. AGAD, PWIS, 1887, 1282, l. 25. The letter, in broken Polish and barely legible, is translated here as close to the original as possible. Some sentence parts are paraphrased.

118. [Written by Pacanowski], AGAD, PWIS, 1884, 977, l. 12. This tactic was only rarely employed in the Warsaw region.

119. "Komitet Robotniczy oskarża Karola Baume," AZHP, 305, I, 1.

120. AGAD, PWIS, 1884, 978, ll. 29-33. Contains original letter and envelope. On the Poznański affair see AGAD, PWIS, 1884, 952.

121. AGAD, PWIS, 1884, 978, ll. 42-43. Contains the original letter and envelope. The master Stanisław Żeranski was also threatened by the Workers' Committee. If he did not change his bearing to the workers, he would be killed. TsGAOR, f. 102, op. 168, d. 9, ll. 39-40.

122. AGAD, PWIS, 1884, 915, l. 5. "Odezwa" (proclamation) printed in Warsaw, Nov. 1883, and found in Zgierz in 1884.

123. *Listok "Narodnoi voli,"* no. 2 (1883), carried the Proletariat death sentence on Śremski. B. Bazilevskii (Bogucharskii), ed., *Literatura partii "Narodnoi voli"* (Paris, 1905), p. 650. When asked by the police why he attacked Śremski, Schmaus replied: "Remember I am a revolutionary

socialist." In an earlier meeting Schmaus is reported to have said — "life or death — to us it is all the same, but a revolutionary should not betray another." He then brandished a revolver and said, "six lead bullets, if someone squeals, one for him and the second for yourself." AGAD, PWIS, 1884, 977, ll. 42–43. Schmaus was also an important smuggler of illegal literature into the Congress Kingdom through Kalisz and Częstochowa. AGAD, PWIS, 1884, 963, l. 43. See Schmaus's papers, AGAD, PWIS, 1884, 975, and the Ministry of Justice summary, TsGIA SSSR, f. 1405, op. 83, d. 11271, ll. 11–40.

124. The prosecutor often noted the immense popularity of terrorism and "social revolutionary ideas" in Zgierz. See, for instance, *Kółka,* p. 858.

125. AGAD, PWIS, 1884, 979, ll. 314–315.

126. AGAD, PWIS, 1884, 941, ll. 9–10.

127. S. Bugajski, "Autobiografia," *ZPW,* no. 4 (1927), p. 14.

128. AZHP, 305, I, 1. AGAD, PWIS, 1884, 980, l. 41. "Zeznanie Pacanowskiego," *ZPW* (London, 1904), p. 221.

129. Baumgarten suggests that Helszer in fact did not betray the party. *Dzieje,* pp. 424–425.

130. AGAD, PWIS, 1884, 977, l. 46.

131. Ibid., l. 45.

132. According to Mańkowski, Bloch and another conspirator, Leon Degórski, were "serious" and "honest," and both "were fathers of large families. Their positions were very hard, but they quickly accepted their sacrifice on the altar of the cause." M. Mańkowski, *U stóp szubienicy* (Kraków, 1905), p. 28.

133. See the collection on the assassination of Helszer (487 pages), AGAD, PWIS, 1884, 979.

134. That the proclamation was intended for the workers of the Piotrków industrial region is attested to by its bilingual (German and Polish) text. "Towarzysze! — Genossen!" AZHP, 305, I, 1. See also the Russian translation in *Narodnaia volia,* no. 10 (1884), *Literatura "Narodnoi voli,"* pp. 706–707.

Chapter 8. *The Proletariat and the Russians*

1. Some Proletariat members like Feliks Kon thought that they should indeed unify with Osvobozhdenie Truda ("Emancipation of Labor") and not with Narodnaia Volia, but there was no real basis for this cooperation in the empire itself. F. Kon, "Soiuz 'Proletariata s 'Narod. voli,'" *KS,* no. 3 (1926), p. 70. Snytko generalizes that those schooled in the empire tended to sympathize with Narodnaia Volia and those in the Congress Kingdom with Black Partition. Snytko, *Russkoe narodnichestvo,* p. 166. In a review of Plekhanov's *Socialism and the Political Struggle* (Geneva, 1883), *Walka Klas* attacks Plekhanov's socialism and supports Narodnaia Volia, *Walka Klas,* no. 2 (1884), pp. 25–26.

2. "Obywatele!" 15 June 1883. AZHP, 305, I, 1.

3. AGAD, PWIS, 1884, 977, l. 10.

4. *Przedświt,* no. 24 (1883), p. 4.

5. "Novyi pol'skii sotsialisticheskii zhurnal'," *Vestnik "Narodnoi voli,"* no. 2 (1884), p. 180.

6. Tikhomirov to Oshanina, 22 May 1883. In B. Sapir, ed., *Lavrov,* II, p. 104. In this letter, Tikhomirov argues against uniting with the Poles, and calls Oshanina's Polish friend, probably Jankowska, "a swine."

7. L. Tikhomirov, *Vospominaniia L'va Tikhomirova* (Moscow, 1927), pp. 319–320.

8. AGAD, WGZŻ, 1884, no. 3, l. 166.

9. For Shchulepnikova's role see the published records from the Kiev judicial archives in L. Berman, "Dopolneniia k stat'e M. P. Shebalina," *Narodovol'tsy 80-kh i 90-kh godov* (Moscow, 1929)¸ p. 84. For Figner and Waryński see *Khronika,* p. 238.

10. See Volk, *Narodnaia volia,* p. 416.

11. Recruits from Russia entered the Proletariat ranks especially after the 1883 Vilna meeting. Some of the financial aid came from Polish radicals in Russia, other from the *narodovol'tsy* coffers. Official sources estimate the sum at around 5,000 rubles. *Khronika,* pp. 269–270. See also W. Jodko-Narkiewicz, *Geschichte der sozialistischen Bewegung in Polen* (Zürich, 1895), p. 11.

12. Krzywicki, *Wspomnienia,* vol. II, p. 157.

13. See Tikhomirov's letters to Oshanina from Nov. 1882 in Sapir, ed., *Lavrov,* II, pp. 92, 94, 96. Apparently, Tikhomirov wanted to use Waryński to reestablish broken ties with the internal Russian movement and provided him with recommendations and identification papers for that purpose.

14. The spring 1883 trip of Waryński to St. Petersburg is the least documented aspect of his career. Baumgarten doubts that Waryński went to St. Petersburg at all. *Dzieje,* p. 235. There is no question, however, that in the spring 1883 high level discussions between an important member of Proletariat and members of the Executive Committee took place. The *narodovolets* I. I. Popov remembered that Bardovskii as well as Waryński took part on the Polish side. The Russians Karaulov, Ivanov, Iakubovich, and Ovchinnikov (as well as Degaev) took part. I. I. Popov, "Revoliutsionnye organizatsii v Peterburge v 1882–1885 godakh," *Narodovol'tsy posle 1-go marta 1881 goda* (Moscow, 1928), p. 61. Dębski unequivocally states that it was Waryński who was in St. Petersburg at this time. A. Dębski, "Wspomnienia o Kunickim i Bardowskim," *ZPW* (1904), p. 86. Perl accepts this in *Dzieje,* p. 185.

15. V. Nevskii, "Iz narodovol'cheskikh vospominanii (S. A. Ivanova)," *Narodovol'tsy 80-kh i 90-kh,* pp. 45–46.

16. M. Iu. Ashenbrenner, "Voennaia organizatsiia partii 'Narodnoi voli,'" *Byloe,* no. 7 (1906), p. 13.

17. The very complex relationship between Degaev and Sudeikin, between Sudeikin and his fellow tsarist police, and in general between liberals and revolutionaries in the tsarist regime complicates any simple explanation of the role of the provocateur. Sudeikin, for instance, was highly ambitious and hoped through Degaev to prompt Narodnaia Volia to spectacular terrorist deeds. Sudeikin, in turn, could take credit for arresting the culprits. He often

worked at cross-purposes with other police organs which, through the legal *narodnik* Drahomanov or Ignatiev-led Sviashcheniia Druzhina ("Holy Battalion"), were trying to bring Narodnaia Volia to some kind of nonterrorist agreement. See *Dnevnik Polovtsova*, vol. I (Moscow, 1966), p. 157; M. G. Sedov, *Geroicheskii period revoliutsionnogo narodnichestva* (Moscow, 1966), pp. 20–25. For the "Degaevshchina" in general, see "Degaevshchina (materialy i dokumenty)," *Byloe*, no. 4 (1906), pp. 18–33; N. A. Troitskii, "Degaevshchina," *Voprosy istorii*, no. 3 (1976), pp. 125–133; and A. Ulam, *In the Name of the People* (New York, 1977), pp. 380–389.

18. For the assassination of Sudeikin, see Sedov, *Geroicheskii period*, p. 339; "Ubiistvo podp. Sudeikina (iz arkhiva V. L. Burtseva)," *Na chuzhoi storone*, vol. IX (1925), pp. 205–219. These latter documents include confessions of participants Konoshevich and Starodvorskii.

19. Degaev made his way to the United States where, under the name of Dr. Alexander Pell, he became a professor of mathematics in South Dakota. See HI, Nicolaevsky Archives, no. 184, folder 9.

20. AGAD, PWIS, 1884, 980, l. 265. Other Russian members of the Proletariat, Mikhail Luri and P. Bardovskii (as well as S. Kunicki), were similarly linked to the Sudeikin killing. Ibid., ll. 258–259. Kon described Rechniewski's stay in Warsaw directly before the Sudeikin killing. Kon, *Narodziny*, p. 52.

21. Kunicki explained to the police that the "Degaevshchina" "in a fatal way, changed the course of his life." He began to think "only about in which form to best express his protest against the existing police system." AGAD, PWIS, 1884, 977, ll. 56–57.

22. B. Szapiro (Besem), *Tadeusz Rechniewski*, p. 30.

23. I. Popov, "Revoliutsionnye organizatsii," *Narodovol'tsy posle l-go marta*, p. 59.

24. Krzywicki, *Wspomnienia*, vol. II, p. 157.

25. For police reaction to the "Degaevshchina" see V. Novitskii, *Iz vospominanii zhandarma*, p. 21.

26. Shebalin, "Peterburgskaia narodovol'cheskaia organizatsiia," *Narodovol'tsy posle l-go marta*, pp. 46–47.

27. Popov wrote, "The committee of our group was extraordinarily interested in the talks between the Proletariatczycy and the *narodovol'tsy*." I. Popov, "Revoliutsionnye organizatsii," *Narodovol'tsy posle l-go marta*, p. 61.

28. Ibid., pp. 59–60.

29. Ibid., p. 62.

30. Ludwik Bazylow is skeptical of the services of the Proletariat to the Russians. "This 'help' for Narodnaia Volia or any other revolutionary organizations in Russia had — it seems, unfortunately — a rather more declarative nature, at least in the majority of instances." Bazylow, *Działalność narodnictwa rosyjskiego*, p. 235. Indeed, aside from the "Degaevshchina," the influence of propagandists among the Workers' Section, and the Proletariat printing operations in Warsaw for *Narodnaia volia*, active especially in 1883, little other help is recorded. For the printing operations see Volk, *Narodnaia*

volia, p. 416; and L. Baumgarten, "Cenny dokument z dziejów 'Proletariatu' i 'Narodnej woli,'" reprint from *Biuletyn Żydowskiego Instytutu Historycznego*, no. 24, pp. 30–34.

31. See W. Jodko-Narkiewicz, *Geschichte der sozialistischen Bewegung in Polen*, p. 12.

32. Kon, *Narodziny*, p. 66.

33. Letter from Bardovskii's mother to her youngest son 13 January 1886. Quoted in Szapiro, *Tadeusz Rechniewski*, pp. 66–67.

34. M. Mańkowski, *U stóp szubienicy* (Kraków, 1905), p. 37.

35. *Khronika*, p. 267.

36. Kon, *Narodziny*, p. 71.

37. AGAD, PWIS, 1884, 980, ll. 86–87, 92.

38. For the detailed titles in the library see AGAD, PWIS, 1884, 977, l. 98.

39. Kon, *Narodziny*, p. 72.

40. That Bardovskii was not a member of the Proletariat is confirmed by the police. AGAD, PWIS, 1884, 977, l. 99.

41. *Khronika*, p. 272.

42. Stepurin was the primary source of funds for the Proletariat from Narodnaia Volia. AGAD, PWIS, 1884, 977, l. 108. This report indicates that Luri received 200 rubles from Stepurin which he passed on to Bardovskii's wife, N. Poll, who turned it over to the Proletariat.

43. AGAD, PWIS, 1884, 977, l. 99. See Ingel'strom's deposition in TsGAOR, f. 102, op. 168, d. 10a (1886), ll. 214–219.

44. Ibid., ll. 13–19; AGAD, PWIS, 1884, 977, l. 99. Also in "Archiwum Bardowskiego," *ZPW*, 1960, pp. 80–84.

45. "Towarzysze," *Przedświt*, no. 3 (1885), pp. 4–6.

46. The career of Marceli Janczewski is especially crucial in this netherland of secret printing operations, the procurement and maintenance of full sets of type, the transfer of funds, and the shipment of illegal material. In 1880–81, Janczewski helped establish a Black Partition underground press in Minsk, moving the press to Grodno and Vilna when the police got too close. In 1882, he moved his headquarters to Vitebsk and in October of that year, became an agent of Narodnaia Volia after meeting with Vera Figner in Kharkov. Before Figner's arrest, he was the intermediary between Waryński and the Russian *narodovol'tsy* leadership. After the Kharkov arrests of the spring 1883, Janczewski moved his headquarters again, this time to Vilna where a Polish-Jewish socialist community centered around the Rabbinical Institute served as a clearinghouse for the transportation of illegal materials. Janczewski provided Waryński with a set of Polish type from Grodno, helped the Proletariat establish a lottery in Łódź, and arranged for the technical side of printing *Narodnaia volia* in Warsaw. He received money from the provocateur Degaev to reestablish a St. Petersburg press and he negotiated with the leaders of the Workers' Section about their own periodical. At the same time, Janczewski can be considered the leader of the Grodno, Vitebsk, Minsk, and Vilna *narodovol'tsy* organizations, all of which leaned towards a more Polish, that is Proletariat-style, concept of revolutionary activities. TsGIA, SSSR, f. 1405,

op. 85, d. 10807, ll. 168–188; AGAD, PWIS, 1884, 977, l. 70. For Janczewski and Jewish *narodovol'tsy* contacts with the Proletariat, see also Krzywicki, *Wspomnienia*, vol. II, pp. 49–50; V. A. Bodaev, "N. M. Flerov i 'podgotovitel'-naia gruppa partii Narodnoi voli,'" *Narodovol'tsy 80-kh i 90-kh godov*, p. 21; and Baumgarten, "Cenny dokument," *Biuletyn Ż.I.H.*, no. 24, p. 30.

47. The police report that the initiative for the negotiations with the Paris Russians came from Rechniewski: AGAD, PWIS, 1884, 977, l. 77.

48. Dłuski and Piekarski left *Przedświt* as a result of their minority position in the beginning of 1884. Especially Piekarski grew closer to Limanowski. When Jankowska reported to Limanowski the final agreement of Narodnaia Volia and the Proletariat in the summer of 1884, Piekarski was with Limanowski. "Piekarski was quiet," wrote Limanowski, "and was drawing something on paper — he had a talent for sketching. Someone picked up the drawing and showed it. It was Narodnaia Volia which pulled up the strings of the Polish socialist personalities portrayed as dolls." Limanowski, *Pamiętniki (1870–1907)*, pp. 318–319.

49. "Prospekt 'Walka Klas'," AZHP, 305, I, 1.

50. Kon, *Narodziny*, p. 35.

51. A. Dębski, "Wspomnienia o Kunickim i Bardowskim," *ZPW* (London, 1904), p. 82. At his trial Kunicki affirmed his support of the assassination of Alexander II, saying, "You may try us, you may convict us, we die with the feeling of having done our duty." A. Dębski, "Stanisław Kunicki," *Światło*, no. 5 (1899), p. 6.

52. A jealous Tikhomirov wrote that the émigré Poles were considerably more active than the Russians in European circles. He maintained as well that he could seldom get any accurate information about the Congress Kingdom movement from the *Przedświt* and *Walka Klas* editors: *Vospominaniia L'va Tikhomirova*, pp. 319, 322.

53. The document was entitled "General principles of the program and organizational activities of the Central Committee of the Social Revolutionary Party 'Proletariat.' Proclamation to the Executive Committee of the Party 'Narodnaia Volia,'" *Walka Klas*, no. 6 (1884), pp. 19–21.

54. Ibid., p. 20.

55. *Vestnik "Narodnoi voli,"* no. 2 (1884), p. 181. Emphasis added.

56. "Odpowiedż Komitetu wykonawczego partii 'Narodnaia volia,'" *Walka Klas*, no. 6 (1884), p. 21. Both the "Odpowiedż" and the "General Principles" were also published in *Narodnaia volia*, no. 10 (1884), *Literatura "Narodnoi voli,"* pp. 677–681. In addition to Tikhomirov's negative disposition to Poles and Polish socialism, German Lopatin, who signed the agreement for Narodnaia Volia, was reported to have had doubts about the Poles. Dębski, "Wspomnienia," *ZPW* (London, 1904), pp. 89–90.

57. *Wielki Proletariat — Materiały i dokumenty z historii ruchu robot- niczego w Polsce* (Warsaw, 1950), pp. 179–182.

58. The idea of combining Russian and Polish forces did not totally disappear. Dębski wrote that after the agreement the Poles considered reorganizing both movements on the basis of function: on the one hand an all-empire

terrorist central with local committees, and on the other, an all-empire propagandist central with similar local committees. The locals would be run by the Proletariat in the Congress Kingdom; in Russia the *narodovol'tsy* would have control. The centrals would be bilaterally administered. Lopatin first completely rejected the idea, then later considered it too difficult to implement. Dębski, "Wspomnienia," *ZPW* (London, 1904), pp. 89–90.

59. Approximately 500 *narodovol'tsy* were arrested as a result of the material found on Lopatin. TsGIA, SSSR, f. 1405, op. 530, d. 1079, l. 131.

60. Plokhotskii [L. Wasilewski], *Vzaimnyia otnosheniia pol'skikh i russkikh sotsialistov* (London, 1902), p. 8.

61. AGAD, PWIS, 1884, 977, l. 12; 976, l. 14.

62. A. Próchnik, "Ideologia Proletariatu," *KRRP* (1936), p. 8.

63. See Kon, *Narodziny*, p. 63.

64. K. Kelles-Krauz, "Polscy i rosyjscy socjaliści," *Pisma wybrane*, vol. II (Warsaw, 1962), pp. 107–108. Wasilewski also uses this argument in support of his PPS position, *Vzaimnyia otnosheniia*, pp. 12–24.

65. *Vospominaniia L'va Tikhomirova*, p. 321.

66. Dejcz, "Pionerzy," *ZPW* (1930), p. 77.

Chapter 9. *The Last Stage: Bohuszewiczówna, Ulrych, and Terror*

1. The account of Waryński's arrest and the contents of both the package and the letter are in AGAD, WGZŻ, no. 6, ll. 5–6, 8, and AGAD, PWIS, 1884, 966, ll. 48–52.

2. AGAD, PWIS, 1884, 974, l. 96.

3. K. Pietkiewicz, "Michał Mancewicz," *Niepodległość* (1931), p. 231.

4. TsGAOR, f. 102, op. 168, 1884, d. 7, "Svod," ll. 9–10.

5. *Kółka*, p. 888; AGAD, PWIS, 1886, 1264, ll. 211–212.

6. *Pamiętnik — Bohuszewiczówna*, p. 32.

7. Ibid.

8. The prosecutor wrote, "The party had a mass of books and brochures of legal as well as social revolutionary content, stored at [the home of] the accused, Maria Bohuszewicz." AGAD, PWIS, 1884, 976, l. 10. On no. 6, *Proletariat*, see ibid., l. 3; on the charters see "Sektsionnyi kassy, utverzhdennyi na sobranii Ts. K., 19 Aprelia 1885 goda," AGAD, PWIS, 1886, 1248, l. 5.

9. *Kółka*, pp. 887–888.

10. AGAD, PWIS, 1884, 918, contains the first archival mention of his socialist activities.

11. *Kółka*, p. 897.

12. According to the police, despite "an entire series of rather serious arrests" illegal printed material still was pouring into the Congress Kingdom, St. Petersburg, and Vilna under the supervision of Mendelson in Paris and border area Jewish "kontrabandistii." TsGAOR, f. 102, op. 168, d. 10a (1886), l. 327.

13. *Kółka*, pp. 890, 897. Baumgarten disputes the prosecutor's report on this issue, asserting, with insufficient evidence, that no Blanquist solution to

the party's organizational structure was offered by Ulrych. Since this is the only extant document on the Ulrych period, Baumgarten's denial is only a guess.

14. *Khronika*, p. 35. For an excellent statement on the functioning of the judicial-administrative system, see A. F. Koni, "Vospominaniia o dele Very Zasulich," *Sobranie sochinenii*, vol. II (Moscow, 1966), pp. 332–334.

15. *Pis'ma Pobedonostseva k Aleksandru III*, vol. II, p. 140. *Khronika*, p. 36.

16. See Appendix: table 56, p. 237.

17. Examples of these cases are in AGAD, PWIS, 1883, 862–863; 1884, 962. The extraordinary thoroughness of the prosecutor's office is revealed most obviously in these isolated cases of individuals completely devoid of any revolutionary ties. When, for instance, illiterate shtetl Jews received a Yiddish socialist newspaper from New York, the authorities doggedly pursued the case until the governor-general himself halted the investigation. AGAD, PWIS, 1884, 954, ll. 6–12.

18. *Dnevnik Polovtsova*, vol. I, p. 244.

19. See R. Arskii, "Iz istorii 'Proletariata'," *KL* (1923), p. 60; F. Kon, *Narodziny*, pp. 56–57.

20. The most serious case of police provocation was that of Edmund Baranowski, who, as a police agent, helped to form the Fighting Squad and spurred it on to increase its terrorist activities.

21. In their enthusiasm the three sometimes worked at cross-purposes, to the benefit of the movement. Numerous calls for unity among these three branches of government — the police, the gendarmerie, and the judiciary — reflected the fact of disunity and lack of coordination. AGAD, PWIS, 1884, 966, ll. 179–189; 973, ll. 238–239.

22. Pacanowski, for instance, felt that Kunicki's devotion to terrorism derived completely from the shock he experienced when he discovered that his socialist mentor and friend, Sergei Degaev, was an agent. See "Zeznanie Pacanowskiego," *ZPW* (London, 1904), pp. 217–234.

23. Details of the correspondence between Warsaw and St. Petersburg on the best manner to try the arrested members of the Proletariat is ably recounted in Baumgarten, *Dzieje*, pp. 597–608. See also Rechniewski's letter to his parents, 23 Feb. 1885, which explained the ministerial hierarchy of responsibility in his case: Szapiro (Besem), *Tadeusz Rechniewski*, p. 45.

24. The regional prosecutor's recommendations for administrative action were passed on to a joint Ministry of Interior–Ministry of Justice committee, whose actions were mostly automatically accepted by the Minister of Interior, in this case Dmitri Tolstoi.

25. "Sprawozdanie z procesu przeciwko 29 oskarżonym przed sądem wojennym w Warszawie," *Walka Klas*, no. 8, 9, 10 (1886), pp. 7–34. See also *ZPW* (Geneva, 1886), pp. 155–163; *ZPW* (London, 1904), pp. 205–208.

26. Administrative action relieved Luri and Schmaus of their sentences; on 27 January 1886, the Russians hanged the others.

27. AGAD, DKGW, 1886–1887, 44, ll. 2–4. The entire verdict of the

military tribunal is in AGAD, PWIS, 1884, 973, ll. 315–368. See also L. Vasilevskii [Wasilewski], "'Proletariat' pered sudom," *Byloe,* no. 7 (1906), pp. 257–282.

28. "Material o shlisselburgskikh zakliuchenykh," HI, Nicolaevsky Archives, no. 122, box 2, folder 11.

29. Dębski, "Wspomnienia," *ZPW* (London, 1904), p. 90.

30. AGAD, PWIS, 1884, 974, ll. 39–40.

31. For the fate of the Proletariat socialists, including reports from prison officials on their behavior and the rules governing their limited prison rights, see AGAD, DKGW, 1885, 265, ref. 1, ll. 1–350. The rules are in ibid., ll. 20–21. AGAD, WGZŻ, no. 9, ll. 56–63, contains several original letters which express the great solidarity among the revolutionary prisoners. See also the collection "Perepiska 'Proletariata'," AGAD, PWIS, 1884, 980, ll. 1–416. Bolesław Onufrowicz describes the fate of the Proletariat members in Siberia in "V mestakh otdalennyia (vospominaniia administrativnogo)," *Minuvshie gody,* no. 8 (1908), p. 285.

32. See Kon's letter to his brother of 3 July 1885 (o.s.), AGAD, PWIS, 1884, 974, ll. 36–37. See also Kon's statement to the police, ibid., 977, ll. 72–73.

33. Zofia z Grabskich Kirkor-Kiedroniowa, *Wspomnienia,* vol. I, maszynopis, Biblioteka Narodowa (National Library), rps. sygn. IV-6399, p. 49.

34. *Bohaterowie 'Proletariatu,'* p. 31.

35. AGAD, PWIS, 1884, 974, ll. 36–37.

36. The defendants after a long discussion agreed to speak at the trial in Polish and not in Russian. Their testimonies, including that of Waryński, were geared to address Polish society as well as the court. M. Mańkowski, *U stóp szubienicy* (Kraków, 1905), p. 24.

37. Waryński's speech is in H. Bicz, *Proletariat: Pierwsza socjalnorewolucyjna partia w Polsce* (Moscow, 1934), pp. 35–37.

38. *Bohaterowie 'Proletariatu',* pp. 31–32. See also *Przedświt,* no. 1 (1886), pp. 1–3; "Od towarzyszy, skazanych w Grudniu, 1885," *ZPW* (Geneva, 1886), pp. 170–180.

39. R. Luxemburg, *Pamięci "Proletariatu"* (Warsaw, 1922), p. 58. L. Blit, *The Origins of Polish Socialism: The History and Ideas of the First Polish Socialist Party* (Cambridge, Eng., 1971), pp. 104–131.

40. F. Kon, *Narodziny wieku,* p. 27.

41. L. Krzywicki, *Wspomnienia,* vol. II, p. 33.

42. Ibid., p. 282. Krzywicki adds here that Waryński was interested primarily in "economic" terror.

43. L. Dejcz, "Pionerzy," pp. 51–52.

44. U. Haustein, *Sozialismus und nationale Frage in Polen,* p. 49.

45. L. Baumgarten, *Dzieje,* p. 41.

46. T. G. Snytko, *Russkoe narodnichestvo i pol'skoe obshchestvennoe dvizhenie, 1865–1881 gg.* (Moscow, 1969), pp. 428–429. Emphasis added.

47. See A. Próchnik, "Ideologia 'Proletariatu'," *KRRP,* no. 1 (5) (1936), p. 15.

48. "O zamachach," *Przedświt,* no. 2 (1884), pp. 1–2.

49. "Przegląd krajowy," *Proletariat,* p. 24.

50. "Notatka redakcyna . . . ," "Archiwum Bardowskiego," *ZPW,* no. 1 (9) (1960), pp. 84–85.

51. AGAD, PWIS, 1884, 977, 1. 32.

52. "Rok 1885," *Przedświt,* no. 12 (1885), p. 2.

53. AGAD, PWIS, 1884, 977, 1. 37.

54. *Walka Klas,* no. 4 (1884), p. 6.

55. "O Terrorze," *Przedświt,* no. 2 (1886), ll. 2–3.

56. The party accused Mehle of bringing the provocateur Skrzypczyński into the party. Either Mehle was to kill the traitor, or he himself "could expect similar punishment." AGAD, PWIS, 1884, 977, 1. 49.

57. A. Dębski, *Krwawe zajście w mleczarni Henneberga w roku 1884* (Warsaw, 1924), pp. 18–19.

58. AGAD, PWIS, 1884, 977, 1. 49.

59. For a police copy of the declaration see AGAD, PWIS, 1884, 980, 1. 201.

60. The investigating gendarme authorities concluded that the Piński verdict was passed by Proletariat members in prison. AGAD, WGZŻ, 1887, no. 9, ll. 39–40, ll. 51–57.

61. AGAD, PWIS, 1887, 1264, 1. 893.

62. AGAD, PWIS, 1886, 1176, 1. 29.

63. Hipszer and Kowalewski were sentenced by a military tribunal. AGAD, PWIS, 1886, 1264, ll. 896–897.

64. Haustein, *Sozialismus und nationale Frage,* p. 49.

65. B. Sławiński, "Niedoszły zamach na gen.-gub. Hurkę," *KRRP,* no. 1 (1936), p. 42.

66. AGAD, PWIS, 1884, 977, ll. 54–55.

67. [B. A. Jędrzejowski], "Ludwik Waryński," *Bohaterowie,* p. 20.

68. AGAD, PWIS, 1884, 977, 1. 36.

69. "Protokół Pacanowskiego," *ZPW* (London, 1904), p. 227.

70. HI, Okhrana Archives, index no. xiv, folder 12A, p. 2. Ksawery Kieffer, a Proletariat member, also mentions plans on the life of Alexander II in AGAD, PWIS, 1884, 980, ll. 103–104.

71. AGAD, PWIS, 1884, 976, 1. 15.

72. Ż. Kormanowa, "Zamach na Aleksandra III w Warszawie," *ZPW,* no. 3 (1963), pp. 110–122.

73. L. Baumgarten, "Czy partia Proletariat organizowała zamach na cara," *ZPW,* no. 4 (1963), pp. 110–122.

74. J. Krzesławski, "Tragiczne losy robotnika-proletaryatczyka (Piotr Dąbrowski, szewc warszawski)," *KRRP,* no. 1 (1936), p. 36.

75. AZHP, 305, I, 1, z. 2, p. 14.

76. AZHP, 305, I, 1, z. 13.

77. AGAD, DKGW, referat I, 1886–87, no. 44, 1. 37. See Dębski's recounting of the incident in *Krwawe zajście,* pp. 18–19. One policeman was wounded. AGAD, PWIS, 1884, 977, ll. 6–7.

78. Dębski, *Krwawa zajście,* p. 8.

79. Ibid.

80. AGAD, PWIS, 1884, 977, l. 37.
81. F. Kon, *Narodziny wieku,* pp. 59–61.
82. AGAD, PWIS, 1884, 977, l. 37.
83. Ibid., ll. 31–32.
84. AGAD, PWIS, 1884, 974, l. 89.
85. AGAD, PWIS, 1884, 977, l. 22.
86. Ibid., ll. 22–23.
87. "Turskii to Burtsev (letters 1924–1925)," HI, Nicolaevsky Archives, no. 211, folder 2, letter 1.

Chapter 10. *Epilogue: The Years of Transition in Polish Politics: 1886–1887*

1. *Khronika,* p. 305.
2. L. Kulczycki, *Dokoła mego życia,* p. 144.
3. TsGIA, SSSR, f. 1405, op. 92, d. 10951, prilozh. 1, l. 58.
4. *Khronika,* p. 305.
5. S. Valk, "Iz arkhiva V. Ia. Bogucharskogo: K biografii L. Varynskogo," *KS,* no. 3 (1927), p. 101.
6. "Walka klas i zmniejszenie dnia roboczego," *Przedświt,* no. 2 (1886), p. 1.
7. "W kwestii programu minimum," *Walka Klas,* no. 4 (1887), p. 1.
8. "Czy jesteśmy patriotami," *Walka Klas,* no. 4 (1887), p. 4.
9. *Walka Klas,* no. 1 (1887), p. 6.
10. The letter ended with a new slogan, "Freedom with bread, bread with freedom!" AGAD, WGZŻ, 1886, no. 9, ll. 37–38.
11. L. Kulczycki and few other students began serious socialist activities in 1886. See Kulczycki, *Dokoła mego życia,* p. 87. Kulczycki was arrested in Warsaw in 1888 for "propaganda among workers." TsGIA, SSSR, f. 1405, op. 92, d. 10919, l. 620.
12. One indication of the serious hiatus of socialist activity in the Congress Kingdom is that not one brochure or proclamation resides in the *Przedświt* archives for the years between 1886 and 1890. AZHP, 305, I, 1.
13. A large number of 1878–1886 socialists later became involved in nationalist activities. It should be noted as well that these "apostates" generally came from student-intelligentsia ranks. See Appendix: tables 50–54, pp. 235–236.
14. Czekanowski, *W domu niewoli,* pp. 103–104. Czekanowski writes with particular acumen about the years 1886–1887. As an acquaintance of both many socialists and new patriots, including the young Dmowski, he relates an atmosphere of searching and discussion, sympathy with socialism but commitment to national unity, and intense discussions between friends and acquaintances from both camps. Czekanowski also writes that all of Warsaw "even those negatively disposed toward socialism . . . were moved" by the trial and sentencing of Proletariat members. Ibid., pp. 57, 95, 103–105. See also Offenberg, *Stan umysłów,* p. 13.
15. "Z naszych stron," *PT,* no. 17 (1885), p. 205.

16. "Życie społeczne," *Prawda*, no. 3 (1886), pp. 27–29.
17. *Prawda*, no. 43 (1886), p. 509.
18. *Prawda*, no. 3 (1886), pp. 28–29.
19. Ibid., p. 28.
20. *Prawda*, no. 42 (1886), p. 495.
21. "Polityka: Etyka samolubstwa," *Prawda*, no. 12 (1886), pp. 158–519.
22. "Prospekt," *Głos*, kwartal IV (1886), p. 1.
23. S. Żeromski, *Dzienniki*, vol. III (Warsaw, 1964), p. 131.
24. "Prospekt," *Głos*, kwartal IV (1886), p. 1.
25. "Nasze pisma," *Głos*, no. 5 (1886), p. 1.
26. Other Głosites included A. Więckowski, M. Brzeziński, Z. Heryng, J. Hłasko, and A. Dygasiński, all of whom to some extent were involved in the development of the Proletariat.
27. "Antysemityzm i sprawa żydowska," *Głos*, no. 6 (1886), pp. 1–2.
28. "Antysemityzm i sprawa żydowska," *Głos*, no. 4 (1886), pp. 51–52.
29. B. Limanowski, *Pamiętniki (1870–1907)*, p. 335.
30. L. Kulczycki, *Dokoła mego życia*, p. 102.
31. Quoted in Mazowiecki [Kulczycki], *Historia*, p. 122.
32. Spector [Erazm Piltz], *Nasze stronnictwa skrajne* (Kraków, 1903), p. 9.
33. P. Brock, *W zaraniu ruchu ludowego* (London, 1956), p. 20. See also Krzywicki, *Wspomnienia*, vol. II, pp. 106–107; O. A. Narkiewicz, *The Green Flag: Polish Populist Politics* (London, 1976), p. 43.
34. W. Pobóg-Malinowski, *Narodowa demokracja 1887–1918: Fakty i dokumenty* (Warsaw, 1933), p. 36.
35. S. Kozicki, *Historia Ligi Narodowej* (London, 1964), pp. 46–47.
36. TsGIA, SSSR, f. 1405, op. 521, d. 438, l. 95.
37. Żeromski, *Dzienniki*, vol. III, p. 135.
38. Pobóg-Malinowski, *Narodowa demokracja*, pp. 37–38.
39. Ibid., p. 38.
40. Ibid., p. 44.
41. Large segments of the program are quoted in ibid., pp. 48–52, followed by an interesting discussion of the newer 1888 program much more oriented towards the "nation" and less concerned with "independence."
42. Mazowiecki [Kulczycki], *Historia*, p. 121.
43. The police were genuinely at a loss to describe Zet's ideology. In one report, the organization was accused of trying to set up an independent Poland "on the bases of social democracy." TsGIA, SSSR, f. 1405, op. 521, d. 439, l. 285. In general, at the end of the 1880s, the police were less well-informed about patriotic activities than about the remaining socialists. On what they call the "patriotic party" see ibid., ll. 93–127.
44. Quoted in Kozicki, *Historia Ligi Narodowej*, pp. 39–40.
45. The reason for this shift towards economism, the authorities astutely noted, was that the workers' groups themselves wanted nothing to do with a terrorist underground organization or, for that matter, with politics. Especially the Związek, wrote the prosecutor with considerable satisfaction, "did not pursue especially dangerous revolutionary goals" and was devoted to the

strike as the "single means" to achieve its primary goal, "the gradual improvement of the life of workers." TsGIA SSSR, f. 1405, op. 92, d. 10951, prilozh. 1, l. 25. For the Second Proletariat and the Związek see ibid., ll. 1–69.
46. U. Haustein, *Sozialismus und nationale Frage in Polen,* p. 57.
47. W. Pobóg-Malinowski, *Narodowa demokracja,* p. 10.
48. See Appendix: table 50, p. 235.
49. A. Dębski to P. Lapin, April 1896, HI, Okhrana Archives, index no. XIX, folder 7.
50. Quoted in F. Perl, *Dzieje,* p. viii.
51. J. Piłsudski, *Jak stałem się socjalistą* (Lwów, 1903), p. 3.

Appendix

1. AGAD, PWIS, 1878–1888, nos. 218–1447. This study would have been considerably more difficult without the use of an alphabetized list of revolutionaries and short biographical sketches in *Kółka socjalistyczne, Gminy i Wielki Proletariat: Procesy polityczne 1878–1888,* ed. Leon Baumgarten (Warsaw, 1966), pp. 1056–1135. Also useful in accumulating data on individual revolutionaries was *Deiateli revoliutsionnogo dvizheniia v Rossii: Bio-bibliograficheskii slovar'* (Moscow, 1929–1933), vol. II, parts 1–4 and vol. III [incomplete], parts 1–2. For comparative statistics on the Russian movement, see I. Avakumovic, "A Statistical Approach to the Revolutionary Movement in Russia, 1878–1887," *The American Slavic and East European Review,* April (1959), pp. 182–186. See also the Soviet critical reworking of Avakumovic's basic approach, V. S. Antonov, "K voprosu o sotsial'nom sostave i chislennosti revoliutsionerov 70-kh godov," *Obshchestvennoe dvizhenie v poreformennoi Rossii* (Moscow, 1965), pp. 336–365. Finally, see N. I. Sidorov, "Statisticheskie svedeniia o propagandistakh 70-kh godov v obrabotke III otdeleniia," *Katorga i ssylka,* no. 1 (38) (1928), pp. 27–58. Further statistical information is available in *Narodnaia volia,* no. 4 (1880), pp. 354–356 and *Narodnaia volia,* no. 4 (1880), pp. 315–322, in *Literatura partii "Narodnoi voli,"* ed. V. I. Bogucharskii. M. G. Sedov, *Geroicheskii period rev. narodnichestva* (Moscow, 1966), p. 361. Avakumovic's and Antonov's works, upon which I most heavily rely, are statistical abstracts from the unfortunately only partly published *Deiateli revoliutsionnogo dvizheniia v Rossii;* vol. II, parts I–IV, on revolutionaries of the seventies is published in complete form, but of vol. III, only parts 1 and 2, A–Z of the Russian alphabet, were published. The authors also make use of biographical data on 1,083 revolutionaries in *La Chronique du Mouvement Socialiste en Russie 1878–1887* (St. Petersburg, 1890).

2. There is no question that some of those listed for arrest were not socialists. There is even less question that not all socialists were listed for arrest or indicted. Rashkovskii, in another study of this type on the Polish socialists, estimates that from the 1860s to the 1880s there were at least 1,012 socialists in all of the partitions of Poland. This number is clearly too low. E. V. Rashkovskii, "Pol'skie revoliutsionnye demokraty i pervye pol'skie sotsialisty k voprosu o dialektike revoliutsionnogo protsessa 60-kh-80-kh godov XIX v,"

Sviazi revoliutsionerov Rossii i Pol'shi v XIX-nachala XX v (Moscow, 1968), pp. 313–331. See also S. Kalabiński, "Członkowie kółek socjalistycznych, gmin i socjalno-rewolucyjnej partii 'Proletariat' w świetle badań ankietowych," *Polska klasa robotnicza,* vol. VI, pp. 7–62.

3. A.F. = absolute frequency, A.F.% = adjusted frequency percentage, that is, the percentage of the sample known.

4. In 1892 the population of the Congress Kingdom broke down into 75.53 percent Catholic; 13.90 percent Jewish; 5.02 percent Orthodox; and 5.46 percent Protestant. *Opis ziem zamieszkanych przez Polaków,* vol. II, "Królestwo Polskie" (Warsaw, 1904), p. 12.

1897	C.K.	Eur. Russia	Empire
Orthodox	6.47%	81.71%	69.35%
Roman Catholic	74.80%	4.65%	9.13%
Jewish	14.05%	4.06%	4.15%
Lutheran	4.41%	3.30%	2.84%

Obshchii svod 1897, vol. I, part 1, p. xv. Of 2,238 revolutionaries arrested from 1873 to 1880 in Russia, 75 percent were Orthodox, 12 percent Catholic, 2.4 percent Protestant, and 4.3 percent Jewish. "K statistike gosudarstvennykh prestuplenii v Rossii," part 2, *Narodnaia volia,* no. 5 (1881), *Literatura,* ed. Bogucharskii, p. 356.

5. In general statistics, though not in police statistics, Jews and Protestants often registered by nationality as Poles and Russians. The 1882 Warsaw census records the following religious and nationality composition of Warsaw:

Orthodox	3.56%	Russian	4.05%
Catholic	58.26%	Pole	90.66%
Protestant	4.60%	German	2.01%
Jewish	33.40%	Jew	2.62%

Rezultaty spisu jednodniowego Warszawy 1882, part 1, pp. 28, 38. In 1883 the Congress Kingdom was 11.83 percent Jewish, 5.8 percent German, 72.1 percent Polish. Łódź itself was more than 40 percent German. See also "A. L.," "Alarmujące cyfry," *Prawda,* no. 50 (1886), p. 582; F. Sulimierski, "Notatka statystyczna," *Ognisko,* p. 61; "Przegląd statystyczny," *PT,* no. 51 (1883), p. 640. By mother tongue the empire (in 1897) broke down into 66.8 percent East Slavic, 6.3 percent Polish, 4.0 percent Jewish, and 1.4 percent German. Of 2,238 arrested in the Russian movement between 1875 and 1880, 56 percent were Great Russian, 19.7 percent Ukrainians, 15 percent Poles, and 4 percent Belorussians. "Stat.," part 2, *Narodnaia volia,* no. 5 (1881), p. 355. Avakumovic, "Statistical Approach," *Slavic Review,* April (1959), pp. 182–183.

6. The 1897 census records the following breakdown of nationality by estate.

	Hereditary Nobles	Personal Nobles
Empire	1,200,000	630,000
Russians	640,000	510,000
Jews	196	3,400
Poles	350,000	62,000

	Townspeople	Peasants
Empire	13,400,000	96,900,000
Russians	6,200,000	72,400,000
Jews	4,800,000	200,000
Poles	1,200,000	6,200,000

Obshchii svod 1897, vol. I, part 1, p. 374.

7. In 1897, Jews in the empire were 38.9 percent literate, Catholics 32.1 percent literate, and Orthodox 19 percent literate. *Obshchii svod 1897,* vol. I, part 1, p. 4.

8. I.P. — Industrial proletariat. See Table 36 and note 23.

9. Of 379 revolutionaries arrested from 1 Jan. to 31 July 1879, 92 percent were male. "Stat.," *Narodnaia volia,* no. 4 (1880), p. 316. Of 1,611 revolutionaries arrested between 1873 and 1877, 85 percent were male. N. I. Sidorov, "Statisticheskie svedeniia," *KS,* no. 1 (38) (1928), p. 29.

10. For statistics on the Russian movement, see Avakumovic, p. 183. According to the 1897 census:

	Cong. King.	Eur. Russia	Empire
Peasant	72.98%	84.16%	77.12%
Noble	1.91%	1.47%	1.47%
Town	23.53%	10.65%	10.66%

Obshchii svod 1897, vol. I, part 1, p. 3.

11. Only those *gubernii* are listed which record 10 or more revolutionaries.

12. The *gubernii* of the Congress Kingdom were: Warsaw, Kalisz, Kielce, Łomża, Piotrków, Płock, Radom, Suwałki, and Siedlce. The *gubernii* of the western borderlands were Kovno, Vilna, Grodno, Minsk, Mogilev, Vitebsk; the southwestern borderlands *gubernii* were Kiev, Podolia, and Volhynia. The largest percentages of Polish population not in the Congress Kingdom were found in the following *gubernii* (1897).

Gub.	Entire Population	Poles	% Poles
Grodno	1,615,815	471,817	29.20
Vilna	1,591,912	375,691	23.60
Minsk	2,156,343	288,949	13.40
Volhynia	2,999,346	316,230	10.61
Podolia	3,031,040	304,619	10.05
Vitebsk	1,502,895	100,840	6.71
Mogilev	1,707,613	76,359	4.46
Kiev	3,564,433	126,537	3.55
Kovno	1,549,972	49,754	3.21
Total	19,719,369	2,100,796	10.60%

Opis ziem, vol. II, pp. 13–14.

In 1902 the Polish population was:

Congress Kingdom	7,300,000
Western and southwestern *gubernii*	2,220,000
Other *gubernii*	400,000
Austrian Emp.	3,665,000
Prussia	3,510,335

Ibid., p. 15. The population of European Russia was in general more stable than that of the Congress Kingdom. Ninety-two percent of the Russian population remained in the *gub.* in which they were born while 87 percent of Congress Kingdom population did. *Obshchii svod.,* vol. I, part 1, p. xx.

The geography of the Russian movement was very different. Of 2,238 revolutionaries arrested between 1875 and 1880, 337 — 15.1 percent — were born in the 10 *gub.* of the Congress Kingdom. Other large representative *gub.* were Iaroslav — 101, Petersburg — 85, Kursk — 84, Kherson — 77, Viatsk — 76, Saratov — 76, Orel — 71, and Samara — 68. The Belorussian region (Kovno, Grodno, Vilna, Vitebsk, Minsk, and Mogilev) had only 91 revolutionaries — 4 percent of the total. The Ukrainian, Moldavian, and Black Sea *gubernii* of Kherson, Poltava, Kharkov, Ekaterinoslav, Chernigov, Kiev, Taurida, Podolia, Volhynia, and Bessarabia had 440 — 19.7 percent. The Great Russian central *gub.* accounted for 545 — 24.5 percent and the Great Russian border *gub.* for 453 — 20.3 percent. Sidorov's sample of 760 (out of 1,054) of the 1870s yields yet different results. Most revolutionaries came from Samara — 49, Vilna — 40, Penza — 35, Tula — 32, and St. Petersburg — 29. Sidorov, "Stat.," *KS,* no. 1 (38) (1928), pp. 53–54. Avakumovic's sample (453/1,083) from 1878–1887 runs, Kherson — 53, Poltava — 28, Kiev — 23, St. Petersburg — 22, Warsaw — 22, Podolia — 19, Moscow — 18, and Volhynia — 16. Avakumovic, "Stat.," *Slavic Review,* April (1959), p. 183.

13. In 1897, the literacy rate of the empire was 21.2 percent, European Russia — 22.9 percent, and the Congress Kingdom — 30.5 percent. Seven out of the ten Congress Kingdom *gubernii* recorded literacy rates above 25 percent. Excluding the Estonian and Latvian *gubernii,* the highest literacy of *gubernii* were: (1) St. Petersburg — 55.1 percent, (2) Kovno — 41.9 percent, (3) Moscow — 40.2 percent, (4) Iaroslav — 36.2 percent, (5) Grodno — 29.2 percent, and (6) Vilna — 28.8 percent. All of these *gubernii* contributed significant numbers of revolutionaries to the Russian and Polish movement. *Obshchii svod* 1897, vol. I, part 2, p. 38.

14. The western and southwestern borderland *gubernii* had predominantly peasant populations: Lithuanian in Kovno, part of Vilna, and the northern part of Vitebsk; Belorussians in Grodno, Minsk, Mogilev, part of Vitebsk; and Ukrainians in Kiev, Podolia, and Volhynia, as well as southern parts of Minsk and Grodno. The town populations of these areas was around 50 to 75 percent

Jewish, the nobility population between 50 and 75 percent Polish. The Jews of this area contributed heavily to the Jewish social democratic movement of the 1890s, the Poles to the Polish social democratic movement of the 1880s and 1890s. *Opis ziem,* vol. II, pp. 12–13.

15. Only those towns listed in which five or more revolutionaries were born. Large populations of Poles in Russian cities were not well represented in the movement. In 1897 there were 30,700 Poles in St. Petersburg, 19,000 in Kiev, 17,500 in Odessa, 15,500 in Minsk, 15,000 in Riga, and 7,500 in Moscow. See Z. Łukawski, *Polacy w rosyjskim ruchu socjaldemokratycznym w latach 1883–1893* (Kraków, 1970), pp. 21–22. These Poles did play an important role in the beginnings of the social democratic movement in Russia 1888–1892.

16. The literacy rate of Warsaw in 1882 was 57.19 percent for males and 44.65 percent for females. *Rezultaty spisu jednodniowego,* part 1, p. 50. In 1897, the literacy rate was 53.5 percent for Warsaw, 30.5 percent for the Congress Kingdom as a whole, and 22.9 percent for European Russia. *Obshchii svod 1897,* vol. I, part 2, p. 38.

17. Eliminating those revolutionaries over forty and under 18, and those years in which no more than four were born in each year, the mean year of birth was 1856, and taking 1882 as the average date of arrest, a mean age of twenty-six. In 1897 the average age in the Congress Kingdom as a whole was 24.36, in the empire, 25.26. *Obshchii svod 1897,* vol. I, part 1, p. x. Of 365 revolutionaries arrested from 1 Jan. to 31 July 1879 ["Stat.," *Narodnaia volia,* no. 4 (1880), p. 316] and of 451 revolutionaries arrested between 1873 and 1877 [Sidorov, "Stat.," *KS,* no. 1 (38) (1928), p. 29], the breakdown of ages was:

1879		1873–1877	
Under 21	— 11%	Under 21	— 26%
21–25	— 14%	21–25	— 44%
25–30	— 16%	25–30	— 21%
30–40	— 27%	over 30	— 9%
over 40	— 31%		

The Polish movement in 1878–1886 shared the youthful character of earlier 1873–77 movement with over 60 percent of its membership between the ages of 21 and 30 and with the largest percentage of participants between the ages of 20 and 25.

18. Those empire citizens in 1897 who had a middle or higher education were a miniscule percentage of the total: European Russia males 1.4 percent, females 0.8 percent, Congress Kingdom males 1.7 percent, females 0.9 percent. *Obshchii svod,* vol. I, part 1, p. 3.

19. [*R.F.%* — *relative frequency percentage,* or how many revolutionaries attended each school to the total of 622. This percentage is used when an individual can often fall into several categories of variables, in this case attend more than one school.] Those schools are listed which more than nine revolutionaries attended. In the 1880s over 2,200 Poles attended school in Russia. Around 60 percent of these came from the Congress Kingdom.

Polish Students in the Empire — 1886

(St. Petersburg)	No. of Poles	No. of students	% Poles
SPb. Univ.	234	2525	9.0
Inst. of Commun.	46	158	29.1
Inst. of Tech.	202	823	24.5
Med.-Surg. Acad.	200	1200	16.6
Inst. Forestry	105	355	29.5
Inst. Engineering	76	254	30.0
Acad. Mining	50	305	16.4
Kiev — Kiev Univ.	395	2030	19.4
Moscow — Inst. of Agr.	72	364	19.8
Riga — Polytech. Inst.	219	744	29.4

Łukawski, *Polacy,* pp. 15–17.

St. Petersburg's Academy of Medical-Surgery and the Institute of Technology were the most active centers of revolutionary activity throughout the 1870s. It is certainly noteworthy that in the Proletariat, students from these schools and from St. Petersburg Univ. formed the largest non-Congress Kingdom contingent. Sidorov's sample of the 1870s rates these schools one and two in revolutionaries who attended them, and Antonov's sample for the 1870s and 1880s also rates them one and two with St. Petersburg Univ. third. Sidorov, "Stat.," *KS,* p. 42. Antonov, "K voprosu," *Obshchestvennoe dvizhenie* (Moscow, 1965), p. 340. St. Petersburg played an abnormally large role in revolutionary activities, which could be both a result and a cause of the large numbers of revolutionary Poles in its schools. Between 1878 and 1886, 35.2 percent of all revolutionaries in the Russian movement were in St. Petersburg. Avakumovic, "Stat.," *Slavic Review,* p. 184. Of Avakumovic's sample of 1,083, the largest number were schooled at the Inst. of Technology in St. Petersburg. A large number were from Kharkov Veterinary Academy, which together with the large number from Warsaw Veterinary Academy, leads one to suspect that specific social groupings which entered veterinary academies were potentially revolutionary.

20. Avakumovic has 45.8 percent of university revolutionaries in the 1880s enrolled in medicine, 28.2 percent in law. Avakumovic, "Stat.," *Slavic Review,* p. 184. The humanities faculties, especially history-philosophy, were seldom involved in revolutionary activity. Sidorov, "Stat.," *KS,* pp. 32–33.

21. Those jobs and professions are listed that were held by ten or more revolutionaries. Out of 76 workers in the Russian movement from 1878–1886, only 3 were textile workers, 1 was a metalworker, 10 were locksmiths, 8 carpenters, and 4 shoemakers. Avakumovic, "Stat.," *Slavic Review,* p. 185.

22. Those jobs and professions are listed which accounted for at least two female revolutionaries.

23. For statistics on the Russian movement, see Antonov, p. 338. Several arguments can be made against the job composition of the variables in this category. Individual jobs often could have been either artisan or industrial

proletariat; indeed, many locksmiths, blacksmiths, tinsmiths, or even cabinet-makers were in the process of being proletarianized. Some continued to work primarily as artisans in small shops, others worked in factories. Because there is information which places numbers of locksmiths, seamstresses, bronze-workers, weavers, ironworkers, and spinners in large factories, I have included them as members of the industrial proletariat. Where there is information to the contrary — shoemakers, blacksmiths, tailors — jobs have been placed in the artisan category. "Unskilled labor" is composed of those revolutionaries who worked as "day laborers" and "common laborers."

24. Here again, some revolutionaries participated in more than one group, so R.F.% — or relative frequency percentage — is used.

25. We have no figures on participants of the 1863 uprising in the 1878–1886 socialist movement. Rashkovskii estimates that 43 and probably many more of the first Polish socialists came from families who participated in the national independence movement of the 1860s. However, he places too great an emphasis on the continuity between the 1860s and the late 1870s movements and too little weight on the continuity between the beginnings of Polish socialism and the political groupings of the 1890s. Rashkovskii, "Polskie revoliutsionnye," *Sviazi,* p. 315.

26. Of Russian socialists arrested between 1879 and the mid-1890s more than 90 percent were as a result of *narodovol'tsy* activities. Twenty of 3,046 socialists accused of revolutionary activities between 1 July 1881 and 1 January 1888 (which does not include the tsar's assassins) were sentenced to death (0.7 percent), and 128 (4 percent) were sentenced to hard labor. *Khronika,* p. 332. Sedov, *Geroicheskii period,* p. 361.

Selected Bibliography

I. Archival Sources

Archiwum Główne Akt Dawnych (AGAD), Warsaw.
Collection: Prokurator Warszawskiej Izby Sądowej (PWIS) 1878–1888: Zeszyt 218–1507.
Collection: Warszawski Gubernialny Zarząd Żandarmeri (WGZŻ) 1878–1886.
Collection: "Delo" Kancelaria Gubernatora Warszawskiego (DKGW) 1878–1886. Referat I.
Archiwum Zakładu Historii Partii (AZHP), Warsaw.
Collection: Archiwum Mikrofilmów (AM).
Collection: Sygn. 305/I/1. "Odezwy Proletariatu."
Collection: Materiały Procesu Krakowskiego, 1880, Sygn. 5/II.
Hoover Institution Archives (HI) Stanford, California.
Collection: Boris Nicolaevsky Archives.
Collection: Okhrana Archives.
Tsentral'nyi Gosudarstvennyi Arkhiv Oktiabr'skoi Revoliutsii i Sotsialisticheskogo Stroitel'stva (TsGAOR), Moscow.
Fond: 102 — Departament Politsii (DP).
Tsentral'nyi Gosudarstvennyi Istoricheskii Arkhiv (TsGIA SSSR), Leningrad.
Fond: 1405 — Ministerstvo Iustitsii.
  op. 83–93 Delo Departamenta Ministerstva Iustitsii Vtorogo Ugolovnogo Otdeleniia.
  op. 521 Vsepoddanneishie Doklady Ministra Iustitsii.
  op. 530 Doneseniia Prokurorskogo Nadzora Sudebnykh Palat'i Okruzhnykh Sudov.
Fond: 777 — Delo St. Peterburgskogo Tsenzurnogo Komiteta.
Fond: 1410, op. 1 — Veshchestvennye Dokazatel'stvo k Delam Ministerstvam Iustitsii.

II. Unpublished Manuscripts

Borodin, N. I. "Pervye glavy: Idealy i deistvitel'nost'." Galley proofs. HI, Nicolaevsky Archives, no. 168, folder 5.
Czekanowski, S. *W domu niewoli, lata 1879–1888.* Memoirs, vol. I. Written 1943–1944. Reworked and typed, 1953. Manuscript Institute Ossoliniani, 13258. Warsaw University Library.

Daniszewski, T. "U kolebki ruchu robotniczego w Polsce." AZHP, 27/II-46. Maszynopis AZHP. B23601.

Himka, J. "Polish and Ukrainian Socialism: Austria, 1867-1890." Ph.D. Dissertation. The University of Michigan, 1977.

Kirkor-Kiedroniowa, Zofia z Grabskich. *Wspomnienia,* vol. I. Rękopis. Biblioteka Narodowa (National Library), Warsaw. Rps. sygn. IV. 6399.

Kulczycki, L. *Dokoła mego życia.* Maszynopis AZHP. (Special Collections.) Handwritten original in Biblioteka Narodowa (National Library) manuscript collection.

"Listy znalezione przy rewizji u Ludwika Straszewicza i załączone do procesu, 1879." AZHP, Materiały procesu krakowskiego. Sygn. 5/II/2. Typed copy.

III. Pamphlets and Brochures

"Adam z pod Krakowa." *Janek Bruzda.* Geneva, 1884. AZHP, AM, 1494.

Bakunin, M. *Mowa miana na zgromadzeniu w Paryżu przy obchodzie rocznym 29 Listopada 1847 roku.* AZHP, AM, 1494.

Bracke, W. *Precz z socjalistami.* Edition 2. London, 1897. AZHP, AM, 1574.

Chrzanowski, L. *O dążeniach i polityce Moskwy oraz o potrzebie stanowczego powstrzymania jej zaborczych działań.* Kraków, 1866.

(Diksztajn, S.) Mlot, Jan. *O konstytucji 3 Maja.* Edition 2, Warsaw, 1917. AZHP, AM, 1349.

Diksztajn, S. and Jodko-Narkiewicz, W. *Polski socjalizm utopijny i na emigracji — dwie rozprawy.* Kraków, 1904.

Franko, I. *Zasady socjalizmu wyłożone w pytaniach i odpowiedzi (Co to jest socjalizm?).* Lipsk (Leipzig), 1878.

Heurich, J. *Jak robotnicy u nas mieszkają: A jak mieszkać mogą i powinni.* Warsaw, 1873.

Kwestionaryjusz robotniczy, Dodatek do 10 i 11 n-ru, *Równości.*

Limanowski, B. *Socjalizm jako konieczny objaw dziejowego rozwoju.* Lwów, 1879.

Nowina, E. *Przyczyny i skutki nierządu Polski.* Lwów, 1875.

Piłsudki, J. *Jak stałem się socjalistą?* Lwów, 1875.

Program socjalistów galicyjskich. Lwów, 1881.

Propaganda socjalistyczna między ludem wiejskim. Kraków, 1879.

Schaeffle, A. *Kwintessencyja socjalizmu.* Geneva, 1881.

Sosnowski, K. *Przemówienie w rocznicę listopadowej rewolucji na obchodzie w Paryżu 1881 r.* Paris, 1881.

———, *Przemówienie Kaz. Sosnowskiego w Stowarzyszeniu Wzajemnej Pomocy Robotników w Paryżu, dnia 14 Października 1882 roku.* Paris, 1882.

Truszkowski, H. (Toporek, W.). *Rozmowa dwu kumotrów: Podsłuchał i spisał dla ludu.* Kraków, 1883.

IV. Newspapers and Periodicals, 1878-1888. Originals, Microfilms, Reeditions.

Atheneum . . . 1878-1880.
Głos . . . 1886-1887.
Głos Więżnia . . . 1879.
Kalendar' "Narodnoi voli" . . . 1883.
Listok "Narodnoi voli" . . . 1880-1886.
Narodnaia volia . . . 1879-1886.
Nowiny . . . 1878-1880.
Praca . . . 1882-1886.
Prawda . . . 1881-1886.
Proletariat . . . 1883-1884.
Przedświt . . . 1881-1886.
Przegląd Tygodniowy . . . 1883-1887.
Rabochii . . . 1885.
Robotnik . . . 1883.
Równość . . . 1879-1881.
Vestnik "Narodnoi voli" . . . 1883-1886.
Walka Klas . . . 1884-1887.
Zemlia i volia . . . 1878-1879.

V. Published Document Collections, Government Publications, Special Collections

"Archiwum Bardowskiego." *Z Pola Walki,* No. 3 (7), 1959, No. 1 (9), 1960.
Arkhiv "Zemli i voli" i "Narodnoi voli." Ed. S. N. Valk. Moscow, 1932.
Bohaterowie "Proletariatu." Warsaw, 1906.
Deiateli revoliutsionnogo dvizheniia v Rossii: Biobibliograficheskii slovar'. Volumes II, III, V. Moscow, 1929-1931.
Gruppa "Osvobozhdenie truda": Iz arkhivov G. V. Plekhanova, V. I. Zasulicha i L. G. Deicha. Volumes I-VI. Moscow, 1924, 1928.
Istoriko-revoliutsionnyi sbornik. Volumes I-III. Ed. V. I. Nevskii. Moscow-Leningrad, 1924-1926.
"K istorii otnoshenii partii 'Narodnoi voli' i partii 'Proletariat'." From the government publication, *Materialy dlia istorii revoliutsionnogo dvizheniia v Tsarstve Pol'skom s 1877 po 1885 g. Byloe.* No. 7, 1906.
"K istorii rabochego dvizheniia 80-90-kh godov." *Krasnyi arkhiv.* Vol. VI, 1938.
Khronika sotsialisticheskogo dvizheniia v Rossii 1878-1887: Ofitsial'nyi otchet. Moscow, 1906.
Kółka socjalistyczne, Gminy i Wielki Proletariat: Procesy polityczne 1878-1888: Żródła. Ed. L. Baumgarten. Warsaw, 1966.

Krusiński, S. *Pisma zebrane.* Intro. T. Kowalik. Warsaw, 1958.

Księga Polaków uczestników Rewolucji Październikowej 1917–1920: Biografie. Warsaw, 1967.

Krakowski komisarz policji na służbie carskiego wywiadu. Ed. L. Baumgarten. Kraków, 1967.

Lavrov; *Gody emigratsii: Arkhivnye materialy v dvukh tomakh.* 2 vols. Ed. B. Sapir. Dodrecht, Holland, 1974.

Literatura partii "Narodnoi voli." Ed. B. Bazilevskii (Bogucharskii). Paris, 1905.

Ministerstvo Finansov. Departament Torgovli i Manufaktur. *Fabrichno-zavodskaia promyshlennost' i torgovlia Rossii.* Edition 2. St. Petersburg, 1898.

Pierwsze pokolenie marksistów polskich; Wybór pism i materiałów źródłowych z lat 1878–1886. 2 vols. Ed. A. Molska. Warsaw, 1962.

Narodovol'tsy posle l-go marta 1881 goda. Moscow, 1928.

Obshchii svod po imperii: Rezul'tatov razrabotki dannykh pervoi vseobshchei perepisi naseleniia, proizvedennoi 28 Ianvaria 1897. 2 vols. St. Petersburg, 1905.

Ognisko: Książka zbiorowa wydana dla uczczenia 25-letniej pracy T. T. Jeża. Warsaw, 1882.

Opis ziem zamieszkanych przez Polaków. Vol. II. *Królestwo Polskie.* Warsaw, 1904.

"Papiery M. Koturnickiego (E. Kobylański)." *Kronika Ruchu Rewolucyjnego w Polsce.* No. 1 (17), 1939.

Postępowa publicystyka emigracyjna 1831–1846. Wybór żródeł. Eds. W. Łukasiewicz and W. Lewandowski. Wrocław, 1961.

Procesy polityczne w Królestwie Polskiem: Materiały do historii ruchu rewolucyjnego w Król. Polskiem. Zeszyt 1: Rok 1878–1879. Kraków, 1907.

Piekarski, W. *Listy z więzienia (1879).* Ed. J. Zathey. Wrocław, 1953.

Rabochee dvizhenie semidesiatykh godov: Sbornik arkhivnykh dokumentov. Ed. E. A. Korol'chuk. Moscow, 1934.

Radykalni demokraci Polacy: Wybór pism i dokumentów. Warsaw, 1960.

Revoliutsionnaia Rossiia i revoliutsionnaia Pol'sha (vtoraia polovina XIX v.). Eds. V. A. D'iakov et al. Moscow, 1967.

Rezultaty spisu jednodniowego ludności miasta Warszawy 1882 roku. Parts 1–3. Warsaw, 1883. In Polish and Russian.

Rozprawa główna przed sądem przysięgłych przeciw Ludwikowi Waryńskiemu i 34 współ. o zbrodnię zaburzenia spokoju publicznego. AZHP, Materialy procesu krakowskiego, sygn. 5/II. Dodatki do *Czas,* 1880.

Sobolewski, M. "Dwa dokumenty w sprawie Krakowskiego procesu Ludwika Waryńskiego." *Zeszyty Naukowe Uniwersytetu Jagiellońskiego.* No. 2, 1955.

Społeczeństwo Królestwa Polskiego: Studia o uwarstwieniu i ruchliwości społecznej. 3 vols. Ed. W. Kula. Warsaw, 1965–1968.

"Sprawy Gminy socjalistów polskich w Kijowie. Wniosek." *Z Pola Walki.* No. 2, 1927.

Sprawozdanie z międzynarodowego zebrania zwołanego w 50-letnią rocznicę listopadowego powstania przez redakcję "Równości" w Genewie. Geneva, 1881.

Svod ukazanii, dannykh nekotorymi iz arestovanykh po delam o gusodarstvennykh prestupleniiakh. May, 1880.

"Sprawozdanie z procesu Proletariatu, w grudniu 1885 r. przed sądem wojennym w Warszawie." *Z Pola Walki,* 1904.

Sviazi revoliutsionerov Rossii i Pol'shi XIX — nachala XX v. Eds. V. A. D'iakov et al. Moscow, 1968.

"Ubiistvo podp. Sudeikina (iz arkhiva V. L. Burtseva)." *Na chuzhoi storone.* Vol. IX, 1925.

"Uwagi o położeniu robotników przemysłu ciężkiego w Królestwie Polskim." Fragment of "Die Arbeiterverhältnisse in den Eisenfabriken und Bergwerken des Königreichs Polen." Z. Broel-Plater. Heidelberg, 1892. Eds. E. Kaczyńska and K. Piesowicz. *Kwartalnik Historyczny.* No. 4, 1962.

Warszawa popowstaniowa, 1864-1918. Zeszyt 1. Warsaw, 1968.

Z dziejów współpracy rewolucyjnej Polaków i Rosjan w drugiej połowie XIX wieku. Eds. L. Bazylow, et al. Wrocław, 1956.

Z Pola Walki: Zbiór materiałów tyczących się polskiego ruchu socjalistycznego. London, 1904.

Z Pola Walki: Książeczka pierwsza. Geneva, 1886.

"Zeznanie Pacanowskiego: Tłumaczenia oryginalnych protokołów żandarmskich." *Z Pola Walki,* 1904.

VI. Memoirs and Diaries

Ashenbrenner, M. Iu. "Voennaia organizatsiia partii 'Narodnoi voli'." *Byloe,* No. 7, 1906.

Brzeziński, E. "Wspomnienia z mojego życia." *Niepodległość.* Vol. IV, 1931.

Bugajski, S. "Autobiografia." *Z Pola Walki.* No. 4, 1927.

Chmielewski, J. E. "Pierwsze lata korporacji studentów Polaków w Kijowie." *Niepodległość.* Vol. XIX, 1939.

Day, W. A. *The Russian Government in Poland: with a Narrative of the Polish Insurrection of 1863.* London, 1867.

Dębski, A. *Krwawe zajście w mleczarni Henneberga w roku 1884.* Warsaw, 1929.

_____. "Stanisław Kunicki." *Bohaterowie "Proletariatu."* Warsaw, 1906.

_____. "Wspomnienia o Kunickim i Bardowskim." *Z Pola Walki.* London, 1904.

_____. "Stanisław Kunicki." *Światło.* No. 5, 1899.

Dejcz, L. "Pionerzy ruchu socjalistycznego w Królestwie Polskim." *Z Pola Walki.* No. 9-10, 1930.

_____. "Chernyi peredel'." *Istoriko-revoliutsionnyi sbornik.* Vol. II. Leningrad, 1924.

Dłuski, K. "Ludwik Waryński." *Z Pola Walki.* London, 1904.

_____. "Wspomnienia z trzech lat (1875-1878)." *Niepodległość.* Vol. I, 1930.

Dnevnik gosudarstvennogo sekretaria A. A. Polovtsova. 2 vols. Moscow, 1966.

(Dukaczewski) "Robotnik." "Z dziejów ruchu robotniczego w Żyrardowie." *Przedświt.* No. 6, 1902.

Dulębina, H. "Z moich wspomnień o Henryku Dulębie." *Kronika Ruchu Rewolucyjnego w Polsce.* No. 1 (5), 1936.

Figner, W. *Trwały ślad.* Parts 1–2. Warsaw, 1962.

Głowacki, W. (Pytagoras). "Ze wspomnień 'Proletariatczyka'." *Z Pola Walki.* No. 2, 1927.

Gostkiewicz, H. "Wspomnienia Proletariatczyka." *Z Pola Walki.* No. 2, 1927. Translated from *Katorga i ssylka.* No. 6 (27), 1926.

Heryng, Z. "W zaraniu socjalizmu polskiego." *Niepodległość.* Vol. III, 1930.

――――. "X-ty Pawilon przed 50-ciu laty." *Niepodległość.* Vol. I, 1929–1930.

(Janowicz, L.). "Ze wspomnień Szlisselburczyka." *Przedświt.* Nos. 1, 2, 1901.

Jędrzejowski, B. A. "Ludwik Waryński." *Światło.* No. 16, 1902.

Kon, F. *Narodziny wieku: Wspomnienia.* Warsaw, 1969.

――――. "Proletariattsy (Vospominaniia)." *Proletarskaia revoliutsiia.* No. 11, 1922.

Koszutski, S. *Walka młodzieży polskiej o wielkie ideały: Wspomnienia z czasów gimnazjalnych i uniwersyteckich (1881–1900).* Warsaw, 1928.

Krzywicki, L. *Wspomnienia.* 3 vols. Warsaw, 1957.

Limanowski, B. *Pamiętniki (1870–1907).* Vol. II. Warsaw, 1958.

Mańkowski, M. *U stóp szubienicy: Urywek ze wspomnień więziennych "proletaryatczyka" (1885–1886 r.).* Kraków, 1905.

Mikołajski, S. "Pierwszy posiew socjalizmu w Galicji (Wspomnienia z procesu Ludwika Waryńskiego i 34 spólników w Krakowie 1878–1880 r.)." *Niepodległość.* Vol. XII, 1935.

Novitskii, V. D. *Iz vospominanii zhandarma.* Ed. P. E. Shchegolev. Leningrad, 1929.

Offenberg, Jan. *Stan umysłów wśród młodzieży akademickiej Uniwersytetu Warszawskiego w latach 1885–1890 (Ze wspomnień kresowca).* Warsaw, 1929.

O(nufrowi)ch, B. "V mestakh otdalennyia (Vospominaniia administrativnogo)." *Minuvshie gody.* No. 8, 1908.

(Pankratów, W.). "M. Z." "Z pobytu Waryńskiego w twierdzy Szliselburskiej." *Niepodległość.* Vol. VII, 1933.

Pamiętnik — Maria Bohuszewiczówna. Ed. D. Wawrzykowska-Wierciochowa. Intro. Ż. Kormanowa. Wrocław, 1955.

Pekarskii, E. "Otryvki iz vospominanii." *Katorga i ssylka.* No. 4 (11), 1924.

Płoski, E. *Wspomnienia: Czasy uniwersyteckie.* Płock, 1938.

Popov, I. I. "Revoliutsionnye organizatsii v Peterburge v 1882–1885 godakh." *Narodovol'tsy posle l-go marta 1881 goda.* Moscow, 1928.

Rechniewski, T. "Henryk Dulęba." *Kuźnia,* 1914.

――――. "Stanisław Mendelson." *Kuźnia,* 1913.

Schmidt, M. *Wspomnienia młodzieży z przed 50-ciu laty.* Warsaw, 1929.

Shebalin, M. G. "Peterburgskaia narodovol'cheskaia organizatsiia v 1882–

1883 godakh: Vospominaniia uchastnika." *Narodovol'tsy posle l-go marta 1881 goda.* Moscow, 1928.

Shvetsov. "Erazm Kobylanskii." *Katorga i ssylka.* No. 10 (59), 1929.

Sieroszewski, W. "O świcie." *Z Pola Walki.* London, 1904.

Sieroszewski, W. *Pamiętniki: Wspomnienia.* Kraków, 1959.

Sławiński, B. "Niedoszły zamach na general-gubernatora Hurkę." *Kronika Ruchu Rewolucyjnego w Polsce.* No. 1 (5), 1936.

Stempowski, S. *Pamiętniki 1870–1914.* Wrocław, 1953.

Stepniak-Kravchinskii, S. T. *Sobranie sochinenii.* Part 2, "Podpol'naia Rossiia." St. Petersburg, 1907.

Świętochowski, A. *Wspomnienia.* Wrocław, 1966.

Tikhomirov, L. *Nachala i kontsy: Liberaly i terroristy.* Moscow, 1890.

Truszkowski, H. "Przyczynek do dziejów 'Proletariatu'." *Kronika Ruchu Rewolucyjnego w Polsce.* No. 1 (5), 1936.

_____. "Z dalekiej przeszłości (Wspomnienia o Ludwiku Waryńskim)." *Kronika Ruchu Rewolucyjnego w Polsce.* No. 1 (5), 1936.

Uziembło, J. "Wspomnienia." *Przedświt.* No. 4–5, 1902.

_____. "Filipina Płaskowicka." *Światło.* No. 16, 1902.

Vospominaniia I. I. Ianzhula o perezhitom i vidennom v 1864–1909 gg. 2 vols. St. Petersburg, 1910.

(Waryński, L.). "Filipina Płaskowicka." *Równość.* No. 8–9, 1880.

(Wojnicz, M.). "Doktor." "Niedoszłe plany." *Przedświt.* No. 11, 1901.

Żeromski, S. *Dzienniki.* Vol. III. Warsaw, 1964.

VII. Books

Baumgarten, L. *Dzieje Wielkiego Proletariatu.* Warsaw, 1966.

Bazylow, L. *Działalność narodnictwa rosyjskiego w latach 1878–1881.* Wrocław, 1960.

Bicz, H. (Bitner, H.). *Proletariat: Pierwsza socjalnorewolucyjna partia w Polsce.* Moscow, 1934.

Blackwell, W. L. *The Beginnings of Russian Industrialization, 1800–1860.* Princeton, 1968.

Blit, L. *The Origins of Polish Socialism: The History and Ideas of the First Polish Socialist Party: 1878–1886.* Cambridge, 1971.

Blum, J. *Lord and Peasant in Russia from the Ninth to the Nineteenth Century.* Princeton, 1961.

Bobińska, C. *Marks i Engels a sprawy polskie.* Warsaw, 1954.

Bogucharskii, V. Ia. *Iz istorii politicheskoi bor'by v 70-kh i 80-kh godakh XIX veka: Partiia "Narodnoi voli," eia proiskhozhdenie, sud'by i gibel'.* Moscow, 1912.

Borejsza, J. W. *W kręgu wielkich wygnańców 1848–1895.* Warsaw, 1963.

Boss, E. *Sprawa robotnicza w Królestwie Polskiem w okresie Paskiewiczowskim 1831–1855.* Warsaw, 1931.

Brock, P. *W zaraniu ruchu ludowego.* London, 1956.

_____. *Z dziejów wielkiej emigracji w Anglii.* Warsaw, 1958.

Buchner, L. *Force and Matter.* London, 1870.

Budkiewiczówna, B. *Ruch robotniczy w Królestwie Polskim w latach 1870–1890.* Minsk, 1934.

Buszko, J. *Narodziny ruchu socjalistycznego na ziemach polskich.* Kraków, 1967.

Charlton, D. G. *Positivist Thought in France during the Second Empire.* Oxford, 1959.

Ciołkoszowie, L. and A. *Zarys dziejów socjalizmu polskiego.* 2 vols. London, 1966, 1972.

Dziewanowski, M. K. *Joseph Piłsudki: A European Federalist, 1918–1922.* Stanford, 1969.

————. *The Communist Party of Poland: An Outline of History.* Cambridge, Mass., 1959.

El'nitskii, A. *Rabochee dvizhenie v Rossii.* Moscow, 1925.

Emmons, T. *The Russian Landed Gentry and the Emancipation of 1861.* Cambridge, Eng., 1968.

Estreicher, S. *Rozwój organizacji socjalistycznej w krajach polskich.* Kraków, 1896.

Feldman, W. *Dzieje polskiej myśli politycznej w okresie porozbiorowym.* Vol. II. Kraków, 1918.

Fischer, G. *Russian Liberalism: From Gentry to Intelligentsia.* Cambridge, 1958.

Gąsiorowska, N. *Kształtowanie się klasy robotniczej.* Warsaw, 1955.

Gershenkron, A. *Europe in the Russian Mirror: Four Lectures in Economic History.* Cambridge, Eng., 1970.

Groniowski, K. *Realizacja reformy uwłaszczeniowej 1864 r.* Warsaw, 1963.

Grosfeld, L. *Z dziejów kapitalizmu w Polsce.* Warsaw, 1948.

Grünberg, K. and Kozłowski, Cz. *Historia polskiego ruchu robotniczego 1864–1918.* Warsaw, 1962.

Haecker, E. *Historia socjalizmu w Galicji i na Śląsku.* Vol. I. Kraków, 1933.

Haustein, U. *Sozialismus und nationale Frage in Polen: Die Entwicklung der sozialistischen Bewegung in Kongress Polen von 1875 bis 1900 unter besonderer Berücksichtungen der Polnischen Sozialistischen Partei (PPS).* Köln, 1969.

Historia Polski. Vol. III, part 1. Eds. Ż. Kormanowa and I. Pietrzak-Pawłowska. Warsaw, 1967.

Historia Polski 1795–1918. Vol. II. Ed. S. Kieniewicz. Warsaw, 1969.

History of Poland. Eds. A. Gieysztor, S. Kieniewicz et al. Warsaw, 1968.

Hornowa, E. *Ukraiński obóz postępowy i jego współpraca z polską lewicą społeczną w Galicji 1876–1895.* Wrocław-Warsaw-Kraków, 1968.

Ihnatowicz, I. *Przemysł łódzki w latach 1860–1900.* Wrocław, 1965.

Janżułł, I. *Przemysł fabryczny w Królestwie Polskiem, studium ekonomiczne.* St. Petersburg, 1887.

(Jędrzejowski), B. A. J. *Ludwik Waryński.* Warsaw, 1919.

(Jodko-Narkiewicz, W.). *Geschichte der sozialistischen Bewegung in Polen.* In *Handbuch des Sozialismus.* Ed. C. Stegmann. Zürich, 1895.

Kempner, S. A. *Rozwój gospodarczy Polski od rozbiorów do niepodległości.* Warsaw, 1924.

Khromov, P. A. *Ekonomicheskoe razvitie Rossii v XIX–XX vekakh.* Moscow, 1950.

Kieniewicz, S. *The Emancipation of the Polish Peasantry.* Chicago, 1969.

Kornilov, A. A. *Obshchestvennoe dvizhenie pri Aleksandre II (1855–1881): Istoricheskie ocherki.* Paris, 1905.

Kozicki, S. *Historia Ligi Narodowej.* London, 1964.

Kozłowski, J. *Wacław Święcicki: Poeta "Proletariatu."* Warsaw, 1953.

Krusiński, S. *Szkice socjologiczne.* Intro. L. Krzywicki. Warsaw, 1891.

Kucharzewski, J. *The Origins of Modern Russia.* New York, 1948. Abridged translation of seven volume *Od białego caratu do czerwonego.* Warsaw, 1923–1925.

Kukiel, M. *Dzieje Polski porozbiorowe 1795–1921.* London, 1961.

Kula, W. *Historia gospodarcza Polski 1864–1918.* Warsaw, 1947.

Kulczycki, L. *Rewolucja rosyjska.* Vol. II. Lwów, 1911.

Kuz'min, D. *Narodovol'cheskaia zhurnalistika.* Moscow, 1930.

Lange, O. *Papers in Economics and Sociology.* Ed. and Trans. P. F. Knightsfield. Warsaw, 1970.

Lenin, V. I. *The Development of Capitalism in Russia.* Moscow, 1956. Translated from *Sochineniia.* Vol. III, edition 4.

Liashchenko, P. I. *History of the National Economy of Russia to the 1917 Revolution.* Trans. L. M. Herman. New York, 1949.

Limanowski, B. *Historia ruchu społecznego w XIX stulecia.* Lwów, 1890.

———. *Rozwój polskiej myśli socjalistycznej.* Warsaw, 1929.

Litwin, J. *Na drogach rozwoju ruchu robotniczego Łódzi w latach 1861–1905.* Łódź, n.d.

Luxemburg, R. *Die industrielle Entwicklung Polens.* Leipzig, 1898.

———. *Pamięci "Proletariatu."* Warsaw, 1922. Reprint from *Przegląd Socjaldemokratyczny,* 1903.

Łepkowski, T. *Początki klasy robotniczej Warszawy.* Warsaw, 1956.

Łukasiewicz, J. *Przewrót techniczny w przemyśle Królestwa Polskiego 1852–1886.* Warsaw, 1963.

Łukawski, Z. *Polacy w rosyjskim ruchu socjaldemokratycznym w latach 1883–1893.* Kraków, 1970.

Marx, K. *Manuscripte über die polnische Frage.* Gravenhage, 1961.

Mazowiecki, M. (Kulczycki, L.). *Historia polskiego ruchu socjalistycznego w zaborze rosyjskim.* Kraków, 1903.

Meloch, M. *Ruch strajkowy w Królestwie Polskim w latach 1870–1886.* Warsaw, 1937. Reprinted from *Przegląd Socjologiczny.* Vol. V, 1937.

Mendelsohn, E. *Class Struggle in the Pale: The Formative Years of the Jewish Workers' Movement in Tsarist Russia.* Cambridge, Eng., 1970.

Mill, J. S. *Auguste Comte and Positivism.* London, 1881.

Molska, A. *Model ustroju socjalistycznego w polskiej myśli marksistowskiej lat 1878–1886.* Warsaw, 1965.

Narkiewicz, O. A. *The Green Flag: Polish Populist Politics 1867–1970.* London, 1976.

Nettl, J. P. *Rosa Luxemburg*. Abridged ed. London, 1969.

Offmański, M. *Charakterystyka rządów Aleksandra III w ziemiach polskich (1881–1894)*. Lwów, 1895.

"B. P." *Ocherki Privislian'ia*. Moscow, 1897.

Perl, F. (Res). *Dzieje ruchu socjalistycznego w zaborze rosyjskim: Do powstania PPS*. Third edition. Warsaw, 1958.

(Piltz, E.). Scriptor. *Nasze stronnictwa skrajne*. Kraków, 1903.

Plokhotskii, L. (Wasilewski, L.). *Vzaimnyia otnosheniia pol'skikh i russkikh sotsialistov*. London, 1902.

Pogodin, A. L. *Istoriia pol'skogo naroda v XIX veke*. Moscow, 1915.

Pogozhev, A. V. *Uchet chislennosti i sostava rabochikh v Rossii: Materialy po statistike truda*. St. Petersburg, 1906.

Pobóg-Malinowski, W. *Narodowa Demokracja 1887–1918*. Warsaw, 1933.

Polevoi, Iu. Z. *Zarozhdenie marksizma v Rossii, 1883–1894 gg*. Moscow, 1959.

Poznanskii, I. *Istoricheskii ocherk ekonomicheskogo polozheniia Pol'shi*. St. Petersburg, 1875.

————. *Proizvoditel'nyia sily Tsarstva Pol'skogo: Sravnitel'naia statistika promyshlennogo, torgovogo i finansovogo polozheniia Pol'shi za 1874, 1878 i 1876 gg*. St. Petersburg, 1880.

Próchnik, A. *Ku Polsce socjalistycznej: Dzieje polskiej myśli socjalistycznej*. Warsaw, 1936.

————. *Studia i szkice 1864–1918*. Warsaw, 1962.

Pukhlov, N. N. *Iz istorii pol'skoi sotsial-demokraticheskoi partii (1893–1904 gg.)*. Moscow, 1968.

Rashin, A. G. *Formirovanie rabochego klassa Rossii: Istoriko-ekonomicheskie ocherki*. Ed. S. G. Strumilin. Moscow, 1958.

————. *Naselenie Rossii za 100 let (1811–1913 gg.): Statisticheskie ocherki*. Moscow, 1956.

Robinson, G. T. *Rural Russia under the Old Regime*. Berkeley, 1967.

Rutowski, T. *W sprawie przemysłu krajowego*. Kraków, 1883.

Schaff, A. *Narodziny i rozwój filozofii marksistowskiej*. Warsaw, 1950.

Schapiro, L. *Rationalism and Nationalism in Russian Nineteenth-Century Political Thought*. New Haven–London, 1967.

Sedov, M. G. *Geroicheskii period revoliutsionnogo narodnichestva*. Moscow, 1966.

Skrzycki, R. (Dmowski, R.). *Młodzież polska w zaborze rosyjskim*. Lwów, 1896. Reprinted from *Przegląd Wszechpolski*. Vol. I, 1896.

Snytko, T. G. *Russkoe narodnichestvo i pol'skoe obshchestvennoe dvizhenie 1865–1881 gg*. Moscow, 1969.

Strobel, G. W. *Die Partei Rosa Luxemburgs, Lenin und die SPD*. Wiesbaden, 1974.

Studnitskii, V. *Pol'sha v politicheskom otnoshenii ot razdelov do nashikh dnei*. St. Petersburg, 1908.

Sviatlovskii, V. V. *Fabrichnyi rabochii: Issledovanie zdorov'ia russkogo fabrichnogo rabochego. Sanitarnoe polozhenie fabrichnogo rabochego v Privislianskom krai i v Malorossii. Iz nabliudenii fabrichnogo inspektora.* Warsaw, 1889.

Szapiro, B. ("Besem"). *Tadeusz Rechniewski 1862–1916.* Warsaw, 1927.

Szpotański, S. *Początki polskiego socjalizmu.* Warsaw, 1907.

Targalski, J. *Ludwik Waryński: Próba zycia.* Warsaw, 1976.

Thun, A. *Geschichte der revolutionären Bewegung in Russland.* Leipzig, 1882.

Tugan-Baranovskii, M. *Geschichte der russischen Fabrik.* Berlin, 1900.

_____. *Statisticheskie itogi promyshlennogo razvitiia Rossii.* St. Petersburg, 1898.

Tvardovskaia, V. A. *Sotsialisticheskaia mysl' Rossii na rubezhe 1870–1880 gg.* Moscow, 1969.

Ulam, A. B. *In the Name of the People: Prophets and Conspirators in Prerevolutionary Russia.* New York, 1977.

Veto (Studnicki, W.). *Dwadzieścia lat walki proletariatu polskiego.* Lwów, 1899.

Volk, S. S. *Narodnaia volia 1879–1882.* Moscow–Leningrad, 1966.

Walczak, S. *Rola Genewskiego ośrodka emigracyjnego polskich socjalistów w kształtowaniu się świadomości socjalistycznej w kraju.* Reprint from *Ze Skarbca Kultury.* No. 1 (7), 1955.

Walicki, A. *The Controversy over Capitalism: Studies in the Social Philosophy of the Russian Populists.* Oxford, 1969.

Wasilewski, L. *Tajna prasa rewolucyjna w zaborze rosyjskim w dobie popowstaniowej.* Kraków, 1924.

Wawrzykowska-Wierciochowa, D. *Mikołaj i Walentyna Archangielscy — zapomniani Rosjanie-Proletariatczycy.* Warsaw, 1954.

Wielki Proletariat i jego dziedzictwo. Eds. A. Czubiński et al. Warsaw, 1974.

Wołkowiczer, I. *Początki socjalistycznego ruchu robotniczego w Królestwie Polskim.* Warsaw, 1955.

Wóycicki, A. *Dzieje robotników przemysłowych w Polsce.* Warsaw, 1929.

_____. *Instytucje fabryczne i społeczne w przemyśle Królestwa Polskiego.* Warsaw, 1914.

Wudzki, L. *O Ludwiku Waryńskim.* Warsaw, 1956.

Zaionchkovskii, P. A. *Krizis samoderzhaviia na rubezhe 1870–1880-kh godov.* Moscow, 1964.

_____. *Rossiiskoe samoderzhavie v kontse XIX stoletiia (politicheskaia reaktsiia 80-kh — nachala 90-kh godov).* Moscow, 1970.

Załęski, W. *Statystyka porównawcza Królestwa Polskiego.* Warsaw, 1876.

VIII. Articles

Antonov, V. S. "K voprosu o sotsial'nom sostave i chislennosti revoliutsionerov 70-kh godov." *Obshchestvennoe dvizhenie v poreformennoi Rossii (sbornik statei k 80-letiiu so dnia rozhdeniia B. P. Koz'mina).* Moscow, 1965.

Arskii, R. "Iz istorii sotsial'no-revoliutsionnoi partii 'Proletariat'." *Krasnaia letopis'*. No. 8, 1923.

Avakumovic, I. "A Statistical Approach to the Revolutionary Movement in Russia, 1878–1887." *The American Slavic and East European Review*. April, 1959.

Baumgarten, L. "Cenny dokument z dziejów 'Proletariatu' i 'Narodnej woli'." Reprint from *Biuletyn Żydowskiego Instytutu Historycznego*. No. 24, 1957.

———. "Na marginesie reedycji pisma 'Proletariat'." *Z Pola Walki*. No. 3, 1958.

———. "'Odkrywczość' więcej niż wątpliwa." *Z Pola Walki*. No. 3, 1960.

———. "Raz jeszcze o potrzebie krytycznego stosunku do żródeł (W odpowiedzi T. Kowalikowi). *Z Pola Walki*. No. 3, 1961.

———. "Czy partia Proletariat organizowała zamach na cara." *Z Pola Walki*. No. 4, 1963.

Bobinskii, S. "Etapy razvitiia kommunisticheskoi partii v Pol'she." *Proletarskaia revoliutsiia*. No. 11, 1922.

Czachowski, K. "Szermierz wolności (Bolesław Limanowski)." *Niepodległość*. Vol. II, 1930.

Giza, S. "Do biografji Józefa Beutha." *Niepodległość*. Vol. XV, 1937.

———. "Do biografji Stanisława Padlewskiego." *Niepodległość*. Vol. XIV, 1936.

Gershenkron, A. "Agrarian Policies and Industrialization: Russia, 1861–1917." *Cambridge Economic History of Europe*. Vol. VI, part 2. Cambridge, Eng., 1965.

———. "Problems and Patterns of Russian Economic Development." *The Transformation of Russian Society*. Ed. C. E. Black. Cambridge, Mass., 1960.

Hałas, I. "Powstanie i rozwój zorganizowanego ruchu robotniczego w Łodzi." *Z dziejów ruchu robotniczego w Łodzi*. Łódź, 1967.

"Iz arkhiva V. Ia. Bogucharskogo: K biografii L. Varynskogo." Ed. S. Valk. *Katorga i ssylka*. No. 3 (32), 1927.

Kelles-Krauz, K. "Polscy i rosyjscy socjaliści." *Pisma wybrane*. Vol. II, Warsaw, 1962.

———. "Niepodległość Polski w programie socjalistycznym." *Pisma wybrane*. Vol. II. Warsaw, 1962.

Kon, F. "Soiuz 'Proletariata' s 'Narod. voli'." *Katorga i ssylka*. No. 3 (24), 1926.

Koni, A. F. "Vospominaniia o dele Very Zasulich," *Sobranie sochinenii*. Vol. II, Moscow, 1966.

Korman(owa), Ż. "Kazimierz Puchewicz i 'Solidarność'." *Niepodległość*. Vol. XIX, 1939.

———. "Odezwy Proletariatu z lat 1882–1885." *Niepodległość*. Vol. XIV, 1936.

———. "Proletariat." *Kronika Ruchu Rewolucyjnego w Polsce*. No. 2 (6), 3–4 (7–8), 1936.

———. "Z pierwszego pokolenia walczących: Przyczynek do działalności braci Józefa i Kazimierza Pławińskich." *Kronika Ruchu Rewolucyjnego w Polsce.* No. 4 (12), 1937.

———. "Zamach na Aleksandra III w Warszawie." *Z Pola Walki.* No. 3, 1963.

Korzec, P. "Dwa bunty łódzkie (1861, 1892)." *Z dziejów ruchu robotniczego w Łodzi.* Łódź, 1967.

Kowalik, T. "W sprawie Krusińskiego i 'Krusińszczyków' (Odpowiedź L. Baumgartenowi i A. Osiadacz-Molskiej)." *Z Pola Walki.* No. 3 (15), 1961.

Kozłowski, J. "Rosjanie-Proletariatczycy." *Kwartalnik Instytutu Polsko-Radzieckiego.* Warsaw, 1953.

Krzesławski, J. (Cynarski). "Spoliczkowanie Apuchtina." *Kronika Ruchu Rewolucyjnego w Polsce.* No. 3 (15), 1938 and No. 1 (17), 1939.

———. "Tragiczne losy robotnika-proletarjatczyka (Piotr Dąbrowski — szewc warszawski)." *Kronika Ruchu Rewolucyjnego w Polsce.* No. 1 (5), 1936.

Kurbatowa, I. N. "J. W. Plechanow a polski ruch robotniczy." *Z Pola Walki.* No. 3 (7), 1959.

Lewak, A. "Rząd Narodowy, 1877 r." *Niepodległość.* Vol. XII, 1935.

Lure, G. "Manifestatsiia bezrabotnykh v Varshave." *Katorga i ssylka.* No. 10, 1931.

Mikhailovskii, Ia. T. "O zarabotnoi plate i prodolzhitel'nosti rabochego vremeni na russkikh fabrikakh i zavodakh." Ministerstvo Finansov. *Fabrichno-zavodskaia promyshlennost' i torgovlia Rossii.* Edition 2. St. Petersburg, 1896.

Miller, I. S. "Nekotorye obshchie problemy istorii russko-pol'skikh revoliutsionnykh sviazei." *Sviazi revoliutsionerov Rossii i Pol'shi XIX — nachala XX v.* Moscow, 1968.

Molska-Osiadacz, A. "W sprawie charakterystyki poglądów Stanisława Krusińskiego." *Z Pola Walki.* No. 3 (11), 1960.

Nevskii, V. "Iz narodovol'cheskikh vospominanii S. A. Ivanova (pis'ma S. A. Ivanova k P. V. Karpovich)." *Narodovol'tsy 80-kh i 90-kh godov.* Moscow, 1929.

Oczak, I. "Działalność serbskiego rewolucyjonisty Andra Bankowicza w Polsce w latach 1885–1886." *Z Pola Walki.* No. 3 (7), 1959.

Olszewski, F. "Sprawa włościańska i służebności." *Ognisko.* Warsaw, 1882.

Pankratova, A. M. "Vstupitel'naia stat'ia," *Rabochee dvizhenie v Rossii v XIX veke.* Vol. III. Part 1. Moscow, 1952.

Pietkiewicz, K. "Do biografji Michała Mancewicza." *Niepodległość.* Vol. V, 1931.

———. "Michał Mancewicz i jego czasy." *Niepodległość.* Vol. III, 1931.

———. "Polacy w rosyjskim ruchu wyzwoleńczym." *Niepodległość.* 1930. Part 1. "Kacper Michał Turski." Vol. I, 1930. Part 2. "Leon Dmochowski w kółku 'Dołguszyńców'." Vol. II, 1930. Part 3. "Polacy w procesie upadku 'Narodowej woli'." Vol. II, 1930.

Próchnik, A. "Działalność wydawnicza 'Proletariatu'." *Kronika Ruchu Rewolucyjnego w Polsce.* No. 1 (5), 1936.

_____. "Ideologia 'Proletariatu'." *Kronika Ruchu Rewolucyjnego w Polsce.* No. 1 (5), 1936.

_____. "Z dziejów wywiadu rosyjskiego i wzajemnych usług rządów zaborczych: Na marginesie procesu krakowskiego." *Niepodległość.* Vol. VII, 1933.

Sidorov, N. I. "Statisticheskie svedeniia o propagandistakh 70-kh godov v obrabotke III otdeleniia. *Katorga i ssylka.* No. 1 (38), 1928.

Świętochowski, A. "Socjalizm i jego błędy." *Nowiny.* Nos. 110, 112, 115, 116, 117, 1878.

_____. "Wskazania polityczne." *Ognisko.* Warsaw, 1883.

Tych, F. "Narodziny masowego ruchu klasy robotniczej w Królestwie Polskim," *Polska klasa robotnicza,* Vol. II, Warsaw, 1971.

Vasilevskii, L. (Plokhotskii). "Pol'skaia s.-r. partiia 'Proletariat' 1882–1886." *Byloe.* No. 4, 1906.

_____. "'Proletariat' pered sudom." *Byloe,* No. 7, 1906.

Wasilewski, L. "Walka o postulat niepodległości w polskim obozie socjalistycznym." *Niepodległość.* Vol. XIX, 1939.

Wierzejski, W. K. "Fragmenty z dziejów polskiej młodzieży akademickiej w Kijowie (1864–1920)." *Niepodległość.* Vol. XIX, 1939.

Wołkowiczer, J. "Strajk żyrardowski (Według dokumentów archiwalnych)." *Z Pola Walki.* No. 2, 1927.

Wścieklica, W. "Rojenia socjalistów polskich wobec nauki ich mistrza." *Ognisko.* Warsaw, 1883.

Zelnick, R. E. "The Peasant and the Factory." *The Peasant in Nineteenth Century Russia.* Ed. W. S. Vucinich. Stanford, 1968.

Zhigunov, E. K., Rashkovskii, E. B. "Iz istorii russko-pol'skikh revoliutsionnykh sviazi." *Obshchestvennoe dvizhenie v poreformennoi Rossii (sbornik statei k 80-letiiu so dnia rozhdeniia B. P. Koz'mina).* Moscow, 1965.

Index